A TON OF CRAP

MEN **WOMEN**

THE BATHROOM BOOK THAT'S FILLED TO THE BRIM WITH KNOWLEDGE

Paul Kleinman

A adamsmedia
Avon, Massachusetts

Published by
Adams Media, a division of F+W Media, Inc.
57 Littlefield Street, Avon, MA 02322. U.S.A.
www.adamsmedia.com

ISBN 13: 978-1-4351-4526-9

Printed in the United States of America.

10   9   8   7   6   5   4   3   2   1

This publication is designed to provide accurate and authoritative information with re-gard to the subject matter covered. It is sold with the understanding that the publisher is not engaged in rendering legal, accounting, or other professional advice. If legal ad-vice or other expert assistance is required, the services of a competent professional person should be sought.
—From a *Declaration of Principles* jointly adopted by a Committee of the American Bar Association and a Committee of Publishers and Associations

Many of the designations used by manufacturers and sellers to distinguish their product are claimed as trademarks. Where those designations appear in this book and Adams Media was aware of a trademark claim, the designations have been printed with initial capital letters.

Interior illustration of head profile © istockphoto.com/MaryLB

Contains material adapted and abridged from

contents

Introduction

Welcome to the Stalls of Academia

This is an education by way of the bathroom visit. It's about time you took your stay in here a little more seriously—well, as seriously as you can with your pants around your ankles. What follows is a digestible re-education in everything you probably learned at one time or another, but forgot because your head is filled with so much crap. Don't worry though; the way the information's presented, the learning won't be too rough, and you'll actually be entertained as you pass the time.

During every visit, you'll be schooled on five academic subjects: History, Language Arts, Math, Science, and Foreign Language. Each subject is broken down into topics like Ancient Egypt, Logarithms, and Poetry. And then each topic is split into six mini-lessons to avoid cramming too much information into one sitting. So you aren't just presented with a brain-dump on the American Revolution all at once; instead, you'll learn about the shot heard 'round the world during your first visit, the Battle of Bunker Hill the next time you drop by, and so on so by the end of the week you'll have a full understanding of the topic. Think of each visit as a day of middle school crammed into one bathroom break.

But don't think you're squeaking out of here without getting tested. This is supposed to be educational after all. Once you've digested the week's worth of information, you'll be quizzed on those particular topics. Don't bother bringing a pencil though. The quick and fun multiple-choice questions don't require any real writing, and you don't have to worry about wiping the page clean when you finish. Just take your time and don't push yourself too hard.

So get comfortable, relax, and get ready to learn. Rather than idle away as you do your business, it's time for a first-class education that finishes when you flush—and picks back up again when you sit back down.

HISTORY: Mesopotamia and the First Civilizations

The Sumerians, Ziggurats, The Akkadians, Babylonia, The Hittites, Inventions

MATH: Numbers

Babylonian Numbers, The Greek Numbers, The Egyptian Numbers, Roman Numerals, Arabic Numerals, Real Numbers

LANGUAGE ARTS: Punctuation

How It Started, The Period, The Comma, The Semicolon, The Colon, The Dash

SCIENCE: Evolution

Charles Darwin Sails to the Galapagos, Darwin's Finches, Natural Selection, *On the Origin of Species*, Genetic Drift, Mutation

Lesson 1

FOREIGN LANGUAGE: Latin

Ancestor of Romance Languages, Classical Latin, Vulgar Latin, Medieval Latin, Renaissance Latin, An Extinct Language and New Latin

MESOPOTAMIA AND THE FIRST CIVILIZATIONS

The Sumerians   Six thousand years ago, the first civilizations developed between the Tigris and Euphrates Rivers in what is now Iraq. The first civilization was known as Sumer, and the different villages developed self-governing city-states with a temple, or ziggurat, at the center of each city-state. As a result of the location, there was seasonal flooding and a hot, dry environment. This led to very fertile ground, which farmers took advantage of, producing crops such as wheat, barley, sesame, and flax.

PUNCTUATION

How It Started   Use of punctuation dates back to Ancient Greece and Rome. Orators placed marks in their speeches to indicate where and when to pause. These marks were given names such as period, comma, and colon, correlating for the kind of pauses needed. Punctuation was used infrequently, and it was not until the fifteenth century, with the introduction and rise of printing in England, that the punctuation we know today began being used.

NUMBERS

Babylonian Numbers   The Babylonians, another civilization of Mesopotamia, created a number system 5,000 years ago. The Babylonians used the cuneiform writing system, and their number system was originally based on a set of tally marks. Their number system was extremely complex, and the Babylonians divided the day into 24 hours, 60 minutes an hour, and 60 seconds a minute. Their system was sexagesimal rather than decimal, meaning all numbers are based on the number 60 and powers of 60. Decimal, or base ten, is the number system we use today.

EVOLUTION

Charles Darwin Sails to the Galapagos   In 1831, twenty-year-old Charles Darwin, a failing medical scholar and naturalist, sailed to the Galapagos Islands on a five-year-long trip. When Darwin landed on San Cristobal, he noticed something peculiar about the animals on the island. Not only were the animals different from those on the mainland, but also, among the islands, animals of the same species behaved differently due to different environments.

LATIN

Ancestor of Romance Languages   Latin is an Indo-European language that was spoken in ancient Rome. It is the ancestor of all modern Romance languages today, including Italian, Spanish, French, Portuguese, and Romanian just to name a few. Although it is officially a dead language, meaning no one speaks it as a native language, Latin is still used in the Roman Catholic Church.

MESOPOTAMIA AND THE FIRST CIVILIZATIONS

Ziggurats   The ziggurats at the heart of each city-state served many purposes. Not only were they there for religious reasons, but they were also the center of daily life for the Sumerian people. The Sumerians believed there were many powerful gods in the sky, and they dedicated these large temples to them with steps leading to the top. The ziggurats were built of mud-brick. At the very top of each, religious ceremonies were held.

 PUNCTUATION

The Period   A period is used at the end of a sentence, creating a statement and completing a thought. A period can also be used at the end of a command, such as, "When you've finished the last part of the exam, put your pencils down." A period is also used when ending an indirect question. For example, "Her boss asked her why she didn't come to work on Monday."

 NUMBERS

The Greek Numbers   The Greek numbers were based on the Greek alphabet, which came from the Phoenicians circa 900 B.C. The Greeks borrowed some of the symbols created by the Phoenicians and also created new symbols. By using the alphabet, they were able to have a more condensed version of their original system, Attic, a technique based on putting symbols in rows. By using letters instead, these numerical values took up less space on clay tablets and were able to be stamped on coins.

⚛ EVOLUTION

Darwin's Finches   The finches of the Galapagos laid the groundwork for understanding evolution. All of the finches Darwin saw shared many qualities. They were the same size and color and had similar habits. The most noticeable difference was the size and shape of their beaks. The difference in beak size and shape was a direct result of the different eating habits the birds had on the different islands.

◑ LATIN

Classical Latin   Classical Latin was used by the ancient Romans at the same time as Archaic Latin. Classical Latin was based on the language that was spoken by the more refined, upper classes of Romans, and was found in the literature of the time. Around 75 B.C. to A.D. 14, from the Republic all the way to the reign of Augustus Caesar, Latin literature was at its peak and was written in Classical Latin. This was referred to as the Golden Age.

MESOPOTAMIA AND THE FIRST CIVILIZATIONS

The Akkadians   The Akkadians were a Semitic people from the Arabic peninsula who increasingly came into more conflict with the Sumerians as they migrated north. In 2340 B.C., Sargon, the Akkadian military leader, conquered Sumerian city-states and established an Akkadian empire over the land. Sargon established his rule in the city of Akkad, and created the largest empire known to man at that time. The empire was short-lived, and in 2125, the Akkadian Empire fell.

PUNCTUATION

The Comma   The comma has many uses. A comma should be used when separating any independent clause that is joined by the conjunctions *and*, *yet*, *so*, *but*, *for*, *nor*, *or*. A comma is also used to separate items in a list or series and after an introductory adverb clause. The comma can also be used to interrupt a sentence to add extra information. For example, "Her dog, which had jumped in the puddle, was soaking wet."

NUMBERS

The Egyptian Numbers   The number system of Ancient Egypt was made up of hieroglyphs. Using this system of writing, where values and words are depicted with images, the Egyptians were able to note numbers all the way to 1,000,000 and perform addition, subtraction, multiplication, and division. The ancient Egyptians also had a very good understanding of fractions, and the use of fractions was so important that scribes would create tables for temple personnel referencing the division of supplies and food.

EVOLUTION

Natural Selection   Darwin's most groundbreaking idea was his theory of natural selection. This theory states that when there is an environmental change, only the organisms with the traits best suiting them to the new environmental conditions will survive. Those organisms that do not have these desirable traits cannot compete, and will die off. If enough traits change, over time, this could lead to a new creature or organism entirely.

LATIN

Vulgar Latin   Vulgar Latin, not Classical Latin, is the closest ancestor to the Romance languages. Vulgar Latin was the Latin spoken by the common people, and was a simpler form of Classical Latin, which was reserved for literature. Vulgar Latin varied across the Roman Empire due to the influence of the languages of local populations. By the time the Roman Empire disintegrated after A.D. 600, the local forms of Vulgar Latin were so distinct, they became the Romance languages.

MESOPOTAMIA AND THE FIRST CIVILIZATIONS

Babylonia As the last Sumerian dynasty fell, the Amorites came to power, basing their capital in Babylon. One of the most notable legal texts in history comes from this time period, when the king, Hammurabi, created one of the first sets of written laws. This is called the Code of Hammurabi. These laws were written out so that all would know the punishments if they disobeyed them. One of the most famous paraphrases of this code is "An eye for an eye, and a tooth for a tooth."

PUNCTUATION

The Semicolon A general rule is you can use a semicolon instead of a period when having two sentences without a conjunction in between them. For example, "Give me your number; I'll call you when I get home." A semicolon should also be used before introductory words like *however*, *therefore*, and *namely*. One can also use a semicolon when, if writing a series, one or more of the items contains a comma, or when two sentences are joined by a coordinating conjunction and there are commas in the first sentence.

NUMBERS

Roman Numerals Roman numerals were at least somewhat influenced by the Greek number system based on the alphabet. Many believe Roman numerals were originally created based on the shape of the hand. One finger representing the number one as I, and V, meaning five, expressed as the whole hand spread out. Reading Roman numerals is fairly simple, as they are read from left to right, with the larger number at the beginning and other numbers added as you move to the right. To subtract, the smaller number is placed in front of the larger number.

EVOLUTION

On the Origin of Species Darwin published his findings and his theory of natural selection in his book, *On the Origin of Species*, in 1859. Darwin stated that as a result of natural selection, organisms must have evolved over time, which led to the wide variety of species. He also stated that all of these organisms must have originated from a common ancestor. His beliefs were quite controversial at the time, as the British scientific world was closely linked to the Church of England.

LATIN

Medieval Latin Medieval Latin was the form of Latin used in the Middle Ages, from A.D. 500 to 1500. While it was primarily used by the Roman Catholic Church, it was also found in literature, law, administration, and science. The major distinction found in the Latin used at this time is that it began to have a wider vocabulary, grammar, and syntax, influenced by the various languages of the time.

MESOPOTAMIA AND THE FIRST CIVILIZATIONS

The Hittites   No one knows the origins of the Hittites, and until recently, their language was undecipherable (it was in the Indo-European family). Their invasion brought the end of the Old Babylonian Empire; however, as they conquered Mesopotamia, they adopted the laws, literature, and religion of Old Babylon. The Hittites are most notable for their work involved in trade and commerce, which spread Mesopotamian literature and thought all over the Mediterranean.

PUNCTUATION

The Colon   A colon is used if one wishes to emphasize the second clause when writing two independent clauses. For example, "The time had passed: his date never showed up." A colon can also be used when introducing a list, a quotation, an appositive (in which two phrases are placed next to each other, with one serving to define or change the other), or another idea related to the independent clause.

NUMBERS

Arabic Numerals   Arabic numerals were developed in India in A.D. 600, and it is the current system we have today. However, until A.D. 952, these numerals were actually written backward. In A.D. 952, this system was brought to Europe and the numerals were flipped. The shape of the numerals is actually derived from the number of angles in the shape of the number. The numeral 1 has one angle, the numeral 2 has two angles, and so on.

EVOLUTION

Genetic Drift   Another important aspect of evolution is genetic drift. However, unlike natural selection, genetic drift does not allow for adaptations. Rather, genetic drift is by chance. In every generation of an organism, chance plays a key part in who lives and who dies. Some individuals may leave behind more descendents than others, meaning the genes of these organisms will be passed on. The genes will pass on simply because of luck, and not because of a genetic advantage.

LATIN

Renaissance Latin   Similar to how the Renaissance in Italy placed emphasis on a return to Classicism, the Latin at this time was used to purge the language of the changes made from Medieval Latin. People wished to return to the language that was used in the Golden Age of Latin Literature during the Roman Empire. The humanists' efforts were successful in education, but ultimately, this wish to return to Classicism would lead to the extinction of the language.

MESOPOTAMIA AND THE FIRST CIVILIZATIONS

Inventions   Many important inventions came out of Mesopotamia. The seeder plow was revolutionary in agriculture and allowed seeding and plowing to occur simultaneously. The people of Mesopotamia also created a writing system based on images called cuneiform, developed irrigation and sanitation methods, created glass, and around 3500 B.C., invented the wheel. They were also the first to harness wind energy by creating sails.

PUNCTUATION

The Dash   An em dash is used to place emphasis on or set content apart from the rest of the text. Named because it is the width of an *M*, this dash is longer and places more importance on text than parentheses do. For example, "A lot of people were in the crowd—Tom and Scott among them." The en dash, which is the width of an *N*, is shorter and is used to indicate a span of values between two numbers. For example, "For ages 3–5."

NUMBERS

Real Numbers   Real numbers are whole numbers, such as 1, 2, 3, etc. Rational and irrational numbers as well as positive and negative numbers are also real numbers. Real numbers get the name "real" because they are not "imaginary." An imaginary number is any number that becomes negative when squared. Imaginary numbers were at one time believed to be impossible, but are actually useful in calculating things such as electricity.

EVOLUTION

Mutation   Mutation is the last crucial part to evolution. Natural selection and genetic drift explain why organisms change, but they don't necessarily explain how. A mutation is a change in the DNA of an organism that affects appearance, behavior, and the organism's physiology. These mutations enable the changes that Darwin mentions. Mutations are random, and not all mutations lead to evolution. If a mutation doesn't occur in reproductive cells, it is somatic and it will not be passed on to offspring.

LATIN

An Extinct Language and New Latin   Because humanists during the Renaissance were writing in an old language, they did not have the proper vocabulary for current issues. This gave the language an old, antiquated feel. Over time, less was written in Latin, until ultimately, the language became extinct. From that point on and to this day, the most common form of Latin is known as New Latin. This is Latin used for international scientific vocabulary, systematics, and the classification of species.

1. **What river or rivers did the Sumerians first develop civilizations on?**
   a. The Nile River
   b. Tigris and Euphrates
   c. The Indus
   d. Amu Darya

2. **What are the Hittites most known for?**
   a. Inventing the wheel
   b. Creating cuneiform
   c. Expanding trade and commerce
   d. Creating the Code of Hammurabi

3. **Which of the following is correct?**
   a. When you've finished the last part of your exam, put your pencils down.
   b. When you've finished the last part of your exam. Put your pencils down.
   c. When you've, finished the last part of your exam; put your pencils down.
   d. When—You've finished the last part of your exam put your pencils down.

4. **When is the en dash used?**
   a. It can be used instead of a comma.
   b. It can be used to place emphasis on one of two connected independent clauses.
   c. To end a train of thought.
   d. To indicate a span of values between two numbers.

5. **What is the current number system we use today?**
   a. Arabic Numerals
   b. Egyptian Numbers
   c. Greek Numbers
   d. Babylonian Numerals

6. **What is an imaginary number?**
   a. A negative number
   b. A number that when multiplied the result is positive
   c. A number that when squared the result is negative
   d. A number that when squared the result is positive

7. **What did Charles Darwin notice about the finches of the Galapagos?**
   a. Their legs were different sizes.
   b. Their beaks were different shapes and sizes.
   c. Their wings were different shapes and sizes.
   d. Their beaks were different colors.

8. **Genetic drift is a result of:**
   a. Chance
   b. Luck
   c. Mutations
   d. A and B

9. **The closest ancestor to the Romance languages is:**
   a. Classical Latin
   b. New Latin
   c. Vulgar Latin
   d. Medieval Latin

10. **Latin became an extinct language because:**
    a. The language blended with other languages until it was unrecognizable.
    b. All of the people who spoke it died.
    c. During the Renaissance, people wanted to return to a time before people spoke Latin.
    d. Latin didn't have vocabulary relevant to current issues and felt old and antiquated.

ANSWER KEY: b, c, a, d, a, c, b, d, c, d

8

HISTORY: Xia Dynasty

Real or Legend?, Yu the Great, The Political Systems, Decline of the Xia Dynasty, Controversies Today, Archaeological Findings

MATH: Zero

A Placeholder, A Number That Means Nothing, The First Use of Zero, The Origins of the Symbol, The Rules of Brahmagupta, Other Rules of Zero

LANGUAGE ARTS: Phonics

What Is Phonics?, Synthetic Phonics, Analytical Phonics, Vowel Patterns, Consonant Patterns, Alphabetic Principle

SCIENCE: Cells

The Basic Unit of Life, Prokaryotic and Eukaryotic Cells, Plant Cells, Animal Cells, Structure of a Cell, The Nucleus

Lesson 2

FOREIGN LANGUAGE: Spanish

The History of the Spanish Language, Making Spanish Official, Spanish Spreads, Framing a Sentence, Spanish Today, Useful Phrases

XIA DYNASTY

Real or Legend?   The Xia Dynasty, said to be the first dynasty of China, is supposed to have lasted from the twenty-first to the seventeenth century B.C. with seventeen emperors. There is little evidence showing the existence of the Xia Dynasty, and whether it actually existed or is merely a legend told in the ancient texts is still up for debate.

PHONICS

What Is Phonics?   Phonics is a method of teaching English. The main idea is that first students are taught the various sounds of the English language, and then they are taught the letters of the alphabet that those sounds correspond to. The advantage to learning English in this way is that once the main sounds have been mastered, one can learn to read many English words much quicker.

ZERO

A Placeholder   The zero has many functions. One very important function zero has is as a placeholder. The difference between 500, 50, and 501 is the placement and amount of zero digits. Even though the value zero is nothing, the digit zero means something. We understand that 501 is not the same thing as 51. The notion of the placeholder was first used by the Babylonians.

CELLS

The Basic Unit of Life   The cell is the smallest unit of life in an organism's body. Each cell has its own unique feature and function. Some organisms, like humans, animals, and plants, are multicellular, meaning they are made of many, many cells (for humans the number is in the trillions). However, other organisms, such as bacteria, are unicellular and consist of a single cell. Both animals and plants are eukaryotes, meaning their cells have a well-defined nucleus.

SPANISH

The History of the Spanish Language   Spanish is an Indo-European language. The earliest ancestor of Spanish was spoken 5,000 years ago around the Black Sea. Indo-European language speakers migrated throughout the land, leading to fragmentation. With the Romanization of Spain in 218 B.C., Latin became the language people used, and it is the direct ancestor of Spanish and all other Romance languages.

XIA DYNASTY

Yu the Great Da Yu, who would come to be known as Yu the Great, was the founder of the Xia Dynasty. He is famous for his involvement in stopping the great flooding of the Yangtze River; a process that lasted thirteen years. Yu the Great united the various ethnic groups, divided the land into nine provinces, and most notably, taught the people methods on how to control floodwater through the building of canals.

PHONICS

Synthetic Phonics Synthetic phonics involves teaching children unfamiliar words through translating the sounds of each letter and blending them together, or synthesizing. This is used particularly when teaching very young children how to read. Synthetic phonics does not focus on names of letters until the sound of each letter is understood. This is to develop phonic awareness, meaning listeners can differentiate the smallest units of sound in a word.

ZERO

A Number That Means Nothing Zero precedes the number one, meaning it represents an absence of value. It is an even number; however, it is neither prime nor composite and neither positive nor negative. The use of zero as a number, meaning a symbol representing a value of nothing, was first found in India around the eighth century A.D.

CELLS

Prokaryotic and Eukaryotic Cells There are two basic types of cells; prokaryotic and eukaryotic. *Prokaryotic* means "before a nucleus," and *eukaryotic* means "possessing a true nucleus." Prokaryotic cells have no nucleus, are usually single-celled organisms, and were the first organisms to live on Earth. Examples of prokaryotic cells are bacteria. On the other hand, eukaryotic cells have a nucleus and organelles, and are the types of cells found in humans, plants, and animals.

SPANISH

Making Spanish Official Early standard Spanish was the direct result of Alfonso X the Learned, king of Castile and Leon. Though Latin was partly abandoned by the previous king, Alfonso X became the first king to establish Castilian, a form of Spanish spoken in northern and central Spain, as the official language to be used in the churches, courts, official documents, and books, instead of Latin.

XIA DYNASTY

The Political Systems   Yu the Great chose to set up the Xia Dynasty under an abdication system, which meant choosing a leader based on ability. Following his death, his son, Qi, made himself emperor, officially ending the abdication system and creating a hereditary system. Fifteen offspring of Qi succeeded him, forming the first imperial dynasty in China.

PHONICS

Analytical Phonics   Analytical phonics relies on looking at word forms. In particular, analytical phonics looks at word groupings or patterns that are common. For example, if a child knows the words *moat*, *boat*, and *goat*, then they should know the word *coat* even if they have never seen that word before. Analytical phonics looks at two parts: the onset and the rime. The onset is the first consonant part of a word, and the rime is the second part of the word that begins with a vowel.

ZERO

The First Use of Zero   In A.D. 825, Persian scientist Khwarizmi used the zero for the first time as a number in an arithmetic book that combined Greek and Hindu mathematics. Also included in the book was an explanation on how to use zero properly, where Khwarizmi explained it was to be used as a placeholder.

CELLS

Plant Cells   Though structurally similar, there are some major differences between the cells found in plants and those found in animals. Plant cells have very rigid walls made of cellulose and contain chloroplasts. Chloroplasts, which contain chlorophyll, utilize the sun's light and enable the process of photosynthesis. They are also responsible for the green color found in plants. Plant cells have a larger central vacuole and contain, within their cell walls, linking pores that connect to transmit the information.

SPANISH

Spanish Spreads   When Christopher Columbus, backed by the Spanish Empire, came to the New World in 1492, he opened the door for the Spanish conquest of what is now known as Central America. Four hundred years of colonization of this new land by the Spanish Empire followed, which included bringing over their culture, religion, and language. The Spanish would come to control Central America, much of North America, Mexico, and much of South America.

XIA DYNASTY

Decline of the Xia Dynasty   The Shang Dynasty followed the Xia Dynasty. The last leader of the Xia Dynasty, Jie, was an oppressive and tyrannical emperor who killed many of his people. Eventually, the people of the Xia Dynasty began to revolt and followed the leadership of Shang Tang, chief of the Shang tribe. The successful uprising led to the demise of the Xia Dynasty and the beginning of the Shang Dynasty, which would hold power from 1766 B.C. to 1122 B.C.

 PHONICS

Vowel Patterns   Short vowels are the sounds that *a*, *e*, *i*, *o*, and *u* create in words like *cat*, *pet*, *hit*, *hot*, and *cup*. They are called short because they aren't diphthongs. Long vowels sound like the names of the letters themselves. Examples of long vowels can be found in words like *cake* or *meter*. Schwa is another sound single vowels produce, and it is an indistinct sound in an unstressed syllable. For example, the sound the *o* makes in the word *lesson* is a schwa.

 ZERO

The Origins of the Symbol   Originally, the Babylonians put a space between numbers and didn't have a symbol representing zero. (For instance, 303 would have been 3 3.) By 300 B.C., the notion of the placeholder was represented by two slanted wedges. In A.D. 130, Greek astronomer Ptolemy represented the zero placeholder as a circle with a long overbar.

CELLS

Animal Cells   Animal cells are much smaller than plant cells and do not have the rigid cell walls that plant cells have. This allows animal cells to take on various shapes. While plants have the ability to make their own food with chloroplasts and sunlight, in animal cells, it is the role of the mitochondria to get energy from food that is consumed.

SPANISH

Framing a Sentence   Unlike English, in Spanish the object of your sentence can come before the verb, and the subject is part of the verb. For example, in English, we would say, "I see you." The word "you" being the object, it is at the end of the sentence. "I see you" in Spanish translates as "Te veo." The object is "te," and "veo" is actually a combination of "I" and "see."

XIA DYNASTY

Controversies Today   In the 1920s, Gu Jiegang created a school of scholars in China called the Skeptical School. It was the first group of people to question whether the Xia Dynasty actually existed or whether it was just a legend; they cited the lack of archaeological findings corresponding to the historical texts. Today, scholar Sarah Al-lan argues that the Zhou Dynasty created Xia to justify their conquest of the dynasty that followed Xia, the Shang Dynasty.

PHONICS

Consonant Patterns   Consonant digraphs are letter combinations that represent consonant phonemes. Examples of these include *ch*, *ph*, *sh*, *th*, and *wh*. Consonant patterns with a short vowel appear in words that have two possible spellings based on how they sound. They can be *ck* or *k*, *tch* or *ch*, and *dge* or *ge*. To determine the spelling in these cases, one must look at the vowel that precedes the sound. If there is not a short vowel, the latter forms are used. For example, in the word "pick," there is a short vowel, so *ck* is used, while in the word "took," a *k* is used because there is no short vowel present.

ZERO

The Rules of Brahmagupta   Rules governing how the zero should be used as a value and not a placeholder first appeared in a book written by the Indian mathematician Brahmagupta in A.D. 628. Though he states some things that modern science disagrees with, he also laid down much of the groundwork for how zero is applied in mathematics. Such examples are:

The sum of a positive number and zero is the positive number.
The sum of a negative number and zero is the negative number.
The sum of zero with zero equals zero.
The sum of a positive number and a negative number equals their difference, and if their absolute values are equal, then the result is zero.

CELLS

Structure of a Cell   The plasma membrane is the outer lining of a eukaryote cell. It protects the cell from the surrounding environment and is composed of lipids and proteins. The nucleus inside of the cell is surrounded by a membrane that separates it from the cytoplasm. Two kinds of genetic material, DNA and RNA, exist inside the cell. The cell's chromosomes are in the nucleus, which is also the location for RNA synthesis and DNA replication.

SPANISH

Spanish Today   Today, Spanish is the native language of 332 million people, and it is the second most popular language in the world. It is the official language of numerous countries including Spain, Colombia, Peru, Cuba, Argentina, Bolivia, Mexico, Honduras, and Costa Rica. By the 1990s, the number of people in the United States who spoke Spanish as their primary language at home was more than 17 million.

XIA DYNASTY

Archaeological Findings   In 1959, a site was excavated in the city of Yanshi. The site included large palaces, and archaeologists at the time believed that this could be the capital of the Xia Dynasty. Over the next twenty years, many sites were uncovered, revealing tombs, urban sites, and bronze implements. These were discovered in areas where the ancient texts claimed the Xia Dynasty to be, and radiocarbon dating places the site to be from around 2100 to 1800 B.C. The debate as to whether this is the Xia Dynasty, or whether the Xia Dynasty even existed at all, continues to this day.

PHONICS

Alphabetic Principle   In English, spelling is based on the alphabetic principle, in which letters are used to represent sounds, or phonemes, and then combined to create words. However, English is much more complicated than just following the alphabetic principle because the same sound can be spelled different ways and the same letters can have different sounds. This is because the language has absorbed several other languages into it, and traces of Classical Latin, Old English, Old Norse, Greek, and Norman can be found in English. For example, even though the words *though* and *enough* both end in *gh*, the words do not follow the same pronunciation rules.

ZERO

Other Rules of Zero   When using zero in math there are several basic rules beyond those mentioned in the Brahmagupta section. When a number is multiplied by zero, the answer will always be zero. A number cannot be divided by zero; this makes the solution undefined. When discussing exponents, x^0 equals one, unless the quality of *x* is zero. In that case, the answer is zero.

CELLS

The Nucleus   The nucleus is responsible for regulating all activity in eukaryotic cells. It contains the hereditary information (DNA and RNA) and controls growth and reproduction. The most prominent structure in the nucleus is called the nucleolus. The nucleolus produces ribosomes, which play a critical role in protein synthesis. These proteins are used for a variety of purposes including, but not limited to, structural support and as enzymes to catalyze a reaction.

SPANISH

Useful Phrases   There are several basic things one should know how to say when traveling in a Spanish-speaking country.

Hello! *¡Hóla!*
Good day. *Buenos diás.*
Thank you very much. *Muchas gracias.*
Good night. *Buenos noches.*
Goodbye. *Adiós.*
Where is the bathroom? *¿Dónde está el baño?*
Can you help me? *¿Me podría ayudar?*
How much does that cost? *¿Cuánto cuesta?*
Can I get on the internet? *¿Puedo conectarme con el internet?*

1. **What is Yu the Great most known for?**
   a. Teaching methods on how to control flood water
   b. Questioning whether the Xia Dynasty existed
   c. Leading a revolt against Shang Tang
   d. Excavating the city of Yanshi

2. **Yu the Great's son, Qi, ended the abdication system and created:**
   a. A hierarchical system
   b. A serfdom
   c. A hereditary system
   d. The Shang Dynasty

3. ***Ch*, *sh*, *th*, and *ph* are examples of:**
   a. The alphabetic principle
   b. Vowel patterns
   c. Analytical phonics
   d. Consonant digraphs

4. **What is synthetic phonics?**
   a. Words having two possible spellings based on how they sound
   b. An indistinct sound that single vowels produce in an unstressed syllable
   c. A method of teaching children unfamiliar words through translating the sounds of each letter and blending or synthesizing them together
   d. A combination of Classical Latin, Old English, Old Norse, Greek, and Norman

5. **Which of the following is NOT one of the rules of Brahmagupta?**
   a. The sum of a positive number and zero is the positive number.
   b. The sum of a positive number and a positive number is zero.
   c. The sum of zero with zero equals zero.
   d. The sum of a negative number and zero is the negative number.

6. **In his book of A.D. 825, Persian scientist Khwarizmi stated that:**
   a. Zero was to be expressed as a circle with a long overbar.
   b. A number cannot be divided by zero.
   c. Zero was to be used as a placeholder.
   d. When a number is multiplied by zero, the answer will always be zero.

7. **What is the difference between prokaryotic cells and eukaryotic cells?**
   a. Eukaryotic cells have a nucleus, prokaryotic do not.
   b. Prokaryotic cells have a nucleus, eukaryotic do not.
   c. Eukaryotic cells have a true nucleus and prokaryotic have a fake nucleus.
   d. Prokaryotic cells have a true nucleus and eukaryotic have a fake nucleus.

8. **Which of the following is true?**
   a. Animal cells are larger than plant cells.
   b. Only animal cells have DNA.
   c. Animal cells get their energy from sunlight.
   d. Animal cells do not have the rigid cell walls that plant cells have, allowing them to take on various shapes.

9. **Who was the first to establish Castilian, a form of Spanish, as an official language instead of Latin?**
   a. Charlemagne
   b. The Hittites
   c. Alfonso X, The Learned
   d. The Sumerians

10. **How do you say "Where is the bathroom?" in Spanish?**
    a. ¿Me podría ayudar?
    b. ¿Cuánto cuesta?
    c. ¿Puedo conectarme con el internet?
    d. ¿Dónde está el baño?

HISTORY: Ancient Egypt

Predynastic Egypt, Early Dynastic Egypt, The Old Kingdom, The Middle Kingdom, The New Kingdom, The Late Period

MATH: Inca Mathematics

A Language Found in Math, The Quipu, How the Quipu Works, The Color-Coding of the Quipu, Local Statisticians, The Yupana

LANGUAGE ARTS: Composition

Parts of Speech, Basic Parts of a Sentence, Modifiers, Prepositional Phrases, Adjective Clauses, Participle Phrases

SCIENCE: The Nervous System

What Is the Nervous System?, Neurons, The Central Nervous System, The Peripheral Nervous System, The Somatic Nervous System, The Autonomic Nervous System

Lesson 3

FOREIGN LANGUAGE: French

The Origins, French Consonants, French Vowels, Articles, French Today, Useful Phrases

⟐ ANCIENT EGYPT

Predynastic Egypt   Egypt's history began similarly to that of Mesopotamia. Civilizations congregated around the Nile River around 5500 B.C. The largest civilization, the Badari, inhabited the northern part of Egypt, and was most known for high-quality stone tools, ceramics, and pottery and their use of copper. In the southern part of Egypt, the Naqada civilization arose. Over the course of 1,000 years, the Naqada controlled the tribes along the Nile, and created a full system of hieroglyphics for writing.

✐ COMPOSITION

Parts of Speech   Knowledge of parts of speech, or word classes, is critical in understanding how composition works. Parts of speech are nouns, such as people, places, or things; pronouns (words like *he*, *she*, and *it* that can replace nouns); adjectives (words that describe nouns); verbs (actions); adverbs (words that modify adjectives, verbs, or nouns by expressing place, manner, time, etc.); conjunctions (words used to connect phrases or sentences); articles (the word that is before the noun); prepositions (words that link nouns, pronouns, or phrases to other parts of the sentence); and interjections (words that show emotion and are not linked to the rest of the sentence).

⊞ INCA MATHEMATICS

A Language Found in Math   The Inca Empire — which in 1532 was extremely large, spanning from present-day Argentina to Ecuador — consisted of many diverse ethnic groups of people. As a result, more than twenty different languages were spoken. With so many different languages and ethnicities, the Incas turned to mathematics to unite their people and to act as a common language among everyone. Their mathematical system was developed before their written language.

✺ THE NERVOUS SYSTEM

What Is the Nervous System?   The nervous system is a complex system that is responsible for sending every electrical impulse and signal throughout your body. These signals are what cause any and all actions, reactions, and thoughts you have, as well as anything you feel. The nervous system is made up of two systems: the central nervous system and the peripheral nervous system.

◉ FRENCH

The Origins   The roots of the French language date back to 154–125 B.C. when Gaul was conquered by the Romans. With the Romanization, Latin became the spoken language, causing the Gaulish language to be looked down upon and only used in more rustic areas. Eventually, the north would split from the south, leading to the creation of many distinct dialects. Over time, and due to the political prestige of the area, the dialect spoken in Paris would become the national language.

 ANCIENT EGYPT

Early Dynastic Egypt Around 3100 B.C., Upper and Lower Egypt united under the pharaoh Menes. Memphis, a part of Lower Egypt, was established as the capital of the land and became critical in trade and agriculture. It also provided a work force. Notable from this time period were the mastaba tombs, which were large rectangular, flat-roofed structures made of stone and mud-bricks that were built to celebrate pharaohs who had died.

 COMPOSITION

Basic Parts of a Sentence There are three main parts found in a sentence; the subject; the verb; and, often, the object. The subject is usually the noun, and it is who or what the sentence is about. The verb then follows the subject, indicating what action takes place. Lastly, the object follows the verb and is what receives the action. In the sentence "Tom threw the ball to Sally," Tom is the subject because the sentence is about him. The throwing of the ball is the verb, and Sally is the object. She receives the ball that the subject threw toward her.

 INCA MATHEMATICS

The Quipu The Incas created a tool called the quipu. This was not a calculator used to add or subtract, but rather a storage device used to record. It is this use of the quipu that allowed the Incas to successfully create roads, sophisticated agriculture, administration, and textile designs. The tool was made entirely of strings that were then tied into knots. Each knot represented a number, with a positional base ten representation, a system that we still use to this day.

⚛ THE NERVOUS SYSTEM

Neurons The nervous system works via nerve cells, or neurons. These cells process and transmit information through chemical and electrical signaling. What makes neurons different from other cells is that they have very specialized extensions called axons and dendrites. Dendrites receive the information, and the axon carries the message to target cells.

◖ FRENCH

French Consonants French consonants are pronounced similarly to the way they are in English. However, there are two major exceptions. Consonants at the end of a word (except *c*, *r*, *f*, and *l*) are not pronounced, and unlike in English, you are not supposed to linger on consonants. They should be short and quick, so that you can move on to the next vowel. The letter *r* is also pronounced from the back of your throat.

ANCIENT EGYPT

The Old Kingdom   The Old Kingdom refers to the rule of the Third Dynasty to the Sixth Dynasty from 2686 to 2181 B.C. This is a time defined by a flourishing economy, a well-defined justice system, and a strong government. It is during this time that the famous pyramids of Giza were built, marking great artistic and technological advancements. A new class of educated scribes also arose.

COMPOSITION

Modifiers   A modifier is any word, clause, or phrase that adds meaning to another word or part of a sentence. There are two types of modifiers, pre-modifiers and post-modifiers. The head is any word that determines the nature of the sentence. A pre-modifier goes before the head, and a post-modifier goes after the head. For example, "history book," is an example of a pre-modifier, and "A book on history" is an example of a post-modifier.

INCA MATHEMATICS

How the Quipu Works   The quipu was used in a truly ingenious way. The knots placed on the string were put in different positions representing the base ten counting system. Knots near the end of the string represented the digits. A space followed by more knots represented the tens. If another space was left and then followed by more knots, this represented the hundreds, and so on. For example, to represent the number 246 on the quipu, there would be six knots, a space, then four knots, a space, and then two knots.

THE NERVOUS SYSTEM

The Central Nervous System   The central nervous system consists of two of the most important parts of the nervous system: the brain and the spinal cord. The brain is considered to be the command center of the nervous system, since it controls all of the workings of your body. The central nervous system collaborates with the peripheral nervous system in controlling the behavior of the body.

FRENCH

French Vowels   Unlike consonants, French vowels are pronounced differently than they are in English. Vowels do not form diphthongs like in English. Instead of closing the vowel with a "y" or "w" sound, the vowels stay constant, and the tongue remains tense while pronouncing them. The letters *a*, *o*, and *u* are hard vowels, and *e* and *i* are soft vowels. When followed by *m* or *n*, vowels sound nasal, meaning that when pronouncing them, air escapes both the mouth and the nose.

ANCIENT EGYPT

The Middle Kingdom The central government of the Old Kingdom collapsed in 2160 B.C., and around 2055 B.C., the prosperity and stability of Egypt was restored when Mentuhotep II came to power beginning what is known as the Middle Kingdom. Once again, art, literature, and great monuments defined this period. One stark contrast between the art of this time and that of the Old Kingdom, is that this work focused more on the individual and a democratization of the afterlife in which every person possessed a soul and was greeted by the gods and goddesses when they died.

 COMPOSITION

Prepositional Phrases A prepositional phrase adds meaning to the verbs and nouns in a sentence. It is composed of two parts; a preposition (a word that expresses the relationship between a noun or pronoun and the other words in the sentence), and the object of the preposition. For example, when looking at the phrase "In the building," the word *in* is our preposition because it indicates the location, and *the building* is the object of the preposition.

 INCA MATHEMATICS

The Color-Coding of the Quipu The Incas did not stop at counting with the strings of the quipu. The quipu had a very functional purpose, and in order to discern what each value represented, a system needed to be in place in order to tell the Incas what was being counted. There were hundreds of strings on the quipu, and yet their system was very easy to understand. What they did was actually color-code the strings. So, for example, a green string might represent a certain type of crop, and the knots on the string would indicate how much of that crop was recorded.

⊛ THE NERVOUS SYSTEM

The Peripheral Nervous System The peripheral nervous system consists of the nerves that receive and send the information from the central nervous system. There are two types of nerves: motor nerves, which send signals from the brain to different tissues in the body; and sensory nerves, which receive information in the form of pain, heat, or touch and then send those impulses to the central nervous system.

◐ FRENCH

Articles In French, there is always an article in front of the noun, and these change according to gender (masculine, feminine), and number (singular and plural). There are three types of articles: definite (equivalent to *the* in English), indefinite (equivalent to *a/an* in English), and partitive (used when a singular noun can represent smaller parts, such as the word *food*). The articles are:

	Definite	Indefinite	Partitive
Masculine	le	un	du
Feminine	la	une	de la
Plural	les	des	
Before Vowel	l'		de l'

ANCIENT EGYPT

The New Kingdom   The New Kingdom lasted from the sixteenth to the eleventh century B.C. and was defined by military campaigns that made the Egyptian empire the largest it had ever been. Amenhotep IV, who changed his name to Akhenaten, instituted new and radical worship of a new sun god, Aten. Attacking the priestly establishment, Akhenaten eventually made the Aten the only god. When Tutankhamen came to power after Akhenaten's death, he returned Egypt to a polytheistis religion.

COMPOSITION

Adjective Clauses   Adjective clauses help indicate which part of a sentence is more important than the rest of the sentence a process known as subordination. The adjective clause is a dependent word group that modifies the noun. These usually include words like *which*, *who*, *whose*, and *that*. For example in "The dog that ate everyone's lunch wanted seconds," *that ate everyone's lunch* is the adjective clause.

INCA MATHEMATICS

Local Statisticians   The Inca king appointed people, called quipucamayocs, to use the quipus, and effectively act as statisticians for the towns. These people were to use and interpret the quipus and keep census records on the population, as well as records of all produce, weaponry, and animals. This information was then sent to the capital, Cuzco, every year.

THE NERVOUS SYSTEM

The Somatic Nervous System   The somatic nervous system, or voluntary nervous system, is part of the peripheral nervous system. It is responsible for processing sensory information — such as pain, heat, and touch — from an external stimuli, and controlling the voluntary muscular systems. The somatic nervous system allows a person to receive sensory information and react to environmental changes. The somatic nervous system is also part of the autonomic nervous system.

FRENCH

French Today   French is the native language for approximately 75 million people worldwide, and it is the national language for over 25 countries including France, Haiti, Luxembourg, and Monaco, and more than 15 countries found in Africa. It is also one of the official languages of Canada, Switzerland, and Belgium, as well as one of the six official languages used by the United Nations today.

ANCIENT EGYPT

The Late Period   The Late Period lasted from 664 to 323 B.C. It is considered to be the end of the once-great Egyptian Empire. From 525 to 404 B.C., Egypt was part of the Persian Empire. The twenty-eighth dynasty, led by Amyrtaeus, saw a revolt against the Persians; however, by the thirtieth Dynasty in 343 B.C., the Persians had once again reoccupied the land.

COMPOSITION

Participle Phrases   A participle is a verb form that is used as an adjective. For example, *cooked*, *cooking*, and *having cooked* are participles of the verb *cook*. A participle phrase is a sentence that consists of a present or past participle, with any modifiers, objects, and complements. For example, in "Running down the aisle, she knocked over the soup display," *running down the aisle* is the participle phrase.

INCA MATHEMATICS

The Yupana   In a letter to the king of Spain, Felipe Guaman Poma de Ayala describes and illustrates a picture of another counting device created and used by the Incas: the yupana. His drawing resembles that of a counting board. Scientists are unsure if the Incas used this as an abacus or some type of calculator, and it is not known whether this was merely just another recording device or a tool for solving mathematical equations.

THE NERVOUS SYSTEM

The Autonomic Nervous System   The autonomic nervous system is part of the peripheral nervous system and controls involuntary body functions. Two important aspects of the autonomic nervous system are the sympathetic nervous system, which comes into effect causing the fight or flight reaction; and the parasympathetic nervous system, which comes into effect in nonemergency situations, causing the body to rest and relax.

FRENCH

Useful Phrases   Here are some helpful phrases to use when traveling to a French-speaking country:

Good morning/Good day. *Bonjour.*
Good evening. *Bonsoir.*
Do you speak English? *Parlez-vous anglais?*
Thank you. *Merci.*
How are you? *Comment allez-vous?*
What time is it? *Quelle heure est-il?*
I need to use the restroom. *J'ai besoin d'utiliser les toilettes.*
Please repeat. *Répétez, s'il vous plaît.*

1. **Around 3100 B.C., the ruler Menes established Memphis as the capital city, uniting:**
   a. Upper and Lower Egypt
   b. Western and Eastern Egypt
   c. Egypt and Mesopotamia
   d. The Nile River and the Yellow River

2. **When Amenhotep IV came to power, he instituted new and radical beliefs. Which of the following was Amenhotep IV responsible for?**
   a. Leading a revolt against the Persians
   b. Creating a class of scribes
   c. Turning the polytheistic religion into a monotheistic one
   d. Creating mastabas

3. **In the sentence "Bobby sees a cat," what is the subject?**
   a. The cat
   b. Seeing
   c. Bobby
   d. There is no subject in this sentence.

4. **"In the store" is an example of:**
   a. A participle phrase
   b. A prepositional phrase
   c. An article
   d. An adjective clause

5. **The quipu had hundreds of strings on it, and yet it was very easy to understand. That is because:**
   a. The strings got progressively shorter.
   b. The knots were made bigger for larger numbers.
   c. The strings got progressively longer.
   d. The strings were color-coded.

6. **The number 45 represented on the quipu would look like:**
   a. 25 knots, a space, then 20 knots
   b. 5 knots, a space, then 4 knots
   c. 10 knots, a space, 10 knots, a space, 10 knots, a space, 10 knots, a space, and 5 knots
   d. 40 knots, a space, 5 knots

7. **The central nervous system consists of the brain and the:**
   a. Blood
   b. Lungs
   c. Arms and legs
   d. Spinal cord

8. **Fight or flight is a result of:**
   a. The central nervous system
   b. The peripheral nervous system
   c. The autonomic nervous system
   d. B and C

9. **In French, an article is always in front of:**
   a. A noun
   b. A verb
   c. An adjective
   d. An adverb

10. **When followed by _____, French vowels sound nasal.**
    a. P and L
    b. M and N
    c. R and Q
    d. K and A

HISTORY: The Huns
Who Were They?, Conquerors, Weaponry, Attila the Hun, After Attila, Legends

MATH: Greek Mathematics
The Ionian School, The Pythagorean School, The Eleatic School, The Sophist School, The Platonic School, The School of Aristotle

LANGUAGE ARTS: The Alphabet
The Phoenician Alphabet, The Aramaic Alphabet, The Greek Alphabet, The Latin Alphabet, Old English Alphabet, Modern English Alphabet

SCIENCE: The Circulatory System
What Is the Circulatory System?, The Heart, Red Blood Cells, White Blood Cells, The Aorta and Arterial System, The Venous System

Lesson 4

FOREIGN LANGUAGE: Italian
The Origins, Vowels, Easy Consonants, Harder Consonants, Articles, Useful Italian Phrases

THE HUNS

Who Were They? In the fourth and fifth centuries A.D., a nomadic group of people from Central Asia spread to the Caspian Sea, coming into contact with the Roman Empire toward the end of its reign. These people were fierce warriors (with a specialty in archery), animal herders, and expert horsemen. The tribes were called the Hsiung-nu; however, in the West, they were referred to as the Huns.

THE ALPHABET

The Phoenician Alphabet By 3000 B.C., there was the cuneiform of Mesopotamia, and the hieroglyphs of ancient Egypt. The Phoenician alphabet, however, was quite a different writing system from either of these. Instead of using pictographs, the Phoenician alphabet was something called abjad. Abjad was a non-pictograph consonantal alphabet that showed symbols representing sounds. This writing system quickly spread throughout the Mediterranean and was adapted by many cultures.

GREEK MATHEMATICS

The Ionian School Founded by Thales in 643 to 546 B.C., the Ionian School was a pre-Socratic group of philosophers that focused on teaching philosophy, science, and the origins of the universe. Thales is credited for being the first mathematician to discover and teach deductive proofs in geometry, using Thales's theorem, which states that if there are three points on a circle and the first and last point make up the diameter, then the angle of the three of them combined is a right angle.

THE CIRCULATORY SYSTEM

What Is the Circulatory System? The circulatory system consists of the heart, blood, and blood vessels. It is the body's transportation and cooling system. Your blood moves from the heart via arteries, and to your heart via veins, delivering oxygen and nutrients throughout your body. The blood also picks up any waste products in your system, so the body can get rid of them.

ITALIAN

The Origins Italian, like the other Romance languages, stemmed from Vulgar Latin, and it most closely resembles Latin. Around the fourteenth century, the Tuscan dialect began to dominate as a result of the aggressive commerce centered in Florence. In 1525, Venetian linguist and lawyer Pietro Bembo set out to make the dialect spoken in fifteenth-century Florence the official language of Italian literature. The first official Italian dictionary was published in 1612.

THE HUNS

Conquerors   The Huns first overcame another nomadic group that lived between the Don and Volga rivers, the Alani. From there, they attacked the Ostrogothic kingdom and in 376, the Huns attacked the Visigoths. During the fifty years following their conquest of the Visigoths, the Huns firmly established their status with both the Western and Eastern Roman Empires through constant raids and attacks.

THE ALPHABET

The Aramaic Alphabet   The Aramaic alphabet was an adaptation of the Phoenician alphabet, and all Middle Eastern alphabets can be traced back to it. Much like the Phoenician alphabet, the letters only represented consonants, but it did also have certain places where long vowels were to be pronounced. To this day, the Hebrew alphabet is the closest relative to the Aramaic script of the fifth century B.C. The inventory of the letters and the shapes of the letters are practically identical.

GREEK MATHEMATICS

The Pythagorean School   The Pythagorean School, taught by Pythagoras, though mystical, placed heavy emphasis on math. Pythagoras's work had a deep impact in mathematical areas such as number theory, proof theory, plane geometry, solid geometry, and proportion. Pythagoras is said to have constructed the first proof of what would become known as the Pythagorean theorem, which states that for a right triangle, the square of the length of the hypotenuse equals the sum of the squares of the lengths of the two other sides. Or to put it simply, $a^2 + b^2 = c^2$.

THE CIRCULATORY SYSTEM

The Heart   The heart is a muscle roughly the size of a clenched fist. It is two sided and has four chambers. Blood enters the heart through the right atrium. The right ventricle pushes the deoxygenated blood to the lungs. The left atrium then receives the oxygenated blood and pumps it to the left ventricle of the heart, which is responsible for pushing the blood out of the heart and into the body's circulation.

ITALIAN

Vowels   Vowels in Italian are short. They should be pronounced very clearly and not drawn out. The letters *a*, *i*, and *u* are always pronounced in the same way. The letter *a* is pronounced like in the word *cat*, the letter *i* is like the *y* in the word *yellow*, and the *u* is pronounced as in the word *fun*. The pronunciation of the letters *e* and *o*, however, will vary depending on which part of Italy you are in and could have an open or closed sound.

THE HUNS

Weaponry   The Huns relied on two very powerful weapons: a composite bow and horses. The Huns were excellent horseback riders and fought as cavalry. The groups they attacked could not escape their hit-and-run tactics, and using their bows and arrows allowed the Huns to attack their enemies and inflict injury from long ranges. Warriors of the Huns also carried swords, lassos, and lances.

THE ALPHABET

The Greek Alphabet   The Greeks adopted the Phoenician alphabet, and by the eighth century B.C., had modified it and created the first true alphabet, meaning both consonants and vowels were represented. The Greeks even used the Phoenician consonant symbols to represent vowels because they did not have the same sounds the Phoenicians did and they needed the symbols for the vowels. The Greek alphabet heavily influenced the Latin alphabet, which is the most widely used alphabet today.

GREEK MATHEMATICS

The Eleatic School   Founded by Parmenides, the Eleatic School focused on opposing the physical theories of early philosophers and paved the way for metaphysics. Zeno, another philosopher in the Eleatic School, proposed challenges to ideas of motion and time, and against multiplicity. What Zeno actually does in his work, however, is invoke the notion of infinity.

THE CIRCULATORY SYSTEM

Red Blood Cells   Blood is constantly flowing through our bodies and carries oxygen, nutrients, water, and waste products to and from our cells. Red blood cells carry oxygen and carbon dioxide. After picking up oxygen from the lungs and delivering it to the cells, the red blood cells transport the carbon dioxide to the lungs, from which it is then exhaled.

ITALIAN

Easy Consonants   The modern Italian alphabet features fewer letters than the English alphabet. Missing from the Italian alphabet are the letters j, k, w, x, and y. The letters b, f, m, n, and v are pronounced the same way they are in English. One drastic difference when it comes to consonants is that the h in Italian is actually silent.

THE HUNS

Attila the Hun   In 432, the Huns became centralized under the leadership of one ruler, Rua. Two years later, Rua died and his throne was passed on to his two nephews: Bleda and Attila. In 445, Attila killed his brother, taking complete control of the government and the Huns. Under Attila's reign, the Huns defeated and conquered several rivals and made several attacks on the Roman Empire. Attila was one of the most feared rulers of the time.

 THE ALPHABET

The Latin Alphabet   The Latin alphabet, or the Roman alphabet, was taken from the Greek alphabet and then modified by the Etruscans and Romans. The Latin alphabet consisted of twenty-one letters: A, B, C, D, E, F, Z, H, I, K, L, M, N, O, P, Q, R, S, T, V, X. This was the alphabet used when writing Latin, and as the Roman Empire spread, so too did the language and the letters. As the Romance languages started to evolve, the languages adapted with these letters.

 GREEK MATHEMATICS

The Sophist School   The Sophist School was founded in Athens around 480 B.C. For a long time, the Sophists were the only source of higher education in cities. The Sophist School placed emphasis on using abstract reasoning to understand the universe. The Sophists applied math to try to solve problems such as how to double a cube, square a circle, and trisect an angle with just a compass and a straight edge.

THE CIRCULATORY SYSTEM

White Blood Cells   White blood cells fight germs. During an infection, the body produces more white blood cells, which will then try to attack and destroy the infection. When someone is prescribed an antibiotic, it is because the white blood cells need help fighting off the infection.

ITALIAN

Harder Consonants   These consonants are different than the ones you previously learned about. In Italian, some consonants have two different pronunciations depending on the letter before it. When a *c* is followed by an *a, o, u,* or a consonant, it is pronounced with a "k" sound, such as in the word *cat*. If it is followed by an *e* or an *i*, it is pronounced with a "ch" sound. If a *g* is followed by an *a, o, u,* or a consonant, it is pronounced like it is in the word *get*. If it is followed by an *e* or and *i*, it is pronounced with a "j" sound, like in the word *gym*.

THE HUNS

After Attila   Upon Attila's death, Ellac, one of his sons, overcame his two brothers and became ruler of the Huns. However, former subjects of Attila began to revolt and united under Ardaric, the ruler of the Gepids. The Huns would fight Ardaric's men in the Battle of Nedao in 454, and lose, ending their supremacy over Europe.

THE ALPHABET

Old English Alphabet   The first alphabet for the English language was the Anglo-Saxon futhorc runic alphabet of the fifth century. It was used by the Anglo-Saxons in what is now England. In the seventh century, Christian missionaries introduced the Latin alphabet to the Anglo-Saxons, and over time, the Latin alphabet began incorporating some of the Anglo-Saxon futhorc alphabet into it. The Old English alphabet was made up of twenty-four letters from the Latin alphabet and five letters from the English alphabet.

GREEK MATHEMATICS

The Platonic School   The Platonic School was founded in 387 B.C. by one of the most famous Greek philosophers: Plato. And though he was not a mathematician, Plato placed great emphasis on mathematics. The most significant mathematical achievements were done by Plato's pupils at this time, and the school was heavily influenced by the work of Pythagoras.

THE CIRCULATORY SYSTEM

The Aorta and Arterial System   The aorta is the largest artery in the body. It originates from the left ventricle and distributes the oxygenated blood. From the aorta, the blood is then sent to the other arteries and arterioles, which are small arteries that deliver oxygen and nutrients to all of the cells in your body. At the end of the arterioles are capillaries, which pass the blood through the venous system.

ITALIAN

Articles   Just like the other Romance languages, nouns in Italian must have a gender and number associated with them.

	Singular	Plural
Masculine	il	i
Masculine	lo	gli
Feminine	la	le
Masculine/Feminine	l'	gli/le

There are two masculine articles. The first row is used for a masculine noun that begins with a consonant, unless that word starts with a z or begins with s and another consonant. In those cases, you use the second row of masculine articles.

THE HUNS

Legends   The stories of the Huns' conquests played an important part in the folk-lore of the Germanic people. In particular, the Old Norse *Volsunga Saga*, an epic poem from thirteenth-century Iceland, and the *Hervarar saga ok Heiðreks* make considerable mention of the Huns and the battles they fought. In the *Hervarar saga*, a battle is depicted between the Huns and the Goths, and in the *Nibelungenlied*, another epic poem, a woman marries Attila the Hun.

THE ALPHABET

Modern English Alphabet   The Modern English alphabet is the current alphabet used in the United States, and it was established around 1550. With the advent of printing, the Old English alphabet evolved into the Modern English alphabet and actually got rid of many of the Anglo-Saxon letters, while maintaining the Latin alphabet. The Old English alphabet looked like this:

A B C D E F G H I K L M N O P Q R S T V X Y Z & ⁊ Ƿ Þ Ð Æ

The Modern English alphabet distinguished the letters *i* and *j* from being a single letter, as well as *u* and *v*, and it is believed the *w* was added at a later time.

GREEK MATHEMATICS

The School of Aristotle   Aristotle described three types of science. There was the theoretical, like math, physics, and logic; the productive, which were the arts; and the practical, which were politics and ethics. He distinguished the basic principles of mathematics into axioms, which include the laws of logic and contradiction, and postulates, which didn't need to be self-evident, but the results from them must sustain their truth.

THE CIRCULATORY SYSTEM

The Venous System   The venous system is responsible for bringing the blood back to the heart. From the capillaries, the blood flows through small veins called venules, and from there, the blood then flows to the veins. The superior and inferior venae cavae are the two largest veins in the body, and both end in the right atrium. The superior vena cava enters on the top while the inferior enters from the bottom.

ITALIAN

Useful Italian Phrases   Here are some helpful phrases to use when traveling to Italy:

Hi. *Ciao.*
Good morning. *Buongiorno.*
Good evening. *Buona sera.*
Where is the bathroom? *Dove posso trovare il bagno?*
How much is this? *Quanto costa questo?*
Thank you. *Grazie.*
Do you speak English? *Parli inglese?*
Can you help me? *Può aiutarmi? / Puoi aiutarmi?* (formal/informal)
When does the train leave? *Quando parte el treno?*

1. **What animal did the Huns use to make them so successful in their attacks on enemies?**
   a. Dogs
   b. Horses
   c. Hawks
   d. Tigers

2. **Attila became the sole ruler of the Huns when he:**
   a. Killed his brother
   b. Killed his uncle
   c. Killed his father
   d. Killed the leader of the Roman Empire

3. **The Phoenician alphabet was the first alphabet to:**
   a. Use hieroglyphs
   b. Use cuneiform
   c. Use symbols representing words
   d. Use symbols representing sounds

4. **What contributed to the change from the Old English alphabet to the Modern English alphabet?**
   a. Influence of the Greek alphabet
   b. The invention of the printing press
   c. Introduction of the Latin alphabet
   d. Christian missionaries introduced Anglo-Saxon futhorc

5. **Thales is credited for being the first mathematician to discover and teach deductive proofs in geometry. He was part of the:**
   a. School of Aristotle
   b. The Ionian School
   c. The Platonic School
   d. The Pythagorean School

6. **Aristotle divided math into two things, axioms and:**
   a. Art
   b. Physics
   c. Postulates
   d. Logic

7. **Your blood moves from the heart via arteries, and to your heart via veins, delivering _____ throughout your body.**
   a. Antibodies
   b. Capillaries and arteries
   c. Superior and inferior venae cavae
   d. Oxygen and nutrients

8. **After picking up oxygen from the lungs and delivering it to the cells, what do the red blood cells then transport to the lungs?**
   a. Carbon dioxide
   b. Nitrogen
   c. Carbon monoxide
   d. None of the above

9. **What vowels are always pronounced the same way in Italian?**
   a. E, O, I
   b. A, I, U
   c. A, E, I
   d. U, O, E

10. **How do you ask "How much is this?" in Italian?**
    a. Quando parte el treno?
    b. Può aiutarmi?
    c. Quanto costa questo?
    d. Puoi aiutarmi?

ANSWER KEY: b, a, d, b, d, c, d, a, b, c

HISTORY: The Ottoman Empire

What the Ottoman Empire Was, Rise of the Ottoman Empire, The Ottoman Empire Expands, Society of the Ottoman Empire, Decline of the Ottoman Empire, Collapse of the Ottoman Empire

MATH: Chinese Mathematics

Before the Qin Dynasty, Math of the Han Dynasty, Math of the Tang Dynasty, Math of the Song and Yuan Dynasties, *Precious Mirror of the Four Elements*, From the Ming Dynasty to the Qing Dynasty

LANGUAGE ARTS: Language

Why Humans Are Different, Linguistics, Semantics, Pragmatics, Phonetics, Syntax

SCIENCE: The Respiratory System

Inhalation, Exhalation, The Lungs, The Nose and Nasal Cavity, Asthma, Chronic Obstructive Pulmonary Disease

Lesson 5

FOREIGN LANGUAGE: German

The Origins, Old German, Middle German, Modern German, German Today, Useful German Phrases

THE OTTOMAN EMPIRE

What the Ottoman Empire Was   The Ottoman Empire was based in Turkey and lasted from 1299 to 1923. In the sixteenth and seventeenth centuries, the Ottoman Empire was at its peak, with territory ranging from North Africa to southwestern Asia and southeastern Europe, across twenty-nine provinces. For six centuries, the empire's capital city, Constantinople, was the center of interaction between the East and the West.

LANGUAGE

Why Humans Are Different   Human language is truly unique, and much different from languages of other animals. Humans can make an extremely wide variety of sounds to create languages, and in fact, the sounds and words we make are arbitrary. For humans, language is something that is learned through social interaction. Other animals, however, have only a very limited set of sounds they can produce, and those are genetically transmitted.

CHINESE MATHEMATICS

Before the Qin Dynasty   Mathematics has been found carved in oracle bones dating back to the Shang Dynasty, which lasted from 1600 to 1050 B.C. From the Shang Dynasty onward, the Chinese developed a full decimal system and showed a basic understanding of equations, arithmetic, algebra, counting rods, and even negative numbers. In the Zhou Dynasty, which lasted from 1122 to 256 B.C., Chinese students were required to study mathematics. There is little to no knowledge of the mathematics of the Qin Dynasty.

THE RESPIRATORY SYSTEM

Inhalation   The function of the respiratory system is to supply the blood with oxygen, which is then transferred to the rest of the body. Oxygen is received through breathing. The oxygen enters through the nose and mouth. From there, it goes through the larynx and trachea to the chest cavity, where the trachea then splits into small tubes called bronchi. The bronchus then divides once more, creating bronchial tubes, which lead to the lungs.

GERMAN

The Origins   German is one of the largest Indo-Germanic languages today. Though it has words based on Latin, it is not a Romance language. The closest relative of German is actually English, but it is also related to Dutch, Norwegian, Danish, and Swedish. The earliest record of the language dates back to 750. The origins of the German language are broken down into three periods: Old German, Middle German, and Modern German.

THE OTTOMAN EMPIRE

Rise of the Ottoman Empire   The Ottoman Empire arose in the early fourteenth century, just as the Roman Empire began to fall. It was originally created when the empire of the Seljuk Turks broke down. As the Ottomans began absorbing other states, by the reign of Muhammad II in 1451, all local Turkish dynasties had ended. Under Osman I and subsequent rulers, many attacks were aimed at the Byzantine Empire.

 LANGUAGE

Linguistics   Linguistics is the study of human languages, and it can be broken down into three categories: grammar (the rules used when speaking the language), meaning (how a language uses references to process and assign meaning), and its context (the evolution of language). Linguists believe the ability to learn and communicate with language is an innate process for humans, similar to our ability to walk.

 CHINESE MATHEMATICS

Math of the Han Dynasty   In the Han Dynasty, which lasted from 206 B.C. to A.D. 220, numbers were developed. These numbers were put into a place value decimal system and used with a counting board. Two famous mathematicians of this time, Liu Xin and Zhang Heng, made many advancements in learning, such as the number pi and astronomy. *The Nine Chapters on the Mathematical Art* was a book from A.D. 179 that taught how to use math in everyday life, as well as advanced lessons such as linear equations.

⚛ THE RESPIRATORY SYSTEM

Exhalation   Inside of the lungs are tiny sacs called alveoli. The inhaled oxygen passes through the alveoli and then diffuses into the arterial blood through the capillaries. As this is happening, the veins send waste-laden blood carrying carbon dioxide into the alveoli and this carbon dioxide comes out as you exhale. Both inhalation and exhalation are made possible by the diaphragm muscle below the lungs, which contracts and relaxes.

◑ GERMAN

Old German   Old German was used from 750 to 1050. Old Low German was known as Old Saxon. This was spoken by people of the northwest coast of Germany and in the Netherlands. During the barbarian invasion, or the migration period, the sound of the German language began to change. This is known as the High German consonant shift, and it's what began to distinguish Old High German from Old Saxon.

THE OTTOMAN EMPIRE

The Ottoman Empire Expands   From the reign of Muhammad II onward, the Ottoman Empire expanded widely over the land. In 1453, the Ottomans took over Constantinople, the capital of the Byzantine Empire. Expansion of the Ottoman Empire reached its peak in the sixteenth century under Sultan Selim I and Süleyman I. The empire expanded to include Hungary, Transylvania, Persia, Egypt, Syria, and Greece.

LANGUAGE

Semantics   Language assigns a meaning to a sign. The lexicon is the array of signs, which are arbitrary and connected to specific meanings. In other words, the lexicon is the words you know in a language. A lexeme is a single sign that is representative of a particular meaning. For example, *dog* only means one thing. A dog can never be mistaken for a cat or an elephant.

CHINESE MATHEMATICS

Math of the Tang Dynasty   By the Tang Dynasty, which lasted from 618 to 907, mathematics became standard in the great schools of China. Mathematician Wang Xiaotong wrote a book which included the first cubic equations. The Chinese of the Tang Dynasty excelled in complex algebra, binomial theorems, and geometry; however, early forms of trigonometry sent over from India, which had been translated into Chinese, were not widely appreciated.

THE RESPIRATORY SYSTEM

The Lungs   The surface area of the lung is larger than the surface area of your skin. If you were to line up all of the airways and air sacs inside of the lungs, the distance would cover more than 100 square yards. The lungs are the second line of defense against harmful materials that are inhaled, second to the nose. Mucus is produced inside of the lungs, which traps inhaled agents and provides white blood cells for protection.

GERMAN

Middle German   From Old Saxon came Middle Low German. This was the language spoken around the North Sea and Baltic Sea, and it had a heavy influence on the Nordic languages. From Old High German came Middle High German, which was used from 1050 to 1350. The High and Low refer to which part of the country the people lived in. During this time, a written language developed and Middle High German replaced Latin in official writings.

THE OTTOMAN EMPIRE

Society of the Ottoman Empire   One of the reasons the Ottoman Empire was so successful was its ability to unify a wide variety of people through its tolerance of other religions. This was done by establishing Millets. Millets were religious groups of people that were able to practice and retain their own laws, language, and traditions of their religions. The many different ethnicities, however, led to a weakness in nationalism, one of the contributing factors of the empire's decline.

LANGUAGE

Pragmatics   Pragmatics studies how the context of an utterance leads to meaning. It is used to explain how humans are able to overcome the ambiguities of language that are so closely related to time, space, manner, etc. An utterance is a concrete example of speech with a specific context, and pragmatics aims to understand how the specific context affects the meaning of the utterance.

CHINESE MATHEMATICS

Math of the Song and Yuan Dynasties   There were many great mathematicians during the twelfth and thirteenth centuries whose work revolved around cubic, quadratic, and root equations. Yang Hui was the first person to have discovered and proved Pascal's triangle. Qin Jiushao introduced zero to mathematics in China. Li Zhi studied algebraic geometry and revolutionized the process of inscribing triangles in a circle, using the Pythagorean theorem to solve his equations.

THE RESPIRATORY SYSTEM

The Nose and Nasal Cavity   The nose and throat are the first line of defense when it comes to protecting the respiratory system. As air is inhaled through the nose, the dirt is cleaned by the hairs in the nose, and further cleaned by mucus. The nasal cavity is lined with tissue that consists of many blood vessels. These blood vessels provide heat, which warms the air as it is taken in. The nasal cavity also adds moisture to this air, making it suitable for the lungs.

GERMAN

Modern German   Modern German began around 1500 and is still being used today. In 1880, the first grammatical rules were established, and in 1901, these were declared the standards for the German language. It is now the official language used in the church, state, education, and the arts.

THE OTTOMAN EMPIRE

Decline of the Ottoman Empire   From the sixteenth to the eighteenth century, the Ottoman Empire faced many wars, rebellions, and treaties. This took a great toll on the empire economically. The Ottoman Empire would come to lose control of Serbia, Montenegro, Bosnia, Romania, Herzegovina, Greece, and Egypt. The once-flourishing Turkey was now being referred to as "The Sick Man of Europe."

LANGUAGE

Phonetics   Phonetics is the study of sounds found in human speech. There are three basic areas of study in phonetics: articulatory phonetics, which studies the production of speech from the articulatory and vocal tract of a speaker; acoustic phonetics, which studies the transmission of speech as it goes from speaker to listener; and auditory phonetics, which studies the reception and perception by the one listening.

CHINESE MATHEMATICS

Precious Mirror of the Four Elements   Written by Chu Shi-jie in A.D. 1303, *Precious Mirror of the Four Elements* was a book that marked the peak of Chinese algebra. In his algebraic equations, Chu Shi-jie says the four elements — man, matter, earth, and heaven — represented four unknown quantities. In his problems, he deals with simultaneous equations, Horner's method, equations with degrees up to 14, and Pascal's triangle.

THE RESPIRATORY SYSTEM

Asthma   Asthma is a chronic inflammatory disease of the lungs, in which the airways tighten and narrow. It is the number one reason children chronically miss school, and it affects more than 20 million people. Asthma flares occur when the muscles contract and the lining of the airways starts to swell. This prevents proper airflow, and can result in wheezing, difficulty in breathing, and sometimes death.

GERMAN

German Today   Today, German is the most widely spoken language in the European Union, and it is one of the three most learned languages. It is the official language of Germany, Austria, Switzerland, Luxemburg, and Liechtenstein, and parts of Belgium, Romania, France, and Italy. German is spoken by more than 100 million people worldwide.

THE OTTOMAN EMPIRE

Collapse of the Ottoman Empire   In 1908, a nationalist and reformist group called the Young Turks forced the restoration of the 1876 constitution. In 1909, the sultan was deposed by Parliament, and replaced by Muhammad V. In the two Balkan Wars, Turkey lost nearly all of its European territory. During World War I, Turkey aligned with the Central Powers, and in 1918, the resistance collapsed, thus ending the Ottoman Empire.

LANGUAGE

Syntax   Syntax is the study of the rules and principles for constructing sentences. There are many theories relating to syntax. One of the most well-known theories is Noam Chomsky's transformational grammar, which recognizes the relationship between the different elements of a sentence and the variety of sentences in a language, and then uses rules to express the relationship.

CHINESE MATHEMATICS

From the Ming Dynasty to the Qing Dynasty   Starting in the mid-fourteenth century, the Ming Dynasty turned away from math, which led to a great decline in its studies. At the end of the sixteenth century, however, mathematical principles from the West spread throughout China. By the time of the Opium War of 1840, Western math was all the Chinese focused on and learned until in the nineteenth century, Chinese mathematicians created new developments in algebra. During the Ming Dynasty, use of the abacus became very popular.

THE RESPIRATORY SYSTEM

Chronic Obstructive Pulmonary Disease   Unlike asthma, which can be treated with medications, Chronic Obstructive Pulmonary Disease (COPD) is a narrowing of the airways that will gradually grow worse over time. It is a co-occurrence of emphysema and chronic bronchitis that is usually caused by an irritation of the lungs. The most common cause of COPD is smoking cigarettes. This can lead to wheezing, shortness of breath, a rapid breathing rate, and a chronic cough. Symptoms usually don't appear until significant lung damage has occurred.

GERMAN

Useful German Phrases   Here are some helpful phrases to know when traveling to a German speaking country:

Good morning. *Guten morgen.*
Hi. *Hallo.*
I'm lost. *Ich habe mich verlaufen.*
Where is the bathroom? *Wo ist das Badezimmer?*
How much is this? *Was kostet das? / Wie teuer ist das?* (formal / informal)
Do you speak English? *Sprechen Sie Englisch?*
What time is it? *Wieviel Uhr ist es? / Wie spät ist es?* (formal / informal)

LESSON 5 QUIZ

1. **One of the reasons the Ottoman Empire was so successful was because:**
   a. They won the two Balkan Wars.
   b. It was tolerant of other religions, allowing a wide variety of people to unify.
   c. The Young Turks forced a restoration of the constitution.
   d. Turkey aligned themselves with the Central Powers in World War I.

2. **At its peak, the Ottoman Empire included:**
   a. Canada, United States, Mexico, Egypt, Syria, and France
   b. Spain, Italy, Germany, Romania, Egypt, and Bulgaria
   c. Hungary, Transylvania, Persia, Egypt, Syria, and Greece
   d. Hungary, France, United States, Egypt, and Greece

3. **A word like *dog*, which can only mean one thing, is an example of:**
   a. A lexeme
   b. Syntax
   c. Noam Chomsky's transformational grammar
   d. Articulatory phonetics

4. **What is acoustic phonetics?**
   a. The study of the speech from the vocal tract of a speaker
   b. The study of speech as it is transmitted from speaker to listener
   c. The study of the perception and reception by the listener
   d. None of the above

5. **Which of the following is NOT one of the four elements described in *Precious Mirror of the Four Elements*?**
   a. Matter
   b. Water
   c. Heaven
   d. Earth

6. **Which of the following were advancements made during the Tang Dynasty?**
   a. Algebra
   b. Binomial theorem
   c. Geometry
   d. All of the above

7. **What is the first defense in protecting the respiratory system?**
   a. The lungs
   b. The nose
   c. The nasal cavity
   d. B and C

8. **What is the most common cause of COPD?**
   a. Wheezing
   b. Smoking
   c. Asthma
   d. Coughing

9. **The history of the German language can be broken down into:**
   a. Old German, Old Saxon, Modern German
   b. Old German, New Old German, Modern German
   c. Old German, Middle German, and Modern German
   d. Old German, New Middle German, Old Middle German

10. **From 1050 to 1350, what replaced Latin in official writings?**
    a. Middle High German
    b. Middle Low German
    c. Old Saxon
    d. Modern German

HISTORY: The Magna Carta

King John of England Taxes His People, King John and the Pope, The Creation of the Magna Carta, Clause 61, The Magna Carta Today, Lasting Effects of the Magna Carta

MATH: Scientific Notation

What Is Scientific Notation?, Example of Scientific Notation, Scientific Notation with Negative Integers, Going from Scientific Notation to Decimal Notation, Order of Magnitude, Engineering Notation

LANGUAGE ARTS: Reading

Literacy, Speed Reading, Subvocalized Reading, Lexical and Sub-lexical Reading, Rapid Automatized Naming, Reading Disorders

SCIENCE: The Digestive System

The Mouth, The Esophagus, The Stomach, The Small Intestine, The Large Intestine, Other Organs

Lesson 6

FOREIGN LANGUAGE: Polish

The Origins, Dialects, Kashubian, Polish Grammar, Polish Today, Useful Polish Phrases

THE MAGNA CARTA

King John of England Taxes His People   King John came to power in 1199 and became one of the most controversial monarchs in the country's history. Though never liked as a ruler, it was after a failed attack on France that King John set in motion the events leading to the creation of the Magna Carta. The mission against the French proved costly, and King John raised taxes on his people, causing outrage.

READING

Literacy   Literacy is the ability to use and understand the symbols of a writing system, be able to interpret what the symbols represent, and then be able to replicate those symbols so that others can understand them and come to the same conclusion. Illiteracy is not having the ability to understand what the symbols represent and derive the meaning.

SCIENTIFIC NOTATION

What Is Scientific Notation?   Scientific notation is a method of writing numbers that makes them easier to work with. These numbers can be any value, and this system is typically used because the numbers are too big or too small. By simplifying normal decimal notation, one can then apply them to other equations and formulas with ease. This is a typical example of scientific notation:

$$x + 10^y$$

x is a real number, and y is an integer representing how far you have to move the decimal point.

THE DIGESTIVE SYSTEM

The Mouth   When a person eats, the saliva in their mouth has enzymes that start to break down the chemicals in the food. As your teeth chew the food, you begin to further break it down into a mushy substance. The tongue then rolls this substance into a ball, and the food is now called bolus, meaning a substance that is broken down to the point that is ready to be swallowed.

POLISH

The Origins   Polish is a West Slavonic language. During the Middle Ages, as the proto-Slavonic tribes settled in Europe, three groups emerged: West, East, and South. The Polish language began to emerge during the tenth century, when the first Polish state was established. As Christianity spread through the land, the Polish adopted the Latin alphabet, which allowed people for the first time to write Polish, a language that until then had only been spoken. Over time, additional letters were added.

THE MAGNA CARTA

King John and the Pope   In 1207, King John fought with the pope over who should become Archbishop of Canterbury. As a result, the pope excommunicated the king, leading to increased tensions between the king and his people. Though the king would come to apologize to the pope, the pope was wary, and in 1214, the pope proclaimed that should anyone try to overthrow King John, they would be legally allowed to do so. That year, King John lost another battle against the French, resulting in England losing its possessions to France.

 READING

Speed Reading   Speed reading is the process of increasing the rate at which one reads without significantly reducing comprehension of the material. There are several methods one can use for speed reading, such as skimming, where one scans sentences for clues to figure out the meaning; or meta guiding, where one guides their eyes by using something (typically their finger) to point to the text.

 SCIENTIFIC NOTATION

Example of Scientific Notation   So now let's look at a simple example of scientific notation.

$$3 \times 10^4 = 30{,}000$$

The 3 can also be shown as 3.0 because there are no numbers following it. From there, we then have to move the decimal point an additional four spots. We move to the right, because the exponent is positive.

Similarly, to show the number 5,000 in scientific notation, it would look like this:

$$5 \times 10^3$$

 THE DIGESTIVE SYSTEM

The Esophagus   The tongue pushes the food to the back of the throat, toward the opening of the esophagus. The esophagus is a pipe responsible for moving food from the throat to the stomach. When a person swallows, a little flap called the epiglottis closes the windpipe, ensuring the food goes down the esophagus. Along the walls of the esophagus, muscles squeeze the food, until it reaches the stomach.

POLISH

Dialects   There are several dialects of Polish. Greater Polish is the dialect of the west, Lesser Polish is spoken in southern and southeastern Poland, Mazovian is spoken in eastern and central parts, Silesian is spoken in the south and southwest, and Highlander is spoken on the border of Poland of the Czech Republic and Slovakia. Highlander is strongly influenced by Romanian, as a result of migrants.

THE MAGNA CARTA

The Creation of the Magna Carta   Following the loss against the French, the English revolted against King John. In 1215, the Magna Carta was created. To this day, it is still one of the most celebrated documents ever written. Literally meaning "The Great Charter," the Magna Carta consisted of thirty-seven laws that greatly reduced the power of the king and allowed for the formation of a parliament. King John of England was forced to sign the document.

READING

Subvocalized Reading   Subvocalization is considered to be a bad habit if one wishes to understand and accomplish speed reading, but it is something that everyone does naturally. Subvocalization is the process of sounding the word out in your head as you read. This internal voice actually slows down the process of reading because you are saying the word at the rate at which you speak, which is not necessary when reading.

SCIENTIFIC NOTATION

Scientific Notation with Negative Integers   For negative integers, you go back the number of spaces the integer indicates.
    For example:

$$500 \times 10^{-1} = 50.$$

    You start at 500, which can be shown as 500.0, and you move the decimal point to the left one space, making it 50. No matter how complex the number may appear, to turn a number into decimal notation, you must follow the exponent.

THE DIGESTIVE SYSTEM

The Stomach   The stomach has three roles: to store food, to break the food down into chyme (a semifluid paste), and to empty the chyme into the small intestine. The stomach breaks the food down with the help of gastric juices that line the walls of the organ. The gastric juices start breaking the food down to its essential nutrients, and kill any harmful bacteria that may be in the food.

POLISH

Kashubian   Kashubian is one of the more commonly spoken variants of Polish. It is spoken in the north of Poland, west of Gdansk, and in Pomerania. The argument over whether Kashubian is a distinct language on its own or another dialect of Polish has long been disputed. It has been decided that Kashubian is in fact another language; however, the similarities between the languages are striking. Nevertheless, those who speak Polish will not understand Kashubian unless it is written down.

THE MAGNA CARTA

Clause 61 A large section of the Magna Carta is referred to today as Clause 61. This established the creation of a committee composed of twenty-five barons who would have the power to overcome the rule of the king at any time should he defy what was written in the Charter. If necessary, these barons could seize the king's possessions and castles. Both King John and the pope refused to allow this, and England entered into a civil war, known as the First Barons' War. The Magna Carta was only valid for three months, and was considered to be a failure.

READING

Lexical and Sublexical Reading Lexical and sublexical processes contribute to how a person learns to read. Sublexical reading involves associating characters with sounds. This is accomplished by learning with the phonics methodology. Lexical reading is acquiring phrases or words without paying attention to the characters those words are made up of. Lexical reading uses a "whole language" approach, which is the opposite of phonics and focuses on the components of sounds found in a language.

SCIENTIFIC NOTATION

Going from Scientific Notation to Decimal Notation To turn a number from decimal notation to scientific notation, you must work backward. You are starting with a number in decimal form, and want to end with the $x \times 10^y$ equation. When doing this, you want to make x as simple a number as you can between 1 and 10.

So for example, 0.003 would be equivalent to 3×10^{-3}

And if the number is more complex, just remember to make it between 1 and 10. For example: .002345 is just 2.345×10^{-3}

THE DIGESTIVE SYSTEM

The Small Intestine From the stomach, the food enters the small intestine, an organ that, outstretched, is 22 feet long in an adult. The small intestine breaks the food down further and it is where the major amount of absorption of nutrients takes place. The nutrients are then sent to the liver, while what's left of the food is passed on to the large intestine.

POLISH

Polish Grammar Grammar in Polish is heavily influenced by the Old Slavic system of grammar. The endings of nouns, pronouns, and adjectives change according to function, with seven distinctions (nominative, genitive, dative, accusative, instrumental, locative, and vocative). There are also two number classes (singular and plural), and like many Slavic languages, there aren't any definite or indefinite articles.

THE MAGNA CARTA

The Magna Carta Today   Today, only three of the original sixty-three clauses are still valid in England. The first clause guaranteed the liberties of the English Church. The second clause declared that London and all of the other cities, towns, ports, and boroughs would be allowed to enjoy their ancient customs and liberties. The last clause, and the most well known of the three, states that no free man shall be imprisoned, seized, or stripped of his rights except by a lawful judgment by his equals and that no one will be denied justice.

READING

Rapid Automatized Naming   Rapid Automatized Naming, or RAN, is the time that it takes someone to name symbols, colors, pictures, and objects out loud, and as quickly as they possibly can. This test can be a good predictor of a child's ability to read later in life, and it is independent from the child's current verbal IQ, phonological awareness, and reading skills that already exist.

SCIENTIFIC NOTATION

Order of Magnitude   The order of magnitude is a number rounded to the nearest power of 10. This enables simple comparisons, estimates, and rough calculations to be performed. So, for example, if something is 1.9 and you need to use it in a calculation, that number is closer to 10^0 than it is 10^1, so when solving your problem, you would use 10^0.

THE DIGESTIVE SYSTEM

The Large Intestine   The large intestine measures five feet long and is fatter than the small intestine. What the small intestine passes on to the large intestine is waste. There is no longer any nutritional value to the substance, so therefore the body can't use it and it must be taken out. The substance passes through a part of the large intestine called the colon, which is the last chance to absorb any water or minerals. The result is feces, and the large intestine then pushes this solid waste to the rectum.

POLISH

Polish Today   There are 50 million Polish speakers worldwide. Polish is the official language of Poland; however, it is used as a secondary language in some parts of Lithuania, Russia, Belarus, Kazakhstan, and Ukraine. This is a result of migration, resettlements, and border changes from the Yalta Agreement following World War II. Today, Polish is the third most widely spoken Slavic language.

THE MAGNA CARTA

Lasting Effects of the Magna Carta The Magna Carta greatly influenced the United States Constitution, the Declaration of Independence, and the Bill of Rights during the writing of these documents. The third clause from the Magna Carta, which stated accused persons shall not be imprisoned until found guilty by their peers is perhaps the most obvious influence, as it appears in the Fifth Amendment of the Bill of Rights. Also, the first clause included the principle of the separation of church and state.

READING

Reading Disorders Reading disorders are the most common forms of learning disabilities. Developmental reading disorder, or dyslexia, is a learning disability that impairs the ability to comprehend accurately in areas such as reading, spelling, and speaking. Dyslexia does not interfere with the ability to think and understand ideas or affect the intelligence of a person. Many common symptoms of dyslexia are having difficulty rhyming, having difficulty recognizing written words, and difficulty determining what a simple sentence means.

SCIENTIFIC NOTATION

Engineering Notation Engineering notation is a form of scientific notation used in civil and mechanical engineering. It is slightly different than scientific notation. In engineering notation, the powers of ten are restricted to be only multiples of three. This is because they are actually powers of a thousand, so instead of writing $1,000^2$, it looks like 10^6.

THE DIGESTIVE SYSTEM

Other Organs The liver, gallbladder, and pancreas also play a key role in the digestive system. These organs send digestive juices to the small intestine. The pancreas is responsible for sending juices that digest protein and fat. Bile, a substance created by the liver but stored in the gallbladder, absorbs fat in the bloodstream. The nutrient-rich blood is then sent to the liver, where waste is filtered out.

POLISH

Useful Polish Phrases Here are some helpful phrases to use when traveling in Poland:

Good morning. *Dzień dobry.*
Good evening. *Dobry wieczór.*
Hello. *Cześć.*
Goodbye. *Do widzenia* (formal) *Do zobaczenia / Narazie! Cześć!* (informal)
I don't understand. *Nie rozumiem.*
I speak English. *Mówię po angielsku.*
Thank you. *Dzięki / Dziękuję / Serdecznie dziękuję.*
Where is the toilet? *Gdzie jest toaleta?*
How much is it? *Ile to kosztuje?/Po ile to jest?*

1. **What did Clause 61 do?**
   a. Made it so that no free man shall be imprisoned or stripped of his rights without lawful judgment by his peers
   b. Allowed London and all of the other cities, towns, ports, and boroughs to enjoy their ancient customs and liberties
   c. Established the creation of a committee composed of twenty-five barons who would have the power to overcome the rule of the king at any time
   d. Guaranteed liberties of the English Church

2. **The Magna Carta had a great influence in the creation of:**
   a. The Bill of Rights
   b. The U.S. Constitution
   c. The Declaration of Independence
   d. All of the above

3. **Methods used for speed reading include:**
   a. Subvocalized reading
   b. Meta guiding
   c. Skimming
   d. B and C

4. **What is the difference between lexical and sublexical reading?**
   a. Lexical involves components of sound, whereas sublexical involves learning the sounds of each symbol.
   b. Lexical is based on phonics and sublexical is not.
   c. Sublexical uses Rapid Automatized Naming and lexical uses phonics.
   d. Lexical uses skimming and sublexical doesn't.

5. **What is 400 in scientific notation?**
   a. 40×10^0
   b. 4×10^{-2}
   c. 4×10^2
   d. 40×10^2

6. **What is 6.4×10^{-3} in decimal notation?**
   a. 6400
   b. -6400
   c. 0.0064
   d. 0.064

7. **What is a bolus?**
   a. The gastric juices in the stomach
   b. The enzymes in the saliva
   c. The waste product created in the liver
   d. Food that has been broken down into a mushy substance and ready to be swallowed

8. **One of the roles of the gastric juices in the stomach is to:**
   a. Kill any bacteria in the food
   b. Absorb nutrients
   c. Turn the food into bile
   d. Absorb bile

9. **What type of language is Polish?**
   a. A Romance Language
   b. A West Slavonic Language
   c. An East Slavonic Language
   d. A North Slavonic Language

10. **How do you say "Where is the toilet?" in Polish?**
    a. Gdzie jest toaleta?
    b. Po ile to jest?
    c. Ile to kosztuje?
    d. None of the above

HISTORY: The Reformation

Power of the Church, Martin Luther's 95 Theses, The Reformation Spreads Throughout the Land, John Calvin, The Day of Placards, The Counter-Reformation

MATH: Operations

Addition, Subtraction, Multiplication, Division, Squaring and the Square Root, Factorials

LANGUAGE ARTS: Writing

Logographies, Syllabaries, Left-Handedness, Right-Handedness, Cross-Dominance, Ambidexterity

SCIENCE: Tissues

What Is Tissue?, Epithelial Tissue, Connective Tissue, Muscle Tissue, Nervous Tissue, Organs

Lesson 7

FOREIGN LANGUAGE: Russian

The Origins, Cyrillic, Peter the Great Reforms the Language, A Need to Change the Language, The Soviet Union's Spelling Reform of 1918, Useful Russian Phrases

THE REFORMATION

Power of the Church   By the beginning of the sixteenth century, Roman Catholicism was the only religion in Western Europe. The Church believed that it alone had the power to interpret the Bible. However, with the Renaissance and the invention of the printing press, people started believing the Church had too much control. In the fourteenth century, a man named John Wycliffe became the first to translate the Bible from Latin into English. This idea was soon picked up by Jan Hus of Bohemia, who began preaching his own sermons.

WRITING

Logographies   Today, the main logographic systems of writing are found in Chinese and Japanese languages. Logograms are written characters or symbols that represent a word. One major disadvantage to a system like this is the amount of characters one has to know and how long it would take to learn so many words. For this reason, there are no languages that are fully logographic, and they all have some phonetic components.

OPERATIONS

Addition   Addition is literally the process of adding, or combining, one thing to another thing. So in the problem 3 + 6, you are adding or combining the two numbers together, leaving you with an end result of 9. The plus sign (+) is actually derived from an abbreviation of the Latin word *et*, which means "and." The plus sign first appeared in print in 1489 in Johannes Widmann's *Mercantile Arithmetic,* or *Behende und hubsche Rechenung auff allen Kauffmanschafft.*

TISSUES

What Is Tissue?   In the body, specific cells group together to perform a certain specialized function, creating tissue. When many tissues group together to carry out a specific function, it becomes an organ. In animals, there are four types of tissue found in the body: epithelial tissue, connective tissue, muscle tissue, and nervous tissue.

RUSSIAN

The Origins   In the sixth century, the Slav people migrated from Old Poland and gradually occupied the Balkans. By the tenth century, Western, Southern, and Eastern Slavonic had emerged as three similar, yet distinct, language groups. Eastern Slavonic is a direct ancestor of what would become Belarusian, Ukrainian, and Russian. The languages shared many grammatical rules, and were able to share one written language (and only a written language), known as Old Slavonic.

THE REFORMATION

Martin Luther's 95 Theses   In 1517, Martin Luther, an Augustinian monk, became fed up with the Church's policies of selling indulgences and misleading people. Luther wrote a series of 95 theses against the practices of the Church (such as indulgences), as well as new ideas for a better religion (such as rejecting the authority of the pope). Luther nailed his 95 theses on the door of the church at Wittenberg.

WRITING

Syllabaries   A syllabary is a set of written characters or symbols (known as syllabograms) that represent syllables. These syllables are then used to make words. A syllabogram is either made up of a consonant with a vowel, or a vowel on its own. The syllabary writing system is used when writing languages that originally had no written form, such as Cherokee, and it is also found in Japanese.

OPERATIONS

Subtraction   Subtraction, the inverse of addition, means to take a certain number away from the original value. So for example, if we subtract 3 from 10 (expressed as $10 - 3$), then we are left with 7. The first time the minus sign appeared in text was also in Johannes Widmann's *Mercantile Arithmetic* or *Behende und hubsche Rechenung auff allen Kauffmanschafft*. It is believed that the minus sign may have come from the tilde ($\sim$) which was used with the letter *m* to represent the Latin word *meno*, meaning minus.

✳ TISSUES

Epithelial Tissue   Epithelial tissue is tissue that covers the entire body, and it forms the covering or lining of internal and external surfaces. It is made up of closely packed cells formed into one or many layers, with close to no intercellular spaces and little intercellular substance. Endothelium is the tissue on the surface of the internal cavities, and its main function is for absorption, excretion, protection, secretion, reproduction, and sensory reception.

◖ RUSSIAN

Cyrillic   In the ninth century, Constantine and Methodius, two missionaries, were ordered to write down the language of Old Slavonic and preach to the people of Moravia about Christianity. Constantine, who on his deathbed changed his name to Cyril, created a Slavonic alphabet that is now known as Cyrillic. The Cyrillic alphabet was closely based on the Greek alphabet, with additional letters added for sounds not found in the Greek system.

THE REFORMATION

The Reformation Spreads Throughout the Land At the same time that Luther's ideas began to spread, Ulrich Zwingli led a similar revolt in Switzerland. The printing press enabled the ideas of Luther and Zwingli to reach the general public; however, there were differences in some of their ideologies. The teachings of Luther would become established as Lutheranism. Soon another voice would rise and become a prominent figure in the Protestant Reformation: John Calvin.

WRITING

Left-Handedness Handedness is more than just which hand feels more comfortable when writing. Hand orientation develops in the fetus. One leading theory suggests that prenatal testosterone impacts brain organization of the fetus, and that higher amounts of it can lead to left-handedness in the child. This theory would help explain why more males are left-handed than females, and why there is a higher rate of left-handedness found in male twins.

OPERATIONS

Multiplication Multiplication is the process of repeated addition. For example, 5×4 is simply saying 5 added to itself 4 times, or $5 + 5 + 5 + 5$. There are many ways to represent multiplication. The first and most common is by using the multiplication sign $\times$. Multiplication can also be expressed as a dot, such as $5 \cdot 4$, or by placing numbers side by side with parentheses between them, such as $5(4)$.

TISSUES

Connective Tissue Connective tissue supports and binds to other tissues in the body. It is the framework that epithelial tissue rests upon, and it is what nerve and muscle tissues are embedded in. The major cells involved in immunological defense are also found in the connective tissue, and connective tissue is where inflammation, the body's defense against invading microorganisms, occurs.

RUSSIAN

Peter the Great Reforms the Language In the early eighteenth century, Peter the Great came to power in Russia. With his political reforms came a reform of the alphabet that modified and simplified it and removed some of the Greek letters. Some vocabulary from Western Europe was introduced, and the language reflected Post-Renaissance Europe instead of the Byzantine Empire's way of pronouncing words.

THE REFORMATION

John Calvin   In 1536, John Calvin, a lawyer, published "Institutes of the Christian Religion," in which he expressed his theology. Calvin's teachings gained in popularity, and soon Calvin would reform the church in Geneva and force its citizens to follow his practices. Although Calvin and Luther were contemporaries and shared many similar beliefs, there were considerable differences. In particular, Calvinism espoused the idea of predestination, that a person was destined at birth to either be saved or doomed to damnation.

WRITING

Right-Handedness   Ninety percent of the world is right-handed. Scientists are still unsure how to explain the dominance of the right hand; however, it has been discovered that the rate of right-handedness in primitive man was less than it is today. In cultures where text is written from left to right, the right hand is considered to be more favorable, and in many religions and cultures, using the right hand shows respect.

OPERATIONS

Division   Division is the opposite of multiplication. It is the process of splitting something into equal parts. Division can be represented in several ways. The most common symbol is ÷, but it can also be expressed with / between two numbers or with a bar between two numbers like in a fraction. So, if 5 × 4 = 20, then 20 ÷ 5 = 4. That problem can also be expressed as 20/5 or $\frac{20}{5}$.

⚛ TISSUES

Muscle Tissue   Muscle tissue can contract and conduct electrical impulses and allow the body to move. Muscle is classified as voluntary or involuntary, and smooth or striated. There are three types of muscle tissue: skeletal muscle (which is voluntary, striated, and attached to the bone); cardiac muscle (which is involuntary, striated, and found in the heart); and smooth muscle (which is involuntary, smooth, and found in the digestive system, respiratory system, eyes, and the walls of blood vessels).

☾ RUSSIAN

A Need to Change the Language   By the middle of the eighteenth century, there was a need for the written Russian language to reflect the actual language spoken. Three distinct styles were distinguished: high style, also known as Church Slavonic, which was to be spoken for religion and poetics; middle style, which was used for science and prose; and low style, which was to be used for low comedies and personal correspondence. The middle style would come to form the Russian language that exists today. It was a combination of East Slavonic and Church Slavonic.

🏛 THE REFORMATION

The Day of Placards On October 18, 1584, citizens of Paris awoke to find the city covered with placards denouncing the Catholic Mass and condemning the Eucharist, among other things. These placards were also posted all around northern France and even on the king's door. A group of Huguenots, French adherents of Calvinism, were deemed the culprits, and were burned. Suppression of Protestantism soon followed.

✍ WRITING

Cross-Dominance Cross-dominance, or mixed-handedness, is when a person favors one hand for some activities and favors the other hand for different activities. Ambidexterity is a rare form of cross-dominance, but in many cases, a person can be left- or right-handed and cross-dominant. There are also cases where people who are cross-dominant are stronger on their less dominant side.

➗ OPERATIONS

Squaring and the Square Root Squaring a number is multiplying that number by itself. It is represented by having a small 2 as the exponent next to the number that you are going to multiply. So, 4^2 is equal to 16, because $4 \times 4 = 16$. The square root is the inverse of squaring and is represented by $\sqrt{}$. Perfect squares are squares of whole numbers. For example, $\sqrt{100} = 10$ because $10^2 = 100$, and that is a perfect square. However, $\sqrt{105} = 10.246951$, and that is not a whole number, and therefore, not a perfect square.

✳ TISSUES

Nervous Tissue Nervous tissue is made up of neurons (cells that transmit messages) and neuroglia cells (cells that protect the neurons). Nervous tissue is specialized to conduct impulses and react to various stimuli, and it is the main part of the nervous system. Nervous tissue consists of the brain, the spinal cord (making up the central nervous system), and the peripheral nerves (making the peripheral nervous system).

☭ RUSSIAN

The Soviet Union's Spelling Reform of 1918 Shortly after the Russian Revolution, and as a direct result of political ideology, the Russian language was simplified once again. This time, four letters were removed, and one silent letter used at the end of words was also removed. New political terminology was introduced, and the politeness characteristic toward the upper classes was also removed. These steps were characteristic of what the new authoritarian regime set out to accomplish.

THE REFORMATION

The Counter-Reformation Initially, the Catholic Church thought nothing of the Reformation, but as it spread from country to country, the Church established the Council of Trent to repair the schism that was occurring. A Spanish nobleman named Ignatius Loyola, who had renounced his military life, founded the Jesuits, a group that made reforms from within the Church. By the end of the sixteenth century, half of the lands lost to Protestant Reform returned to the Catholic Church, a divide that still exists today.

WRITING

Ambidexterity Ambidexterity is the ability to be equally adept at using both the left and the right hand. It is a rare form of cross-dominance, and though it can be taught, only 1 out of 100 people are born naturally ambidextrous. Because many items are made for right-handed people, left-handed people learn to use their right hands, and are more likely to become ambidextrous than right-handed people.

OPERATIONS

Factorials Factorials are a very simple concept to understand. It is expressed by having an exclamation point following a number (for example, 5!). Factorials are the product (meaning result from multiplication) of all of the positive integers less than or equal to that number. So, 5! is really saying $5 \times 4 \times 3 \times 2 \times 1 = 120$.

TISSUES

Organs Organs are groups of tissues that work together to perform a specific function. In organs, there is usually a main tissue called the parenchyma, which is unique to the specific organ, and sporadic tissues called the stroma, such as connective tissue or blood. Groups of organs that work together to perform a specific function form organ systems.

RUSSIAN

Useful Russian Phrases Here are some helpful phrases to use when traveling to Russia. Note that these are not written with the Russian alphabet, but rather pronunciations that have been written in English.

Good day. *Dobry den.*
Hi/Hello. *Privet.*
Do you speak English? *Govorite li vy po angliyski?*
I need to use the restroom. *Mne nuzhno otoyti v tualet.*
What time is it? *Kotoryy chas?*
Goodbye. *Do svidaniya.*
Yes. *Da.*
No. *Net.*

1. **Which one of the following did Martin Luther include in his 95 Theses?**
   a. Rejection of Christianity
   b. Rejection of Protestantism
   c. Rejection of the pope
   d. Rejection of the Trinity

2. **Which of the following is true?**
   a. By the beginning of the sixteenth century, Roman Catholicism was the only religion in Western Europe.
   b. By the beginning of the sixteenth century, Protestantism and Calvinism were the only religions in Western Europe.
   c. By the beginning of the sixteenth century, Lutheranism was the only religion in Western Europe.
   d. By the beginning of the sixteenth century, Lutheranism and Calvinism were the only religions in Western Europe.

3. **Ambidexterity is an example of:**
   a. Right-handedness
   b. Left-handedness
   c. Syllabaries
   d. Cross-dominance

4. **What is one reason why there are no fully logographic languages?**
   a. Words do not sound the way they are written.
   b. With the amount of characters, it would take too long to learn every word.
   c. There are too many consonants in each word.
   d. There are too many vowels in each word.

5. **What operation is being expressed in the following problem: 9(6) = 54**
   a. Division
   b. Square root
   c. Factorial
   d. Multiplication

6. **Which of the following is a perfect square?**
   a. $\sqrt{97}$
   b. $\sqrt{43}$
   c. $\sqrt{49}$
   d. $\sqrt{67}$

7. **The major cells involved in immunological defense are found in the:**
   a. Connective tissue
   b. Nervous tissue
   c. Epithelial tissue
   d. Organs

8. **Which of the following is a main function of the endothelium?**
   a. Absorption
   b. Protection
   c. Secretion
   d. All of the above

9. **Who invented Cyrillic?**
   a. Peter the Great
   b. Constantine
   c. Methodius
   d. B and C

10. **Which of the following was not a change made in the Soviet Union Spelling Reform of 1918?**
    a. Four letters were removed.
    b. One silent letter that was put at the end of words was removed.
    c. New political terminology was introduced.
    d. New vowels were introduced.

HISTORY: Rome
The Founding Myth, The Roman Kingdom, The Roman Republic, The Roman Empire, The Fall of Rome, The Colosseum

MATH: Decimals

Naming Numbers with Decimals, Addition and Subtraction with Decimals, Multiplying with Decimals, Division with Decimals, Rounding Decimals, Finding the Percent of a Number

LANGUAGE ARTS: Speaking
The Vocal Folds, The Voice, Volume, The Pitch of a Voice, Diction, Speech Impediments

SCIENCE: Reproduction
The Human Reproductive System, Gametes, The Male Reproductive System, The Female Reproductive System, Fetal Development, Asexual Reproduction

Lesson 8

FOREIGN LANGUAGE: Greek
Mycenaean Greek, Classical Greek, Hellenistic Greek, Medieval Greek, Modern Greek, Useful Greek Phrases

ROME

The Founding Myth   According to legend, Romulus and Remus were the children of the god Mars. Mars feared they would one day kill him, and decided to drown them. They were rescued by a she-wolf and raised by her until ultimately being found by a shepherd and his wife. When the boys grew older, they decided to build a city. In a fight over who would rule the city, Romulus killed Remus with a rock. Romulus then named the city after himself and called it Rome.

SPEAKING

The Vocal Folds   Vocal folds, or what are commonly referred to as vocal cords, are responsible for producing your voice. Vocal folds are a pair of tissue flaps stretched across the trachea. The vocal folds open when breathing and close while swallowing food. During the process of speaking, the tissues vibrate and change the flow of air that comes from your lungs. This modification of airflow produces the sound of your voice.

DECIMALS

Naming Numbers with Decimals   Decimals are another way of expressing a fraction. The fraction $\frac{8}{10}$ is equivalent to 0.8. Each number after the decimal is based on the number 10. Therefore, 0.8 is actually eight-tenths. A number in the next spot to the right would make it hundredths, and the next spot to the right would make it thousandths. For example, 0.54 is the same as saying fifty-four-hundredths, and 0.986 is the same as saying nine-hundred eighty-six-thousandths.

REPRODUCTION

The Human Reproductive System   The reproduction system is a system of organs that work together and allow humans to reproduce. In order for reproduction to occur, two different types of reproduction systems must be present: the male reproduction system and the female reproduction system. The differences between these systems allow for the genetic material of both individuals to be passed on to the offspring.

GREEK

Mycenaean Greek   Mycenaean Greek is the oldest form of the Greek language. It was spoken from the sixteenth to eleventh centuries B.C. in Mycenae and Crete. The Linear B script tablets, which showed a system of writing based on a syllabic alphabet, is the only record of Mycenaean Greek. The language consisted of eighty-eight signs representing syllables and made no distinction between long and short vowels, or double consonants.

ROME

The Roman Kingdom   The Roman Kingdom lasted from 753 to 509 B.C. Rome was established as a village on the Tiber River and was ruled by seven kings (with Romulus as the first), who were elected by the village to serve for life. According to legend, Romulus's followers were mostly men from all classes, including slaves, and the shortage of women brought about the abduction of women from the neighboring tribe, the Sabines. The Kingdom of Rome expanded to 350 square miles at this time. Most notably, a Senate of 100 men was created to act as an advisory council to the king.

SPEAKING

The Voice   To create your voice, air is blown from the lungs against the loosely closed vocal folds. As the air pushes through the small space between the vocal folds, it covers the vocal folds. The air then passes through a constriction and speeds up, creating suction. The suction draws part of the vocal folds in toward the center, and they are then pushed by more air from the lungs. This repeated movement is known as the mucosal wave, and its regularity is essential to the production of your voice.

DECIMALS

Addition and Subtraction with Decimals   When adding decimals, it is important to line the decimals up. The numbers are then added in their respective rows starting from the right, and the decimal is carried over. So for example:

$$\begin{array}{r} 3.4 \\ +1.4567 \\ \hline 4.8567 \end{array} \quad \text{and} \quad \begin{array}{r} 4.5 \\ -3.2 \\ \hline 1.3 \end{array}$$

When subtracting decimals with multiple places, be sure to add zeros to the number with less digits. For example:

$$\begin{array}{r} 4.5 \\ -3.234 \end{array} \quad \text{can also appear as} \quad \begin{array}{r} 4.500 \\ -3.234 \end{array}$$

Now it appears as any other subtraction problem.

REPRODUCTION

Gametes   There are two types of gametes, or sex cells, involved in human reproduction. The male gamete is called the sperm and the female gamete is called the ovum, or egg. The gametes are produced in organs called gonads. In the male, the sperm is produced in the testes, and in the female, the ovum is produced in the ovaries. Each gamete carries twenty-three chromosomes. The ovum carries only an X chromosome, and the sperm can carry either an X or a Y chromosome. During sexual intercourse, the gametes come together in fertilization. If both have an X chromosome, the zygote will grow to become a female. If the sperm has a Y chromosome, it will become a male.

GREEK

Classical Greek   Classical Greek, or Ancient Greek, was widely spoken throughout the Roman Empire, and it is the language found in the works of Homer and all of the famous Athenian philosophers. There were three distinctive forms and dialects of the language based on the different tribes and their locations: Dorian (the coast of Peloponnesus), Aeolian (the Aegean islands), and Ionian (the west coast of Asia Minor).

ROME

The Roman Republic   After the last king, Tarquin the Proud, was overthrown, a republican system based on elected magistrates was put into effect, and along with the Senate, there was a new focus on separation of powers and a system of checks and balances. The Roman Republic lasted from 500 to 30 B.C. During this time, Rome expanded throughout the Mediterranean and into North Africa, Greece, and the Iberian Peninsula. Toward the end of this time period, one of the most famous rulers, Julius Caesar, came to power and attempted to become a dictator of Rome.

SPEAKING

Volume   The volume of a voice is a result of the pressure of the air that is blown past the vocal folds. The higher the amount of air, the higher the pressure will be and the louder the volume. The vocal cords must tense up to create such pressure and people who suffer from vocal fold paralysis are unable to raise the volume of their voice because they lack this pressure.

DECIMALS

Multiplying with Decimals   Multiplying with decimals requires a few extra steps. Let's take a look at a problem.

$$
\begin{array}{r}
5.46 \\
\times\ 0.6 \\
\hline
\end{array}
$$

The first thing you do is start from the number on the bottom, the 0.6. Starting from the right, take the 6 and multiply it by each of the numbers on top, starting from the right and moving to the left.

$$
\begin{array}{r}
3 \\
5.46 \\
\times\ 0.6 \\
\hline
6
\end{array}
$$

6 × 6 equals 36, so you put the 6 down, and then place the 3 above the 4. After multiplying 6 by 4, you then add that three. So your problem now looks like this:

$$
\begin{array}{r}
5.46 \\
\times\ 0.6 \\
\hline
76
\end{array}
$$

Then continue moving to the left until you have:

$$
\begin{array}{r}
5.46 \\
\times\ 0.6 \\
\hline
3276
\end{array}
$$

Do the exact same thing with the next digit on the bottom row. In this case, because it is zero, the result will be 000. You then add the two numbers you got, leaving 3276, and then count up the numbers that are behind decimals. In this case there are three total numbers behind decimals, so starting from the end of the number, you move to the left three spaces and your answer will be 3.276.

REPRODUCTION

The Male Reproductive System   The role of the male reproductive system is to produce semen, which transports the sperm during sexual intercourse. The external structures of the male reproduction system include the penis, the organ used during sexual intercourse; the scrotum, a sac that holds and moderates the temperature of the testicles; and the testicles, which make testosterone and generate sperm. There are several internal structures involved in the male reproduction system including the epididymus, a tube that transports, stores, and matures the sperm; and the vas deferens, a tube that transports the mature sperm to the urethra, which gets urine and semen out of the body.

GREEK

Hellenistic Greek   Hellenistic Greek, or Koine Greek, is traced back to the Hellenistic colonization created by the conquests of Alexander the Great. It was the first common Greek dialect, and it was developed from a mixture of the Attic dialect (a subdialect of Ionic spoken in Athens) and other Greek dialects. It became the lingua franca across the Mediterranean, meaning the common language among people who spoke various languages. This was also the language used in the translation of the Christian New Testament.

ROME

The Roman Empire   The Roman Empire, which lasted from 27 B.C. to A.D. 1453, began when Octavian took control of the empire after Julius Caesar was assassinated by a group of senators. The republic was never re-established, as the emperor held most of the power, but the Senate continued. Rome continued to expand, and by the time Trajan ruled (A.D. 98–117), the Roman Empire had expanded 6.5 million square kilometers. To better control the vast empire, authority was divided between four co-emperors. These divisions would ultimately divide the Roman Empire into a Western Empire and an Eastern Empire.

SPEAKING

The Pitch of a Voice   The pitch of your voice is determined by the frequency of the mucosal wave, and by altering the tension of your vocal folds. Vocal folds have the ability to get longer and shorter, and this leads to the tension in the vocal folds. Tension of the vocal folds must be symmetrical and must be altered in this way. The notion of tension leading to pitch is similar to that of a guitar, in which as the string is pulled tighter the pitch is higher.

DECIMALS

Division with Decimals   The process of dividing a whole number by a decimal is similar to any long division problem. Just remember to bring the decimal over and work it out normally. For example:

$$9\overline{)0.326} \text{ would be } 9\overline{)0.3260}$$

$$\begin{array}{r} 0.0362 \\ \hline 27 \\ 56 \\ 54 \\ \hline 2 \end{array}$$

The answer is 0.0362

When dividing a decimal by a decimal, the process requires one extra step. In order to divide, you need to make the divisor into a whole number by multiplying it by either 10, 100, 1000, or whatever is needed to make it whole, and whatever you do to the divisor, you must also do the dividend. So for example:

$.86\overline{)0.567}$ would become $86\overline{)56.7}$ and then you would solve it normally.

✸ REPRODUCTION

The Female Reproductive System   The female reproductive system is responsible for producing the egg cells and hormones and transporting the egg cells to the site of fertilization; if conception occurs, the beginning stages of pregnancy take place. If fertilization does not happen, the system is designed to shed the uterine lining, or menstruate. The female reproductive system is located internally in the pelvis and consists of the vagina, the cervix, the uterus (the major organ that accommodates the growing fetus and pushes the fetus out during delivery), the fallopian tubes (the source of fertilization), and the ovaries.

◗ GREEK

Medieval Greek   Medieval Greek, also known as Byzantine Greek, was spoken during the Byzantine Empire from 600 to the Ottoman conquest of Constantinople in 1453. It was the only language used in government and it is still the language used in the Greek Orthodox Church. Medieval Greek is considered to be the link between Ancient Greek and Modern Greek. Over time, neighboring languages and the languages of conquerors came to influence and shape the language.

ROME

The Fall of Rome   The Western Empire of Rome collapsed in 476 with an attack from the Visigoths. In 1453, the Eastern Empire collapsed, thus ending the great Roman Empire. There were several contributing factors that led to the fall of Rome, including its grand size, making it hard to control its people; the influence and spread of the newly formed religion, Christianity; the spread of Islam; attacks from barbarians; inflation; and even lead poisoning.

SPEAKING

Diction   Now that you understand how your voice works, it is important to know useful tools to help in using your voice. Diction means two things. It is the pronouncing of the words clearly so as to be understood by those listening to you, and it also relates to one's choice of words while speaking or writing so that what you are saying relates to the audience or listeners and has meaning.

DECIMALS

Rounding Decimals   Rounding with decimals is similar to rounding with any other kind of numbers. If the number in the thousandths is 4 or less, then that number is dropped and the number in the hundredths place remains. For example, 0.983 would be rounded to 0.98. If the number in the thousandths is 5 or higher, then the number is rounded to the nearest hundredth. For example, 0.986 would turn into 0.99. This same rule applies whether you are rounding from the tenths, the hundredths, or the thousandths.

REPRODUCTION

Fetal Development   Immediately upon fertilization, the sex of the child is determined. In the first four weeks, neural tubes, the foundation of the nervous system, will develop and the heart and a primitive circulatory system will form. By the third week, the embryo has developed along with a placenta, and its heart begins to beat. By day 40, the embryo is the size of a raspberry and has five fingers on each hand, and its brain waves can be detected. By week 12, the fetus breathes amniotic fluid, exercises, sleeps, awakens, and can open and close its mouth. By week 21, the fetus now weighs one pound. By week 36, the baby will weigh anywhere from six to nine pounds. By week 38, its heartbeat can be heard from outside of the womb and the baby is ready to come out.

GREEK

Modern Greek   Modern Greek refers to the language spoken from the fall of the Byzantine Empire in 1453 until now. There were two forms of the language spoken: Demotic and Katharévusa. Katharévusa was used for literature, scientific, administrative, and juridical purposes, and it was an imitation of the Classical Greek language. In 1976, Demotic was announced as the official language of Greece, and this is now known as Standard Modern Greek.

ROME

The Colosseum   Construction of the Colosseum, one of the best-known monumental structures associated with Rome, began in A.D. 72 and was completed eight years later. The amphitheater could seat 55,000 spectators and was 159 feet tall. Free games were held in the Colosseum for the public, representing power and prestige, and the events included comedy acts and gladiatorial fights to the death with animals and other gladiators.

SPEAKING

Speech Impediments   Speech impediments, or speech disorders, are disorders that disrupt the process of speaking normally. Speech impediments include stuttering, lisping, fronting (where "K" is replaced with "T," "G" is replaced with "D," "NG" is replaced with "N") and gliding ("R" and "L" are replaced with "W" and "Y"). Speech disorders are developmental and occur because children develop different sounds at different stages during childhood.

DECIMALS

Finding the Percent of a Number   Finding the percent of a number is very easy. If you are asked, "What percent of 98 is 32?" you must first divide 32 by 98. The answer is 0.32653061. Choose the first four numbers, and remember to round. You now have 0.3265. Then multiply this number by 100, leaving you with 32.65, and then round to the nearest whole number. So, 32 is 33 percent of 98.

✸ REPRODUCTION

Asexual Reproduction   What was just described was reproduction for humans; however, plants and even certain animals reproduce in a different way—asexually, or without a mate. This is done through mitosis. Mitosis is a process of cell division that involves replicating chromosome material. During asexual reproduction, genetic mixing does not happen, and it is sometimes referred to as cloning because the copies are identical.

◑ GREEK

Useful Greek Phrases   Here are some helpful phrases to use when traveling in Greece:

Hello (singular). *Yia sou.*
Hello (plural). *Yia sas.*
Thank you. *Efharisto.*
Excuse me. *Signomi.*
Please. *Parakalo.*
Where is the toilet, please? *Pou ine i twaleta, parakalo?*
Where is the beach? *Pou ine i paralia?*
Sorry, I don't speak Greek. *Signomi, ala then milao elinika.*
How much is it? *Poso kani?*

LESSON 8 QUIZ

1. **Which of the following didn't lead to the fall of Rome?**
   a. The spread of Christianity
   b. Lead poisoning
   c. Attacks from barbarians
   d. Attacks from the Byzantine Empire

2. **What event led to the rule of a succession of emperors in Rome?**
   a. Caesar's assassination
   b. Octavian's assassination
   c. Construction of the Coliseum
   d. The fall of the Western Roman Empire

3. **What is diction?**
   a. Replacing the "K" sound with a "T" sound
   b. Pronouncing words clearly
   c. When the vocal folds tighten
   d. The pitch of the voice

4. **What is the result of the pressure of the air that is blown past the vocal folds?**
   a. Stuttering
   b. Pitch
   c. Volume
   d. Gliding

5. **What can 0.982 be rounded to?**
   a. 0.983
   b. 0.98
   c. 0.99
   d. 1.98

6. **What does 9.2 × 0.8 equal?**
   a. 73.6
   b. 0.736
   c. 736
   d. 7.36

7. **How many chromosomes does each gamete carry?**
   a. 23
   b. 46
   c. 21
   d. 2

8. **Which of the following is not part of the male reproductive system?**
   a. Epididymus
   b. Vas deferens
   c. Fallopian tubes
   d. Urethra

9. **The first common Greek dialect is known as:**
   a. Ionian
   b. Koine
   c. Dorian
   d. Aeolian

10. **The two forms of Modern Greek spoken today are:**
    a. Koine and Katharévusa
    b. Demotic and Aeolian
    c. Demotic and Katharévusa
    d. Ionian and Katharévusa

HISTORY: The Middle Ages

The Early Middle Ages, The High Middle Ages, The Late Middle Ages, The Black Death, Science of the Middle Ages, Inventions of the Middle Ages

MATH: Measurement

The Metric System, The United States Custom Units, Length, Mass, Volume, Temperature

LANGUAGE ARTS: Listening

How We Hear, Active Listening, Active Listening Barriers, Informational Listening, Reflective Listening, Tips for Being a Good Listener

SCIENCE: Genetics

Gregor Mendel's Plants, Mendel's Laws of Inheritance, Inheritance Patterns, DNA, Gene Expression, Genetic Mutations

Lesson 9

FOREIGN LANGUAGE: Bulgarian

About Bulgarian, Old Bulgarian, Middle Bulgarian, Modern Bulgarian, Dialects, Useful Bulgarian Phrases

THE MIDDLE AGES

The Early Middle Ages   The Early Middle Ages, also known as the Dark Ages, followed the collapse of the Western Roman Empire, and lasted from the fifth century to the tenth century. From 400 to 700, Europe was greatly divided, and there was a great migration of Germanic and Slavic people. Besides the increase in migration, this time period was marked by an economic decline. Many empires rose and fell during this time, never being able to achieve the status or success of the Roman Empire. It is also during this time that feudalism starts to appear.

LISTENING

How We Hear   The ear is divided into three parts (the outer ear, the middle ear, and the inner ear) that lead to the brain. The outer ear is made up of the eardrum and the ear canal. As sound travels down the ear canal, the sound strikes the eardrum and causes it to vibrate. The middle ear is a space behind the eardrum where a chain of three bones, called ossicles, are. This chain of bones connects the eardrum to the inner ear, and as these bones vibrate, the fluid in the inner ear, or cochlea, begins to move. The movement of the cochlea causes hair cells to move, which sends electric messages up the auditory nerve. From there, the message is sent to the brain, which interprets these signals as sound.

MEASUREMENT

The Metric System   Though there are many systems of measurement found throughout the world, the Metric System is one of the most common systems used worldwide, with the notable exception of the United States. The metric system is a decimal system that measures with a base of ten. Weight is measured in grams, volume is measured in liters, dimensions are measured in meters, and Celsius is used to measure temperature.

GENETICS

Gregor Mendel's Plants   Austrian monk Gregor Mendel is considered to be the father of genetics. In 1856, Mendel conducted a series of studies on pea plants observing seven traits he found in the plants: the color and shape of the seed, the color of the flower, the color and shape of the pod, the position of the flower, and the height of the plant. Mendel performed tests in hybridization and cross-pollination and found that the first generation of plants only resembled one parent, but in the next generations, dominant and recessive traits appeared.

BULGARIAN

About Bulgarian   Bulgarian is a South Slavic language spoken by 9 million people today. It is the official language of the Republic of Bulgaria, though there are also Bulgarian-speaking minorities in neighboring countries such as Greece, Turkey, Macedonia, and the Ukraine. Bulgarian is believed to be the first Slavic language that was written, and the language evolved in three periods: Old Bulgarian, Middle Bulgarian, and Modern Bulgarian.

THE MIDDLE AGES

The High Middle Ages   The High Middle Ages, which lasted from the eleventh to the thirteenth century, was defined by urbanization, a unifying religion in Christianity, and a rise in population and military expansion. It is during this time that the Crusades, a series of wars fought between Christians and Muslims over the Holy Land occurred. From the Crusades came contact with Arab science, math, and philosophy, which had been developed from the classical works of Ancient Greek philosophers. The contributions made by the Muslim world were passed on to Europe.

LISTENING

Active Listening   There is a difference between hearing and listening. Hearing is a physiological process, but listening requires work. To actively listen, one must understand, interpret, and evaluate what has just been heard. There are three elements involved in active listening: comprehending, retaining, and responding. Comprehension involves the listener discerning the sounds and determining the context. Retaining uses memory to create a meaning of the words one hears. Responding can be both verbal and nonverbal.

MEASUREMENT

The United States Custom Units   There are only three countries in the world that have not adopted the metric system: Myanmar, Liberia, and the United States (though the metric system is used for scientific and medical measurements). The measurement system in the United States is based on the imperial system used in England (though England has since converted to the metric system). The system is not a base ten system.

GENETICS

Mendel's Laws of Inheritance   From his findings, Mendel came up with three laws regarding inheritance. The law of dominance states that if there is a pair of genes, the one that appears in the offspring is most likely the dominant one because that is passed on more often than the recessive gene. Mendel's principle of segregation states that an individual inherits an allele (or a unit of information) about a trait from both parents, and during the formation of the gamete, these alleles segregate from one another. Mendel's law of independent assortment states that the factors for characteristics are distributed independently to the reproductive cells.

BULGARIAN

Old Bulgarian   Old Bulgarian was also known as Old Church Slavonic (which you might recall from the lesson on Russian). It was spoken from the ninth century to the eleventh century, and it was the first written Slavic language that was used universally throughout the land. Old Bulgarian shared many qualities that other Slavic languages had; however, certain sounds were solely found in Bulgarian.

THE MIDDLE AGES

The Late Middle Ages   The Late Middle Ages, which lasted from 1300 to 1500, was a time defined by climate change, famine, disease, war, and social upheaval. The Great Famine of 1315 to 1317 and the Black Death led to an incredibly large loss of life. It is during this time that the Hundred Years' War was fought between England and France, and it is in the Late Middle Ages that the schism in the Catholic Church occurs.

LISTENING

Active Listening Barriers   There are several barriers that can interrupt active listening, and they can be anything from outside distractions to one's own emotions. Daydreaming or glazing over while a person speaks is one example of a barrier to active listening, as are interruptions and shift response. In shift response, instead of passively listening, the listener turns the conversation into one about him- or herself and no longer actively listens but focuses on the self.

MEASUREMENT

Length   The units of length used every day in the United States are inch, foot, yard, and mile. In this system, 12 inches makes 1 foot, 3 feet equals 1 yard, and 1 mile is 5,280 feet. In the metric system, 1 yard measures to be 0.9144 meters and 1 inch is measured to 2.54 centimeters.

GENETICS

Inheritance Patterns   There are three types of inheritance patterns: single-gene inheritance, multifactorial inheritance, and mitochondrial inheritance. These are all useful in understanding disease. In single-gene inheritance, also known as Mendelian inheritance, a single gene is mutated and then follows the predictable pattern of inheritance. In multifactorial inheritance, it is not due to a single gene but rather several genes and environmental factors. In mitochondrial inheritance, disease is transmitted by the mitochondria, organelles that are inherited only from the mother's egg.

BULGARIAN

Middle Bulgarian   From the twelfth century to the fifteenth century, the language changed dramatically. Middle Bulgarian was the official language used in the administration of the Second Bulgarian Empire. Many vowels lost their nasal quality, and consonants were harder in the West, while in the East, there was still a difference between hard and soft consonants. Also during this time, a new class of verbs developed.

THE MIDDLE AGES

The Black Death   In 1347, Europe was struck by the Black Death (now known to have been the bubonic plague). It is believed that one-third to one-half of the entire population of Europe was killed by this plague. The common belief is that rats in ships arriving from Asia were infected with the disease. The disease would then move from rats to fleas, and then the fleas would bite humans, infecting them. From there, the disease would spread from human to human.

LISTENING

Informational Listening   Informational listening concentrates on the ability to understand the message of someone that is speaking. Confirmation bias and the vividness effect can be barriers to informational listening. Confirmation bias involves taking particular parts of a conversation or message so that it fits your own personal beliefs or standards. The vividness effect relates to the impact of dramatic or highly graphic events and how they can affect the perception of a situation.

MEASUREMENT

Mass   There have been four systems to measure mass in the United States: Tower weight, Troy weight, avoirdupois weight, and apothecaries' weight. Today, avoirdupois is the main system used. Troy, apothecaries', and avoirdupois are all based on the same unit of measurement, the grain. In today's system, one grain equals 64.79891 mg, one dram equals 1.772 grams, one ounce equals 16 drams or 28.35 grams, one pound equals 16 ounces or 453.59237 grams, one hundredweight equals 100 pounds, and one ton equals 20 hundredweights.

GENETICS

DNA   Deoxyribonucleic acid, or DNA, is a double helix structure that carries all of the genetic information and is the hereditary material. The double helix structure is crucial in genetics. DNA can copy and replicate itself, and each strand in the double helix serves as a pattern for duplication. When cells divide, each new cell gets an exact copy of the old cell's DNA.

BULGARIAN

Modern Bulgarian   Modern Bulgarian started in the sixteenth century and borrowed many words from Greek and Turkish. The present-day written language, which was based on the vernacular language, was standardized in the nineteenth century and included Russian, German, and French words. There are no definite rules when it comes to stress in language, so the accent of each word must be learned. Unlike other Slavic languages, Bulgarian has definite articles and has dropped almost all case forms for nouns, using prepositions and positions like English.

THE MIDDLE AGES

Science of the Middle Ages   Science during the Middle Ages focused on the natural world. Much of the scientific advancements were from the Islamic world, learned by Europeans as they traveled during the Crusades. One of the major fields of science Europeans learned from the Arab world was the study of astronomy. Another important field of science studied during this time was known as alchemy (or what we refer to as chemistry today).

LISTENING

Reflective Listening   Reflective listening shows the speaker that you are listening and comprehend what is being said. The first step is to understand what you are listening to, and then the next step is to confirm that you understand by presenting the idea back to the speaker. There are several ways to show reflective listening, such as engaging in the conversation actively, empathizing with the point of view of the speaker, mirroring the speaker's mood, and summarizing what has been said using their words.

MEASUREMENT

Volume   Measurements of volume in the United States are the cubic inch, cubic foot, and cubic yard. Volume is also separated into two categories: volume of dry material and volume of liquids. Measurements of liquid volume and dry material include cups, pints, quarts, and gallons; however, the measurements are different. For example, one pint in dry volume is 550.610 mL, but one pint in liquid volume is 473.176 mL.

GENETICS

Gene Expression   Gene expression is the process of converting the gene's information into messenger RNA (mRNA) through a process called transcription, and then converting the information to a protein in a process called translation. Gene expression is responsible for interpreting the genetic code in the DNA, which gives rise to the organism's traits or phenotype.

BULGARIAN

Dialects   Even though the written language is used across the entire country, there are several variations in the spoken language. The differences in pronunciation of consonants that was found in Middle Bulgarian between the East and West still holds true today. Another one of the main differences can be found in the pronunciation of vowels, and there are even words only used in certain areas.

THE MIDDLE AGES

Inventions of the Middle Ages   There were many major technological advancements made during the Middle Ages. Among the most important inventions were the use of gunpowder, vertical windmills, the mechanical clock, the printing press, eyeglasses, and improvements on water mills. Advancements were made in agriculture as well, with the introduction of the heavy plough and three-field crop rotation.

LISTENING

Tips for Being a Good Listener   Here are some helpful tips for being a good listener:

- Pay attention to the speaker, and do not get distracted by outside noises or disturbances.
- Don't interrupt. Let the speaker finish his or her thought before talking and finish listening before speaking. If the whole time the person is talking you're thinking about what you are going to say, then you're not listening.
- Listen for the main ideas the speaker is trying to get across.
- Make sure to ask questions and repeat what you are hearing so that you are truly understanding what is being said.
- Give physical cues that you are listening: Maintain eye contact and nod your head, smile, laugh, etc. at the appropriate times.

MEASUREMENT

Temperature   Temperature in the United States is measured in degrees Fahrenheit. Both Celsius and Fahrenheit use the same reference points — the boiling point and freezing point of water — to make their measurements. However, in Celsius, the freezing point is 0°, and in Fahrenheit, 32°. In Celsius, the boiling point is 100°, and in Fahrenheit, 212°. To convert from Fahrenheit to Celsius, subtract the number by thirty-two and then multiply by five, and divide by nine. To convert from Celsius to Fahrenheit, multiply the number by nine, divide by five, and then add thirty-two.

GENETICS

Genetic Mutations   Genetic mutations are permanent changes found in the genetic sequence of an organism that alter the nucleic acids, which alter the DNA. Mutations are the main cause of diversity and can lead to evolution, but they can also lead to genetic diseases and cancers. Mutations can either be inherited by parents, or can occur during an organism's lifetime.

BULGARIAN

Useful Bulgarian Phrases   Here are some helpful phrases to use when traveling to Bulgaria:

Hello/Hi. *Zdravey/Zdrasti.*
Good morning. *Dobro utro.*
Good evening. *Dobar vecher.*
Yes. *Da.*
No. *Ne.*
Thank you. *Blagodarya.*
I do not understand. *Ne razbiram.*

Where is the bathroom? *Kade e baniata?*
How much is this? *Kolko struva tova?*
Can you help me? *Moje li da mi pomognete?*
Do you speak English? *Govorite li angliiski?*
My Bulgarian is bad. *Balgarskiiat mi e losh.*
Goodbye. *Chao.*

1. **Which of the following occurred in the Late Middle Ages?**
   a. Climate change
   b. Famine
   c. Disease
   d. All of the above

2. **Which of the following was not invented during the Middle Ages?**
   a. Gunpowder
   b. The mechanical clock
   c. The printing press
   d. Water mills

3. **Showing the speaker that you are listening and comprehending what is being said is an example of:**
   a. Confirmation bias
   b. Vividness effect
   c. Reflective listening
   d. Shift response

4. **There are three elements involved in active listening: comprehending, retaining, and what?**
   a. Responding
   b. Daydreaming
   c. Interrupting
   d. Understanding

5. **In the metric system, what is weight measured in?**
   a. Liters
   b. Meters
   c. Degrees Celsius
   d. Grams

6. **What is 50° Celsius in Fahrenheit?**
   a. 10º
   b. 122º
   c. -10º
   d. -122º

7. **What does the law of dominance state?**
   a. In a pair of genes, the one that appears in the offspring is most likely the recessive one because that is passed on more often than the dominant gene.
   h. In a pair of genes, only the dominant genes get passed on.
   c. In a pair of genes, only the recessive genes get passed on.
   d. In a pair of genes, the one that appears in the offspring is most likely the dominant one because that is passed on more often than the recessive gene.

8. **What does Mendel's principle of segregation state?**
   a. An individual inherits an allele from one parent, and during the formation of the gamete, the allele segregates from itself.
   b. An individual inherits an allele from both parents and during the formation of the gamete, these alleles segregate from one another.
   c. An individual inherits three alleles from both parents and during the formation of the gamete, these alleles segregate from one another.
   d. An individual inherits five alleles from both parents and during the formation of the gamete, these alleles segregate from one another.

9. **What was the official language used in the administration of the Second Bulgarian Empire?**
   a. Old Bulgarian
   b. Middle Bulgarian
   c. Modern Bulgarian
   d. Old Slavonic

10. **How do you say "Can you help me?" in Bulgarian?**
    a. Kade e baniata?
    b. Kolko struva tova?
    c. Govorite li angliiski?
    d. Moje li da mi pomognete?

HISTORY: The Crusades
The First Crusade, The Second Crusade, The Third Crusade, The Fourth and Fifth Crusades, The Sixth and Seventh Crusades, The Eighth and Ninth Crusades

 MATH: Graphs
Line Graphs, Bar Graphs, Pie Charts, Flow Charts, Organizational Charts, Pictographs

LANGUAGE ARTS: Thinking
Cognition, The Brain, Sentience, Consciousness, Imagination, Creativity

SCIENCE: The Earth's Layers
The Crust, The Upper Mantle, The Lower Mantle, The Outer Core, The Inner Core, The Atmosphere

Lesson 10

FOREIGN LANGUAGE: Albanian
The Origins, Influences, Dialects, The Albanian Alphabet, Grammar, Useful Albanian Phrases

THE CRUSADES

The First Crusade   The First Crusade lasted from 1096 to 1099. It was an attempt by Western Christians to recapture Jerusalem, the Holy Land, from the Muslims. Fearing that his country would fall to the Muslims, Alexius I of Constantinople called on Pope Urban II for help. The pope urged people to volunteer and repel the invading Turks, and the armies consisted of knights and, largely, of peasants. Eventually, Jerusalem was captured and the Kingdom of Jerusalem was created.

THINKING

Cognition   Cognition refers to the mental processes or functions involved in thinking, gaining and comprehending knowledge, remembering, problem solving, and judging. Cognitive processes can be conscious or unconscious, natural or artificial. Cognition is related to abstract ideas such as intelligence, the mind, memory, perception, and imagination.

GRAPHS

Line Graphs   Line graphs are useful for showing data that changes over a period of time. By plotting the dips and peaks on the graph and then connecting them to make a line, you are able to compare, monitor, and analyze improvement and decline of the data. Line graphs use an x axis and a y axis, the x axis going horizontally, and the y axis going vertically.

THE EARTH'S LAYERS

The Crust   The outermost layer of the Earth, the layer we are living on, is called the crust. It is the thinnest layer of the Earth, and is composed of two types of rock: granite (otherwise known as the continental crust) and basalt (also known as oceanic crust). Basalt is found underneath the oceans, and granite is the crust of the continents. Granite is also older than basalt.

ALBANIAN

The Origins   Albanian does not belong to any other family of the Indo-European languages. The vocabulary of Albanian is distinct, though the language does borrow from Germanic, Balto-Slavic, and Greek. Albanian is believed to have originated from Illyrian, a language spoken in the Western Balkans until the sixth century; however, others believe it is a descendent from Dacian or Thracian, languages spoken in the Balkans until the fifth century. Albanians call their language Shqip.

 THE CRUSADES

The Second Crusade   The Second Crusade took place from 1145 to 1149, and occurred after the County of Edessa, a Crusader state established in the First Crusade, fell. This Crusade was announced by Pope Eugene III, and it was led by European kings from France and Germany. The armies of the two kings marched separately and were each defeated by the Seljuk Turks and the Crusade was considered a failure.

THINKING

The Brain   Thinking is a complex and abstract idea, but one thing that is not abstract is the location of where we think. In our brain, the cerebral hemispheres are divided into lobes, which specialize in performing different functions. The two frontal lobes are used when imagining, planning, and making reasoned arguments. Broca's area on the left frontal lobe is responsible for transforming thoughts into words.

GRAPHS

Bar Graphs   Bar graphs are excellent for presenting and comparing data. The values are represented by rectangular bars that differ in height according to the values they represent. Whereas line graphs are used to show a change in time, bar graphs are used to show different amounts. Similar to line graphs, bar graphs also make use of the *x* and *y* axes, and bar graphs can be presented either horizontally or vertically.

THE EARTH'S LAYERS

The Upper Mantle   The layer underneath the crust and above the core is known as the mantle. Mantle rock makes up around 84 percent of the Earth's volume. The mantle begins around 19 miles below the continental crust and 6 miles below the oceanic crust. It can be divided into two parts: the upper and lower mantle. In the upper mantle is the asthenosphere, which is involved in plate tectonic movement. Part of the lithosphere, the outermost shell of the planet, is also in the upper mantle.

ALBANIAN

Influences   The earliest language that Albanian borrowed from was Doric Greek, and from the second to the fifth centuries, Albanian also began absorbing Greek and Latin. Latin had the largest influence on the language. From the seventh to the ninth centuries, the language absorbed Southern Slavic and Proto-Romanian, a result of tribes settling in the Balkans.

THE CRUSADES

The Third Crusade   Also known as the King's Crusade, the Third Crusade lasted from 1189 to 1192. The Third Crusade was an attempt to reconquer the Holy Land after it was retaken by Saladin. The king of France and the king of England ended their conflict and united to fight Saladin; however, they achieved little beyond capturing the city of Acre. As the king of France left, the king of England and Saladin eventually came to a truce in which Jerusalem would remain under Saladin's control but unarmed Christian pilgrims were allowed to visit the city.

THINKING

Sentience   Sentience is the ability to perceive, be conscious, experience, and feel. *Qualia* is the term used to describe the way things seem to someone. For example, the taste of a cookie, the redness of an apple, the pain of a cut, are all qualia. Sentience is the ability to have an experience with qualia.

GRAPHS

Pie Charts   Pie charts are very easy to use and do not require an x or y axis. They are used when representing categorical data or values in proportion to the whole. Essentially, a pie chart is a circle that is divided into segments that reflect the values or categories that they are supposed to represent.

THE EARTH'S LAYERS

The Lower Mantle   The lower mantle plays a key role in controlling the planet's thermal evolution; it can be found 190 to 1,800 miles below the crust, with an average temperature of 5,400°F. The lower mantle is mostly made of perovskite, a magnesium silicate mineral, which can change into a high-pressure form.

ALBANIAN

Dialects   There are two dialects found in Albanian, Tosk and Gheg, and the two have diverged for at least a millennium. Gheg is spoken to the north of the Shkumbin River, and Tosk is spoken south of the river. The Tosk dialect is considered the official language of the country. There is a transitional language that is spoken in central Albania.

THE CRUSADES

The Fourth and Fifth Crusades   The Fourth Crusade lasted from 1202 to 1204 and was an attempt to once again conquer Jerusalem by going through Egypt. Instead of Jerusalem, however, the Crusaders sacked Constantinople and established the Latin Empire. The Fifth Crusade, from 1217 to 1221, was an attempt to conquer Jerusalem by defeating the Ayyubid Sultanate in Egypt. The Ayyubid Sultan launched an attack that would lead to the surrender of the crusaders, and an eight-year peace agreement was made.

 THINKING

Consciousness   Consciousness refers to an awareness or ability to sense feelings, memories, sensations, or thoughts. It is can also be understood as a feeling of being "awake." One's consciousness is an unbroken stream of ever-changing thoughts. You might be doing something one minute, and then your mind will think about something else the next. This continues forever, without any breaks or stops.

 GRAPHS

Flow Charts   Flow charts are used to describe how all of the steps in a process fit together. They represent a progression and are useful in depicting the various stages that go into a project. Flow charts use three symbols that are all labeled according to their description. There are elongated circles, representing the start and finish; rectangles, which show the steps or instructions; and diamonds, which show the decisions that have to be made. Arrows connect the symbols to one another, showing the progression in the process.

⚛ THE EARTH'S LAYERS

The Outer Core   The core of the Earth is about 15 percent of the Earth's volume, made of iron-nickel, and is roughly the size of Mars. The outer core is 1,800 to 3,200 miles below the surface and is made of mostly molten iron. The temperature of the molten core ranges from 7,200°F to 9,032°F. The motions of the molten core create the Earth's magnetic field.

◑ ALBANIAN

The Albanian Alphabet   Over the course of history, the Albanian alphabet has been written in several different ways, including using the Greek alphabet, the Turkish alphabet, and Cyrillic. In the 1900s, the Albanian government made a form of the Latin alphabet the standard alphabet. The Albanian alphabet appears as:

A B C Ç D Dh E Ë F G Gj H I J K L Ll M N Nj O P Q R Rr S Sh T Th U V X Xh Y Z Zh

THE CRUSADES

The Sixth and Seventh Crusades   The Sixth Crusade was from 1228 to 1229, and though there was very little fighting, control of Jerusalem was regained temporarily by the crusaders. The Seventh Crusade lasted from 1248 to 1254, and was led by King Louis IX of France. The Christians were defeated by the Egyptian army led by the Ayyubid sultan, with support from the Mamluks, and the king and thousands of European soldiers were captured.

THINKING

Imagination   Imagination is the ability to create mental sensations, images, concepts, and ideas without these things having been seen, felt, touched, heard, or tasted. It is the work of the mind that gives meaning to experiences and knowledge. Imagination allows people to think outside of the confines of the reality that is presented to them and it is crucial in the thought process.

GRAPHS

Organizational Charts   Organizational charts are used to show the formal and informal relationships in an overall structure. They are mostly used in the workforce, showing the ranks and relationships between employees. Organizational charts also show how different departments can be connected. Generally, they are shaped like pyramids, with the top rectangle representing the highest position such as the president or CEO, and other rectangles descending according to rank. The size of the rectangles relates to the level of authority, and arrows are used to represent the flow.

THE EARTH'S LAYERS

The Inner Core   The inner core is 3,200 to 3,960 miles below the surface and is the hottest part of the Earth, with a temperature of 9,032°F to 10,832°F. There is so much pressure in the inner core that it is actually solid metal, and it is believed to be made of a nickel-iron alloy. The extreme heat of the core directly affects the movement of plate tectonics and the Earth's magnetic field.

ALBANIAN

Grammar   Nouns in Albanian have a case, a gender, and indefinite and definite forms. Definite and indefinite articles (such as the word *the*) are attached to the words as suffixes, and not stand-alone words. Adjectives come after the nouns, and match the gender and number of the nouns. The conjugation of verbs shows tense and person.

 THE CRUSADES

The Eighth and Ninth Crusades The Eighth Crusade of 1270 only lasted one year and was led by King Louis IX once again. It was originally meant to aid Crusader states but was diverted to Tunis, where two months later, King Louis IX died. The Ninth Crusade was the final Crusade, and it lasted from 1271 to 1272. Prince Edward of England led the Crusade following the death of Louis IX. It failed due to the rising power of the Mamluks in Egypt and low morale among the Crusaders.

THINKING

Creativity Creativity is the process where a person creates something new and the end result has some sort of value. The value might be anything from personal growth to monetary value. Some researchers believe creativity is a result of the cognitive processes involved in intelligence. It is believed that the frontal lobe of the brain is the most important area for creativity.

GRAPHS

Pictographs Pictographs use picture symbols to represent data and compare trends. The symbols used represent a specific quantity, and are repeated a certain number of times along the chart. Pictographs do not provide precise information but rather give a general representation. An example of a pictograph would be a chart showing the amount of apples four students have eaten. The key on the bottom might say that for every picture of an apple, four apples have been eaten. So on the chart, if the students have three apples pictured by their names, it means they've actually eaten twelve apples each.

THE EARTH'S LAYERS

The Atmosphere The final layer is not on the ground, but above it. The atmosphere is what surrounds the planet and what gives life to the planet. There are several layers in the atmosphere, and it is about 500 miles thick. It is composed of various gases, dust, and water. The atmosphere provides warmth and even protection from the sun's rays and meteorites.

ALBANIAN

Useful Albanian Phrases Here are some helpful phrases to use when traveling to Albania:

Hello. *Tungjatjeta.*
Goodbye. *Mirupafshim.*
Thank you. *Faleminderit.*
Yes. *Po.*
No. *Jo.*
I don't speak Albanian. *Nuk flas Shqip.*
I don't understand. *Nuk kuptoj.*
Do you speak English? *Flisni Angisht?*

Excuse me. *Më falni.*
Good morning. *Mirëmëngjes.*
Good afternoon. *Mirëdita.*
Good evening. *Mirëmbrëma.*
Good night. *Natën e mire.*
What is your name? *Si ju quheni?*

LESSON 10 QUIZ

1. **What happened during the Third Crusade?**
   a. The king and thousands of his troops were captured and defeated by the Egyptian army led by the Ayyubid Sultan, with support from the Mamluks.
   b. The king of England and Saladin eventually came to a truce in which Jerusalem would remain under Saladin's control but unarmed Christian pilgrims were allowed to visit the city.
   c. The Ayyubid Sultan launched an attack that would lead to the surrender of the crusaders and an eight-year peace agreement was made.
   d. None of the above.

2. **Which of the following is true?**
   a. The Crusades were only led by popes.
   b. The Crusades were only led by kings.
   c. The Crusades were led by popes at first and then kings later on.
   d. The Crusades were led by kings initially and then popes later on.

3. **An awareness or ability to sense feelings, memories, sensations, or thoughts is:**
   a. Consciousness
   b. Creativity
   c. Imagination
   d. Qualia

4. **Which of the following represents qualia?**
   a. The taste of an apple
   b. Making up a story in your head
   c. An unconscious stream of thoughts
   d. Creating something new that has an end value

5. **What kind of chart would you use to show categorical data or values in proportion to the whole?**
   a. Bar graph
   b. Line graph
   c. Flow chart
   d. Pie chart

6. **Which of the following is true?**
   a. Line graphs are used to show a change in time; bar graphs are used to show different amounts.
   b. Line graphs are used to show different amounts; bar graphs are used to show a change in time.
   c. Both line graphs and bar graphs don't use an *x* and *y* axis.
   d. Bar graphs are shaped like pyramids and show how different departments in a workforce are connected.

7. **What is the uppermost layer of the Earth?**
   a. The outer mantle
   b. The inner mantle
   c. The crust
   d. The outer core

8. **What type of rock is continental crust?**
   a. Basalt
   b. Granite
   c. Magma
   d. Nickel-iron alloy

9. **What do Albanians call their language?**
   a. Thracian
   b. Dacien
   c. Proto-Romanian
   d. Shqip

10. **How do you say "excuse me" in Albanian?**
    a. Më falni.
    b. Nuk kuptoj.
    c. Natën e mire.
    d. Mirëmbrëma.

HISTORY:
The Renaissance
What Led to the Renaissance, The Medici Family, Early Renaissance, High Renaissance, Northern Renaissance, Advancements in Technology and Science

MATH: Pi
The Symbol, The Definition, Early History of Pi, Pi Gets More Accurate, An Irrational Constant, The Not-So-Accurate Pi

LANGUAGE ARTS:
Visual Literacy
What Is Visual Literacy?, Why Visual Literacy Is Important, Data Visualization, Typography, Color, The Power of Photography

SCIENCE: Natural Disasters
Earthquakes, Hurricanes, Tornadoes, Avalanches, Tsunamis, Volcanic Eruptions

Lesson 11

FOREIGN LANGUAGE:
Portuguese
The Origins, Dialects, Related Languages, The Portuguese Language Orthographic Agreement of 1990, Portuguese Today, Useful Portuguese Phrases

🏛 THE RENAISSANCE

What Led to the Renaissance   The Renaissance was a return to the classicism and humanism of Ancient Greece in Europe following the Middle Ages. Following the Black Death, there was a great change in the European economy. That, along with the invention of the printing press, the fall of the Byzantine Empire, and the Crusades all led to the birth of the Renaissance, where Classic Greek and Roman art, literature, and philosophy were reintroduced into European culture.

📷 VISUAL LITERACY

What Is Visual Literacy?   Visual literacy is a method of teaching based on the principle that visual images are a language that must be learned, and one should be able to understand, apply, and create visual messages. The term was created by Jack Debes. In a world of mass media, visual literacy has become increasingly more important; however, visual literacy is not limited to simply media.

➕ PI

The Symbol   Pi is a mathematical constant. Pi is always equal to the ratio between the area of a circle to its radius that is squared. Pi is represented by the Greek letter π. This symbol's name is pi, and it is the symbol still used today. The letter stems from the Greek word $\pi\varepsilon\rho\acute{\iota}\mu\varepsilon\tau\rho o\varsigma$, meaning "perimeter." The first to use the symbol as the mathematical constant was William Jones in 1708. The mathematical constant is always represented by the lowercase π, because the capital version, $\prod$, has an entirely different meaning.

✳ NATURAL DISASTERS

Earthquakes   The Earth's crust and the mantle slowly move in separate pieces called tectonic plates. The edges of these tectonic plates are called boundaries, and the boundaries are made of faults. As the plates move, the edges get stuck as the rest of the plate continues to move. When the plate finally moves far enough away, the edges of the plate get unstuck on one of the faults, and this release of energy creates an earthquake.

🌐 PORTUGUESE

The Origins   Portuguese is the sixth most-spoken language in the world. It is a Romance language that evolved from Latin, which was spoken on the western coast of the Iberian Peninsula. From A.D. 409 to 711, Germanic people inhabited the land, which led to regional variation. From the ninth to eleventh centuries, Portuguese-Galician was first being used in official administrative documents. In the eleventh century, the Christians of the region took over the land, and Portuguese and Galician split.

🏛 THE RENAISSANCE

The Medici Family   The Renaissance began in Florence, Italy. Much of the great artwork in the Early Renaissance can be traced back to a family of the noble class, the Medici family. In the thirteenth century, the Medici acquired great wealth as bankers and became the wealthiest family in all of Italy. With their wealth, they sponsored many artistic endeavors, such as the great paintings and architecture of this time.

📷 VISUAL LITERACY

Why Visual Literacy Is Important   Today's world is increasingly visual, and in order for people to get a true grasp of a situation, they must be able to grasp an understanding of visual imagery such as photographs. Through expressing thoughts and ideas in visual form and translating the meaning of visual forms, students become visually literate, which allows them to have a greater understanding of the world around them.

PI

The Definition   To put it simply, π is the ratio of a circumference of a circle to the diameter of the circle. In other words, the equation looks like this:

$$\pi = \frac{C}{d}$$

Regardless of the size of the circle, this ratio will always equal π. There is another way to define π by using a circle's area, and that is by this equation:

$$\pi = \frac{A}{r^2}$$

In this equation, r represents the radius of the circle, which is half of the diameter.

⚛ NATURAL DISASTERS

Hurricanes   Hurricanes, also known as typhoons or cyclones, develop in the summer and early fall months. Hurricanes develop over warm waters. The humid air travels upward, forming clouds and leaving a low pressure area below it. Any warm air left in this area pushes into the low pressure area and begins to rise. This process continues as the air and clouds spin. When the wind speeds of this low-pressure system reaches 75 miles per hour, it is no longer a tropical storm and is officially a hurricane.

🌐 PORTUGUESE

Dialects   There are many types of dialects found in Portuguese, but the two main ones can be broken down into Brazilian and European. The differences between the two involve different grammatical forms and phonology. The European dialect is more like that spoken by Portugal's former Asian and African colonies. The Brazilian dialect is primarily spoken in Brazil, and is the most common form.

THE RENAISSANCE

Early Renaissance   The Early Renaissance was from 1330 to 1450, and took place in Florence, Italy. Artwork sponsored by the Medici family placed great focus on the art of Ancient Greece and Rome. The artwork once again focused on humanism, naturalism, and realism, with new ideas introduced into art such as depth of field, linear perspective, and new types of shading. The most well-known artists to come out of the Early Renaissance are Sandro Botticelli (*La Primavera*), Domenico Ghirlandaio (*An Old Man and His Grandson*), and Piero della Francesca (*The Baptism*).

VISUAL LITERACY

Data Visualization   Data visualization is a method of presenting data graphically with shapes, proportions, dimensions, textures, and direction. A graphic that is proportionately large to the paper it is on can convey a sense of importance and will draw the eye in before anything else. Direction of a shape can lead to many different emotional states. A vertical shape might present stability, while a diagonal shape might show movement or change.

PI

Early History of Pi   The Rhind Mathmatical Papyrus, a famous piece of Egyptian papyrus dated around 1650 B.C., from Egypt shows the use of pi written by the scribe Ahmes. He states: "Cut of $\frac{1}{9}$ of a diameter and construct a square upon the remainder; this has the same area as the circle." According to his calculations, pi equaled 3.16049. In the nineteenth century B.C., the Babylonians believed the value to be 25/8, which is only 0.5 percent below the actual value of π.

NATURAL DISASTERS

Tornadoes   The most common and dangerous tornadoes form from a supercell thunderstorm, meaning it lasts longer than an hour and feeds off of a rising current of air that is rotating and tilted. Non-supercell tornadoes form without the updraft of air. A gustnado is a form of a non-supercell tornado that forms near the ground from dust or debris, and a landspout is a non-supercell tornado that forms near the ground, doesn't have a rotating updraft, and forms a funnel when the thunderstorm cloud is growing. Waterspouts are like landspouts, but they form over water.

PORTUGUESE

Related Languages   Portuguese is a West Iberian Romance language, and is closely related to Spanish, Galician, Fala, Leonese, and Mirandese. Galician and Fala are the closest languages to Portuguese. Galician and Portuguese used to be one language called Galician-Portuguese, and the vocabulary of Galician is still very similar to Portuguese. Fala is a descendant of Galician-Portuguese, and is spoken in several small towns in Spain.

THE RENAISSANCE

High Renaissance   The artwork of the High Renaissance, which was from 1490 to 1530, made advances on the techniques of artists of the Early Renaissance. The center of the High Renaissance was Rome, and artwork was now being commissioned by the popes. It is during the High Renaissance that the best-known works of Renaissance painters appeared. The most well-known artists to come out of the High Renaissance are Leonardo da Vinci (*Last Supper*), Michelangelo Buonarroti (*The Creation of Adam*), and Raphael (*Sistine Madonna*).

VISUAL LITERACY

Typography   The size, arrangement, and style of letters can give different meanings, and also determine an image's legibility. This is especially important in understanding advertising, websites, or media pieces. Typography does not just rely on what font looks the best, but rather what font will convey the message you want to get across to the viewer. Typography also gives value. Not all words are given the same meaning or value, and use of typography allows for distinctions and emphasis to be made.

PI

Pi Gets More Accurate   At first, pi was believed to have less than ten digits. Aryabhata, an Indian mathematician and astronomer from the fifth century, came to the realization that pi is in fact an irrational number; that is, the decimals go on forever without repeating. Around 1600, Ludolph van Ceulen, a German mathematician, correctly identified the first 35 decimals in pi. In 1789, a Slovene mathematician calculated to the first 140, though only the first 126 numbers were correct. In 1873, the first 527 numbers were calculated correctly. And in 2005, with the use of a supercomputer, the first 1.24 trillion places were claimed to have been calculated correctly.

❀ NATURAL DISASTERS

Avalanches   Avalanches occur because of gravity's pull on the snow on a mountainside. In mild weather, water vapor can slide down the snow, flake, and refreeze at the center, creating a cohesive and solid mass. When it is cold, the water vapor goes to the bottom of the snow on the ground, and forms angular crystals, which weaken snow. Sunlight and light rain produce a thin surface crust, and that makes bonding of new snow more difficult. Instability of the snowpack can be triggered by a storm, wind, temperature, and even a person's weight. Sluffs are avalanches of loose snow, and slab avalanches occur when a strong layer is on top of a weak layer. Sluffs are the more deadlier type of avalanche.

◖ PORTUGUESE

The Portuguese Language Orthographic Agreement of 1990   In 1990, an international treaty was made to unify the writing system of Portuguese that would be used by all Portuguese-speaking countries. The treaty made changes in the spelling of both European and Brazilian Portuguese. Some letters were removed, the letters *k*, *w*, and *y* were added to the Portuguese alphabet, and guidelines were made for the use of the hyphen and capitalization.

THE RENAISSANCE

Northern Renaissance   The Northern Renaissance was from 1500 to 1600, and it took place outside of Italy. The ideas of the Renaissance quickly spread throughout Europe, and some of the most notable artwork of the time came from the Netherlands and Germany. This artwork is distinctively different than the work produced in Italy, due to the increasing disenchantment with the Church. The figures appeared less classical, and more realistic. The most well-known artists to come out of the Northern Renaissance are the Flemish painter Jan Van Eyck (*The Arnolfini Portrait*), the German painter Albrecht Durer (*The Knight, Death, and the Devil*), and the Dutch painter Hieronymus Bosch (*The Garden of Earthly Delights*).

VISUAL LITERACY

Color   Color shapes emotions and perceptions of a visual image. In terms of visual literacy, an important distinction needs to be understood when it comes to colors, and that is the difference between warm and cool colors. Hues can express mood. Red, a warm color, will evoke anger or passion, while blue, a cool color, is more passive and is often used to represent truth. Color saturation and contrast of light and dark also play a key role in understanding the role of color.

PI

An Irrational Constant   Pi is an irrational constant, which means that it cannot be expressed as a fraction or ratio of two integers. Pi is also a transcendental number, meaning that it is not the root of any algebraic numbers. When pi is calculated out into numbers, the decimal representation does not repeat or end. For example, the number truncated to 50 decimals is 3.14159265358979323846264338327950288419716939937510. So for basic mathematic equations, many people shorten pi to 3.14.

NATURAL DISASTERS

Tsunamis   Tsunamis are caused by shifts in the seafloor, and are generally the results of earthquakes, landslides, or volcanic eruptions. For a tsunami to occur, the earthquake must occur near or under the ocean, with vertical movements in the seafloor. Large amounts of energy are dispersed in an upward bottom movement, and a wave forms. The largest tsunami ever recorded had waves up to 1,640 feet high and occurred in Alaska in 1958.

PORTUGUESE

Portuguese Today   Around 240 million people speak Portuguese today, and it is the official language of nine countries. Portuguese is the most widely spoken language of the Southern Hemisphere. Attempts have been made to turn Portuguese into an official language of the United Nations; however, it has faced several challenges, such as the fact that many Portuguese speakers all live on the same continent.

🏛 THE RENAISSANCE

Advancements in Technology and Science   Not only was the Renaissance a time of great achievements in art, but there were also great advancements made in technology. It is during this time period that the first portable clocks, eyeglasses, printing press, microscope, telescope, and even the first flush toilet were created. With the rise of technology and science, ideas such as gravity and the ability to study the universe led to the notion that the universe was not simply centered around mankind.

📷 VISUAL LITERACY

The Power of Photography   Photography is one of the greatest sources for understanding past events, and helps tell the story of what occurred in ways other methods cannot. A photograph is not just a still of everyday life, but rather a scene that was specifically chosen and highly edited. With every photograph comes the opinion of the photographer. It is a natural part of photography, because the photographer chooses what should and should not be seen in the photograph. Understanding how to interpret photographs leads to visual literacy.

➗ PI

The Not-So-Accurate Pi   Less accurate depictions of pi can be found in sources as early as the Bible, which states that pi equals 3. More recently, the Indiana Pi Bill of 1897 was an attempt to turn into law the notion that pi equaled 3.2 in the state of Indiana. The bill never passed the Indiana General Assembly, and never became a law.

❋ NATURAL DISASTERS

Volcanic Eruptions   Volcanoes are mountains that were formed from folded continental plates. The magma that is erupted from the volcano comes from 150 kilometers below the Earth's crust, where there is enormous pressure. This pressure forces the magma to rise, creating the eruption. When magma is released, it is then referred to as lava. Volcanoes do not always have to erupt from the top. Mount St. Helens was a volcano that erupted from the side.

🗣 PORTUGUESE

Useful Portuguese Phrases   Here are some helpful phrases to use when traveling to a Portuguese-speaking country:

Hello. *Olá.*
Goodbye. *Adeus.*
Good day. *Bom dia.*
Good evening. *Boa tarde.*
Yes. *Sim.*
No. *Não.*
Thank you. *Obrigado.*

How much? *Quanto?*
I don't speak Portuguese. *Eu não falo*
     Português.
Hey, ref! Where's the penalty? *Oí, árbitro!*
     Cadê o penalty?
Brazil is magnificent! *O Brasil é lindo*
     maravilhoso!

1. **Which of the following is true?**
   a. The Northern Renaissance took place in Rome and the High Renaissance took place in Florence.
   b. The Early Renaissance took place in Florence and the High Renaissance took place in Germany.
   c. The Early Renaissance took place in Florence and the High Renaissance took place in Rome.
   d. The Early Renaissance took place in Rome and the High Renaissance took place in Florence.

2. **What was one quality of Northern Renaissance paintings?**
   a. They were more realistic.
   b. They were more idealized.
   c. They were religion oriented only.
   d. They were sponsored by the Medici family.

3. **What is visual literacy?**
   a. A method of teaching how to take photographs
   b. A method of teaching how to read on television screens
   c. A method of teaching how to create typography
   d. A method of teaching based on the principle that visual images are a language that must be learned

4. **Which of the following aids in understanding visual literacy?**
   a. Color
   b. Typography
   c. Photographs
   d. All of the above

5. **Which of the following is a formula for pi?**
   a. Area/diameter
   b. Circumference/diameter
   c. Diameter/area
   d. Area/circumference

6. **What is a transcendental number?**
   a. A number truncated to 50 decimals
   b. A number that is not the root of any algebraic numbers
   c. A number that cannot be expressed as a fraction or ratio of two integers
   d. Number that has less than ten digits

7. **What is the difference between sluffs and slabs?**
   a. Sluffs are avalanches of loose snow and slabs have a strong layer on top of a weak layer.
   b. Slabs are avalanches of loose snow and sluffs have a strong layer on top of a weak layer.
   c. Sluffs are tropical storms; slabs are hurricanes.
   d. Sluffs are hurricanes; slabs are tropical storms.

8. ***Typhoons* and *cyclones* are other words used to describe:**
   a. Avalanches
   b. Tsunamis
   c. Tornadoes
   d. Hurricanes

9. **What letters were added in the Portuguese Language Orthographic Agreement of 1990?**
   a. q, x, and b
   b. k, w, and y
   c. k, w, and c
   d. q, x, and y

10. **The closest language to Portuguese is:**
    a. Spanish
    b. Galician
    c. Leonese
    d. Mirandese

HISTORY: The Ming Dynasty

Founding of the Ming Dynasty, The Early Reign, The Golden Age of the Ming Dynasty, The Decline and Fall of the Ming Dynasty, The Economy of the Ming Dynasty, The Great Wall of China

MATH: Angles

What Is an Angle?, Different Types of Angles, Complementary and Supplementary Angles, Measuring Angles, The Trigonometric Functions, Positive and Negative Angles

LANGUAGE ARTS: Braille

The History of Braille, Derivation, How Braille Works, Reading with Touch, Grade II Braille, Grade III Braille

SCIENCE: The Solar System

What Is the Solar System?, The Planets, The Sun, The Asteroid Belt, The Milky Way, Dwarf Planets

Lesson 12

FOREIGN LANGUAGE: Dutch

The Origins, Dialects, Changes to the Language, Polder Dutch, Dutch Today, Useful Dutch Phrases

THE MING DYNASTY

Founding of the Ming Dynasty   The Yuan Dynasty, led by Mongols, left the economy and state of agriculture in shambles. A group of peasants, the Han Chinese, who were discriminated against during the Yuan Dynasty, rose up and revolted. Zhu Yuanzhang came to lead the group of rebels, and as the last Yuan leader fled north, Zhu Yuanzhang founded the Ming Dynasty. Zhu took control of the capital city, Yuan, officially ending the Yuan Dynasty.

BRAILLE

The History of Braille   Braille was invented in 1825 by Louis Braille, a blind Frenchman. The system was originally based on a military code created by Charles Barbier that Napoleon had ordered so that soldiers would be able to communicate at night in silence. Barbier's code was rejected as too difficult. In 1821, Barbier visited the National Institute for the Blind in Paris, France, and it is there that he met Louis Braille. Braille simplified Barbier's code and created the six-dot cell, which would turn into Braille.

ANGLES

What Is an Angle?   Angles are used in geometry. An angle is formed when two rays, an order of points in a line, share the same endpoint. The size of an angle refers to the value of the arc between the two lines, or the value of the rotation. There are five basic types of angles to know: acute, right, obtuse, reflex, and perigon.

THE SOLAR SYSTEM

What Is the Solar System?   The solar system consists of the Sun, the Earth, Mars, Mercury, Venus, Jupiter, Saturn, Neptune, Uranus, the moons orbiting the planets, dwarf planets, and the asteroid belt. The solar system has an elliptical shape and is always in motion. The largest object in the solar system is the Sun, which all other objects in the system orbit around. The solar system is believed to be about four billion years old.

DUTCH

The Origins   Dutch is a part of the West Germanic dialect, and more specifically, it is a West Low Franconian language. Dutch can be traced back to A.D. 500, when Old Frankish was split by the High German consonant shift. The Dutch language is broken down into periods: Old Dutch, which lasted from 500 to 1150; Middle Dutch, which lasted from 1150 to 1500; and Modern Dutch, which began in 1500 and is still spoken today.

 THE MING DYNASTY

The Early Reign   When he came to power, Zhu Yuanzhang instituted a series of policies aimed to reduce the burden on the peasants, and placed great attention on punishing court officials involved in corruption and ending corruption. When Zhu Yuanzhang died, his son came to power; however, his son was soon overthrown in a coup led by Zhu Di, who would come to be known as Emperor Chengzu. The reign of Emperor Chengzu would be considered the most prosperous time in the Ming Dynasty.

 BRAILLE

Derivation   Braille was derived from the Latin alphabet, and the points were positioned according to the positions of letters in the alphabet. For example *a* has one dot, *b* has two dots, etc. The numbers also follow this pattern. Braille is the first binary encoding scheme that represents the characters of a system of writing.

⊟ ANGLES

Different Types of Angles   As angles increase, their names change. Acute angles have values that are greater than zero but less than 90 degrees. A right angle is exactly 90 degrees. An obtuse angle is any angle greater than 90 degrees but less than 180 degrees. A reflex angle is larger than an obtuse angle, and it is any angle that is more than 180 but less than 360. A perigon is a full rotation that equals 360 degrees exactly.

✳ THE SOLAR SYSTEM

The Planets   There are eight planets in the solar system. Mercury, Venus, Earth, and Mars are known as rocky inner planets. These are smaller and denser, contain less gas, and are primarily composed of rock or metals. In fact, Mercury and Mars do not even have atmosphers. The other four planets, known as outer planets, are larger, with dense atmospheres and small cores.

◑ DUTCH

Dialects   Dialects in Dutch are extremely diverse, and there is said to be about twenty-eight distinct dialects. *Flemish* is the term used for the type of Dutch spoken in Belgium, and in Flanders there are four types of Flemish: West Flemish, East Flemish, Brabantian, and Limburgish. Flemish is considered a softer dialect, and it favors older words. Netherlandish Dutch, in contrast, is considered to be harsh and even hostile sounding. In the east of the country, Dutch Low Saxon is spoken, and in Holland, Hollandic is spoken.

THE MING DYNASTY

The Golden Age of the Ming Dynasty   Emperor Chengzu's reign was known as the Yongle Period, and is considered the Golden Age of the Ming Dynasty. Emperor Chengzu launched a series of five wars against Mongolia, and most notably, it is during this time that the Forbidden City was constructed. Relations with minorities and different nationalities were strengthened, and Chengzu was the first to make Beijing the capital, a title it would hold for 500 years.

BRAILLE

How Braille Works   There are a total of six dots that can represent a letter or number. The first ten letters of the alphabet only use the top four dots. The next ten letters are identical to the first ten, except an additional dot is added. Letters *u, v, x, y*, and *z* are like letters *a* through *e*, only different dots are added. The *w* is the only letter that is not in an order like this because the language was originally written in French, which didn't have a *w*.

ANGLES

Complementary and Supplementary Angles   Complementary and supplementary angles involve combining two angles. Complementary angles are any two angles that when added up, the sum is equal to 90 degrees. This means that if you put them together, they will form a right angle. A supplementary angle is the sum of any two angles that equals 180 degrees. This means that when they are added together, they make a straight line.

THE SOLAR SYSTEM

The Sun   The Sun is the center of the solar system, the closest star, and the largest object in the solar system. It makes up 99.8 percent of the mass of the solar system. The power of the Sun is produced through nuclear fusion reactions. The energy from the nuclear fusion travels into space in the form of light and heat. The surface of the Sun has a temperature of 5800 Kelvin.

DUTCH

Changes to the Language   Pronunciation has changed over the past century in Dutch. Voiceless pronunciation with some letters — meaning saying hard sounds instead of using one's voice — has started to become the standard for the language. This change mirrors a movement to make the spelling of Dutch words as phonological as possible. Another change that has not been declared an official change to the standard language, but rather has begun appearing in the younger generation is known as Polder Dutch.

THE MING DYNASTY

The Decline and Fall of the Ming Dynasty   The Ming Dynasty began to decline under the reign of Emperor Shenzong. When his chancellor, Zhang Juzheng, died, state affairs began to be neglected, and later, his army was defeated by the "Latter-Jin" regime. The last ruler was Emperor Weizong, whose reign was defined by corruption and extreme hardship due to natural disasters. In 1628, rebel forces began attacking. In 1644, Beijing fell to a rebel army. Emperor Weizong hanged himself, thus ending the Ming Dynasty.

 BRAILLE

Reading with Touch   Braille relies on the sense of touch rather than the sense of sight. While reading, you move your index finger from left to right over the text with one hand, while the other hand searches for the next line of text. The text is a series of raised dots arranged in cells, and there are sixty-four possible combinations for one cell.

ANGLES

Measuring Angles   The angle is defined by the theta symbol, θ. The length of the arc is represented by the lowercase letter s, and the radius of a circle is represented by the lowercase letter r. The lowercase letter k is used to represent a scaling constant, and that depends on the units of measurement in the problem. The basic formula for finding the value of an angle is:

$$\theta = k\frac{s}{r}$$

THE SOLAR SYSTEM

The Asteroid Belt   Asteroids are bits of rock that were left over after the formation of the Sun and the planets. These asteroids are most often found orbiting the Sun between Mars and Jupiter. This area is known as the asteroid belt, and more than 7,000 asteroids have been discovered in it. The total mass of the asteroids found in the asteroid belt is less than the mass of the Moon.

 DUTCH

Polder Dutch   Polder Dutch is a variation of Dutch spoken by the younger generation. In Polder Dutch (a term coined by Jan Stroop), diphthongs are pronounced with a wider mouth, and are pronounced lower. Polder Dutch seems to have begun around the 1970s, and originally it was middle-aged women and the upper-middle class who were pronouncing these diphthongs in this way. It has since spread.

THE MING DYNASTY

The Economy of the Ming Dynasty   The economy of the Ming Dynasty showed an end of feudalism and the beginnings of capitalism. From the reign of Zhu Yuanzhang and onward, porcelain making was the major source of finance, and there was a wide interest in foreign commodities from both Europe and America. Urbanization and commercial metropolises also arose during this time in cities such as Beijing, Nanjing, and Yangzhou.

BRAILLE

Grade II Braille   Grade II Braille is an extension of Braille used in English. Beyond just letters and numbers, it includes punctuation marks, composition signs, single-cell words, contractions, short-form words, and abbreviations. Whereas Grade I Braille used a cell to represent each letter, symbol, or number, in Grade II Braille, a single cell can represent whole words.

ANGLES

The Trigonometric Functions   In trigonometry, sine, cosine, and tangent are used to find the relation of the angles of a triangle to the sides of the triangle. The basic equations are:

$$\sin\theta = \frac{\text{opposite of angle}}{\text{hypotenuse}}$$

$$\cos\theta = \frac{\text{adjacent line}}{\text{hypotenuse}}$$

$$\tan\theta = \frac{\text{opposite of angle}}{\text{adjacent line}}$$

THE SOLAR SYSTEM

The Milky Way   The Milky Way is the spiral-shaped galaxy that is the home to our solar system. Whereas the solar system revolves around one Sun, the Milky Way contains at least 400 billion other stars (with their planets and other objects in orbit). The Milky Way is just one of 200 billion galaxies that have been observed from Earth.

DUTCH

Dutch Today   Dutch is currently the native language of Belgium, the Netherlands, and the Republic of Suriname. Dutch is said to be somewhere in between German and English; however, it most closely resembles German. It is spoken by 22 million people worldwide and was standardized in the seventeenth century. The Dutch of today has started to sound more like the dialect found in Holland.

THE MING DYNASTY

The Great Wall of China   The majority of the Great Wall of China that exists today is from the Ming Dynasty, which lasted from 1368 to 1644. The project took over 100 years to complete, and the wall was made in an effort to protect the citizens of the Ming Dynasty from outside Yuan tribes such as the Wala and the Dada.

BRAILLE

Grade III Braille   Grade III is the last system of Braille, and it allows for reading shorthand. Grade III has not yet been standardized and is typically used for the convenience of the person reading. In Grade III, a lot of the vowels are omitted, and the spacing between words and paragraphs is much smaller. Sometimes, combinations of punctuation symbols are substituted for words.

ANGLES

Positive and Negative Angles   If an angle is counterclockwise, the angle (θ) will have a positive value. If the angle is in a clockwise motion, then the value of θ will be negative. θ equaling -50 and θ equaling 50 do not mean the same thing. Angles have degrees of rotation and directions of rotation. Even though both of those numbers have the same degree of rotation, their directions are the opposite, making them different angles.

THE SOLAR SYSTEM

Dwarf Planets   Until fairly recently, Pluto was referred to as another planet in our solar system; however, it is now referred to as a dwarf planet. Dwarf planets orbit around the Sun, have a mass that gravity has turned round, cannot be satellites to other planets, and have a mass that is larger than an asteroid but not large enough to be considered a planet. Dwarf planets are not categories of planets, but rather different objects entirely. There are three dwarf planets in our solar system: Pluto, Ceres, and Eris.

DUTCH

Useful Dutch Phrases   Here are some helpful phrases to use when traveling in a Dutch-speaking country:

Hello. *Hallo.*
Good morning. *Goedemorgen.*
Good afternoon. *Goedemiddag.*
Good evening. *Goedenavond.*
Have a nice day. *Nog een prettige dag.*
I don't understand. *Ik begrijp het niet.*
Excuse me. *Neem me niet kwalijk.*
How much is this? *Hoeveel kost dit?*
Thank you. *Dank U.*
Where's the toilet? *Waar is de WC?*
Goodbye. *Tot ziens.*

1. **One of the achievements during Emperor Chengzu's reign was:**
   a. Trading with Europe and America
   b. Defeating the "Latter-Jin" regime
   c. Reducing the burden on peasants
   d. The building of the Forbidden City

2. **Which of the following occurred during the reign of Zhu Yuanzhang?**
   a. A major source of finance was in porcelain making.
   b. There was wide trade with Europe and America.
   c. Urbanization and commercial metropolises appeared.
   d. The burden on peasants was reduced.

3. **In Braille, how many possible combinations are there in one cell?**
   a. 89
   b. 64
   c. 46
   d. 98

4. **Which of the following is true?**
   a. Grade I Braille uses a cell to represent each letter, Grade II Braille sometimes uses a cell to represent whole words.
   b. Grade I Braille uses a cell to represent words; Grade II Braille uses a cell to represent letters.
   c. Grade I Braille uses a cell to represent each letter; Grade II Braille uses a cell to represent numbers.
   d. Grade I Braille uses a cell to represent each number; Grade II Braille uses a cell to represent letters.

5. **What are complementary angles?**
   a. Two angles that add up to 180°
   b. Two angles that are obtuse
   c. Two angles that add up to be greater than 90°
   d. Two angles that add up to be 90°

6. **Which measurement is an example of an acute angle?**
   a. 91°
   b. 90°
   c. 89°
   d. 100°

7. **What is the largest object in the solar system?**
   a. Jupiter
   b. The Sun
   c. The asteroid belt
   d. Ceres

8. **Pluto, Ceres, and Eris are examples of:**
   a. Outer planets
   b. Inner planets
   c. Dwarf planets
   d. Galaxies

9. **What type of language is Dutch?**
   a. West Slavic
   b. East Germanic
   c. West Germanic
   d. East Slavic

10. **How many distinct dialects of Dutch are there?**
    a. 16
    b. 28
    c. 7
    d. 12

ANSWER KEY: d, d, b, a, d, c, b, c, c, b

HISTORY: Columbus and the New World

Columbus Decides to Travel to the East, The First Voyage, The Second Voyage, The Third Voyage, The Fourth Voyage, The Impact on the Native Americans

 **MATH:** Pythagorean Theorem

What Is the Pythagorean Theorem?, Proof with Triangles That Are Similar, Euclid's Proof, Algebraic Proof, Proof with Differentials, The Pythagorean Triple

LANGUAGE ARTS: Dialects

What Is a Dialect?, Standard Dialects, Social Dialects, Geographic Dialects, Interlingua, Focal and Relic Areas

 SCIENCE: The Big Bang

From Nothing to Something, The Universe Expands, Evidence for the Big Bang, Misconceptions, Other Theories, Does God Have a Role?

Lesson 13

FOREIGN LANGUAGE: Swedish

The Origins, Old Swedish, Modern Swedish, Contemporary Swedish, Dialects, Useful Swedish Phrases

COLUMBUS AND THE NEW WORLD

Columbus Decides to Travel to the East   Christopher Columbus spent much of his life sailing the Atlantic Ocean. He became very interested in traveling to the far East, which he believed was just across the Atlantic Ocean. His idea was to create a sea route to India and attain the gold and spices of the East Indies. Columbus met with King John II of Portugal to support his journey, but was soon rejected. He then met with the monarchs of Spain, King Ferdinand and Queen Isabella, who, although they had rejected him initially, would eventually agree to support his journey.

DIALECTS

What Is a Dialect?   A dialect is a variety of a particular language that is characteristic within a certain group of speakers of that language. It refers to differing speech patterns within the same language, and is often representative of social, geographic, and economic factors, as well as background. Dialects are distinguished by the use of grammar, syntax, morphology, and vocabulary.

PYTHAGOREAN THEOREM

What Is the Pythagorean Theorem?   The Pythagorean theorem is one of the most well-known formulas ever written:

$$a^2 + b^2 = c^2$$

The letters a and b represent the sides of the triangle, and the letter c represents the hypotenuse, which is opposite of the right angle. The Pythagorean theorem can only be used when dealing with right triangles (which as you might recall, means an angle of 90 degrees). There are at least 370 ways to prove the Pythagorean theorem.

THE BIG BANG

From Nothing to Something   The big bang is the most widely accepted theory that explains how the universe began. Before the universe started, there was literally nothing. Then, 13.7 billion years ago, the universe came into existence. This was known as a singularity. Singularities are thought to exist inside black holes and defy the laws of physics that we understand. Black holes have intense pressure from gravity, and finite matter was squished together, forming the singularity.

SWEDISH

The Origins   Swedish is a North-Germanic language, influenced by Middle Low German. It originally stemmed from Old Norse, which, in the ninth century, split into Old West Norse and Old East Norse. Old East Norse consisted of Sweden and Denmark, and in the twelfth century, the language between those two lands began to change, turning into Old Swedish and Old Danish.

COLUMBUS AND THE NEW WORLD

The First Voyage   Columbus prepared three ships, the *Nina*, the *Pinta*, and the *Santa Maria*, for their journey. Columbus was the captain of the *Santa Maria* and his brothers were the captains of the other ships. On August 3, 1492, they set sail. On October 12, they landed on what is now the island of San Salvador in the Bahamas and took possession of the island. Columbus soon found Cuba (which he believed to be China), and in December, he reached Hispaniola (which Columbus believed to be Japan), and established a colony of thirty-nine men. In March of 1493, Columbus returned to Spain with riches, spices, and "Indian" captives.

DIALECTS

Standard Dialects   A standard dialect, also known as a standard language, is a dialect that begins to be used in other ways, rather than just by the small group of people who speak it. Standard dialects appear in literature and administrative work, for example, and also have support from institutions. Standard English, Standard Australian English, and Standard Canadian English are all dialects of the English language.

PYTHAGOREAN THEOREM

Proof with Triangles That Are Similar   The simplest way to prove the Pythagorean theorem is by using similar triangles. In similar triangles, corresponding parts are proportional, regardless of how big or small the two triangles are. This type of proof depends on length and not on area. The equation for this proof is:

$$\frac{a}{c} = \frac{e}{a} \text{ and } \frac{b}{c} = \frac{d}{b}$$

From there, $a^2 = c \times e$ and $b^2 = c \times d$

If you add them together, you get

$$a^2 + b^2 = c \times e + c \times d$$

which leads to

$$a^2 + b^2 = c^2$$

THE BIG BANG

The Universe Expands   Once the singularity formed, it began to expand and inflate (the big bang). The big bang was not an expansion of matter in space, but rather the creation and expansion of the space that carried matter. The big bang started at extremely hot temperatures, and as it expanded it began cooling. The universe is still expanding and cooling even to this day.

SWEDISH

Old Swedish   Old Swedish was the language spoken in 1225, and it lasted until the late fourteenth century. The language was much more complex than what is spoken today, and the influence from Middle Low German was very clear. The Christian Church played an important role in society, and documents were written in Latin script. Words from Latin, Greek, and Dutch were all incorporated into Old Swedish.

COLUMBUS AND THE NEW WORLD

The Second Voyage   In October of 1493, Columbus set sail with a fleet of seventeen ships and 1,500 colonists. In November, they landed in the Lesser Antilles and discovered Puerto Rico and the Leeward Islands. Upon returning to Hispaniola, Columbus found that the original colony had been killed by the natives. Columbus established another colony and then set sail once again, exploring Cuba and finding Jamaica. As Columbus left for Spain, his brother stayed in Hispaniola and founded Santo Domingo, which was the first permanent European settlement of the Americas.

DIALECTS

Social Dialects   Difference in dialects is directly related to social status. Those that are highly educated tend to belong to a higher social class and use the standard dialect, whereas the lower classes, which tend to be less educated, preserve the original dialect of the region. In urban areas, innovations in the dialect tend to be made, whereas the dialect spoken in rural areas is more of the traditional geographic dialect.

PYTHAGOREAN THEOREM

Euclid's Proof   In Euclid's proof, a large square is divided into two rectangles, one large, one small. Of the larger rectangle, a triangle is created that is half of the area of the rectangle. The same thing is done with the smaller rectangle, so you have two congruent triangles.

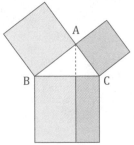

After working through a set of rules, you will end up with $AB^2 + AC^2 = BC^2$

THE BIG BANG

Evidence for the Big Bang   There are many pieces of evidence that lead to the big bang theory as correct regarding the origins of the universe. Scientists are certain that the universe did have a beginning. Hubble's law, discovered in 1929, states that galaxies are moving away at speeds that are in proportion to their distance, which would mean that the universe was once compact and is now expanding. Scientists have also found remnants of heat traveling through the universe, which is believed to be from the initial heat of the big bang.

SWEDISH

Modern Swedish   With the printing press and the Reformation, the Swedish language began to undergo changes. Gustav Vasa, the king of Sweden, ordered that the Bible be translated into Swedish; this remained the most common Bible in Sweden until 1917; blending Old Swedish with the colloquial Swedish of the time. During this time, changes were made to certain sounds in the language, such as the softening of certain consonants and assimilation of consonant clusters.

COLUMBUS AND THE NEW WORLD

The Third Voyage   In 1498, Columbus set sail on his third voyage, and due to bad reports from Hispaniola, was forced to bring convicts to the New World. Columbus sailed farther south, finding Trinidad, and continued sailing until he realized that he had found a land mass. Columbus had to return to Hispaniola before exploring it any further, however. In 1500, due to the bad reports from Hispaniola, the monarchy sent a royal commissioner to survey the situation, which resulted in Columbus being sent back to Spain in chains.

DIALECTS

Geographic Dialects   The widespread differentiation in dialects is mostly due to geographical factors. Speech in one locality will always differ in some way from that of another locality. An isogloss is a geographic boundary between regions that shows a difference in linguistic features. Isoglosses are frequently grouped together in bundles, the result of migration and political borders. An example of an isogloss is the La Spezia-Rimini line, which divides the Central Italian dialects from the Northern Italian dialects.

PYTHAGOREAN THEOREM

Algebraic Proofs   The Pythagorean theorem can also be proven by using algebra. To do so, the equation looks like this:

$$(b-a)^2 + 4(ab/2) = (b-a)^2 + 2ab = a^2 + b^2$$

When solved, this problem simply turns into:

$$c^2 = a^2 + b^2$$

Another proof related to this was actually created by President James Garfield.

THE BIG BANG

Misconceptions   The big bang was not an explosion, as many believe it to be. Rather, it was an expansion (which continues today). Some believe the singularity to be a ball of fire in space, but in all reality, there was no space, time, energy, or matter prior to the big bang. Space actually started in the singularity. Scientists still do not know where the singularity appeared if space did not exist.

SWEDISH

Contemporary Swedish   Nusvenska, literally meaning "Now-Swedish," is the Swedish language spoken today. It began toward the end of the nineteenth century, and much of the written language appeared closer to the spoken language, moving away from formal restrictions. By the time of the spelling reform of 1906, the language was standardized, and in the 1960s, a major change was made, known as du-reformen (the "you-reform"), replacing standard titles and surnames with "du."

COLUMBUS AND THE NEW WORLD

The Fourth Voyage   Columbus managed to get four ships together in 1502 for his fourth journey, which he hoped would restore his reputation. Columbus hit the coast of Honduras and was later marooned on Jamaica in an attempt to return to Hispaniola. Upon being rescued, Columbus was forced to return to Spain in 1504. Columbus died two years later, still believing he had reached Asia.

DIALECTS

Interlingua   From 1937 to 1951, Interlingua was developed as a language that would use the languages of Western civilization as its dialects. Realizing that many words in different languages are similar, linguists used words from English, Spanish, Portuguese, Italian, French, Russian and German to create a spoken and written language that would be able to be understood by all. Interlingua is known as an international auxiliary language.

PYTHAGOREAN THEOREM

Proof with Differentials   A proof using differentials employs principles of calculus to prove the Pythagorean theorem. This type of proof involves studying how changes to a side of the triangle affect the hypotenuse. This is considered to be a metric proof, and instead of using areas, the proof is based on lengths.

THE BIG BANG

Other Theories   The big bang is not the only scientific theory regarding the origins of the universe. Physicist Robert Gentry proposed another theory in 2003, claiming that the foundation of the big bang was a faulty paradigm. Gentry's theory was based on Einstein's static-spacetime paradigm, with the notion that there is a center that neither expands nor contracts. Gentry believes this also explains the evidence that has been found.

SWEDISH

Dialects   There are six main dialects found in the Swedish language: North Swedish, South Swedish, Finland Swedish, Svealand Swedish, Götaland Swedish, and Gotland Swedish. These dialects are separate from the standard language and developed independently from as far back as Old Norse. The dialects are very localized, and speakers of these dialects also speak the standard language.

COLUMBUS AND THE NEW WORLD

The Impact on the Native Americans   Over the course of a century, the population of natives on the island of Hispaniola was completely destroyed in a genocide brought on by the Spanish. In 1493, policies regarding slavery and mass extermination were implemented, and within a three-year time span, 5 million Native Americans were killed. Mass numbers of Native Americans were hanged, stabbed, shot, and worked to death as slaves.

DIALECTS

Focal and Relic Areas   Focal areas are locations where innovations in dialect occur. They usually coincide with urban areas or areas with great cultural and economic activity. Relic areas are locations that the innovations from focal areas spread to but haven't arrived yet. Relic areas also have innovations; however, they do not spread as widely geographically as focal areas. Boston is an example of a focal area, while Cape Cod is an example of a relic area.

PYTHAGOREAN THEOREM

The Pythagorean Triple   The Pythagorean triple is a series of three whole numbers, such as 3, 4, and 5 that work when put into the Pythagorean theorem, and can be the sides of a right triangle. Other examples of Pythagorean triples include 5, 12, 13 and 7, 24, 25. To create a Pythagorean triple, take any odd number and square it. Then find two consecutive numbers that add up to that number.

THE BIG BANG

Does God Have a Role?   The big bang is a controversial issue because it puts into question the role of God in the creation of the universe. While some religions have welcomed and incorporated the big bang theory into their beliefs, others have refused to believe it. In 1951, Pope Pius XII declared that the big bang theory was in accordance with Catholic beliefs.

SWEDISH

Useful Swedish Phrases   Here are some helpful phrases to use when traveling to Sweden:

Hello. *Hej.*

Good morning. *God morgon.*

Good afternoon. *God eftermiddag.*

Good evening. *God kväll.*

Good night. *God natt.*

I don't understand. *Jag förstår inte.*

How much is this? *Hur mycket kostar det?*

Where's the toilet? *Var är toaletten?*

Cheers! *Skål!*

Excuse me. *Ursäkta.*

Thank you. *Tack.*

Goodbye. *Hej då.*

1. **What was the name of the first permanent European settlement in the New World?**
   a. Hispaniola
   b. Leeward Islands
   c. Santo Domingo
   d. Santa Maria

2. **In 1493, policies regarding slavery and mass extermination were implemented on the Native Americans. Within a three-year time span, how many Native Americans were killed?**
   a. 2 million
   b. 9 million
   c. 5 million
   d. 500

3. **Which of the following affects dialects?**
   a. Social status
   b. Geographic location
   c. Urbanization
   d. All of the above

4. **The standard forms of English spoken in America, Australia, and England are examples of:**
   a. Standard dialects
   b. Relics
   c. Focals
   d. Interlingua

5. **In the Pythagorean theorem, the letter *c* represents:**
   a. The left side
   b. The right side
   c. The long side
   d. The hypotenuse

6. **Which of the following is a Pythagorean triple?**
   a. 7, 24, 25
   b. 9, 18, 27
   c. 7, 8, 9
   d. 7, 25, 26

7. **Which of the following is true?**
   a. Before the big bang, there was nothing.
   b. The big bang led to the creation and expansion of the space that carried matter.
   c. The big bang began from a singularity.
   d. All of the above.

8. **What does Hubble's law state?**
   a. That the universe does not expand
   b. That the universe is expanding
   c. That heat is moving through the universe
   d. That the universe never contracted

9. **What important event was Gustav Vasa, the king of Sweden, responsible for?**
   a. He turned Götaland Swedish into Gotland Swedish.
   b. He united the North Swedish and South Swedish dialects.
   c. He created the du-reformen.
   d. He ordered the Bible to be translated into Swedish.

10. **How do you say "Thank you" in Swedish?**
    a. Hej då.
    b. Tack.
    c. Ursäkta.
    d. Hej.

ANSWER KEY: c, c, d, a, d, a, d, b, d, b

HISTORY: The American Revolution

The Battle of Lexington and Concord, The Battle of Bunker Hill, The Evacuation of Boston, The Battle of Trenton, The Battle of Saratoga, The Battle of Yorktown

MATH: Fibonacci Sequence

What Is the Fibonacci Sequence?, The Golden Ratio, The Fibonacci Sequence in Nature, The Fibonacci Sequence in Music, The Man Behind Fibonacci, Leonardo Pisano Bogollo's Rabbits

LANGUAGE ARTS: Figures of Speech

What Is a Figure of Speech?, Simile, Metaphor, Hyperbole, Oxymoron, Other Common Figures of Speech

SCIENCE: Galileo Galilei

Who Was Galileo Galilei?, The Telescope, The Moon, Jupiter, Galileo and the Church, Copernicanism and Galileo

Lesson 14

FOREIGN LANGUAGE: Finnish

The Origins, Finnish During the Middle Ages, The Writing System, Modernization of Finnish, Dialects, Useful Finnish Phrases

THE AMERICAN REVOLUTION

The Battle of Lexington and Concord   It is unknown which side the "Shot Heard 'Round the World" came from, but on April 19, 1775, the British troops and the American colonists fought the first battle of the Revolutionary War. A rumor was circulating that the Massachusetts Militia had been storing weapons in Concord, and 700 British soldiers were sent to quell their mission. The colonists quickly learned of the oncoming British troops, leading to Paul Revere's famous horseback ride. Though both sides faced casualties, more British soldiers were left dead or wounded.

FIGURES OF SPEECH

What Is a Figure of Speech?   Figures of speech are a literary device used to add interest, emphasis, freshness, or special meaning to words. A figure of speech can also be referred to as a rhetorical device or locution. Figures of speech are used in figurative (meaning not literal) language, allowing for imagination and more creative ways to describe something.

FIBONACCI SEQUENCE

What Is the Fibonacci Sequence?   The Fibonacci sequence is a series of numbers that follows the very simple rule that any number in the sequence is the sum of the previous two numbers. The first ten numbers in the sequence are:

$$0, 1, 1, 2, 3, 5, 8, 13, 21, 34$$

The Fibonacci sequence is written as:

$$x_n = x_{n-1} + x_{n-2}$$

GALILEO GALILEI

Who Was Galileo Galilei?   Galileo was an Italian mathematician, physicist, philosopher, and astronomer who played a key role in the Scientific Revolution that began toward the end of the Renaissance and continued through the Enlightenment period of the eighteenth century. Galileo lived from 1564 to 1642. He is considered to be the "father of modern science" and his contributions to the world of science are still extremely relevant to this day.

FINNISH

The Origins   Finnish is a Uralic language. It came from the Proto-Finnic language Sámi. The Proto-Finnic language was not actually spoken in Finland, but rather around present-day St. Petersburg. As the language began to spread north, one of the daughter languages turned into Finnish. Around the first century, the Finnic languages separated, which still has great influence on the Finnish dialects.

THE AMERICAN REVOLUTION

The Battle of Bunker Hill   Following the Battle of Lexington and Concord, the colonists besieged Boston from the surrounding hills. When they heard news of the British planning to attack Bunker Hill and Breed's Hill, the colonists sent 1,600 militiamen to set up fortifications. On June 17, 1775, 2,600 British soldiers attacked. Most of the fighting took place on Breed's Hill. By the third charge from the British, the colonists had to retreat, and though the British gained control of Breed's Hill, they suffered a great amount of losses and casualties.

FIGURES OF SPEECH

Simile   A simile is one of the most common figures of speech. In similes, one thing is described to be like another thing. The important part about similes is their use of the words *like* or *as*. For example, "He eats like a pig" and "It's as light as a feather" are both examples of similes. Other forms of similes can be found in sentences with *as if* and *than*. For example, "I completely forgot how to work the machine, as if it were my very first time" and "larger than life."

FIBONACCI SEQUENCE

The Golden Ratio   The Golden Ratio, expressed as φ, is a mathematical constant with a value of 1.6180339887. If the ratio between the sum of two quantities and the larger quantity equals the ratio of the larger quantity and the smaller quantity, it is called the Golden Ratio. In other words:

$$\frac{a+b}{a} = \frac{a}{b} = \varphi$$

Any two successive numbers from the Fibonacci sequence will have a ratio close to the Golden Ratio.

GALILEO GALILEI

The Telescope   In 1609, Galileo heard news of an invention in the Netherlands that would make faraway objects appear close — the spyglass. Determined to figure out how the invention worked, Galileo tried making his own, and in only 24 hours, without ever having seen the object and going by only the rumors he had heard, he created a 3-power telescope. After making some changes, he brought the now 10-power telescope to the Senate of Venice and demonstrated how it worked.

FINNISH

Finnish During the Middle Ages   Before the Middle Ages, Finnish was only an oral language. During the Middle Ages, Finland was annexed to Catholic Sweden. The administrative language was Swedish, the language used in religion was Latin, and business was transacted Middle Low German, leaving little room for Finnish to be spoken. However, the first evidence of Finnish writing is found from this time period, dating to around 1450.

THE AMERICAN REVOLUTION

The Evacuation of Boston   The evacuation of the British from Boston was a very important victory for the colonists, and also the first victory for General George Washington. As a result of the battle of Bunker Hill, though the British won, they desperately needed reinforcements. To support Washington, Henry Knox, the chief artillery officer, brought fifty cannons from Fort Ticonderoga and positioned them to aim at the British fleet in Boston Harbor. On March 5, 1776, the British general saw the cannons aimed at them and took his men to Halifax, Canada.

FIGURES OF SPEECH

Metaphor   Metaphors are very similar to similes, only they do not include the words *like*, *as*, *as if*, or *than*. Instead, they simply state that one thing is another thing. In the sentence "Her home is a pigsty," we understand that this does not mean her home is a literal pigsty, but rather a very messy place. The differences between metaphors and similes is that even though they mean the same thing, they are worded differently. For example, "He is a snake" is a metaphor, but the same idea put as "He is like a snake" is a simile.

FIBONACCI SEQUENCE

The Fibonacci Sequence in Nature   Fibonacci sequences appear in the natural world with astounding frequency. The number of petals on a flower, branching in trees, how leaves are arranged on a stem, the spirals of a pinecone, and even the scales of a pineapple all show Fibonacci sequences. One particular example of the Fibonacci sequence in nature is with the reproduction of the honeybee. The sequence of honeybee parents and ancestors correlates exactly with the Fibonacci sequence.

GALILEO GALILEI

The Moon   During Galileo's time, the widespread belief was that the Moon was actually completely smooth and polished. As Galileo focused his new invention on the Moon, he began noticing a surface that was anything but smooth. The landscape of the Moon was rough, full of cavities and craters, and uneven. People dismissed Galileo's findings, and some even argued that the surface of the Moon was covered with an invisible layer of smooth crystal.

FINNISH

The Writing System   In the sixteenth century, Finnish bishop Mikael Agricola created the first comprehensive Finnish writing system. The orthography was based on Latin, Swedish, and German, and Agricola created the system to translate the Bible. Agricola's system was revised to make a more phonemic system at a later time, and certain phonemes were lost.

THE AMERICAN REVOLUTION

The Battle of Trenton   Following a defeat, General George Washington decided to plan a surprise attack on the British and Hessian soldiers on Christmas day of 1776. Washington led 2,500 soldiers across the Delaware River in a great snowstorm under treacherous conditions to reach Trenton, New Jersey. While the British soldiers slept, Washington and his men attacked, taking 1,000 prisoners and killing over 100 men without a single American killed.

 FIGURES OF SPEECH

Hyperbole   Hyperbole is a form of exaggeration used to elicit a strong response. Hyperboles are not to be taken literally and are often used for humor. For example, "He is older than the dinosaurs" and "I'm a million times smarter than you" are both hyperboles. There is great exaggeration to these sentences. Hyperbole is very common in media and advertising.

 FIBONACCI SEQUENCE

The Fibonacci Sequence in Music   The Fibonacci sequence can also be found in music. In any octave, thirteen notes can be played. A scale is made up of eight notes, and the third and fifth notes in the scale are the foundation of the chords. These are based on a whole tone, which is two tones away from the root tone, which happens to be the first note.

GALILEO GALILEI

Jupiter   By January of 1610, Galileo's telescope was now 30-power. As Galileo fixed his telescope on the stars, he began to focus on Jupiter, noticing three bright stars in a straight line near the planet. When looking the following evening, the three stars had moved to the west of the planet, while still maintaining the straight line. Over time, Galileo came to the conclusion that these were satellites of Jupiter that rotated around the planet. The implications meant that if satellites rotated around another planet, perhaps the Earth was not the center of the universe as many believed.

FINNISH

Modernization of Finnish   In the nineteenth century, there was a great need to improve the Finnish language. Since Agricola's writing system first appeared, written Finnish was almost solely used for things pertaining to religion. As support for a national language grew, efforts were made to modernize and improve the language. By the end of the nineteenth century, Finnish, with Swedish, became the official language of journalism, literature, science, and administration.

THE AMERICAN REVOLUTION

The Battle of Saratoga   The Battle of Saratoga is considered to be one of the major victories in the Revolutionary War and a turning point for the Americans. The British army wished to control the Hudson River and cut New England off from the other colonies. British troops had planned to join with other troops along the way to quell the colonists; however, intervention from the Americans prevented this. On September 19, 1777, the first battle of Saratoga occurred, and on October 7, the second battle occurred, resulting in the surrender of the British troops.

FIGURES OF SPEECH

Oxymoron   An oxymoron pairs two opposite or contradicting ideas together to create a new meaning or paradoxical image. For example, in "bittersweet chocolate" *bitter* and *sweet* are opposites of each other, and yet when put together, they take on a whole new meaning. Other examples of oxymora include *deafening silence*, *jumbo shrimp*, and *freezer burn*.

FIBONACCI SEQUENCE

The Man Behind Fibonacci   The Fibonacci sequence was named after the Italian Leonardo Pisano Bogollo, who lived from 1170 to 1250. His nickname was Fibonacci, meaning "son of Banacci." Though the sequence was described earlier by Indian mathematicians, it was Leonardo Pisano Bogollo who helped spread the sequence to Western Europe. He also helped spread the Hindu-Arabic numerals (the current system used today) across Europe, replacing the Roman Numeral system.

GALILEO GALILEI

Galileo and the Church   Galileo continued to discover things about the various planets, and his findings started to contradict the beliefs of the Church. Galileo was, in fact, quite religious and believed in the Bible, but he believed they were wrong in this matter and that the Bible should not be taken so literally. This led to charges of heresy from the Church. He was eventually found innocent; however, sixteen years later he was put under house arrest until his death for a book he had written expressing Copernican theory.

FINNISH

Dialects   There are two types of dialects found in the Finnish language: Western and Eastern. The two dialects are fairly similar, but do have slight differences in diphthongs, rhythms, and vowels. The most obvious distinguishing factor between the two dialects is how the letter *d* is pronounced. Otherwise, much of the same grammar, vocabulary, and phonology are the same.

THE AMERICAN REVOLUTION

The Battle of Yorktown   Though the battle of Yorktown did not end the American Revolution, it was the last major battle fought. On September 5, 1781, the French fleet arrived and defeated the British Navy. The British general, Lord Cornwallis, found his men trapped between the American colonists and the French, and on October 19, 1781, he and his 8,000 troops surrendered. The surrender had a huge impact on the British government, as the war was being lost.

FIGURES OF SPEECH

Other Common Figures of Speech   Other common examples of figures of speech include alliteration, where there is a repetition of the beginning consonant; anaphora, the repetition of a single word or phrase in a sentence; onomatopoeia, the use of words that imitate the sounds they are referring to; and antithesis, which juxtaposes opposite ideas in a single, balanced sentence.

FIBONACCI SEQUENCE

Leonardo Pisano Bogollo's Rabbits   Leonardo Pisano Bogollo first mentioned the sequence in his book *Liber Abaci*. In it, he examined the growth of an unrealistic rabbit population. Bogollo wondered how many pairs of rabbits would there be in one year if a male and a female rabbit can mate at one-month old, by the end of the second month the female can produce another pair, the rabbits do not ever die, and a new pair is produced every month from the second month on.

GALILEO GALILEI

Copernicanism and Galileo   Galileo was a believer and teacher in Copernicanism, the idea, first posed by Nicolaus Copernicus, that the Earth was not the center of the universe. The ban of Galileo's book that ended in his house arrest was eventually lifted from the Catholic Church in 1822, and in 1992 the Vatican publicly and formally cleared Galileo of doing anything wrong.

FINNISH

Useful Finnish Phrases   Here are some helpful Finnish phrases to use when traveling to Finland:

Hello. *Terve.*
Good morning. *Hyvää huomenta.*
Good afternoon. *Hyvää päivää.*
Good evening. *Hyvää iltaa.*
Yes. *Kyllä.*
No. *Ei.*
Thank you. *Kiitos.*

Do you speak English? *Puhutteko englantia?*
I don't speak Finnish. *Minä en puhu suomea.*
I don't understand. *Minä en ymmärrä.*
Where's the toilet? *Missä on WC?*
Goodbye. *Näkemiin.*

1. **Which of the following describes the Battle of Trenton?**
   a. On Christmas of 1776, Washington led 2,500 soldiers across the Delaware River in a great snowstorm under treacherous conditions for a surprise attack on the British and Hessians.
   b. British troops planned to join with other troops along the way to quell the colonists; however, intervention from the French prevented this.
   c. The British evacuated Boston.
   d. The Shot Heard 'Round the World occurred.

2. **Which of the following did the Americans lose?**
   a. Battle of Yorktown
   b. Battle of Bunker Hill
   c. Battle of Trenton
   d. Battle of Saratoga

3. **Which of the following is a metaphor?**
   a. He's like a pig.
   b. He's as messy as a pig.
   c. He's a million times messier than a pig.
   d. He's a pig.

4. **Which of the following is an example of hyperbole?**
   a. He's like a pig.
   b. He's as messy as a pig.
   c. He's a million times messier than a pig.
   d. He's a pig.

5. **What is the next number in the Fibonacci sequence: 0, 1, 1, 2, 3, 5...**
   a. 9
   b. 5
   c. 7
   d. 8

6. **Which of the following is an example of the Fibonacci sequence in nature?**
   a. Leaves arranged on a stem
   b. The spirals of a pinecone
   c. The scales of a pineapple
   d. All of the above

7. **What was one conclusion Galileo came to when he found the satellites orbiting around Jupiter?**
   a. If satellites rotated around another planet, perhaps the Earth was not the center of the universe as many believed.
   b. The satellites were new planets.
   c. The satellites were comets.
   d. The Earth was the center of the universe, contrary to what others believed.

8. **With his new telescope, Galileo noticed that the moon:**
   a. Was smooth and even
   b. Was rough and uneven
   c. Had a layer of invisible crystal around it
   d. Was not made of cheese

9. **Before the Middle Ages, Finnish was:**
   a. Only a written language
   b. Only spoken on the western half of the country
   c. Only an oral language
   d. None of the above

10. **In Finnish, the most obvious distinguishing factor between the two dialects is how this letter is pronounced:**
    a. B
    b. G
    c. C
    d. D

ANSWER KEY: a, b, d, c, d, d, a, b, c, d

114

HISTORY:
The Constitution

The Declaration of Independence, The Articles of Confederation, The Constitutional Convention of 1787, Articles of the Constitution, The Bill of Rights, Amendments to the Constitution

MATH: Square Roots

Simplifying Square Roots, Multiplying Square Roots, Adding and Subtracting with Square Roots, Division with Square Roots, Rationalizing Denominators, Higher Index Roots

LANGUAGE ARTS:
Literary Terms

Genre, Allegory, Catharsis, Motif, Ambiguity, Metanoia

SCIENCE:
Stephen Hawking

About Stephen Hawking, Theory of Singularity, Work with Black Holes, Unified Field Theory, *A Brief History of Time*, The Thorne-Hawking-Preskill Bet

Lesson 15

FOREIGN LANGUAGE:
Icelandic

The Origins, Middle Icelandic, Modern Icelandic, Influences on Icelandic, Phonology, Useful Icelandic Phrases

THE CONSTITUTION

The Declaration of Independence   Before the Constitution was ever written, the Declaration of Independence needed to be drafted, declaring the colonies' freedom from the British. The Continental Congress met in the summer of 1776 to discuss the writing of the important document, and on June 11, Thomas Jefferson began the first draft. The final draft was submitted to the Continental Congress on June 28, and by July 2, the Continental Congress took a vote regarding their independence. On July 4, the document was released to the public.

LITERARY TERMS

Genre   In literature, a genre is a specific category that literature follows. It is instantly recognizable and follows common conventions pertaining to that genre. Types of genres include nonfiction, in which everything written is true; mystery, in which all stories follow a crime or event that is not solved until the end; and fantasy, which features elements that are not realistic.

SQUARE ROOTS

Simplifying Square Roots   For simplifying square roots, you begin by taking out any perfect squares. For example:

$$\sqrt{25} = \sqrt{5^2} = 5$$

When the number is not a perfect square, there might be a perfect square within the number. First you must factor the problem, and then take out the perfect square. For example:

$$\sqrt{400} = \sqrt{100 \times 4} = \sqrt{100} \times \sqrt{4} = 10 \times 2 = 20$$

If there is no perfect square, you break it down to its simplest form. For example:

$$\sqrt{98} = \sqrt{49} \times \sqrt{2} = 7 \times \sqrt{2} = 7\sqrt{2}$$

STEPHEN HAWKING

About Stephen Hawking   Stephen Hawking is a British mathematician and physicist who has made astounding discoveries in the fields of cosmology, and especially pertaining to understanding how our universe works. Hawking studied physics at Oxford, graduating with a first class honors in 1962. While studying physics in graduate school at Cambridge, Hawking was diagnosed with ALS (also known as Lou Gehrig's disease), the disease that would leave him wheelchair-bound for the rest of his life.

ICELANDIC

The Origins   Icelandic is a Northern Germanic language, and is actually a dialect of Norwegian. During the ninth century, settlers from Norway came to Iceland, speaking Old Norse. Due to the geographic location of Iceland, over time, the language began to diverge from Norwegian. The language also had influence from other Scandinavian settlers and as a result, the common traits to all of the different languages were reinforced, with the differences disappearing gradually.

THE CONSTITUTION

The Articles of Confederation   Upon winning their freedom, the thirteen states began to operate under their own rules, and a centralized government was strongly opposed, fearing another monarchy could arise. As a compromise, the Articles of Confederation were drafted in 1776 and ratified in 1781. Essentially, this was the country's first constitution. Each state would retain its freedom, and a committee of representatives — a Congress — would be responsible for declaring war, dealing with foreign affairs, and maintaining an army and navy. Though the document had a lot of good ideas, it had many shortcomings, and these led to the creation of the Constitution.

LITERARY TERMS

Allegory   In literature, an allegory is a narrative that is symbolic of something else. With allegories, behind the literal translation of the story, a second, more meaningful story or idea can be found. For example, the literal story of *Lord of the Flies* is about children stranded on an island where chaos ensues; however, the allegory is about civilization as a whole and the evil of humankind.

SQUARE ROOTS

Multiplying Square Roots   When multiplying square roots, simplify the problem into its basic form. For example:

$$\sqrt{10} = \sqrt{5} \times \sqrt{2} = \sqrt{5}\sqrt{2}$$

When working in the other direction, the problem must be simplified by writing no more than one radical. For example:

$$\sqrt{3}\sqrt{12} = \sqrt{3} \times \sqrt{3} \times \sqrt{4} = \sqrt{3} \times \sqrt{3} \times 2 = 3 \times 2 = 6$$

STEPHEN HAWKING

Theory of Singularity   Stephen Hawking's theory of singularity was his first major contribution to the world of physics. Using the work of Albert Einstein and Roger Penrose (with whom he collaborated), Hawking proved that the origin of our universe was in a singularity that has no end. Hawking's research supported the big bang theory and began his lifelong interest in black holes.

ICELANDIC

Middle Icelandic   From 1350 to 1550, the differences between Norwegian and Icelandic grew significantly. There was a dichotomy in Icelandic: Part of the Icelandic language remained pure and the other went through a significant transformation. Among the changes made was a diphthongization of long vowels, short vowels became less tense, previously absent consonant phonemes appeared, and unvoiced consonants were now aspirated. These changes were never written, but were phonetic.

THE CONSTITUTION

The Constitutional Convention of 1787   In 1787, the delegates from all of the states except Rhode Island met in Philadelphia to create a more centralized government. Two plans, the Virginia Plan and the New Jersey Plan, were presented. The Virginia Plan consisted of a powerful centralized government that had executive, legislative, and judicial branches. The New Jersey Plan would make changes to the Articles of Confederation and allow Congress to control taxes and trade to some degree. A compromise was reached, combining parts of both plans.

LITERARY TERMS

Catharsis   In literature, a catharsis is a point in the narrative when there is a release of negative emotions, which in turn ends up either helping the character or helping the audience in understanding the character. The term comes from the Greek *kathoros*, which means "to make clean or purify." Use of the term applied to literature first appeared in Aristotle's *Poetics*, in which he describes the impact of drama on a viewer.

SQUARE ROOTS

Adding and Subtracting Square Roots   With addition, if the root is the same, you just have to add the numbers before it. For example:

$$3\sqrt{5} + 2\sqrt{5} = 5\sqrt{5}$$

If a square root can be simplified into whole numbers, then they should be, and then continue with the problem. For example:

$$3\sqrt{25} + 2\sqrt{25} = 3(5) + 2(5) = 25$$

Only like radicals can be combined in the end, so if you end with a problem like $2\sqrt{3} + 3\sqrt{7}$, then that is your answer.

STEPHEN HAWKING

Work with Black Holes   Hawking's work with black holes has been critical in understanding our universe. Hawking proved that when two black holes merge, the new hole's surface area is larger than the sum of the two black holes, and that surface area only increases and does not decrease. The two most important discoveries made by Hawking concerning black holes are that black holes give off heat and that there exist millions of small black holes created from the big bang.

ICELANDIC

Modern Icelandic   Modern Icelandic formed around 1550 with the introduction of the printing press, the Lutheran Reformation, and the translation of the Bible. Several changes have been made to both the vowel system and the consonant system. The modern alphabet was established in the nineteenth century and based on that of the twelfth century, with some changes made to fit Germanic conventions. In the twentieth century, *é* was adopted, replacing *je*, and the letter *z* was abolished.

THE CONSTITUTION

Articles of the Constitution   Currently, the Constitution has a preamble, seven original articles, a list of twenty-seven amendments, and a certification from the Constitutional Convention. The first article establishes the legislative branch, defining Congress as a bicameral body with a House of Representatives and a Senate. Article II establishes the role of the presidency. Article III describes how the court system will work, and includes the Supreme Court.

LITERARY TERMS

Motif   A motif is a recurring image, phrase, element, expression, word, action, or object that has some sort of symbolic significance to the story. Motifs can help produce the theme of the narrative. A motif can also be a situation, character, image, idea, or incident that is found in other literature. For example, a love triangle or the corruption of power are both examples of motifs.

SQUARE ROOTS

Division with Square Roots   Division is very simple. Begin by simplifying the problem from inside the square root. For example:

$$\frac{\sqrt{32}}{2} = \sqrt{16} = 4$$

You can also split the division into radicals and then work from there, simplifying and canceling numbers out. For example:

$$\sqrt{\frac{3}{36}} = \frac{\sqrt{3}}{\sqrt{6 \times 6}} = \frac{\sqrt{3}}{6}$$

⚛ STEPHEN HAWKING

Unified Field Theory   In the 1980s, Stephen Hawking was able to answer one of Albert Einstein's most famous theories that had been left unanswered, the unified field theory. This theory provides an explanation for conditions present at the beginning of our universe and the physical laws of nature. The theory consists of four main interactions: a strong nuclear force, electromagnetism, radioactivity's weak nuclear force, and gravity.

☾ ICELANDIC

Influences on Icelandic   Though at one point in time Danish was the official language of Iceland, little of the language has stuck. In the nineteenth century, the language was purified to get rid of any Danish influence, and only a few Danish words are still used today. Though Latin influences can be seen from its Germanic roots, Icelandic has not been heavily influenced by any other languages with the exception of English, which the younger generation has adapted to the Icelandic morphological and phonetic system.

🏛 THE CONSTITUTION

The Bill of Rights   The Bill of Rights are the first ten amendments made to the Constitution. These amendments establish the specific rights every American citizen has. The Bill of Rights was created due to the fears of Anti-Federalists who were wary of the Constitution and feared the presidency could turn into a monachy. These rights include the freedom of speech and religion, the right to bear arms, and the right to have a fair trial by a jury.

📖 LITERARY TERMS

Ambiguity   Ambiguity leaves room for different interpretations. It creates an openness in the text. Ambiguity can sometimes be considered a flaw in literature due to a lack of detail or vague characterization; however, it can also be used skillfully and can work to the advantage of the story.

➗ SQUARE ROOTS

Rationalizing Denominators   The denominator can never contain a radical. To fix this problem, you must find the common denominator, the exact same way you were taught to do with fractions growing up.

For example, to simplify

$$\frac{8\sqrt{2}}{\sqrt{3}}$$

You must first find the common denominator and multiply it by both the top and the bottom.

$$\frac{8\sqrt{2}}{\sqrt{3}} = \frac{(\sqrt{3})}{(\sqrt{3})} = \frac{8\sqrt{6}}{\sqrt{3\times3}} = \frac{8\sqrt{6}}{3}$$

⚛ STEPHEN HAWKING

A Brief History of Time   Stephen Hawking has written many books. His most well-known book is *A Brief History of Time: From the Big Bang to Black Holes*, which was first published in 1988. The book explains immensely complex issues such as the big bang, black holes, and light cones so that the nonscientist can understand it. The book is so immensely popular, a documentary was made about it, and the New York Metropolitan Opera is turning it into an opera.

🌐 ICELANDIC

Phonology   Due to the fact that Icelandic is spoken by a small number of speakers in one concentrated area, there are relatively few dialects of the language. The language features diphthongs, monophthongs (pure vowels with a fixed articulation), and consonants that can be both voiced and unvoiced. In Icelandic, there is a contrast of aspiration (burst of air) between plosives (a consonant sound that stops airflow).

THE CONSTITUTION

Amendments to the Constitution During the writing of the Constitution, the framers were aware that over time, certain changes would be necessary, and included the ability to amend the constitution. There have only been twenty-seven amendments to the U.S. Constitution. Some of the most well known are the Thirteenth Amendment, which abolished slavery; the Nineteenth Amendment, which established women's suffrage; and the Eighteenth Amendment, which prohibited the sale of alcohol. The Eighteenth Amendment was then repealed by the Twenty-first Amendment.

 LITERARY TERMS

Metanoia Metanoia, which comes from the Greek *metanoiein*, meaning to change one's mind, is when a character goes through a complete breakdown, and then begins the process of healing or a change of mind or transformation. Metanoia is one form of catharsis.

 SQUARE ROOTS

Higher Index Roots Operations with higher roots such as cube roots, fourth roots, etc., are similar to square roots. With cube roots, take out factors that occur in threes. With a fourth root, take out factors that occur in fours, etc.

For example:

$$\sqrt[4]{16} = \sqrt[4]{2 \times 2 \times 2 \times 2} = 2$$
$$\sqrt[3]{54} = \sqrt[3]{3 \times 3 \times 3 \times 2} = 2\sqrt[3]{3 \times 2} = 2\sqrt[3]{6}$$

⚛ STEPHEN HAWKING

The Thorne-Hawking-Preskill Bet The Thorne-Hawking-Preskill bet was a public bet made in 1997 between three physics theorists: Kip Thorne, John Preskill, and Stephen Hawking. The bet regarded the black hole information paradox. Hawking and Thorne argued that quantum mechanics needed to be rewritten due to the fact that the information carried by Hawking radiation must be new, and Preskill believed the opposite to be true. In 2004, Hawking conceded. In 2008, Hawking announced that he believed he had solved the paradox.

🗣 ICELANDIC

Useful Icelandic Phrases Here are some helpful phrases to use when traveling to Iceland:

Hello. *Halló.*
Good morning. *Godan dag.*
Good afternoon. *Godan daginn.*
Good night. *Goda nott.*
Thank you. *Takk.*
I don't understand. *Eg skil ekki.*
Do you speak English? *Talardu ensku?*
How much is it? *Hvad kostar?*
Goodbye. *Bless.*

1. **Which of the following is true?**
   a. The Virginia Plan consisted of a powerful centralized government that had executive, legislative, and judicial branches. The New Jersey Plan would make changes to the Articles of Confederation and allow Congress to control taxes and trade to some degree.
   b. The New Jersey Plan consisted of a powerful centralized government that had executive, legislative, and judicial branches. The Virginia Plan would make changes to the Articles of Confederation and allow Congress to control taxes and trade to some degree.
   c. Both plans featured executive and legislative branches, but no judicial branch.
   d. Both plans featured legislative and judicial branches, but no executive branch for fear that the presidency would turn into another monarchy.

2. **What did the Thirteenth Amendment do?**
   a. Gave women the right to vote
   b. Prohibited alcohol
   c. Abolished slavery
   d. Repealed the prohibition of alcohol

3. **What is a motif?**
   a. When a character goes through a complete breakdown, and then begins the process of healing or a change of mind or transformation
   b. When there is room for different interpretations
   c. A narrative that is symbolic for something else
   d. A recurring image, phrase, element, expression, word, action, or object that has some sort of symbolic significance to the story

4. **Which of the following is an example of a genre?**
   a. Science fiction
   b. Romance
   c. Fantasy
   d. All of the above

5. **What is $5\sqrt{7} + 4\sqrt{7}$?**
   a. $9\sqrt{14}$
   c. $9\sqrt{49}$
   b. $9\sqrt{7}$
   d. 9

6. **What does $\sqrt{8\dfrac{1}{3}}$ equal?**
   a. 9
   c. 3
   b. $\sqrt{27}$
   d. $\sqrt{3}$

7. **Stephen Hawking proved that when two black holes merge:**
   a. The surface area of the new hole is larger than the sum of the two black holes.
   b. The surface area of the new hole is equal to the sum of the two black holes.
   c. The surface area of the new hole is equal to the difference of the two black holes.
   d. The surface area of the new hole stays the same.

8. **Stephen Hawking's theory of singularity proved:**
   a. The origins of our universe was in a singularity that ends.
   b. The origins of our universe was in a singularity which has no end.
   c. The origins of our universe was not in a singularity.
   d. The origins of our universe was in a singularity that stopped moving.

9. **Modern Icelandic formed around 1550 with the introduction of:**
   a. The printing press
   b. The Lutheran Reformation
   c. Translation of the Bible
   d. All of the above

10. **What type of language is Icelandic?**
    a. East Germanic
    b. West Slavonic
    c. Northern Germanic
    d. Southern Germanic

ANSWER KEY: a, c, d, d, b, c, a, b, d, c

HISTORY: The Industrial Revolution

What Was the Industrial Revolution?, Textiles, Steam Power, Transportation, Iron and Coal, The Cotton Gin

MATH: Geometry

Polygons, Area, Perimeter, Circumference, Volume, Surface Area

LANGUAGE ARTS: Literary Elements

Plot, Protagonist, Antagonist, Foreshadowing, Point of View, Setting

SCIENCE: The Periodic Table

What Is the Periodic Table?, The History of the Periodic Table, Groups, Periods, Blocks, Names of the Elements

Lesson 16

FOREIGN LANGUAGE: Croatian

The Origins, Attempt at Standardizing Croatian, The Illyrian Movement and Forward, Phonology, Croatian Today, Useful Croatian Phrases

THE INDUSTRIAL REVOLUTION

What Was the Industrial Revolution? The Industrial Revolution can be broken into two parts: the first Industrial Revolution, which started in England and lasted from 1750 to 1850; and the second Industrial Revolution, which took place in America and lasted from 1850 to 1940. The Industrial Revolution was a great burst of technological advancement that changed the world from a rural, agricultural economy to that of an urban and industrial one.

LITERARY ELEMENTS

Plot Simply put, the plot is the story found in literature, film, television, or other narrative work. It is the sequence of events that make up the story. German novelist Gustav Freytag considered the plot to any story to be composed of five parts: exposition, which introduces the main characters and their stories and relationships; a rising action, which begins with a conflict of some sort (this generally involves the character striving for a certain goal); the climax, which is the turning point of the story; the falling action, where loose ends are tied up; and lastly, the resolution or denouement.

GEOMETRY

Polygons Geometry is the study of shapes and their properties. Polygons are particular types of shapes used in geometry. Polygons have many straight sides. With regular polygons, all of the angles and sides have to be the same. A shape with three sides and angles is called a triangle. A shape with four sides and angles is called a quadrilateral. A shape with five sides and angles is a pentagon, six makes a hexagon, and so on. A shape that has two pairs of parallel lines is called a parallelogram.

THE PERIODIC TABLE

What Is the Periodic Table? The periodic table is a table displaying the various elements. There are currently 118 known elements. The elements are placed along the grid in accordance with how they look and how they act. Rows and columns also have particular meaning in the Periodic Table. If elements are in the same row (each row is considered a period), that means they have something in common. The elements in the center of the table are known as transition elements.

CROATIAN

The Origins Croatian is a South Slavic language. The language developed from Old Church Slavonic which, in the ninth century, became the official language of the land. Based on the local dialect of Old Church Slavonic, Croatian developed and used three alphabets: Cyrillic, Glagolithic, and Latin. Over time, the language was strongly influenced by Slovenian and Serbian.

THE INDUSTRIAL REVOLUTION

Textiles   In 1750 England, the modern factory system developed in textiles as a result of power-driven machinery. Prior to these machines, textile work was done completely by hand. With the spinning machine, however, a person would just have to operate a foot pedal and let the machine do the rest. The most famous model of the spinning machine was the spinning jenny. In the 1740s, the first textile mills began appearing in England, and by the 1780s, there were over 120 textile mills.

LITERARY ELEMENTS

Protagonist   The protagonist is the main character found in the story. It is who the entire plot of the story revolves around. For example, even though in *The Wizard of Oz*, the story is about finding the Wizard of Oz, whose name is the title of the book, the story's protagonist is actually Dorothy, because the story is about her journey, not the Wizard. The protagonist can sometimes be the narrator of the story. A false protagonist is a dramatic device where the protagonist is disposed of unexpectedly. A famous example of this can be found in Hitchcock's *Psycho*, where halfway through the movie, the main character is killed.

GEOMETRY

Area   The area is the amount of space inside a shape. To find the area of a square or any other plane shape, the formula is simple. You multiply the length by the height of the object. To find the area of a parallelogram, you multiply the base by the height of the object. For trapezoids — shapes with four sides but only one pair of parallel sides — you add the lengths of the two parallel sides, divide by two, and then multiply that number by the height.

THE PERIODIC TABLE

The History of the Periodic Table   The periodic table of today was created by Dmitri Mendeleev in 1869; however, he was not the first. In 1789, a list of thirty-three chemical elements was published. These were organized by earths, gases, metals, and nonmetals. In 1829, Johann Wolfgang Döbereiner came to the realization that based on chemical properties, elements could be grouped into groups of three, or triads. By 1869, there had been several attempts at perfecting the table, and what made Mendeleev's table so special was that it left gaps for elements not yet discovered. Also, it occasionally ignored the order by atomic weight to better classify into chemical families.

CROATIAN

Attempt at Standardizing Croatian   In the seventeenth century, there was an attempt to unify Croatia, which at the time had been ruled by two dynasties. Ikavian-Kajkavian was chosen to be the unifying dialect because it was an intermediate between all of the other dialects. However, when the dynasties were overtaken by the Holy Roman Emperor, the standard language was abandoned and replaced by Neo-Shtokavian.

THE INDUSTRIAL REVOLUTION

Steam Power   The steam engine provided an efficient and cheap source of power. The first practical steam engine was created in 1712, and it was later perfected by Scottish inventor James Watt in the 1770s. The steam engine was an integral part of the Industrial Revolution. It provided power for machinery and soon moved from the factories to being used in locomotives and ships.

LITERARY ELEMENTS

Antagonist   The antagonist is the character in opposition to the protagonist. The antagonist may also represent a threat or opposing idea to the protagonist. For example, if the superhero is the protagonist, the evil villain is the antagonist. A classic example of an antagonist is Voldemort or Snape from the Harry Potter series. Harry is the protagonist, and they are his antagonists.

GEOMETRY

Perimeter   Perimeter is a very simple idea, with a very simple solution to finding it. The perimeter of an object is the distance around the outside of the shape. The easiest way of finding the perimeter is by adding up all of the sides. For example, if a rectangle has two sides that are 7 inches and two sides that are 3 inches, then the perimeter would be $7 + 7 + 3 + 3 = 20$.

THE PERIODIC TABLE

Groups   The vertical columns in the periodic table are called groups. The groups are the most important way to classify elements. In the current format, the groups are numbered 1 to 18 from the left to the right. Elements in a group share similar configurations of the atom's outermost electron shells. The groups are given names such as alkali metals, alkaline earth metals, halogens, pnictogens, and chalcogens, to name a few.

CROATIAN

The Illyrian Movement and Forward   In the nineteenth century, there was an attempt to create a common South Slavic literary language. This was known as the Illyrian movement. The Shtokavian dialect was chosen as the standard language to be used among Croats and Serbs, and the Serbo-Croatian language was standardized. In 1954, the Novi Sad Agreement established Serbo-Croatian as one language with two variants. The Novi Sad Agreement remained until the collapse of the Socialist Federal Republic of Yugoslavia in 1991, which led to several disputes.

THE INDUSTRIAL REVOLUTION

Transportation   Prior to the Industrial Revolution, transportation was limited to horse-drawn carriages and boats. In the 1800s, the first steamboat was created by an American inventor. Within just a few years, steamboats appeared both in the United States and in England and traveled the Atlantic with goods and raw materials. Technological advancements soon led to better roads and the first steam-powered rail systems.

LITERARY ELEMENTS

Foreshadowing   Foreshadowing is used to suggest developments that will be found later on in the plot. Formal patterning is a form of foreshadowing where certain events, actions, and gestures let the reader anticipate the plot. A red herring is a hint given to the reader that intentionally misleads the reader.

GEOMETRY

Circumference   Circumference is the same idea as perimeter, only it applies to circles. The formula for finding the circumference requires a little more work however. To find the circumference, multiply the diameter of the circle by π, which as you may recall, is simplified to 3.14. If only the radius is provided, multiply the radius by 2 to find the diameter, and then solve for the circumference.

THE PERIODIC TABLE

Periods   The horizontal rows in the periodic table are known as periods. All the elements in a period have the same number of electron shells. Currently, the maximum number of electron shells for any type of element is seven. As you move across a period, the atomic number increases. The atomic number is the number of protons found in the atom's nucleus.

CROATIAN

Phonology   Croatian has a total of thirty letters in its alphabet (which stems from the Latin alphabet), with twenty-five of those letters being consonants and only five being vowels. Vowels can be long or short, and when they are stressed, they carry a rising or falling tone. Understanding consonants is a bit more difficult, and they are affricate (begin as a stop and end with a sound of incomplete closure) and palatal (where the tongue is raised to the hard palate).

THE INDUSTRIAL REVOLUTION

Iron and Coal   Without iron and coal, there would not have been an Industrial Revolution. Coal provided the power for the steam engines as well as energy to fuel the smelting of iron. The iron was then used to build and improve machinery, ships, and bridges. The reason Great Britain became a leader in the Industrial Revolution, and in fact, the first industrialized nation, was due to their large coal and iron ore deposits.

LITERARY ELEMENTS

Point of View   The point of view is the perspective the story is being told from. A narrator can tell the story in first person, where it is the narrator who is experiencing it (use of the word *I*), and sometimes is limited to the information in the moment. The third-person narrator is objective, an unattached observer that does not take a character's perspective. An omniscient narrator can relate multiple characters' perspectives, knowing all, including characters' thoughts. And a limited omniscient narrator knows all, like an omniscient narrator, but only about one or two of the characters.

GEOMETRY

Volume   Whereas area deals with two-dimensional figures, volume is the amount of space in three-dimensional figures. To find the volume of a rectangular prism, multiply the length by the width by the height. To find the volume of a triangular prism, you do the same formula and then multiply by ½. As the shapes get more advanced, so too does the formula for volume. For example, the formula for finding the volume of a cone is ⅓ times the area of the base times the height.

THE PERIODIC TABLE

Blocks   A set of adjacent groups is known as a block or family. There are five blocks: s-block (the first two groups), p-block (the last six groups except for helium), d-block (the transition metals), f-block (part of the lanthanoids and actinoids), and g-block (which is hypothetical; no elements exist in the g-block yet). These blocks reflect the configuration of the electrons.

CROATIAN

Croatian Today   Croatian is spoken by 6 million people today, and is the national language of Croatia. The language is also spoken in Herzegovina, Bosnia, Slovakia, Italy, Austria, and Hungary. Though Croatian, Bosnian, and Serbian are extremely similar, speakers emphasize differences between the languages as a result of a deep and complicated cultural, political, and religious history.

🏛 THE INDUSTRIAL REVOLUTION

The Cotton Gin   In America, the cotton gin, created by Eli Whitney, was revolutionary in the American cotton industry. Prior to his invention, farming cotton required hundreds of hours separating the raw fibers from the cottonseed, which was all done by hand. With this new invention however, up to 50 pounds of cotton could be cleaned in one day. Though its technological advancement was great, the cotton gin would ultimately revitalize slavery in the South.

📖 LITERARY ELEMENTS

Setting   The setting of a story is more than just a backdrop for the actions to occur. It also sets the mood and tone of the entire story, as well as any context that needs to be understood. The setting establishes the time period, the culture, and the geography, and in some cases the setting can be just as important as the characters.

➗ GEOMETRY

Surface Area   The surface area is the sum of all of the areas. For rectangular prisms, finding the surface area requires finding the area of each side and adding them together (this of course can be simplified by finding the area of one side and then multiplying it by two because there are two sides, and then doing the same thing for the other sides). To find the surface area of a cylinder, the formula is: $2\pi r^2 + 2\pi rh$

✳ THE PERIODIC TABLE

Names of the Elements   The naming of the elements is complex. Sometimes it is just the first letter of the element (such as oxygen, O; or hydrogen, H), sometimes it's the beginning of the Latin word (gold is Au, from the Latin *aurum*), while other times it is named for the person who discovered it or for a whole slew of other reasons (polonium is Po, which stands for Poland, named after the country that the people who discovered the element were from).

🗣 CROATIAN

Useful Croatian Phrases   Here are some helpful phrases to use when traveling to Croatia:

Hello. *Zdravo.*	Please. *Molim.*
Pleased to meet you. *Drago mi je.*	Thank you. *Hvala.*
Good morning. *Dobro jutro.*	Excuse me. *Oprostite.*
Good day. *Dobar dan.*	I don't understand. *Je ne razumijem.*
Good night. *Laku noć.*	How much is it? *Koliko kosjta?*
Yes. *Da.*	Where's the toilet? *Gdje je zahod?*
No. *Ne.*	Goodbye. *Zbogom.*

1. **One result of the Industrial Revolution was:**
   a. A shift from urban and industrial to rural and agricultural
   b. A shift from rural and agricultural to urban and industrial
   c. A shift from rural and industrial to urban and agricultural
   d. A shift from industrial and rural to industrial and agricultural

2. **One reason Great Britain became the first industrialized nation was due to their:**
   a. Use of steam
   b. Large amount of spinning jennies
   c. Large amount of cotton gins
   d. Large coal and iron ore deposits

3. **If the narrator says "I" in the story and is talking about his or her own experience, this is an example of:**
   a. First person
   b. Third person
   c. Omniscient narrator
   d. Limited omniscient narrator

4. **What is a red herring?**
   a. When you only know the perspective of one or two characters
   b. Where the story takes place
   c. A hint given to the reader with the intention of misleading the reader
   d. The character in opposition of the protagonist

5. **What is the perimeter of a square with sides that measure 6 inches?**
   a. 12 inches
   b. 24 inches
   c. 36 inches
   d. 18 inches

6. **What is the area of a rectangle with sides that measure 7 inches and 9 inches?**
   a. 63
   b. 32
   c. 58
   d. 16

7. **What is the atomic number?**
   a. The number of neutrons found in the atom's nucleus
   b. The number of atoms
   c. The number of protons found in the atom's nucleus
   d. The number of electrons found in the atom's nucleus

8. **A set of adjacent groups is called:**
   a. A period
   b. A block
   c. A chalcogen
   d. A and C

9. **What was the Illyrian movement?**
   a. Turning the alphabet into only thirty letters
   b. An effort by the Holy Roman Emperor to make Latin the official language
   c. Uniting of the two dynasties
   d. An attempt to create a common South Slavic literary language

10. **How do you say "Hello" in Croatian?**
    a. Hvala
    b. Zbogom
    c. Molim
    d. Zdravo

HISTORY: The French Revolution

The Tennis Court Oath, Storming of the Bastille, Women's March on Versailles, Overthrow of the Monarchy, The September Massacres, A New Republic

MATH: Basic Algebra

What Is Algebra?, Addition and Subtraction with Algebraic Expressions, Multiplication with Algebraic Expressions, Division with Algebraic Expressions, Solving for x, Rearranging Formulas

LANGUAGE ARTS: Developing a Paragraph

What Is a Paragraph?, The Topic Sentence, Supporting Sentences, The Concluding Sentence, Making Sure Your Paragraph Is Well Developed, When to Start a New Paragraph

SCIENCE: Chemical Formulas

What Is a Chemical Formula?, Polymers, Ions, Isotopes, The Empirical Formula, The Hill System

Lesson 17

FOREIGN LANGUAGE: Belarusian

The Origins, Grammar Reforms, The Impact of World War II, Dialects, Alphabets, Useful Belarusian Phrases

THE FRENCH REVOLUTION

The Tennis Court Oath   Pre-Revolutionary France practiced a class system. The higher classes were given special privileges, such as not paying taxes. At a time of great debt, King Louis XVI refused to change the system. The Third Estate, which represented the underprivileged class, formed a National Assembly. On June 20, 1789, when the Third Estate was locked out of their meeting hall, they moved to a nearby tennis court. There, they took an oath to never separate until there was a constitution in France.

DEVELOPING A PARAGRAPH

What Is a Paragraph?   A paragraph is a group of sentences that are related in the subject they are discussing. Good paragraphs are crucial to being a good writer or just having your writing make sense to the reader. Paragraphs organize sentences so that the main idea can get across in an easy and coherent way. A good rule of thumb to follow is to always keep one idea for every paragraph.

BASIC ALGEBRA

What Is Algebra?   In algebra, equations are given with unknown numbers. These unknown numbers are represented with letters. Based on the equation laid out, one has to figure out the missing value. The letters can be variables, where the value of the letter can change, or they can be constants, which have a fixed value (such as π).

CHEMICAL FORMULAS

What Is a Chemical Formula?   A chemical formula is a method of expressing how a chemical appears in a simple and easy-to-understand way based on the atoms that make up chemical compounds. When writing out the elements involved in a chemical, if there is more than one atom present in a particular element, then it is indicated by a subscript number after the symbol, showing how many atoms there are. For example, water is H_2O. This means there are two hydrogen atoms and one oxygen atom present in water.

BELARUSIAN

The Origins   Belarusian is an East Slavic language, and is a predecessor of Old Belarusian. Old Belarusian was spoken from the fourteenth to seventeenth centuries. The modern form of Belarusian was based on the vernacular of Old Belarusian. The development of the modern language was a result of increased political conflict in the surrounding area of Belarus, and the language, once considered a peasant's language, started appearing in state offices in the nineteenth century.

THE FRENCH REVOLUTION

Storming of the Bastille   The Bastille was a royal prison that became a symbol of oppression. It was also where the arms and gunpowder were held. On July 14, 1789, hundreds of angry citizens demanded the weapons. When they were refused, they stormed the prison. After gunfire from the prison guards left 100 men dead, some prison guards defected, shooting open the prison doors. The governor of the Bastille surrendered and was beheaded. His head was put on a stake.

DEVELOPING A PARAGRAPH

The Topic Sentence   The topic sentence tells the reader what the rest of the paragraph will be about. Though the topic sentence does not need to be the very first sentence in the paragraph, it certainly is a good approach to take. The idea is that one would be able to summarize from the topic sentence what that paragraph is about. The sentence doesn't have to blatantly state the topic at the beginning, as long as the paragraph is understandable.

BASIC ALGEBRA

Addition and Subtraction with Algebraic Expressions   An example of a single algebraic expression is $6x$, where 6 represents the coefficient and x represents the variable, and these numbers are being multiplied together. You can only add and subtract like terms. For example, in $7x + 9z$ x and z are unlike terms and the problem thus cannot be simplified further; however, with $7x + 9x$, since the variables are both x, we can work the problem out and get $16x$.

CHEMICAL FORMULAS

Polymers   Polymers are macromolecules made up of structural units that repeat. When writing the formula of a polymer, you do not have to write out every one of the repeating units. Instead, parentheses are used followed by a subscript to show how many times it repeats. For example, in a hydrocarbon molecule $CH_3(CH_2)_{50}CH_3$ the CH_2 repeats 50 times.

BELARUSIAN

Grammar Reforms   The language has undergone two official grammar reforms, once in 1933, and again in 1959. The 1933 reform simplified grammar, got rid of any Polish influences that were believed to be corrupting the language, maintained artificial barriers between Russian and Belarusian, and removed vulgarisms and neologisms. In 1959 further changes were made to the grammar, resulting in the Belarusian grammar that exists today with a few changes made throughout the years.

THE FRENCH REVOLUTION

Women's March on Versailles   The women's march on Versailles is one of the most significant events of the French Revolution. On October 5 and 6, 1789, some 7,000 women of the marketplace marched to the king's palace demanding the price of bread and food be brought down. The crowd forced the king and the French Assembly to return to Paris. The authority of the king had effectively been ended and the balance of power began to shift toward the common folk.

DEVELOPING A PARAGRAPH

Supporting Sentences   Supporting sentences do just that; they support. If the topic sentence is the main idea of the paragraph, then the supporting sentences should provide the necessary information (images, data, analysis) to back up that statement. A good rule of thumb when writing paragraphs is they should be five to seven sentences long. That should provide enough support for the main idea you are trying to get across.

BASIC ALGEBRA

Multiplication with Algebraic Expressions   With multiplication it is a matter of following the laws regarding exponents.

For example:

$$x^4(x^3 + 6a) = x^7 + 6ax^4$$

This is the simplest answer we can get from a problem like this. With problems with two sets of equations in parentheses, break the first set up as such:

$$(x + 7)(a - 2)$$
$$x(a - 2) + 7(a - 2)$$

You add or subtract the problems based on whether the second part of the problem is positive or negative. So that gives us:

$$xa - 2x + 7a - 14$$

We cannot break that down any further, so that is our answer.

CHEMICAL FORMULAS

Ions   Ions are atoms that have a positive or negative charge. This is due to the fact that the number of electrons in the atom is not the same as the number of protons. Ions can be represented with a superscript on the right hand side showing whether it is positive or negative. For example, Na^+. In more complex ions, brackets are used (and parentheses can be used inside of the brackets).

BELARUSIAN

The Impact of World War II   Following World War II, Russian became the official national language of Belarus under the Soviets, and it was the principal language for communication. The teaching and use of the Belarusian language was limited to rural areas, and Russian would stay the official language until the 1980s. When Perestroika began, political control was more relaxed, and support for the Belarusian language grew.

THE FRENCH REVOLUTION

Overthrow of the Monarchy   On August 10, 1792, French citizens numbering as many as 30,000 marched to the Tuileries Palace in an effort to capture King Louis XVI. The king had heard of the oncoming mob and moved himself and his family to the Legislative Assembly building. The Swiss Guard protecting the castle was never made aware of these plans, and when the mob approached, they attempted to defend the palace, but ultimately surrendered. As the mob stormed the castle, they killed anyone inside. Leaving the castle, they advanced toward the Legislative Assembly building where King Louis XVI was found and arrested. This was the end of the monarchy.

DEVELOPING A PARAGRAPH

The Concluding Sentence   The concluding sentence is kind of like the reverse of the topic sentence. Instead of beginning a topic for discussion, this is meant to conclude the main idea of the paragraph. One type of concluding sentence would be to summarize all that was said in the topic sentence and supporting sentence. Not every paragraph needs a concluding sentence, but if the paragraph is long or has lots of information, a concluding sentence can be very useful.

BASIC ALGEBRA

Division with Algebraic Expressions   When dividing algebraic expressions, you should first write the problem out as a fraction. The next step is to then simplify the coefficient, and then cancel out like variables in both the numerator and the denominator.

For example:

$$8ab^4 \div 2ab = \frac{8 \times a \times b \times b \times b \times b}{2 \times a \times b} = 4b^3$$

CHEMICAL FORMULAS

Isotopes   Isotopes are different versions of the same element having different numbers of neutrons. Isotopes are indicated with a superscript number on the left-hand side of the formula. For example, the isotope Uranium 235 is expressed as ^{235}U. The 235 refers to the number of neutrons and protons combined, or the mass number.

BELARUSIAN

Dialects   Though some consider Belarusian to be a dialect of Russian, many consider it to be a different language altogether. In Belarus, there are two main types of dialects: South-Western and North-Eastern. These dialects are separated by Ashmyany–Minsk–Babruysk–Homyel, a hypothetical line. The South-Western dialect is characterized by a harder "r" sound, and the North-Eastern has a softer sounding "r."

🏛 THE FRENCH REVOLUTION

The September Massacres Starting on September 2, 1792, a mass killing of prisoners took place. Following the overthrow of King Louis XVI, there was an imminent threat of invasion by Austrian and Prussian forces to restore the monarchy. The French feared the political prisoners were going to join together and create a counter-revolution. The killings lasted for five days, and 1,200 prisoners were killed.

DEVELOPING A PARAGRAPH

Making Sure Your Paragraph Is Well Developed It can be hard to know when a paragraph has enough information or perhaps too little information. To make sure your paragraph is well developed, here are some helpful tips. Make sure you describe the topic you're going to talk about, analyzing it and citing any information that helps get your idea across. Cite facts and details, talk about causes and effects, use stories or anecdotes, define terms, and compare and contrast when you can.

➗ BASIC ALGEBRA

Solving for x When solving for x, you want to get x all by itself. For example:

$$2x = 10$$

To get x by itself, you have to divide $2x$ by 2, and whatever you do on one side, you must do on the other side. So you end up with $x = 5$. No matter how complex the problem might get, as long as you remember to get x by itself, you will be able to solve the problem.

⚛ CHEMICAL FORMULAS

The Empirical Formula The empirical formula is the simplest way of expressing the ratio of the elements present in a compound. For example, the molecular formula for glucose is $C_6H_{12}O_6$. However, the empirical formula breaks that down further into its simplest form. So glucose expressed in the empirical formula is CH_2O.

👤 BELARUSIAN

Alphabets Due to such a complex history full of conflict, the Belarusian alphabet is actually a combination of two influences, Cyrillic and the Latin alphabet. Old Belarusian was originally written in Cyrillic, and during the sixteenth century, with the Reformation and the Counter-Reformation, Belarusian began appearing in the Latin alphabet. By the nineteenth century, Belarusian was written in both alphabets, and spelling became an issue of controversy, as some wanted words spelled like Russian and others wanted words spelled like Polish. When the Soviets came to power, Cyrillic became the official alphabet; however, when Belarus gained independence in 1991, efforts were made to return to the Latin alphabet.

🏛 THE FRENCH REVOLUTION

A New Republic   On September 22, 1792, the French First Republic was founded by the National Convention. The National Convention abolished the monarchy, created a new constitution, and a day later, declared France to be a Republic. The Republic would only last fourteen years, however, before Napoleon Bonaparte rose to power and established the First French Empire.

📖 DEVELOPING A PARAGRAPH

When to Start a New Paragraph   There are a couple of ways you know you need to start a new paragraph. The most obvious is when you begin discussing a new topic or a new idea. Similarly, if the material contrasts to the material before it, that should be a new paragraph. Even if the idea of your content is continuing, however, if the paragraph goes on for too long, it can make it hard to read. Use another paragraph to give the reader's eyes a break. Lastly, you want a new paragraph when beginning your introduction and your conclusion.

BASIC ALGEBRA

Rearranging Formulas   Rearranging formulas is essentially taking all that you have learned, and working backward. It is very similar to the last lesson where you solved for x, only you are not limited to just one number. You can solve any part of the problem. For example, if you have a formula that states $2b = c$, and then you are asked to solve for b, you can just divide both sides by 2. So, $b = c/2$.

❋ CHEMICAL FORMULAS

The Hill System   Another system of writing chemical formulas is called the Hill system. With the Hill system, you first indicate the number of carbon atoms, then hydrogen, and then you go down the list of elements alphabetically. For example, uranium oxide in the chemical formula is written as U_3O_8. In the Hill system, it appears as O_8U_3. This system is commonly used for databases.

🗣 BELARUSIAN

Useful Belarusian Phrases   Here are some helpful phrases to use when traveling to Belarus. Note that these are written phonetically.

Hello. *Vitayu.*
How are you? *Jak spravy?*
Pleased to meet you. *Pryiemna paznajomicca.*
Good morning. *Dobray ranitsy.*
Good evening. *Dobry vechar.*
Good night. *Dabranach.*
Cheers! *Za zdarou'e!*
I don't understand. *Ne razumeyu.*
Where's the toilet? *Dze tualet?*
Goodbye. *Da pabachen'nya.*

LESSON 17 QUIZ

1. **Which major event of the French Revolution signified that the authority of the king had effectively been ended and a balance of power toward the common folk was beginning?**
   a. The National Convention
   b. The September massacres
   c. The storming of the Tuileries Palace
   d. The Women's march on Versailles

2. **In French society, the Third Estate represented:**
   a. The king
   b. Nobles
   c. The upper class
   d. The common people

3. **When is it appropriate to start a new paragraph?**
   a. When starting a new idea
   b. When the paragraph is too long and the reader needs a break
   c. When beginning your introduction and conclusion
   d. All of the above

4. **Which of the following is an example of a supporting sentence?**
   a. A sentence that analyzes and cites information regarding the topic
   b. A sentence that introduces a new topic
   c. A sentence that introduces the conclusion
   d. A sentence that introduces the topic of the paragraph

5. **If $x + 4 = y$, then what does x equal?**
   a. $x = y + 4$
   b. $x = y - 4$
   c. $x = 4$
   d. $x = y/4$

6. **What does $x^4(x + 7)$ equal?**
   a. $2x + 7$
   b. $x^5 + 7$
   c. $x^5 + 7x^4$
   d. $5x + 7x^4$

7. **Which of the following is an example of an ion?**
   a. Na^+
   b. H_2O
   c. CO_2
   d. ^{235}U

8. **Which of the following is an example of a polymer?**
   a. ^{235}U
   b. $CH_3(CH_2)_{50}CH_3$
   c. Na^+
   d. H_2O

9. **Which of the following is true about Belarusian?**
   a. The South-Western dialect is characterized by a harder "s" sound, and the North-Eastern has a softer-sounding "s."
   b. The South-Western dialect is characterized by a harder "g" sound, and the North-Eastern has a softer-sounding "g."
   c. The South-Western dialect is characterized by a harder "r" sound and the North-Eastern has a softer-sounding "r."
   d. The South-Western dialect is characterized by a harder "p" sound, and the North-Eastern has a softer-sounding "p."

10. **How do you say "Pleased to meet you" in Belarusian?**
    a. Za zdarou'e.
    b. Da pabachen'nya.
    c. Dobry vechar.
    d. Pryiemna paznajomicca.

HISTORY: The Civil War
Secession from the Union, First Battle at Bull Run, The Battle of Shiloh, The Emancipation Proclamation, The Gettysburg Address, The Surrender of Robert E. Lee

MATH: Linear Algebra
What Is Linear Algebra?, Linear Equations, Matrices, Vector Space, Complex Numbers, Useful Theorems

LANGUAGE ARTS: Virginia Woolf
About Virginia Woolf, The Bloomsbury Group, *The Voyage Out*, *Mrs. Dalloway*, *To the Lighthouse*, Virginia Woolf's Death

SCIENCE: John Dalton
About John Dalton, Color Blindness, Atomic Weights, Atomic Theory, Dalton's Law, Impact of the Atomic Theory

Lesson 18

FOREIGN LANGUAGE: Czech
The Origins, The Fifteenth Century, The "Peasant Tongue," Czech and Slovak, Dialects, Useful Czech Phrases

THE CIVIL WAR

Secession from the Union   Before Abraham Lincoln even took office as president of the United States, the state of South Carolina perceived his election as a threat and called all state delegates to a meeting. The delegates voted to remove South Carolina from the United States in December of 1860. Mississippi, Alabama, Florida, Louisiana, Georgia, and Texas followed South Carolina's move, forming the Confederate States of America on February 4, 1861. Four more states, Virginia, Tennessee, Arkansas, and North Carolina would join the Confederate States of America.

VIRGINIA WOOLF

About Virginia Woolf   Born Adeline Virginia Stephen in 1882, Woolf was educated at home by her father, who wrote *Dictionary of English Biography*. Woolf suffered from depression and severe mental illness all of her life. Her first series of nervous breakdowns started after her mother's death when she was just thirteen. When her father died in 1904, she had to be hospitalized. Her writing is considered to be some of the best feminist and modernist work.

LINEAR ALGEBRA

What Is Linear Algebra?   Linear algebra is a field of mathematics that studies the theory of linear equations and linear transformation. A problem in linear algebra begins in geometry, dealing with lines, space, and vectors, and it is then translated into an algebraic equation so that it can be solved. Once solved, the results go back into the geometry. Linear algebra is essential to modern mathematic and scientific applications.

JOHN DALTON

About John Dalton   It is because of the work of John Dalton that chemistry is a separate science. Dalton was born September 6, 1766, to a Quaker family in Cumberland, England. Dalton grew quite interested in meteorology and began keeping a diary recording weather conditions like atmospheric pressure and temperature. He maintained the diary until his death, a total of fifty-seven years.

CZECH

The Origins   Czech is a West Slavonic language that was known as Bohemian until the nineteenth century. The earliest written documents in Czech date back to the eleventh century, and they were written in the Latin alphabet. Due to geographical location and a turbulent political history, the Czech language is greatly influenced by German and has grammatical and phonetic features of both German and Slavonic.

🏛 THE CIVIL WAR

First Battle at Bull Run   Though the events at Fort Sumter started the Civil War, the first major battle was at Bull Run on July 21, 1861. As pressure to crush the rebellion in the South grew, the Union army started to march toward Richmond, Virginia, the capital of the Confederacy. The Union army and the Confederate army met at Manassas. Though initially losing, the Confederates had reinforcements and Union soldiers began withdrawing. It was thought at the time that this would be the only battle of the war; however, as the battle came to a close, many came to the realization that this war was going to last much longer.

VIRGINIA WOOLF

The Bloomsbury Group   Following her second nervous breakdown, Virginia's sister Vanessa and brother Adrian bought a house in Bloomsbury. Woolf became friends with several intellectuals of the time such as Roger Fry and Duncan Grant, and they formed what was known as the Bloomsbury Group, an artistic and literary circle of intellectuals. The Bloomsbury Group gained notoriety from the Dreadnought Hoax of 1910, in which they tricked the Royal Navy, making them believe they were Abyssinian royals. Virginia participated, dressed as a man. The Bloomsbury Group was very liberal regarding sex, and Virginia started a relationship with a fellow female writer.

➕ LINEAR ALGEBRA

Linear Equations   A linear equation is an algebraic equation that features a constant (or product of a constant) and a single variable that is only the first power. For example, $x + 6$, $4x + 7y$, and $5x + 3$ are all linear equations. However x^2 is not because it is not the first power; $4xy + 6$ is not because there can't be two variables multiplied; and $6x/8y$ is not because you cannot divide two different variables.

JOHN DALTON

Color Blindness   Dalton was colorblind. He wrote a paper concerning the topic in which he hypothesized that the shortage of color perception was due to a discoloration of the liquid medium in the eyeball. Many had not even known of color blindness at that time, and much of his theory lost credence. However, Dalton's work had a lasting impact, and color blindness became known as Daltonism. In 1995, researchers examined Dalton's preserved eyeball and discovered that he had a less common type of color blindness in which he was only able to recognize blue, purple, and yellow colors of the spectrum.

CZECH

The Fifteenth Century   In the fifteenth century, Jan Hus, a religious reformer, standardized the spelling of the language. In his reform, he attributed one letter to every sound. By adding certain accents (in the form of dots or lines) to certain letters, Hus was able to create a standard of spelling based on the Latin alphabet. This system is still in use to this day.

THE CIVIL WAR

The Battle of Shiloh   The Battle of Shiloh is known as one the deadliest battles of the Civil War. Approximately 23,750 soldiers were killed or wounded, 13,000 being from the Union side. The Confederate army attacked General Ulysses S. Grant's soldiers by surprise at Pittsburg Landing in Shiloh, Tennessee, on April 6, 1862. Though not prepared, the Union army was able to fight until reinforcements could come. The next day, Grant led a counterattack, forcing the Confederates to retreat and securing a victory for the Union.

VIRGINIA WOOLF

The Voyage Out   *The Voyage Out* came out in 1915, and was Virginia Woolf's first published novel. The book was written at a time when Virginia was seriously struggling with her depression and she had even attempted suicide at least once during the process. Her feelings of domestic repression and the impact of the Bloomsbury Group can be found in the book. *The Voyage Out* also contains the beginnings of a focus on sexuality, female consciousness, and death, themes that would later become prevalent in her work.

LINEAR ALGEBRA

Matrices   A matrix is a rectangular assortment of numbers, expressions, or symbols. The numbers inside of the matrix are known as elements and they can be the coefficients used to solve the linear equation. Matrices that are the same size can be added and subtracted one element at a time, and matrices that are compatible in size can be multiplied. An example of a matrix is:

$$\begin{vmatrix} 3 & 5 & 8 \\ 4 & 11 & 7 \end{vmatrix}$$

JOHN DALTON

Atomic Weights   Dalton's first published table of atomic weights featured six elements: hydrogen (with a weight of one), oxygen, carbon, nitrogen, phosphorus, and sulfur. Convinced that all gases had atoms, Dalton tried to measure the diameter of the atoms. Dalton's research on the weight of the atoms led him to his greatest scientific discovery: the atomic theory.

CZECH

The "Peasant Tongue"   Up until the fourteenth century, the Czech language was suppressed. It was considered to be a language spoken by peasants, not worthy of literature or any kind of standardization. For the first time, following the work of Jan Hus, Czech appeared in literature. In the nineteenth century, a movement to standardize the dialect to an older form of Czech took place. In Moravia and Silesia, this dialect is still spoken.

THE CIVIL WAR

The Emancipation Proclamation In September of 1862, a preliminary form of the Emancipation Proclamation was ordered declaring that any slaves in the Confederate states would be freed unless the states rejoined the Union by January 1. The Confederate states did not take the offer, and on January 1, 1863, President Lincoln issued the Emancipation Proclamation, stating that slaves in all of the states would be granted freedom. The Emancipation Proclamation did not actually free all slaves however. Rather, it freed the slaves who were living in the Confederate states and allowed blacks to fight for the Union. Though ending slavery was never a major goal of the Civil War, the Emancipation Proclamation turned it into one.

 # VIRGINIA WOOLF

Mrs. Dalloway One of Virginia Woolf's most well-regarded novels is *Mrs. Dalloway*, published in 1925. The book examines a single day in the life of a woman, Clarissa Dalloway, in post–World War I England. The narrative structure jumps in and out of the character's mind and forward and back in time. The book features themes of mental illness, depression, homosexuality, feminism, and existential issues.

 # LINEAR ALGEBRA

Vector Space A structure formed by a collection of vectors is known as a vector space. When objects can be added together or multiplied, they are known as scalars, meaning they can be scaled. Axioms provide the set definition of vector space, and include formulas and rules such as $u + (v + w) = (u + v) + w$ and $v + w = w + v$, where v, u, and w represent arbitrary vectors.

JOHN DALTON

Atomic Theory Dalton's greatest achievement was his atomic theory. His theory states that atoms are tiny particles that make up elements; atoms of different elements are different and have different atomic weights; all atoms of a particular element are the same; chemical compounds are atoms from one element combined with atoms from another; and lastly, that atoms cannot be divided, created, or destroyed.

 # CZECH

Czech and Slovak The Czech language and the Slovak language are very similar. The two countries were once a single country, Czechoslovakia. However, when the Communist regime fell, they broke apart, becoming the Czech Republic and Slovakia. Though there are slight differences, speakers of Czech can understand and read Slovak, and vice versa.

THE CIVIL WAR

The Gettysburg Address   On November 19, 1863, President Lincoln issued one of the most famous speeches in American history: the Gettysburg Address. The speech was delivered in Gettysburg, Pennsylvania, four and a half months after the Battle of Gettysburg, where the Union had defeated the Confederates. The speech paid tribute to all lost soldiers, and featured no hatred or ill will but emphasized the principles of democracy.

VIRGINIA WOOLF

To the Lighthouse   *To the Lighthouse* is considered to be one of Virginia Woolf's greatest works, and a modernist masterpiece. The structure of the narrative is less plot-centric and more focused on character introspection and consciousness. There is no narrator in the story, but rather the story is told through shifting from one consciousness to another. The existence of God is discussed and questioned.

LINEAR ALGEBRA

Complex Numbers   A complex number is a number that consists of two parts: a real part and an imaginary part. Complex numbers allow problems that would not otherwise be solved with real numbers to be solved. The imaginary number is introduced by using the letter i, and is based on the formula $a + bi$. The letters a and b represent real numbers and i equals Ö-1.

JOHN DALTON

Dalton's Law   Dalton's interest in weather led to the announcement in 1803 of his law of partial pressures, otherwise known as Dalton's law. This law states that the total of the pressure from a gaseous mixture equals the sum of the partial pressures of the individual components. In other words:

$$P_{Total} = p_1 + p_2 + p_3 \ldots$$

CZECH

Dialects   Two major dialects can be found in the Czech language relating to geographic location. The most commonly used dialect is called Common Czech, which is used around Bohemia. The other dialect pertains to Moravia and Silesia, which is based on standard Czech. Moravia and Silesia have more localized dialects than Common Czech. In Silesia, for example, there exists a community that speaks a combination of Czech and Polish.

THE CIVIL WAR

The Surrender of Robert E. Lee   In the spring of 1865 Confederate General Robert E. Lee fled with his army to Appomattox County with Grant's army in pursuit. Seven days after the capture of Richmond, on April 9, 1865, Lee knew that Grant would win another battle, and decided to meet with Grant at Appomattox Courthouse. The two men showed great respect for one another, and Robert E. Lee surrendered. Though this did not end the war immediately, the loss of Robert E. Lee's army would lead to the surrender of the other Confederate armies.

VIRGINIA WOOLF

Virginia Woolf's Death   After Virginia Woolf completed another manuscript, she once again became greatly depressed. Her condition worsened as World War II quickly approached and her London home was destroyed by a bomb. On March 27, 1941, Virginia's husband took her to see a doctor. She told the doctor that everything was normal, even though she had been hearing voices. The next day, she wrote two notes to her husband and one note to her sister, placed stones in the pockets of her coat, and walked into the River Ouse, drowning herself.

LINEAR ALGEBRA

Useful Theorems   All vector spaces have a basis, meaning a set of vectors that can represent every vector in the vector space. Of the same vector, any two bases have the same cardinality, meaning the number of elements in a set. If a set is [4, 6, 8], the cardinality is three because there are three elements in the set.

JOHN DALTON

Impact of the Atomic Theory   Dalton's atomic theory paved the way in understanding chemicals and physics, and Dalton is referred to as the "Father of Chemistry." Though his theory had flaws, it opened the world to a new kind of science. Dalton's work has had a truly lasting effect, leading to the eventual discovery of subatomic particles.

CZECH

Useful Czech Phrases   Here are some helpful phrases to use when traveling to the Czech Republic:

Hello. *Dobrý den.*
Good morning. *Dobré ráno.*
Good evening. *Dobrý večer.*
What's your name? *Jak se jmenujete?*
I don't speak Czech. *Nemluvím česky.*
I don't understand. *Nerozumím.*
Thank you. *Děkuji.*
Where is the bathroom? *Kde jsou toalety?*
How much is this? *Kolik to stojí?*
Goodbye. *Na shledanou.*

1. **What was the purpose of the Emancipation Proclamation?**
   a. It was the South's announcement of secession.
   b. It was the Union declaration of war on the South.
   c. It freed the slaves who were living in the Confederate states and allowed blacks to fight for the Union.
   d. It freed the slaves who were living in the Union states and allowed blacks to fight for the Confederates.

2. **What was the deadliest battle of the Civil War?**
   a. The Battle of Shiloh
   b. The Battle of Gettysburg
   c. First Battle at Bull Run
   d. The Battle at Fort Sumter

3. **The work of Virginia Woolf focused on what theme(s)?**
   a. Sexuality
   b. Female consciousness
   c. Death
   d. All of the above

4. **Shortly before her tragic death, Virginia Woolf lied to the doctor about:**
   a. Having a stomach ache
   b. Hearing voices
   c. Having a headache
   d. Having trouble seeing

5. **When objects can be added together or multiplied, they are known as:**
   a. Scalars
   b. Axioms
   c. Complex numbers
   d. Matrices

6. **If a set is [4, 7, 9], the cardinality is:**
   a. 7
   b. 20
   c. 9
   d. 3

7. **Daltonism is another word for:**
   a. Dalton's Law
   b. Dalton's theory of atomic weight
   c. Color blindness
   d. Dalton's atomic theory

8. **$P_{Total} = p_1 + p_2 + p_3 \ldots$ is an example of:**
   a. Dalton's atomic theory
   b. Dalton's law
   c. Daltonism
   d. Dalton's theory of atomic weight

9. **What is Jan Hus responsible for?**
   a. Breaking Czechoslovakia apart
   b. Standardizing the spelling of the Czech language
   c. Creating a combination of Czech and Polish
   d. Making German the official language of Czechoslovakia

10. **Which of the following is true?**
    a. The official language of the Czech Republic is Slovak.
    b. Czech was the official language of Germany during the fourteenth century.
    c. Czech was considered a rich man's language, worthy of the king and nobility.
    d. Until the fourteenth century, Czech was considered to be a language spoken by peasants, not worthy of literature or any kind of standardization.

ANSWER KEY: c, a, d, b, a, d, c, b, b, d

HISTORY: The Spanish-American War

Cuba's Struggle for Independence, Yellow Journalism, Sinking of the USS *Maine*, Declaration of War, The Philippines, The Treaty of Paris

MATH: Modern Algebra

What Is Modern Algebra?, History of Modern Algebra, Groups, Rings, Fields, Universal Algebra

LANGUAGE ARTS: Jane Austen

About Jane Austen's Life, The Sentimental Novel, *Sense and Sensibility*, *Pride and Prejudice*, *Emma*, Reactions Then and Now

SCIENCE: Weather

The Water Cycle, Clouds, Thunder, Lightning, Wind, Weather Forecasting

Lesson 19

FOREIGN LANGUAGE: Hungarian

The Origins, Turkic Influences, The Four-Tiered Level of Politeness, Writing System, Dialects, Useful Hungarian Phrases

THE SPANISH-AMERICAN WAR

Cuba's Struggle for Independence   Cuba had always been a colony of Spain since 1492. By the mid-nineteenth century, Cuba grew dissatisfied with Spain's corruption and sought independence. The Spanish denied the Cubans any freedom, and Cuban nationalists fought the Spaniards in the Ten Years War from 1868 to 1878. In 1896, the Spanish sent over General Weyler, aka "The Butcher," who established concentration camps where thousands of Cubans died. As news spread to the United States, President Cleveland vowed that even should Congress declare war he would not send the military to Cuba.

JANE AUSTEN

About Jane Austen's Life   The biography of Jane Austen is not fully known. Jane Austen was born on December 16, 1775, in Hampshire, England, and by 1787, Jane began writing plays, poetry, and stories. By the time she was twenty-three, she had already completed the original versions of *Pride and Prejudice*, *Sense and Sensibility*, and *Northanger Abbey*. Her sense of humor was evident from the beginning, and she keenly watched the interactions of the social classes. Jane Austen's work was known for its realism, humor, and social commentary.

MODERN ALGEBRA

What Is Modern Algebra?   Modern algebra, also known as abstract algebra, is a branch of mathematics that involves abstract algebraic structures (complex numbers, real numbers, matrices, vector spaces) instead of number systems. In modern algebra, the most important features are rings, groups, and fields. Linear algebra is considered to be one of the branches of modern algebra.

WEATHER

The Water Cycle   There is a limited amount of water on Earth, which is recycled again and again. This is known as the water cycle. The first step in the process is evaporation, where the sun heats up the water until it turns into steam or water vapor, which then rises into the air. As the water vapor in the air gets cold, it turns back into water, forming clouds. This process is known as condensation. When there is so much water that the air can no longer hold it, precipitation occurs in the form of rain or snow.

HUNGARIAN

The Origins   The Hungarian language, called Magyar, is a Uralic language. Uralic languages are not related to Indo-European languages and emerged in the Urals of Russia. The history of the language can be broken down into five periods: Proto-Hungarian, when the Hungarian language first came to be; Old Hungarian (during the Middle Ages); Middle Hungarian (the language turned into a form similar to today's); New Hungarian (when the language underwent some reforms); and Modern Hungarian (the language as it is spoken today).

THE SPANISH-AMERICAN WAR

Yellow Journalism   *Yellow journalism* was the name given to sensational news stories being reported in the United States about the Spanish treatment of Cubans. Though based on truth, the articles were written to elicit strong responses. The two men most responsible for yellow journalism were William Randolph Hearst of the *New York Journal* and Joseph Pulitzer of the *New York World*. Yellow journalism would galvanize public opinion about wanting to go to war.

JANE AUSTEN

The Sentimental Novel   The sentimental novel was a popular literary genre of the eighteenth century that celebrated emotions and sensibility. These novels focused on the emotional response, both in terms of the reader and the characters. Plots were created to further the emotions of the story rather than the events. Jane Austen's *Sense and Sensibility* was a satire of this type of literature of the time.

MODERN ALGEBRA

History of Modern Algebra   Toward the end of the nineteenth century and the beginning of the twentieth century, there was a great shift in mathematical methodology, and mathematicians moved toward general theory and away from concrete objects. Among others, the work of Ernst Steinitz, David Hilbert, Emmy Noether, and Emil Artin came to define abstract, or modern, algebra.

WEATHER

Clouds   Clouds are large collections of droplets of ice crystals or water so small that they can float in the air. As warm air rises, it cools down and expands. The moisture begins to condense and forms water droplets. As billions of the droplets come together, they begin to form a cloud. Clouds can be classified into three groups: cirrus (clouds above 18,000 feet), alto (clouds that are 6,500 feet to 18,000 feet in the air), and stratus (clouds that go up to 6,500 feet).

HUNGARIAN

Turkic Influences   From 400 to 896, the Hungarians lived as nomads. When they settled on the coast of the Black Sea, they came into contact with the Turkic people. The Huns had come to the area after the fall of Attila and settled there, ruling over the Hungarians. Between the sixth and the eighth centuries, the Huns fell into decline and were replaced by the Turks. Hungarians were introduced to the Turkic writing system, which the Old Hungarian writing system was based on. The word *Magyar* comes from the Turkic *onugor*, and the phonetic language was extremely influenced by the Turkic language.

THE SPANISH-AMERICAN WAR

Sinking of the USS *Maine* In 1897, the United States sent a warship, the USS *Maine*, to Cuba to investigate what was going on and to provide rescue to any Americans. On February 15, 1898, an explosion on the USS *Maine* left 266 Americans dead. Though the explosion was an internal problem with the ship and not an attack by Spain, the newspapers quickly placed blame on the Spanish, creating great anti-Spanish fervor among Americans.

JANE AUSTEN

Sense and Sensibility *Sense and Sensibility* was Jane Austen's first published novel. The book came out in 1811, and Austen credited herself with the pseudonym, "A Lady." Jane Austen would continue to publish anonymously until the day she died, with only her family knowing it was she who was writing the books. The book follows two sisters who relocate to a new home after their father's death, and experience romance and heartbreak. The book sold out all 750 copies in its first edition.

MODERN ALGEBRA

Groups Groups are sets of elements, both finite and infinite, that together with a binary operation (an operation that applies to two expressions) satisfy the properties of closure, the inverse property, the identity property, and associativity. In closure, if a and b are elements in G, then ab, the product, is also in G. The inverse property states that for each element, there must be an inverse, or $(a \times b) = (b \times a) = 1_G$. The identity property states e, an element, exists in G. For every a in G, the equation is $e \times a = a \times e = a$. Lastly, associativity states that $(a \times b) \times c = a \times (b \times c)$.

WEATHER

Thunder The sound of thunder is actually caused by lightning. As a bolt of lightning passes through the cloud, it creates a channel, or a small hole in the air. When the lightning is gone, the air collapses back in again, which creates a sound wave. Because light travels faster than sound, we see the lightning before we hear the thunder.

HUNGARIAN

The Four-Tiered Level of Politeness In Hungarian, there are four different ways to express levels of politeness. Uses of the different levels include when showing respect to the person being addressed; when distancing oneself from the person being addressed; a system similar to the previous two but with additional words (this would be used when talking to the family friends of parents, for example); and a form of being polite that doesn't fit into the other three categories.

THE SPANISH-AMERICAN WAR

Declaration of War   Though President McKinley did not want war, the pressure from the public, including the assistant secretary of the navy, Theodore Roosevelt, grew. On April 11, 1898, McKinley told Congress he supported going to war with Spain. On April 24, Spain declared war on the United States, and the next day, the United States declared war on Spain. To justify going to war, Congress passed the Teller Amendment, in which the United States promised to liberate Cuba.

JANE AUSTEN

Pride and Prejudice   *Pride and Prejudice* was published in 1813. The book, like much of Austen's work, uses free indirect speech (meaning in the third person with the essence of first person) to tell the story. The book focuses on the importance of one's environment and how it affects upbringing and the fact that wealth and a high social status do not necessarily mean one has an advantage.

MODERN ALGEBRA

Rings   A ring is a set, represented by S, that is with two binary operations (commonly addition and multiplication). An example of a ring is $R = (S, 01, 02, I)$. In this problem, S is a set of real numbers, 01 is addition, with its inverse being subtraction, 02 is multiplication, and I is identity element zero.

WEATHER

Lightning   In a thundercloud, frozen raindrops hit each other while moving around in the air. These collisions begin to form an electric charge, and soon the entire cloud is full of electrical charges. The protons form at the top while the electrons form at the bottom. A positive charge builds up below the cloud on the ground, and eventually the charges connect, creating a bolt of lightning.

HUNGARIAN

Writing System   When Stephen I of Hungary came to power in the year 1000, the Old Hungarian system of writing was gradually replaced by the Latin alphabet. The Hungarian system of today still uses the Latin alphabet, although it has expanded, modifying characters with accents (such as *á, é, í, ú, ö,* and *ü*) to represent sounds not present.

THE SPANISH-AMERICAN WAR

The Philippines   Without permission, Theodore Roosevelt, the assistant secretary of the navy, ordered the officer in control of the U.S. Asiatic Squadron to attack the Spanish fleet in the capital of the Philippines should the United States declare war. The fleet was quickly defeated. At the same time, Filipino rebel forces continued fighting the Spanish.

JANE AUSTEN

Emma   *Emma* was published in December of 1815. Once again, the book focuses on misconstrued romance among genteel women. When starting the novel, Austen said, "I am going to take a heroine whom no one but myself will much like." Emma is a spoiled woman who overestimates her matchmaking abilities. Emma is the first heroine of any of Austen's books that does not have financial problems, and Emma is a major shift away from themes common in Austen's work (such as finding a husband and financial security).

MODERN ALGEBRA

Fields   A field is a commutative ring (meaning it has an operation of multiplication) that has nonzero elements that form a group under multiplication. It is an algebraic structure that touches on addition, subtraction, multiplication, and division. Every field must have two or more elements.

WEATHER

Wind   Wind is simply the air put in motion. Because the surface of the Earth is very dynamic and is not even, the Sun's radiation is absorbed unevenly. This uneven spread of the Sun's rays makes some areas hotter than others. Warm air weighs less than cold air, and it begins to rise. Cold air then replaces the warm air as it rises. This creates wind.

HUNGARIAN

Dialects   There are eight major dialects in Hungarian: Alföld, Danube-Tisza, West Danube, King's Pass Hungarian, Northwest Hungarian, Northeast Hungarian, Székely, and West Hungarian. These are all mutually intelligible. The most significant dialect is Csángó. Due to its isolation (it is located in the Romanian area of Bacău), it has the most differences of any of the dialects.

THE SPANISH-AMERICAN WAR

The Treaty of Paris   In 1898, the war officially ended with the Treaty of Paris. The Spanish-American War lasted a total of six months. Under the treaty, Guam and Puerto Rico fell under American control, Cuba was granted its independence, and for $20 million, America got control of the Philippines. Due to the Platt Amendment, the United States was granted a military base at Cuba's Guantanamo Bay.

JANE AUSTEN

Reactions Then and Now   When Austen's books first came out, they were well received. Her work received published reviews praising her realism and narrative qualities. In the nineteenth century, as Victorian and Romantic literature appeared, Austen's work became less popular, and those that still liked her considered themselves the elite. When James Edward Austen-Leigh's *A Memoir of Jane Austen* came out, the work of Jane Austen was reintroduced and once again grew in popularity. By the twentieth century, Austen's work became a major focus of academic studies, as well as a source for media adaptations (the movie *Clueless* is a modernization of *Emma*).

MODERN ALGEBRA

Universal Algebra   Universal algebra studies the actual algebraic structures, and not the models of algebraic structures. In universal algebra, an algebraic structure is a set, known as A, and there are a collection of operations performed on A. An n-ary operation takes n elements of the structure, or A, and returns a single element of the structure. Once operations have been specified, the structure can be limited even further into axioms.

WEATHER

Weather Forecasting   By understanding how air masses react, one is able to predict how the weather will turn out. One way of doing this is by looking at fronts. Two basic types of front are cold fronts and warm fronts. A cold front is a mass of cold air moving into a mass of warm air. As the cold air contracts, it becomes heavier and pushes below the warm air. When warm air moves into a mass of cold air, the warm air replaces the cold air.

HUNGARIAN

Useful Hungarian Phrases   Here are some helpful phrases to use when traveling to Hungary:

Good morning. *Jó reggelt kívánok.*
Good afternoon. *Jó napot kívánok.* (also used as "hello")
Good evening. *Jó estét kívánok.*
Good night. *Jó éjszakát.*
Thank you. *Köszönöm.*
I don't understand. *Nem értem.*
I can't speak Hungarian. *Nem beszélek magyarul.*
Excuse me. *Elnézést.*
Where's the toilet? *Hol van a mosdó?*
Goodbye. *Szia.*

1. **How did yellow journalism portray the explosion of the USS *Maine*?**
   a. The Yellow Newspaper was the first to publish a story on it.
   b. The story was sensationalized and blame was placed on the Spanish.
   c. Newspapers said the explosion was caused by an accident on the ship.
   d. None of the above.

2. **As a result of the Treaty of Paris, America gained control of:**
   a. Guam
   b. Puerto Rico
   c. Spain
   d. A and B

3. **Jane Austen maintained anonymity throughout her writing career. In her first book, *Sense and Sensibility*, she used the pseudonym:**
   a. J. A.
   b. A Woman
   c. A Lady
   d. Anonymous

4. **Which of the following was NOT a theme found in Jane Austen's work?**
   a. Realism
   b. Great displays of emotions
   c. Humor
   d. Social commentary

5. **Another name for modern algebra is:**
   a. Linear algebra
   b. Abstract algebra
   c. Elementary algebra
   d. Algebra II

6. **What rule states if a and b are elements in G, then ab, the product, is also in G?**
   a. The property of closure
   b. The inverse property
   c. The identity property
   d. Associativity

7. **Which of the following accurately describes the steps in the water cycle?**
   a. Evaporation, condensation, precipitation
   b. Condensation, evaporation, precipitation
   c. Evaporation, precipitation, condensation
   d. Precipitation, condensation, evaporation

8. **Which of the following is NOT a group clouds are classified into?**
   a. Cirrus
   b. Stratus
   c. Cumulonimbus
   d. Alto

9. **Which Hungarian dialect is most significantly different?**
   a. Northeast Hungarian
   b. Székely
   c. West Hungarian
   d. Csángó

10. **In Hungarian, how many different ways are there to express levels of politeness?**
    a. 2
    b. 3
    c. 4
    d. 9

HISTORY: The War of 1812

What Was the War of 1812?, Invasion of Canada, Surrender of Detroit, Hartford Convention, Treaty of Ghent, The Battle of New Orleans

MATH: Curves

What Is a Curve?, Conics, Circles, Ellipses, Parabolas, Hyperbolas

LANGUAGE ARTS: Debating

Know Your Facts, Causality, Regression to the Mean, Innuendo, Clarity, Emotionalism

SCIENCE: Global Warming

Greenhouse Gases, The Greenhouse Effect, The Role of the Industrial Revolution, Impact of Global Warming, The Clean Air Act, Fact or Fiction?

Lesson 20

FOREIGN LANGUAGE: Korean

The Origins, The Korean Writing System, Vocabulary, Dialects, Differences Between North Korean and South Korean, Useful Korean Phrases

THE WAR OF 1812

What Was the War of 1812?   The War of 1812 began in 1812 and lasted until 1815. The British, who were in a war with France, wanted to restrict trade between the newly formed United States of America and France. This was considered illegal by the Americans. Following years of Britain's restrictions and attacks on American ships, as well as their funding Native Americans' attacks on American settlements, war was declared on Britain and their Canadian colonies. This new war with Britain reaffirmed the stance that the United States had to be independent from Britain.

 DEBATING

Know Your Facts   One of the very first steps in becoming a great debater is understanding your facts. The source of the material can help or hurt your argument. If a source is taken from a newspaper or magazine, make sure the information is not formed on some sort of bias. It is always a good idea to check your information with multiple sources that have different backgrounds (for example, international newspapers present a very different perspective from local newspapers).

CURVES

What Is a Curve?   A curve is similar to a line in that it is a continuously moving point, but it does not have to be straight. A curve starts out like a straight line then begins to deform in a smooth and continuous formation. The shape the curve takes on is the result of a particular equation. Closed curves repeat and open curves have infinite length.

GLOBAL WARMING

Greenhouse Gases   The Earth's atmosphere is made up of many different gases. Greenhouse gases are particularly important because they let visible light through while not letting heat through. These gases absorb the extreme energy and heat coming from infrared light. The major greenhouse gases in the atmosphere are carbon dioxide, water vapor, nitrous oxide, methane, and ozone. Without the greenhouse gases, life would not be able to survive on Earth.

KOREAN

The Origins   The Korean language is a Ural-Altaic language. Ural-Altaic languages originated in northern Asia and include the Turkic, Mongol, Finnish, Hungarian, and Manchu languages. Despite grammatical similarities, a relationship between Korean and Japanese has not been discovered yet. From 108 B.C. to A.D. 313, the Chinese occupied northern Korea, and by the fifth century, Classical Chinese was the written language and much of the Chinese language was borrowed.

⏛ THE WAR OF 1812

Invasion of Canada   When war was declared against the British, the War Hawks (members of Congress who wanted to go to war with Britain and the Native Americans) set their sights on an attack of the British in Canada. The American forces divided into segments at Niagara, Lake Champlain, and Detroit. On July 12, 1812, the Americans invaded. The divided American troops were no match for the British, and fighting was pushed into American territory.

DEBATING

Causality   Avoid causal relationships that are "post hoc ergo propter hoc." In other words, relationships that state because A happened, and right after, B happened, that must mean A was the cause of B. If you sneezed and then the light went on, it would not be smart to assume that because you sneezed the light went on. You should also avoid the idea that correlation proves causality. For example, if you say people who own dogs are not allergic to dogs, this doesn't mean that if we give dogs to people they will not be allergic.

⊞ CURVES

Conics   Conics are algebraic forms that are curved. They are the result of a cone being sliced by a plane. Four common conics are the circle, the ellipse, the parabola, and the hyperbola. All conics can be written by using the formula:

$$Ax^2 + Bxy + Cy^2 + Dx + Ey + F = 0$$

GLOBAL WARMING

The Greenhouse Effect   The greenhouse effect is a natural process that heats the Earth's surface and atmosphere. As the energy passes through the atmosphere, 26 percent of it is reflected and scattered back into space from the clouds. The clouds absorb 19 percent of the energy and another 4 percent is reflected from the Earth's surface and sent back to space. Fifty-one percent of the Sun's energy that reaches the Earth's surface is used in a number of processes such as heating the surface. The majority of this energy is absorbed by the greenhouse gases and then sent back in a continuous cycle, further heating the planet until it is no longer available for absorption.

◑ KOREAN

The Korean Writing System   The Korean alphabet, Hangul, was created in 1444. The consonants got their shape based on the shape the mouth made when the sound was pronounced. The writing direction (vertically and right to left) and method of writing the symbols in blocks was taken from the Chinese. After Hangul was created, most Koreans could write in both Hangul and Classical Chinese, and during the nineteenth and twentieth centuries, a mix of the two systems (Hanja) became popular until 1945 when use of Chinese characters diminished.

THE WAR OF 1812

Surrender of Detroit   On August 15, 1812, the British forces captured Detroit. In fact, no actual fighting took place. The British general Isaac Brock, along with the Native American British allies, tricked the American general William Hull. Though his men outnumbered the British and Native Americans, Hull thought otherwise and surrendered the fort and town of Detroit.

DEBATING

Regression to the Mean   When debating, it's important to take into account the regression to the mean, sometimes known as chance or luck. The less reliable a measurement, the more regression to the mean there is. If you take a measurement from a large sample, and then choose the individuals with the highest and lowest scores and do the measurement again, the high-scoring individuals will get a lower average score, and the individuals who scored low will have a higher average score.

CURVES

Circles   The most common curve is the circle. The circle is made up of determinate lines. They do not extend forever, but rather have an ending point. When drawing curves on a graph with an x and y axis, a basic formula that tells you the curve will be a circle is $x^2 + y^2 = a^2$. Both values are squared, making them positive, and both have the same coefficient, making them equal distances. Another formula for making a circle is:

$$(x - h)^2 + (y - k)^2 = r^2$$

In this formula, h and k represent the x and y coordinates that are found in the center of the circle, and r is the radius. For example, if you have coordinates (8,5) with a radius of 10, your circle would be $(x - 8)^2 + (y - 5)^2 = 100$.

GLOBAL WARMING

The Role of the Industrial Revolution   When the Industrial Revolution began, not only did it have huge impacts down on the ground, but it also had huge impacts up in the atmosphere. The burning of fossil fuels such as coal, gas, and oil pours greenhouse gases such as carbon dioxide into the atmosphere. As a result, the Earth is absorbing and holding more heat than is being radiated into space.

KOREAN

Vocabulary   The vocabulary of the Korean language is a blend of pure Korean words and Sino-Korean words, which were taken from written Chinese or Korean words in Chinese characters. This is similar to how Indo-European languages infused Greek and Latin into their languages. Today, many of the loanwords found in the language are from the English language. The vocabulary of North Korea favors the native Korean vocabulary over the Sino-Korean vocabulary.

THE WAR OF 1812

Hartford Convention   On December 14, 1814, Federalist delegates from Massachusetts, Connecticut, Vermont, New Hampshire, and Rhode Island met to discuss opposition to the war, and even the possibility of New England seceding. As a result of the Hartford Convention, constitutional amendments were proposed. These amendments stated that war and laws that restricted Congress needed a two-thirds majority in Congress, successive presidents could not be from the same state, presidents were limited to a single term, and the three-fifths clause would be eliminated.

 DEBATING

Innuendo   Innuendo is alluding to something that is not being said outright, often a rumor or popular belief. Though it is not necessarily nice, innuendo is certainly effective when debating. Innuendo is an easy way to work from prejudices without having to make overt statements that would require facts to back it up, or that might be difficult to defend.

 CURVES

Ellipses   An ellipse is another form of a closed curve. Its appearance resembles a circle, only it is squashed and is an oval. Ellipses are defined by two points, known as Focus 1 (F1) and Focus 2 (F2). At any point of the ellipse, if the distances of the focus points are added up, they are constant. The basic formula for an ellipse is:

$$\frac{(x-h)^2}{a^2}+\frac{(y-k)^2}{b^2}=1$$

GLOBAL WARMING

Impact of Global Warming   With the increase in greenhouse gases, the average temperature of the Earth begins to increase. Global warming can have serious effects on the planet. Oceans will rise, hurricanes will become more frequent as the temperature of the oceans increases, there will be an increase in droughts and heat waves, and of course maybe the most well-known result of global warming, the polar ice caps will melt, which can throw the Earth's ecosystems completely out of balance.

KOREAN

Dialects   There are many dialects found in Korean. In South Korea, the standard language is based on the dialect of Seoul. In North Korea, the standard language is based on the dialect of Pyongyang. The dialects found in both North Korea and South Korea are mutually intelligible. The dialect that is most noticeably different is that of Jeju Island, which features many archaic words that have since been lost in the Korean language of today.

🏛 THE WAR OF 1812

Treaty of Ghent   The War of 1812 ended on December 24, 1814, with the signing of the Treaty of Ghent between the United States and Britain. The treaty called for amnesty for all Native American participants, the return of prisoners of war and territory, the return of slaves, and a commitment to end the international slave trade.

✍ DEBATING

Clarity   When debating, you are arguing against someone who opposes your opinions and wants to make you look bad. That is why clarity is so essential to being a good debater. Your words can and will be interpreted by the other person, so choosing your words wisely is essential. Stay away from generalizations or ambiguous terms. Be precise and make your opinion clear so it can't be misconstrued later on.

➗ CURVES

Parabolas   A parabola is a curve that is U-shaped. It is the locus of a point that is always the same distance from the focus and a given line, called the directrix. The standard equations for making parabolas are:

$$y - k = a(x - h)^2 \quad \text{and} \quad x - h = a(y - k)^2$$

If a is greater than zero, the parabola opens upward, and if it is less than zero, it opens downward.

⚛ GLOBAL WARMING

The Clean Air Act   The Clean Air Act, first passed in 1963, is a United States federal law enacted to control air pollution. Since 1963, it has had two significant amendments, one in 1970 and the other in 1990. In 2007, the U.S. Supreme Court stated global warming emissions are air pollutants and would be subject to regulation by the EPA under the Clean Air Act if it was proven they were an endangerment to the public's health. In 2009, the EPA released their findings, claiming that global warming emissions were a danger to public health. In 2010, the Senate rejected the findings, and an effort to have it passed is still ongoing.

◐ KOREAN

Differences Between North Korean and South Korean   Though North Korea and South Korea speak the same language, the lasting separation from one another has created subtle differences in the languages. While they both use the same letters, called jamo, some of the letters have different names. Also, the North uses a different stroke in one jamo than the South, and compound vowel and tense consonant jamos are not treated separately in South Korea but are in North Korea, and some jamos have different names.

 THE WAR OF 1812

The Battle of New Orleans   Two weeks after the Treaty of Ghent, news of the treaty had not yet spread to the United States, and the United States fought in the Battle of New Orleans, its greatest military victory of the war. The British were 7,500 strong, while the Americans were only 5,000. A total of 2,036 British soldiers were killed, with only twenty-one American casualties; turning Andrew Jackson, the general of the battle, into a national hero.

DEBATING

Emotionalism   Though a debate is essentially an argument, emotion-charged words and arguments will do more harm than good. Do not stoop to heated personal attacks or labeling your opponents with broad titles (for example, socialist, baby killer). That discredits you and your argument. You need to prove the other person wrong with facts and information, not by criticizing the person's lifestyle or personality.

 CURVES

Hyperbolas   A hyperbola is kind of like two parabolas put together, making a sort of X shape. There are two types of hyperbolas: vertical and horizontal. The formula for a horizontal hyperbola is:

$$\frac{(x-h)^2}{a^2} - \frac{(y-v)^2}{b^2} = 1$$

The formula for a horizontal hyperbola is:

$$\frac{(y-v)^2}{a^2} - \frac{(x-h)^2}{b^2} = 1$$

GLOBAL WARMING

Fact or Fiction?   Even today there are those who do not believe global warming is real. They claim there is not enough evidence to prove greenhouse gases are heating the planet or will in the future, reliable sources of temperature data do not show a trend of global warming, the computer models are too crude to predict the future climates, and even that should global warming occur, it would be beneficial to society.

KOREAN

Useful Korean Phrases   Here are some helpful phrases to use when traveling to Korea. Note that these are written out phonetically.

Hello. *Annyeonghaseyo.*
How are you? *Eotteohke jinaeseyo?*
Pleased to meet you. *Mannaseo bangapseumnida.*
Good morning/afternoon/evening. *Annyeong hashimnikka.*
I don't understand. *Moreugesseumnida.*
How much is this? *Ige eolmayeyo?*
Thank you. *Kamsahamnida.*
Where's the toilet? *Hwajangsiri eodiyeyo.*
Excuse me. *Shillehagessumnida.*
Goodbye. *Annyeonghi gyeseyo.*

1. **Which of the following was NOT a constitutional amendment proposed from the Hartford Convention?**
   a. Declaration of war and laws that restricted Congress needed to be passed with a two-thirds vote in Congress.
   b. Successive presidents could not be from the same state.
   c. Presidents were limited to a single term.
   d. New England would secede.

2. **Two weeks after the signing of the Treaty of Ghent, word of the treaty had not yet come to America, and Americans and British engaged in:**
   a. The Battle of New Orleans
   b. The Battle of Detroit
   c. The Battle of Hartford
   d. The Battle of Niagara

3. **What is the following statement an example of? "If you take a measurement from a large sample, and then choose the individuals with the highest and lowest scores and do the measurement again, the high-scoring individuals will get a lower average score, and the individuals who scored low will have a higher average score."**
   a. Hyperbola
   b. Innuendo
   c. Regression to the mean
   d. Causality

4. **Heated personal attacks are an example of:**
   a. Causality
   b. Innuendo
   c. Clarity
   d. Emotionalism

5. **What is the name for a U-shaped curve?**
   a. Hyperbola
   b. Parabola
   c. Ellipse
   d. Circle

6. **The formula $x^2 + y^2 = a^2$ will produce a:**
   a. Hyperbola
   b. Parabola
   c. Ellipse
   d. Circle

7. **Which of the following is a result of global warming?**
   a. A rise of oceans
   b. An increase in droughts and heat waves
   c. Polar ice caps will melt
   d. All of the above

8. **Which of the following is true?**
   a. Greenhouse gases let visible light through while not letting the heat through.
   b. Greenhouse gases absorb the extreme energy and heat coming from infrared light.
   c. The major greenhouse gases in the atmosphere are carbon dioxide, water vapor, nitrous oxide, methane, and ozone.
   d. All of the above

9. **What is Hanja?**
   a. The dialect of Seoul
   b. The Korean alphabet
   c. A mix of the Korean alphabet and Classical Chinese writing
   d. The dialect of Pyongyang

10. **The most noticeably different dialect in Korean is:**
    a. The dialect of Jeju Island
    b. The dialect of North Korea
    c. The dialect of South Korea
    d. The dialect of Pyongyang

ANSWER KEY: d, a, c, d, b, d, d, d, c, a

HISTORY: The Salem Witch Trials

About Salem, Strange Occurrences with the Children, The Witch Hunt Begins, Bridget Bishop, The Trials, An End to the Witch Trials

MATH: Precalculus

What Is Precalculus?, Functions, Polynomials, Quadratics, Completing the Square, Permutations

LANGUAGE ARTS: Poetry

Rhythm, Metrical Patterns, Stanza, Narrative Poetry, Epic Poetry, Sonnets

SCIENCE: Isaac Newton

About Isaac Newton, Newton's Law of Universal Gravitation, Newton's First Law of Motion, Newton's Second Law of Motion, Newton's Third Law of Motion, The Spectrum of Colors

Lesson 21

FOREIGN LANGUAGE: Japanese

The Origins, The Writing System, Sounds of the Language, Politeness, Dialects, Useful Japanese Phrases

THE SALEM WITCH TRIALS

About Salem   In Salem, Massachusetts, from 1692 to 1693, a series of witchcraft trials occurred, and nineteen people were executed. In Europe, from the 1300s to the 1600s, there was a strong belief in witchcraft and that the Devil could give people the power to harm others. At the time of the Salem witch trials, these feelings had pretty much subsided in Europe. During this time, however, a war between England and France brought conflict between the countries' respective colonies and Native American allies. The fighting displaced many people to Salem, leading to tensions and strain in the town. The villagers believed this strain and tension to be from the Devil.

POETRY

Rhythm   Rhythm, also known as measure, is the equivalent of beat in music. In poetry, certain words may be held longer or pronounced with more force than other words. A rhythmic effect is produced from this pattern of emphasis. Sometimes rhythm is obvious, but rhythm can also be more muted and subtle.

PRECALCULUS

What Is Precalculus?   Precalculus was created in math education to better prepare students for calculus. It is a more advanced form of algebra that gives students the information needed for the full transition from algebra into calculus. Some of the most important notions of precalculus are functions, polynomials, quadratics, completing the square, and permutations.

ISAAC NEWTON

About Isaac Newton   Sir Isaac Newton lived from 1642 to 1727. Newton is most known today for his law of universal gravitation, his laws of motion, being the inventor of calculus, and discovering the spectrum of colors. He attended Cambridge University in 1661 but had to return home because of a plague epidemic. Six years later, he would return to Cambridge University, and in 1668, he invented the reflecting telescope. In 1687, his greatest work, *Philosophiae Naturalis Principia Mathematica* was published, in which he described the role of gravity.

JAPANESE

The Origins   Japanese is a Japonic language, and is related to Altaic and Ryukyuan languages. The Japanese language has gone through four distinct phases, known as Old Japanese (which ended around the eighth century A.D., a period that saw the beginning of significant influence from Chinese); Early Middle Japanese (from 794 to 1185); Late Middle Japanese (from 1185 to 1600, where European languages began influencing the language); and Modern Japanese (from 1600 to today).

THE SALEM WITCH TRIALS

Strange Occurrences with the Children   In January of 1692, the Puritan minister of Salem's daughter, Elizabeth Parris, and niece, Abigail Williams, began having bizarre fits in which their bodies contorted, and they screamed, threw things, and uttered strange noises. Another girl, Ann Putnam, was also having these fits. The local doctor blamed it on supernatural causes. When pressured to give names, the children accused Tituba, the Parris's slave; Sarah Good, a homeless woman; and Sarah Osborne, a poor elderly woman.

POETRY

Metrical Patterns   Meter is the recurring pattern of stressed and unstressed syllables in lines of verse. For example, if a line of poetry contains fifteen syllables, the first syllable is unstressed, the second stressed, the next unstressed, and so on. A foot is a set combination of unstressed and stressed syllables. Different meters are used for different types of poetry. Iambic poetry has unstressed and then stressed syllables, while dactylic has a stressed syllable followed by two unstressed syllables.

PRECALCULUS

Functions   Functions are essential to mathematic equations, and even though you might not know what they are called, you have already seen and worked with examples of functions. For example, $7x + 3 = y$. To find y, you need to find x. When y depends on finding x, and only one possible answer can be found, that is a function. No matter what x equals, there can only be one value for y.

ISAAC NEWTON

Newton's Law of Universal Gravitation   Newton's law of universal gravitation is perhaps best known by the story of the apple falling from the tree. From noticing the apple fall, Newton concluded that a force, or gravity, must be acting on the apple. Even when the apple tree is the tallest apple tree, this force of gravity still applies. His law of universal gravitation states that every object attracts other objects with a force pointed along the line of centers for the objects. This is in proportion to the product of the masses, and is also inversely proportional to the square of the space between them.

His formula looks like this: $F_g = G \dfrac{m_1 m_2}{r_2}$

F_g = Gravitational force
m_1 and m_2 = masses
r = distance between the masses
G = Gravitational constant

JAPANESE

The Writing System   The Japanese writing system of today is a blend of the Chinese writing system, two kana syllabaries (alphabets based on symbols developed during the ninth century to simplify writing), and Roman numerals and letters. From the third to the fifth century, Japanese used Classical Chinese as the official writing system. As the language evolved, several distinct differences separated the Japanese form of writing from the Chinese. One notable difference is that Chinese is a monosyllabic language (all words are one syllable), and Japanese is polysyllabic.

THE SALEM WITCH TRIALS

The Witch Hunt Begins   Osborne and Good declared their innocence, but Tituba confessed that the Devil had come to her and made her serve him. She described images of a black man making her sign a book and she told them there were other witches seeking to destroy the Puritans. The three women were put in jail and paranoia spread throughout Salem. Dozens of villagers were brought in for questioning. While in prison, Tituba's bail was paid by an unknown person, and Tituba disappeared, never being heard from again.

POETRY

Stanza   A stanza is two or more lines of a poem that form one of the divisions. They are usually the same length and follow the same patterns of meter and rhyme. Couplets are examples of stanzas that are only two lines and that rhyme. Tercets are made of three lines of poetry which may or may not rhyme. If they rhyme, that is known as a triplet. Quatrains have four lines and are written in any type of rhyme scheme.

PRECALCULUS

Polynomials   Polynomials are expressions that are the sum of exponents and variables. Each section of the polynomial is considered a term. To be considered a polynomial, terms must follow strict rules. There cannot be any square roots of variables, fractions, or fractional powers. There must be variables that are raised to a whole number exponent or a regular number. A polynomial looks like this:

$$7x^2 + 8x - 9$$

And do not be fooled by the $8x$. It still follows the rules of terms because that is just saying $8x^1$.

ISAAC NEWTON

Newton's First Law of Motion   Newton's first law of motion deals with inertia. It states that objects at rest stay at rest, and objects in motion stay in a straight line at a constant speed unless an unbalanced force acts on it. If the sum of all of the forces, or net force, is zero, there will be no acceleration or change in velocity. If the net force does not equal zero, there will be acceleration and a change in velocity.

JAPANESE

Sounds of the Language   The Japanese language does not have any diphthongs. Instead, it is composed of monophthongs, meaning the vowels in the language are pure. There are five vowels in Japanese — *a, i, u, o,* and *e* — and each has a long and short form. Most of the syllables in Japanese end with a vowel sound. Japanese has a pitched accent, meaning pitch falls following the syllable that is accented.

THE SALEM WITCH TRIALS

Bridget Bishop   On May 27, 1692, a special court was established. The first trial was that of Bridget Bishop. When she was asked if she had committed witchcraft, Bishop said, "I am as innocent as the child unborn." She was found guilty, and on June 10, she was hanged; the first of the Salem executions for witchcraft.

POETRY

Narrative Poetry   Narrative poetry is like a story because it has a plot, but it is told in verse form. These include epic poems, ballads, and idylls. Narrative poems can be long or short, intricate and complex or more simple. They usually are nondramatic and have a regular meter. One example of a narrative poem is *The Canterbury Tales* by Geoffrey Chaucer.

PRECALCULUS

Quadratics   Polynomials that follow the pattern $ax^2 + bx + c$ have a special name. These are called quadratics. To factor quadratics, you need to find numbers that when multiplied equal c, but when added equal b. For example:

$$x2 + 6x + 8$$

You first break it down into two sets to multiply:

$$(x + ?)\ (x + ?)$$

Then plug in numbers and test:

$$(x + 4)\ (x + 2) = x^2 + 2x + 4x + 8 = x^2 + 6x + 8$$

Therefore, your answer is: $(x + 4)\ (x + 2)$

ISAAC NEWTON

Newton's Second Law of Motion   Newton's second law explains how when pushed or pulled, an object's velocity will change. Newton states that if one puts force on an object, its acceleration, or velocity, will change in the direction you force it to. The acceleration is directly proportional to force (if you push twice as hard on something, it goes twice as fast). The acceleration is inversely proportional to the mass. His second law can be summarized as $F = ma$, where F is force, m is mass, and a is acceleration.

JAPANESE

Politeness   There is a very complex system in the Japanese language when dealing with the issue of politeness, and at least four different levels of how to address a person. How to address someone is based on a variety of factors such as age, job, and experience, and there is even a different form of politeness when asking someone for a favor. There are differences between the polite language, teineigo, the respectful language, sonkeigo, and the humble language, kenjōgo, as well as differences between honorific and humble forms.

🏛 THE SALEM WITCH TRIALS

The Trials   Five days after the hanging of Bridget Bishop, a respected minister requested that the court not allow testimony about dreams and visions. His request was ignored, and in July, five more people were hanged. Another eleven more were hanged and some, like Giles Corey, were tortured to death. A total of nineteen people were killed.

✐ POETRY

Epic Poetry   Epic poems are longer narrative poems, and are usually centered around a hero and details of his heroic journey and deeds. Epics have a history in oral poetry, but even as far back as ancient Greece, these types of poems have been written. One of the most famous epic poems was the *Odyssey* by Homer, which followed Odysseus's journey back home following the Trojan War.

⊟ PRECALCULUS

Completing the Square   Some quadratic equations cannot be factored. To solve these, a method called completing the square is used. This turns $ax^2 + bx + c$ into $ax^2 + bx + c = (a + b)^2$.

For example:

$$x^2 + 2x + 1 = 0$$

Begin by transposing the constant term

$$x^2 + 2x = -1$$

Then you have to add a square to both sides. To do so, you have to take half of coefficient of x and then square it. So, half of 2 is 1, and then 1^2 is 1.

$$x^2 + 2x + 1 = -1 + 1$$
$$x^2 + 2x + 1 = 0$$

Now you have $(x + 1) (x + 1) = 0$
Break these up into two individual problems:

$$x + 1 = 0 \text{ and } x + 1 = 0$$

Solve for x. In both cases, x equals -1. Your answer will go in brackets and look like this:

$$\{-1, -1\}$$

❋ ISAAC NEWTON

Newton's Third Law of Motion   Newton's third law deals with more than one object. The law states that with every force, there is an opposite and equal force. In other words, for every F, there is a $-F$. If you push on something, it will push back. When two objects collide, an opposite and equal force is present.

◗ JAPANESE

Dialects   Due to the mountainous terrain and a history of internal and external isolation, there are many dialects of Japanese. These differ in vocabulary, pitch accent, morphology of certain types of words, and sometimes pronunciation. Though there are dozens of dialects, they can be broken into two main categories: Eastern and Western. Eastern dialects emphasize the sounds of consonants more, and the Western dialects emphasize vowels more.

THE SALEM WITCH TRIALS

An End to the Witch Trials   In response to the Massachusetts governor's own wife being questioned for witchcraft, the governor halted further arrests, released many of the accused, and dissolved the court. In May of 1693, the governor pardoned all who were accused of witchcraft. All in all, nineteen people were hanged, one man was tortured to death, and others died in prison. Nearly 200 people had been accused of witchcraft. Many involved with the trials and accusations issued public apologies, and in 1702 the trials were declared unlawful. In 1957, the state of Massachusetts apologized for the events that had happened more than 250 years before.

 POETRY

Sonnets   One of the most common forms of poetry is the sonnet, perhaps most famously written by William Shakespeare. Sonnets must be fourteen lines and written in iambic pentameter with one of the various rhyme schemes. The first quatrain of the poem must be expositional and discuss the main theme and metaphor. The second quatrain complicates or extends the theme. The third quatrain introduces a twist, and then finally the couplet summarizes the poem, leaving the reader with a new image to end on.

 PRECALCULUS

Permutations   Permutations are all of the possible arrangements you can make of a set. For example:

The permutation of abc is:

abc
bac
acb
cba
bca
cab

There are six permutations. The more letters you have, the more permutations there are. In order to solve these larger problems, this is where you use the factorials you learned about earlier. Permutations are set up like this: $_8P_3$

The number on the left is the same thing as saying 8!, and the number on the right is how many number places you will go. So that really means 8 × 7 × 6 = 336.

⚛ ISAAC NEWTON

The Spectrum of Colors   Sir Isaac Newton also discovered that white light is made up of the variety of colors in the spectrum. With a prism, he separated the light into the spectrum, and then using another prism, he rejoined the colors to create white light. He theorized light was made up of particles, but to explain refraction, he associated the property of light with waves.

◗ JAPANESE

Useful Japanese Phrases   Here are some useful phrases to use when traveling in Japan. Note, these are spelled out phonetically.

Hello/Good morning. *Konnichiwa.*
How are you? *O genki desu ka?*
Pleased to meet you. *Hajimemashite.*
Good morning. *Ohayō gozaimasu.*
Good evening. *Konbanwa.*

Excuse me. *Sumimasen.*
How much is this? *Ikura desu ka?*
Thank you. *Dōmo.*
Where's the toilet? *Benjo wa doko desu ka?*
Goodbye. *Sayōnara.*

1. **During the initial arrests prior to the witch trials, who confessed that the Devil had visited her?**
   a. Sarah Good
   b. The Parris's slave, Tituba
   c. Sarah Osborne
   d. Bridget Bishop

2. **How many people were killed as a result of the Salem witch trials?**
   a. 11
   b. 9
   c. 19
   d. 21

3. **Which of the following is the recurring pattern of stressed and unstressed syllables in the lines of a poem?**
   a. Rhythm
   b. Meter
   c. Sonnet
   d. Polynomial

4. **Which of the following must be fourteen lines and written in iambic pentameter, using one of the various rhyme schemes?**
   a. Sonnets
   b. Epic poetry
   c. Narrative poetry
   d. Stanzas

5. **What does $_8P_3$ equal?**
   a. 24
   b. 512
   c. 6,561
   d. 336

6. **Solve: $x2 + 6x + 8$**
   a. $(x + 2)(x + 2)$
   b. $(x + 4)(x + 2)$
   c. $(x + 4)(x + 4)$
   d. $(x)(x + 8)$

7. **Which law states that for every force, there is an opposite and equal force?**
   a. Newton's first law of motion
   b. Newton's second law of motion
   c. Newton's third law of motion
   d. Newton's law of universal gravitation

8. **Which law states that objects at rest stay at rest, and objects in motion stay in a straight line at a constant speed, unless an unbalanced force acts on it?**
   a. Newton's first law of motion
   b. Newton's second law of motion
   c. Newton's third law of motion
   d. Newton's law of universal gravitation

9. **Teineigo, sonkeigo, and kenjōgo are examples of:**
   a. Eastern dialects
   b. Western dialects
   c. Monophthongs
   d. Politeness

10. **Which of the following is true?**
    a. There are only five vowels in Japanese
    b. Most of the syllables in Japanese end with a vowel sound
    c. Japanese has a pitched accent
    d. All of the above

ANSWER KEY: b, c, b, a, d, b, c, a, d, d

HISTORY: Gandhi

Gandhi's Early Life, Gandhi in South Africa, Spiritual Development and Departure from South Africa, Nonviolent Civil Disobedience, The Dandi March, Quit India

MATH: Calculus

What Is Calculus?, Derivatives, Rules of Differentiation, Limits, Maxima and Minima, Integration

LANGUAGE ARTS: Horror

Gothic Horror, Robert Louis Stevenson, Bram Stoker, Mary Shelley, H. P. Lovecraft, Stephen King

SCIENCE: Quantum Mechanics

What Is Quantum Mechanics?, Heisenberg's Uncertainty Principle, Black Body Radiation, Bohr's Model, Schrödinger's Cat, The Photoelectric Effect

Lesson 22

FOREIGN LANGUAGE: Mandarin

The Origins, Old Mandarin, The Language Becomes Standardized, Differences in Phonology, Dialects, Useful Mandarin Phrases

GANDHI

Gandhi's Early Life   Mohandas Gandhi was born in a town north of Bombay on October 2, 1869. At thirteen years old, he was married under an arranged marriage. Though he wished to study medicine, this went against his caste, and his father urged him to study law. In September 1888, Gandhi went to England to study law. When he finished his studies, he returned to Bombay and Rajkot to practice law and briefly served as a lawyer for the prince of Porbandar.

HORROR

Gothic Horror   Gothic fiction is one of the most famous genres of horror fiction. It began with Horace Walpole's *The Castle of Otranto, A Gothic Story* of 1765, and became incredibly popular during the eighteenth and nineteenth centuries. Gothic fiction combined elements of horror, romance, and emotionalism, with an emphasis on atmosphere. Gothic fiction also focused on monsters, and it is from this genre that some of the most famous horror books ever written are descended.

CALCULUS

What Is Calculus?   Calculus is the study of change over time through using advanced forms of geometry and algebra, and it has many real-world applications. It provides the framework to understanding why things change, how to model things, and learning how to predict change in models. Calculus deals with the concept of infinity. If something is always changing, that means it is changing infinitely.

QUANTUM MECHANICS

What Is Quantum Mechanics?   Quantum mechanics is the study of particles at the atomic and subatomic level — such as protons, electrons, photons, and atoms — and their movements. According to quantum mechanics, particles at such microscopic levels behave counterintuitively. There are major differences between quantum mechanics and Newton's laws, including the notion that a particle can only have one value for its energy, and only the probability of a particle's location can be determined.

MANDARIN

The Origins   There are many variations in the Chinese language. Mandarin is spoken in southwestern and northern China and is a Sino-Tibetan language. It began as the language of the courts starting in the Ming Dynasty, with the dialect of Beijing being very influential. By the seventeenth century, schools were set up to teach the Beijing style, and this dialect was established as the national language in 1909. The Beijing style continued to be the national language when the Republic of China came to power and there was a greater need for a common language.

GANDHI

Gandhi in South Africa   In 1893, Gandhi was offered a job in South Africa. While traveling in the first-class compartment in a train, a white man asked him to leave. It was then that Gandhi decided he would work on eradicating prejudice based on race, and launched a campaign to improve the legal status of Indians in South Africa. In 1896, Gandhi made a return trip home to bring his wife and children to South Africa. As he informed others about what Indians faced in Africa, news of his work began to spread. Upon returning to South Africa, an angry mob formed, with the intention of lynching Gandhi.

HORROR

Robert Louis Stevenson   Robert Louis Stevenson wrote many famous books. One of his most famous works was a horror novella by the name of *The Strange Case of Dr. Jekyll and Mr. Hyde*, published in 1886. The book, which tells the tale of a doctor who takes a new drug he had been testing and turns into a horrible monster, deals with the dual nature of humanity, the human capacity for good and evil.

CALCULUS

Derivatives   The derivative is one of the core concepts used in calculus. In calculus, derivatives are represented in two ways. In geometric terms, derivatives are the slope of a line. The other way to show a derivative is physically, in which it is the rate of change. In a straight line, the slope indicates the speed at which the function changes. With a curved line, however, the slope changes, and this is where derivatives are used.

QUANTUM MECHANICS

Heisenberg's Uncertainty Principle   One of the fundamental principles of quantum mechanics is Heisenburg's uncertainty principle. German physicist Werner Heisenberg came to the conclusion that every part of observing particles actually affects particles. Even the light that is shone to help physicists see affects how the particles react and change velocity. To understand a particle, it has to be measured, but measuring it affects it. To make up for this, quantum physicists have to create thought experiments that prove or disprove the interpretations of quantum theory.

MANDARIN

Old Mandarin   From 960 to 1127 B.C., Emperor Taizu of the Northern Song Dynasty conquered the lands that we now know as China. When the Northern Song Dynasty came to an end, what is referred to as Old Mandarin, a new common speech, developed. Literature and art flourished during this time, and were written in this vernacular form. Much of the grammatical elements, rules, and syntax are retained in the Mandarin spoken today.

GANDHI

Spiritual Development and Departure from South Africa   Gandhi began doing unpaid, menial work for castes outside of his own, and began to live a simpler life. He began fasting, and in 1906, took a vow of celibacy and began living a life of voluntary poverty. He developed Satyagraha, a concept of the pursuit of truth. In 1907, Gandhi was imprisoned after he urged the Indians of South Africa to defy a law in which Indians had to register and be fingerprinted. He was soon released, and following the work of Leo Tolstoy, he created the Tolstoy Farm, a commonwealth of civil resisters. Before leaving South Africa, Gandhi was also responsible for a law that declared that Indian marriages were valid, and an abolition of taxes placed on former Indian indentured servants.

HORROR

Bram Stoker   Bram Stoker is responsible for introducing one of the most famous horror creatures of all time: Count Dracula. Vampire novels had been around before Stoker's *Dracula* of 1872; however, none has left as much of an impact as Stoker's gothic novel. The book follows Jonathan Harker, who travels to Transylvania to help Count Dracula with a real estate transaction and soon witnesses the horrors of the famous vampire. The book touches on sexuality, religion, and superstition, and introduces the world to famous characters like Van Helsing.

CALCULUS

Rules of Differentiation   Differentiation is the process of finding the derivatives. There are several rules of differentiation. Among these rules are the constant rule, which states if $F(x) = C$, then $F'(x) = 0$ (for example, if $F(x) = 5$, then $F'(x) = 0$) and the power rule, which states $F(x) = nx^{n-1}$, where n equals the exponent. For example, if $F(x) = X^4$, then $F'(x) = 4X^3$.

QUANTUM MECHANICS

Black Body Radiation   A black body is the idea of something that absorbs the radiation from all of the wavelengths falling on it. It is the perfect absorber and it appears black because it does not reflect light at normal temperatures. According to Prévost's theory of exchanges, not only is the black body the best absorber of radiation, but it is also the best emitter of radiation. A black body that is hotter will emit radiation with shorter wavelengths, and will appear blue at a higher temperature, and red at a lower temperature.

MANDARIN

The Language Becomes Standardized   Even when the Qing Dynasty fell and the Republic of China came to power, Mandarin remained the official language. When the People's Republic of China came to power in 1949, the effort to make Mandarin the national language continued, and the Beijing dialect became the official language, now known as Standard Chinese. Mandarin is the official language used in the media and in education. Though Taiwan and some of mainland China (such as Hong Kong) still speak Cantonese, Mandarin is spoken fluently as well. Officially, there are two types of Mandarin, one that the PRC government refers to, and one that the ROC government refers to.

GANDHI

Nonviolent Civil Disobedience   In January of 1915, Gandhi returned to India and was now known as Mahatma, meaning "great soul." The Rowlatt Acts of 1919, which allowed the British to try political cases without juries and allowed for the internment of suspects without a trial, enraged the people of India, and Gandhi called for a strike (though it was eventually called off due to violence toward the English). Following this, the Amritsar Massacre occurred, in which on a high holy day, the British began firing on unarmed men, women, and children, killing from 300 to 1,500 people. After the Amritsar Massacre, Gandhi began a noncooperation movement, urging the people to boycott, resign from employment by the British, and refuse to pay taxes.

HORROR

Mary Shelley   In 1818, Mary Shelley brought to life a monster that is still one of the most well-known creatures to this day with her book, *Frankenstein; or, The Modern Prometheus*. *Frankenstein* infuses elements of gothic horror and romance, and is one of the earliest forms of science fiction. Shelley began the book at eighteen years of age as a bet with other writers about who could write the better horror novel. Three years later, the tale of Dr. Frankenstein's monster was published.

CALCULUS

Limits   Limits are the intended height of a particular function. The formula for limits looks like this:

$$\lim_{x \to c} f(x) = n$$

Limits deal with the process of moving up the graph, and are not concerned with the value of *c*. For example, if $f(x) = x^2$, we know that $x = 2$, we can just plug it into the formula to figure out the answer and arrive at *c*. What limits do is figure out where the line is as it moves to the constant.

QUANTUM MECHANICS

Bohr's Model   The Bohr Model of the atom was modified from the Rutherford Model by Niels Bohr in 1915. The model features negatively charged electrons orbiting around a positively charged nucleus. According to the Bohr Model, the orbits of the electrons have a specific size and energy; energy is related to the orbit's size, with the lowest energy in the smaller orbit; and when electrons move from orbit to orbit, radiation is emitted or absorbed. There are several problems with this model, such as not taking Heisenburg's uncertainty principle into account, and it doesn't predict the intensities of the spectral lines.

MANDARIN

Differences in Phonology   Mandarin is known as a stress-timed language. What this means is that syllables, as in English, can last for different lengths of time, but there is still a constant amount of time between the stressed syllables. Mandarin differs from other Chinese languages such as Cantonese and Min Nan for this very reason. Cantonese and Min Nan are known as syllable-timed languages, where each syllable takes the same amount of time.

🏛 GANDHI

The Dandi March   After six years in prison, Gandhi took part in his most famous act of nonviolent civil disobedience: the Dandi March. The march was 240 miles in protest of British taxes on salt. In Dandi, Gandhi and the protesters made their own salt from the seawater, breaking the law. The march lasted twenty-four days and over 60,000 people were imprisoned.

👹 HORROR

H. P. Lovecraft   H. P. Lovecraft is not as well known as Mary Shelley or Bram Stoker, but he has become a cult figure, often compared to the likes of Edgar Allan Poe. He is most widely known for his "Cthulhu Mythos," a shared literary universe about which he and fellow authors wrote horror stories. One of his most well-known books was *The Call of Cthulhu*.

CALCULUS

Maxima and Minima   Maxima and minima (known as extrema) are the largest and smallest values a function has within a specific area (local), or as a whole (global or absolute). Local maximum is the height at a point that is greater than or equal to any other points in the interval. The formula for local maximum is $f(a) \geq f(x)$. Local minimum is the opposite, with a formula of: $f(a) \leq f(x)$.

❂ QUANTUM MECHANICS

Schrödinger's Cat   One of the most famous paradoxes found in quantum theory was created by Erwin Schrödinger. He proposed a theoretical experiment where a cat is placed into a steel box with a vial of a radioactive substance, hydrocyanic acid. If even one atom decays, the vial will break, and the cat will be dead. The observer, however, does not know whether the cat will be dead or alive until opening the box, and in calculations, the cat has to be considered both dead and alive. This is called quantum indeterminacy, and it means there aren't any outcomes until a measurement is observed.

⊙ MANDARIN

Dialects   Mandarin is one of the most widely spoken languages in the world, and due to China's size and population, there are many Mandarin dialects spoken. The dialects include the Northeastern dialect, the Southwestern dialect, the Beijing dialect (which Standard Chinese is based on), the Zhongyuan dialect, and the Ji-Lu dialect. Almost all of the cities in China have their own variation on Mandarin.

GANDHI

Quit India   As World War II began to encroach, Gandhi declared that India would not help the British in a war for independence when they themselves were not granted that freedom. Gandhi's demands for independence grew, and he drafted Quit India, a resolution that would make the British exit India. Gandhi's actions were met with great support by the Indian protesters, and great oppression by the British. Thousands were killed, and Gandhi and the Congress were imprisoned. Though Quit India didn't achieve its goal, it left a dramatic impact. Shortly after the end of World War II, British control over India was to end.

HORROR

Stephen King   Of the past forty years, one name in horror fiction has stood out above the rest, and is forever associated with horror novels: Stephen King. King has won six Horror Guild awards, six Bram Stoker awards, three World Fantasy awards, five Locus awards, and a Lifetime Achievement Award. Some of his most famous works include *The Shining*, *Carrie*, *Salem's Lot*, and *It*.

CALCULUS

Integration   Integration in calculus deals with two things. The first is to find the antiderivative, which is the inverse transform of the derivative. The other thing integration does is find the value of the area below the curve. Integration is represented by $\int f(x)\,dx$. And dx equals the difference of x_n and x_{n-1}. Two common equations for integration are:

$$\text{If } f(x) = x^n, \text{ then } f(x)\,dx = x^{n+1}/(n+1)$$
$$\text{If } f(x) = cx^n, \text{ then } f(x)\,dx = cx^{n+1}/(n+1)$$

QUANTUM MECHANICS

The Photoelectric Effect   The photoelectric effect was explained by Albert Einstein and led him to win the Nobel Prize in 1921. The photoelectric effect explains that when light shines on a piece of metal, a current will flow through it. The light provides energy to the electrons of the metal's atoms, which makes them move around and create a current. Not all lights will have this effect, however. Einstein concluded that instead of light being thought of as a wave, light was made of photons that acted like particles.

MANDARIN

Useful Mandarin Phrases   Here are some useful phrases to use when traveling to China. Note that these are written in pinyin, which is a phonetic spelling that uses the Latin alphabet (with the inclusion of *zh*, *ch*, *sh*, and no *v*):

Hello. *Nǐ hǎo.*
Good morning. *Zǎoān.*
Good afternoon. *Wǔān.*
Good evening. *Wǎnān.*
I don't understand. *Wǒ tīngbùdǒng.*
Excuse me. *Duìbùqǐ.*
Where's the toilet? *Cèsuǒ zài nǎli?*
How much is this? *Zhège duōshǎo qián?*
Goodbye. *Zàijiàn.*

1. **Gandhi developed Satyagraha, which was:**
   a. Another name for Quit India
   b. A march in protest of the British taxing salt
   c. A concept of truth
   d. A commonwealth of civil resisters

2. **Which of the following concerning the Dandi March is true?**
   a. The march was 240 miles long and in protest of British taxes on salt.
   b. In Dandi, Gandhi and the protesters made their own salt from the seawater, which was breaking the law.
   c. The march lasted twenty-four days and over 60,000 people were imprisoned.
   d. All of the above.

3. **Robert Louis Stevenson is the author of:**
   a. *Strange Case of Dr. Jekyll and Mr. Hyde*
   b. *The Castle of Otranto, A Gothic Story*
   c. *Dracula*
   d. *The Shining*

4. **Bram Stoker created:**
   a. Frankenstein's Monster
   b. Cthulhu
   c. Dracula
   d. It

5. **The largest value a function has within a specific area is called the:**
   a. Minima
   b. Maxima
   c. Limit
   d. Derivative

6. **What does the equation $\int f(x)\, dx$ represent?**
   a. Limit
   b. Integration
   c. Power rule
   d. Constant rule

7. **According to quantum mechanics, particles at such microscopic levels behave:**
   a. Counterintuitively
   b. According to Newton's laws
   c. Only like protons
   d. Only like electrons

8. **Which of the following explains that when light shines on a piece of metal, a current will flow through it?**
   a. Schrödinger's Cat
   b. Black body radiation
   c. Bohr's Model
   d. The photoelectric effect

9. **Which dialect of Mandarin is Standard Chinese based on?**
   a. The Northeastern dialect
   b. The Southwestern dialect
   c. The Beijing dialect
   d. The Zhongyuan dialect

10. **What is pinyin?**
    a. The phonetic spelling of Mandarin that uses the Latin alphabet
    b. How you say "Excuse me"
    c. A dialect of Mandarin
    d. A form of Mandarin introduced by the Qing Empire

ANSWER KEY: c, d, a, c, b, b, a, d, c, a

HISTORY: The Russian Revolution

A Century of Repression, The February Revolution, The Bolsheviks, The Summer of 1917, The October Revolution, The Aftermath

MATH: Trigonometry

Ratios, The Law of Cosines, The Law of Sines, Radian Measure, Reciprocal Identities, Inverse Trigonometric Functions

LANGUAGE ARTS: Humor

Mark Twain, John Kennedy Toole, P. G. Wodehouse, Terry Pratchett, Douglas Adams, David Sedaris

SCIENCE: Albert Einstein

About Albert Einstein, Theory of Relativity, $E = mc^2$, Total Eclipse, Brownian Motion, His Brain

Lesson 23

FOREIGN LANGUAGE: Cantonese

The Origins, Differences Between Cantonese and Mandarin, Writing System, Phonology, Cantonese Today, Useful Cantonese Phrases

THE RUSSIAN REVOLUTION

A Century of Repression   Following the Napoleonic wars, ideas of democracy began to spread throughout Europe. Russians, under the rule of Czar Alexander I, began calling for a constitution guaranteeing basic rights. Though Alexander I granted Poland a constitution, he never made his mind up about Russia. Following Alexander's death, there was great chaos as Nicholas I, the Czar's younger brother, came to power. The reign of the son of Nicholas I, Alexander II, brought heavy police repression, creating resentment among the people.

HUMOR

Mark Twain   Mark Twain is one of the most well-known American humorists. He is the author of such classic books as *The Adventures of Tom Sawyer*, and *Adventures of Huckleberry Finn*. The latter is regarded as one of the greatest books in American literature. Even to this day, Twain's impact in humor can be seen. Every year since 1998, the Kennedy Center has awarded the Mark Twain Prize to those comedic voices that have left an impact on the world. Past winners include Bill Cosby, Richard Pryor, Tina Fey, and George Carlin.

TRIGONOMETRY

Ratios   *Trigonometry* literally means "measurement of triangles," and that is exactly what it is: the study of triangles. Trigonometry is based on the measurements of right triangles, meaning triangles with right angles, and the ratios of each side. In ratios, you use cardinal and ordinal numbers. Cardinal numbers are the numbers that you use for counting (1, 2, 3, 4, etc.), while ordinal numbers are in the form of first, second, third, fourth, etc. When a large number is a multiple of another smaller number, that smaller number is part of the larger number. For example, 3 is the first multiple of 3, and 9 is the second multiple of 3. A ratio of two numbers is the relationship regarding the relative size. This is expressed in a sentence. For example, if you were asked what ratio has 3 to 9, the answer would be 3 is the third part to 9.

ALBERT EINSTEIN

About Albert Einstein   Perhaps one of the most famous scientists of all time, and deservedly so, Albert Einstein lived from 1879 to 1955. Einstein, born in Germany, studied physics and mathematics at Zurich, and he became a Swiss citizen in 1905. In 1909, he became a professor in theoretical physics at the University of Zurich, and a year later, he held the same position at the German University of Prague. In 1913, he was elected to the Prussian Academy of Science in Berlin, and, as he taught at the University of Berlin, he once again became a German citizen. When the Nazi party began to rise in Germany, Einstein left for the United States. He taught at the Institute of Advanced Study in Princeton, New Jersey, until his death.

CANTONESE

The Origins   Cantonese originated in southern China. It is the most prestigious dialect of the Yue language. It is believed to have formed following the fall of the Han Dynasty in A.D. 220, due to isolation. By the Tang Dynasty in A.D. 618, Cantonese was its own distinct dialect. Because Hong Kong was a British colony from the mid-nineteenth century to the late twentieth century, it was shielded from many of the linguistic reforms of China, most notably, the shift to Mandarin as the standard language.

THE RUSSIAN REVOLUTION

The February Revolution   Throughout 1916 and 1917, as Russia suffered greatly in World War I and had food shortages, there were many strikes and protests, often leading to violence. February 23, 1917, was the International Women's Day Festival. The festival turned into a citywide protest of men and women from factories and industries. As Czar Nicholas II ordered the military to attack, many in the military, no longer loyal to the czar, joined the protesters. Chaos broke out in the city. By February 27, over 80,000 troops had mutinied. Nicholas II abdicated, giving power to his brother; however, his brother wouldn't accept unless chosen by the representative assemblies. The next day, he resigned, and Russia did not have a head of state.

HUMOR

John Kennedy Toole   John Kennedy Toole lived from 1937 to 1969. He wrote one of the most well-known comedic novels of the twentieth century, *A Confederacy of Dunces*. The book was published posthumously in 1980, eleven years after Toole committed suicide at the age of thirty-one. When Toole had finished writing the manuscript of *A Confederacy of Dunces*, the publisher he sent it to rejected the book. After his death, Toole's mother insisted that author Walker Percy read the book. He finally did, and fell in love with it. The book was published and the next year, John Kennedy Toole was posthumously awarded the Pulitzer Prize.

TRIGONOMETRY

The Law of Cosines   When solving triangles that do not have right angles (known as oblique triangles), the laws of sines and cosines are used. If you need to find the third side, and the other two sides of a triangle and the angle are known, then you use the law of cosines. The formula for the law of cosines is:

$$c^2 = a^2 + b^2 - 2ab \cos \theta$$

For example, if we are given a triangle ABC, side a = 9 inches, side b = 11 inches, and the angle of C is 60°, what is the value of c?

The formula would look like this:

$$c^2 = 9^2 + 11^2 - 2(9)(11) \cos 60$$
$$c^2 = 202 - 99$$
$$c^2 = 103$$
$$c = \sqrt{103}$$

ALBERT EINSTEIN

Theory of Relativity   Einstein's theory of relativity can be broken up into two parts: the special theory of relativity, first published in 1905; and the general theory of relativity, published in 1915. The special theory of relativity states that regardless of total velocity, the laws of physics remain the same, and the speed of light is always constant. In other words, you cannot know whether you are moving, unless you see another object, but the laws of physics always apply. The general theory of relativity expands upon the ideas from the special theory of relativity, including gravity in the picture. This theory states you cannot know the difference between gravity and inertia, and that gravity, which acts like a force, is not one. Gravity bends space-time.

continued on next page

CANTONESE

Differences Between Cantonese and Mandarin   Though both Cantonese and Mandarin share the same basic alphabet, the two languages have very distinct sounds when spoken. Cantonese is thought to be more complex than Mandarin, with up to nine tones compared to Mandarin's four. The most obvious difference is the location of people who speak these languages. Whereas Mandarin is used in mainland China and Taiwan, Cantonese is spoken in southern China. It is said that when comparing the two, it is like having a duck try to talk to a chicken. Though they are both birds, the species are very different.

THE RUSSIAN REVOLUTION

The Bolsheviks Vladimir Lenin, an intellectual who had been known as a revolutionary and socialist, had been living in exile in Switzerland. Lenin saw the political unrest in Russia as the perfect opportunity for him and his party, the Bolsheviks. Lenin negotiated with Germany to be brought back to Russia, and in April of 1917, Lenin returned to great applause. Lenin delivered the April Theses, in which he advocated an end to the war and no cooperation with non-Communists.

HUMOR

P. G. Wodehouse Sir P. G. Wodehouse lived from 1881 to 1975. His first comedic book, *Something Fresh*, came out in 1915. Wodehouse wrote ninety-six books in his career, and he is most known for his Jeeves and Wooster stories, his very eccentric characters, and multiple layers involved in the plots. Also a playwright and lyricist, Wodehouse wrote lyrics for musicals such as *Anything Goes.*

TRIGONOMETRY

The Law of Sines For the law of sines, we are dealing with triangles where the sides are the same ratio as the sines of opposite angles. So $a : b : c = \sin A : \sin B : \sin C$.

So, side a is to b, is to $\sin A$ is to $\sin B$, and the same with b to c. In other words:

$$\frac{a}{b} = \frac{\sin A}{\sin B} \quad \text{and} \quad \frac{b}{c} = \frac{\sin B}{\sin C}$$

ALBERT EINSTEIN

$E = mc^2$ From Einstein's special theory of relativity came one of the most famous mathematical formulas of all time: $E = mc^2$. What this means is that energy (represented by E), equals mass (represented by m) multiplied by the speed of light (represented by c) squared. The speed of light, 186,000 miles per second, is a gigantic number when squared. So, a small amount of mass will create a lot of energy. This equation essentially says that mass is another form of energy.

CANTONESE

Writing System Cantonese literature is more developed than any other Chinese language. Though the writing system uses the same characters as the standard language, it also has additional characters, and some characters even have different meanings. There are also words in Cantonese that do not have any meaning in Mandarin. Instead of a new or different written language, Cantonese is written in the same system as Mandarin, and the words are just pronounced differently.

THE RUSSIAN REVOLUTION

The Summer of 1917   During the summer of 1917, Lenin attempted to overthrow the Provisional Government. The coup failed, and many Bolsheviks were arrested as Lenin fled to Finland. However, when it was feared that the minister of war was trying to create a military dictatorship, the Bolsheviks, who had created a military force, the Red Guard, were needed for support. By the fall, the Bolsheviks were gaining popularity, and Leon Trotsky was elected as president of the Petrograd.

HUMOR

Terry Pratchett   Sir Terry Pratchett was born in 1948. Pratchett's work combines humor and fantasy, and his first novel, *The Carpet People*, was published in 1971. Pratchett's most well-known books are from his *Discoworld* series, of which there are currently thirty-six different titles. In 1990, he collaborated with Neil Gaiman on the book *Good Omens*, a parody of the film *The Omen* and the end of the world.

TRIGONOMETRY

Radian Measure   One revolution in a circle is measured as 2π. This means that half of a circle is π, and that every right angle in a circle is $\pi/2$. $\pi/4$ is half of a right angle, and thus, it equals 45°. So this means that 2π is actually 360°. To find degrees in radians, the equation you have to follow is:

$$\text{Radians} = \frac{\text{Degrees}}{180} \bullet \pi$$

So to convert 90° into radians, you do:

$$\frac{90}{180} \bullet \pi = \frac{\pi}{2}$$

ALBERT EINSTEIN

Total Eclipse   Light photons do not have any mass. They do, however, have energy. And according to Einstein's formula of $E = mc^2$, energy behaves like mass. This means that light from stars is also bent by the Sun's gravity. On May 29, 1919, there was a total eclipse. British astronomer Arthur Eddington studied the location of the stars during the eclipse. What he found was that Einstein's theory was in fact true, and that when looking at the stars during the eclipse, it appeared as if the stars had changed positions, and that the Sun's gravitational field was in fact affecting the light.

CANTONESE

Phonology   The pronunciation of Cantonese is based on the language spoken in the capital of the Guangdong Province, Canton. In the Cantonese syllabary, there are around 630 sounds and 1,760 syllables. The nine different tones have different meanings when combined with syllables. From a phonological standpoint, Cantonese is a much more difficult language to understand than Mandarin.

🏛 THE RUSSIAN REVOLUTION

The October Revolution   Lenin planned a coup d'état to overthrow the Provisional Government, which was increasingly more ineffective, and replace them with the Bolsheviks. Lenin met with twelve party leaders to persuade them that revolution was necessary. With only ten backing him, Lenin began plotting the revolution. On October 24, 1917, troops that were loyal to the Bolsheviks began taking over government buildings. On October 26, the Provisional Government was arrested and a new provisional government was created with only Bolshevik members.

HUMOR

Douglas Adams   Douglas Adams was the creator of the immensely popular *Hitchhiker's Guide to the Galaxy* series. Adams, who was discovered by Graham Chapman of Monty Python fame, started his career writing for BBC radio programs. *The Hitchhiker's Guide to the Galaxy* originally began as a radio show on the BBC. The show would eventually turn into a book, and Adams wrote five books in the series. Since its conception, *The Hitchhiker's Guide to the Galaxy* has been immensely popular, and has been turned into a television series, a video game, a major motion picture, and a comic book series.

➗ TRIGONOMETRY

Reciprocal Identities   Identities are true no matter what value the variable is. For example, the problem $(x + 3)(x - 3) = x^2 - 9$ is always true. That makes it an identity. In trigonometry, there are several reciprocal identities one has to know.

The reciprocal identities are:

$$\sin\theta = \frac{1}{\csc\theta} \quad \csc\theta = \frac{1}{\sin\theta}$$

$$\cos\theta = \frac{1}{\sec\theta} \quad \sec\theta = \frac{1}{\cos\theta}$$

$$\tan\theta = \frac{1}{\cot\theta} \quad \cot\theta = \frac{1}{\tan\theta}$$

⚛ ALBERT EINSTEIN

Brownian Motion   In 1905, Einstein's third paper concentrated on the random movement of small particles in liquids and gases. Brownian motion gets its name from Robert Brown, who in 1827, reported on the motion of pollen particles in water. Brown, however, was never able to figure out why the motion happened. Einstein figured out that the motion was due to water molecules hitting the pollen. Though the pollen grains were visible, the water molecules weren't, and so it appeared that these particles were jiggling. Einstein was also able to show the speed the water molecules were moving in and how many molecules hit a single grain of pollen, as well as what properties of atoms could be tested.

continued on next page

CANTONESE

Cantonese Today   A total of 71 million people speak Cantonese, and it is spoken in Hong Kong, Guangdong, Macau, Hainan, and Guangxi. Through Western colonialism, migration, and trade, the majority of Chinese who have traveled abroad have been speakers of Cantonese. Today, Cantonese-speaking communities appear more in other countries than in most of China. The United States and Canada have the most Cantonese-speaking communities outside of Hong Kong and mainland China, and in San Francisco, there are a total of 180,000 Cantonese speakers.

🏛 THE RUSSIAN REVOLUTION

The Aftermath   Lenin's peace policy with Germany was widely unpopular and ended in Russia ceding large territories to the Germans. Following the October Revolution, a civil war broke out between the Whites (the anti-Bolsheviks) and the Reds (the Communists). The Reds eventually won after four years, and in 1922, the Soviet Union was established. When Lenin died in 1923, Joseph Stalin came to power.

HUMOR

David Sedaris   David Sedaris (whose sister is comedian Amy Sedaris) is one of the most prolific humorists writing today. His books usually consist of short essays full of biting, absurdist, and slightly neurotic commentary, based on his life. One of his most famous pieces, "Santaland Diaries," was a memoir of his seasonal job working as an elf for Macy's during the holiday season. He has published many books of his essays, one of his most well known being *Me Talk Pretty One Day*.

➗ TRIGONOMETRY

Inverse Trigonometric Functions   When given the value of a function and asked to find the value of the angle, this is referred to as an inverse trigonometric function. The terms used for inverse functions are *arcsin*, *arccos*, *arctan*, *arccsc*, *arcsec*, and *arccot*. If $f(x) = \sin x$ and $g(x) = \arcsin x$, then the formula for finding the inverse trigonometric functions is $f(g(x)) = x$ or $g(f(x)) = x$. So arcsin $x = y$, which leads us to the formula $x = \sin y$.

⚛ ALBERT EINSTEIN

His Brain   Albert Einstein died on April 18, 1955, at the age of seventy-six. His body was cremated, but his brain was saved for research. Until 1999, it was decided that Einstein's brain was really no different than any other person's brain. In 1999 however, it was discovered that Einstein's brain lacked a certain wrinkle, called the parietal operculum. To compensate for this lacking wrinkle, other parts of his brain, such as the inferior parietal lobes, had to compensate. This part of the brain plays a role in mathematical thinking and visual imagery.

CANTONESE

Useful Cantonese Phrases   Here are some helpful phrases to use when traveling to Hong Kong. Note that these are written in Yale Romanization, a phonetic English alphabet:

Hello. *Néih hóu.*
Pleased to meet you. *Hóu hòisàm yihngsīk néih.*
Good morning. *Jóusàhn.*
Good day. *Ńgh ōn.*
Good evening. *Máahn ōn.*
Excuse me. *m̀hgòi.*
How much is this? *Nīgo géidō chín a?*
Thank you. *Dòjeh.*
Where's the toilet? *Chisó hái bīndouh a?*
Do you speak English? *Neih sīkm̀hsīk góng yìngmán a?*
Can you translate it for me? *Néih hóm̀hhóyíh bòng ngóh fáanyihk a?*
Goodbye. *Joigin.*

1. **Lenin's successful coup d'état, in which he and the Bolshevicks overthrew the Provisional Government, describes which of the following events?**
   a. The February Revolution
   b. The October Revolution
   c. The events of International Women's Day Festival
   d. The Summer of 1917

2. **Which of the following happened after Lenin came to power?**
   a. A peace policy with Germany that was widely unpopular
   b. Russia ceding large territories to the Germans
   c. A civil war between the Whites and the Reds
   d. All of the above

3. **Which of the following was written by Mark Twain?**
   a. *Adventures of Huckleberry Finn*
   b. *A Confederacy of Dunces*
   c. *Me Talk Pretty One Day*
   d. A and C

4. ***The Hitchhiker's Guide to the Galaxy* was written by:**
   a. P. G. Wodehouse
   b. Terry Pratchett
   c. Douglas Adams
   d. David Sedaris

5. **What is 60° in radians?**
   a. $\pi/3$ c. $\pi/2$
   b. $\pi/4$ d. π

6. **There is an oblique triangle ABC with side a = 9 inches, side b = 11 inches, and the angle of C is 60°. What is the value of c?**
   a. 103
   b. 10609
   c. Ö103
   d. Ö10609

7. **What can we derive from Einstein's special theory of relativity ($E = mc^2$)?**
   a. Mass is not energy.
   b. Mass is another form of energy.
   c. Light is another form of energy.
   d. The speed of light is not as fast as we thought.

8. **Einstein's theory of relativity can be broken up into what two parts?**
   a. Special theory of relativity and Brownian motion
   b. General theory of relativity and Brownian motion
   c. Special theory of relativity and parietal operculum
   d. Special theory of relativity and the general theory of relativity

9. **Which of the following is true?**
   a. Though Cantonese is written in the standard language, it also has additional characters.
   b. There are words in Cantonese that do not have any meaning in Mandarin.
   c. Cantonese-speaking communities appear more in other countries than in China.
   d. All of the above.

10. **Which of the following is true?**
    a. Cantonese has four tones and Mandarin has up to nine.
    b. Cantonese has up to nine tones and Mandarin only has four.
    c. Cantonese and Mandarin have the same number of tones.
    d. Cantonese has four tones and Mandarin has five.

HISTORY: World War I

The Assassination of Archduke Franz Ferdinand, The First Battle at the Marne, The Battle of Tannenburg, The Battle of Cambrai, The United States Enters the War, The Treaty of Versailles

MATH: Logic

What Is Logic?, Shorthand Sentences, Connectives, Use of Parentheses, The Rules of Logic, Modus Ponens, Modus Tollens, and Hypothetical Syllogism

LANGUAGE ARTS: Mystery

Edgar Allan Poe, Sherlock Holmes, The Golden Age of Detective Fiction, Dorothy Sayers, Agatha Christie, Louise Penny

SCIENCE: The Copenhagen Interpretation

Quantum Suicide, The Many-Worlds Theory, What Is the Copenhagen Interpretation?, Wave Function, The Nature of Collapse, Criticism

Lesson 24

FOREIGN LANGUAGE: Vietnamese

The Origins, Role of the Chinese, Quốc Ngữ, Dialects, Speech Patterns, Useful Vietnamese Phrases

WORLD WAR I

The Assassination of Archduke Franz Ferdinand   On June 28, 1914, Archduke Franz Ferdinand, heir to the Austro-Hungarian Empire, was assassinated by a member of the Serbian terrorist group known as the Black Hand. This event would lead to the beginning of the Great War. Following the murder, the government of Austria-Hungary had to impose their authority on Serbia, and they called on Germany for support. On July 23, an ultimatum was delivered to Serbia to wipe out terrorist groups and anti-Austrian sentiment or encounter military action. Serbia called on Russia for support, and on July 28, Austria-Hungary declared war on Serbia. On August 1, Russian forces began mobilizing in support of Serbia, and Germany declared war on Russia. Russia's allies Great Britain and France then joined in.

MYSTERY

Edgar Allan Poe   Perhaps more widely known for his dark poetry such as "The Raven," or his horror stories like "The Tell-Tale Heart," Edgar Allan Poe is actually considered the father of the mystery genre. His story, "The Murders in the Rue Morgue," published in 1841, is considered the very first mystery story. It focuses on detective C. Auguste Dupin, as he tries to solve the murders of two women by gathering and analyzing clues. Many elements of modern mysteries can be found in such works of Edgar Allan Poe as "The Purloined Letter" and "The Gold Bug."

LOGIC

What Is Logic?   Logic is the study of correct reasoning, or inference. The origins of logic can be traced back to Aristotle, who viewed logic as a tool to be used, rather than an actual philosophy. This is still the view mathematicians and philosophers take. In order to establish something, such as a philosophy, as true, one needs logic to demonstrate a proof and to have it accepted. And that is exactly what logic is used for.

THE COPENHAGEN INTERPRETATION

Quantum Suicide   Similar to how the cat from Schrödinger's experiment was both dead and alive, the quantum suicide theory poses this hypothesis: a man sits with a gun to his head. The gun measures the spin of a particle and every time the man pulls the trigger, the particle's spin, or quark, is measured. Based on this measurement, the gun will go off or won't go off. If the quark spins clockwise, the gun will go off, and if it is spinning counterclockwise, there will only be a click, but no firing of the gun. As the man pulls the trigger, he hears click after click, meaning the quark is spinning counterclockwise, and the gun will never go off. However, if you start from the beginning and the quark is clockwise, the man will die. Because we can have both situations, the man is both dead and alive. The universe is split in two every time he pulls the trigger.

VIETNAMESE

The Origins   Vietnamese is an Austro-Asiatic language, belonging to the Mon-Khmer branch. The political history of Vietnam greatly impacted the formation of the language. Prior to the second century B.C., two communities along the Red River came together to become the Viet-Muong. In the second century B.C., the Chinese came to power, importing their language and grammar rules (even today, 60 percent of the language has Chinese roots). From 1884 to 1946, Vietnam was colonized by the French, which also influenced the language.

WORLD WAR I

The First Battle at the Marne   The First Battle at the Marne was the first significant battle fought that proved that the war would not be short and introduced the fighting style most characteristic of World War I: trench warfare. By the end of August 1914, three of Germany's armies were moving toward Paris to take control of the city and conquer France. By September 3, 500,000 French civilians had left the city. The commander-in-chief of the French forces planned an attack on the German First Army, and they attacked on September 6. By splitting the German armies, the French and the British were able to advance, and German forces couldn't break through. On September 9, the Germans retreated, and by September 10, the battle was over.

MYSTERY

Sherlock Holmes   Sherlock Holmes is one of the names that immediately comes to mind when thinking about mystery fiction. Created by Sir Arthur Conan Doyle, Holmes's first case was featured in the book *A Study in Scarlet*, published in 1887, and Doyle's most known book was *The Hound of the Baskervilles* of 1902. When creating the character, Doyle actually used Poe's C. Auguste Dupin as an influence for Sherlock. Sherlock Holmes was featured in four novels and countless stories, and is still adapted for film and television to this day.

LOGIC

Shorthand Sentences   An example of logic might be:
   Assuming: The cat is orange.
   And assuming: The cat is a female.
   I conclude: The cat is orange and the cat is a female.
   In logic, shorthand sentences are essential. Instead of writing out full-length sentences all the time, a letter is chosen to represent that sentence. So the sentence "The cat is orange" would be represented by the letter A, and the sentence "The cat is a female" would be represented by the letter B.

THE COPENHAGEN INTERPRETATION

The Many-Worlds Theory   First proposed in 1957, the many-worlds theory was not taken seriously until the quantum suicide theory. The many-worlds theory states that for every outcome that is possible, the world splits into copies and each of the actions are taken. The person is not aware of the other version of the universe. So, with the case of quantum suicide, if the man dies, his self in the other universe lives on, ready to test the gun once again. Every time he dies, the universe splits once more. The Copenhagen interpretation contradicts the many-worlds theory.

VIETNAMESE

Role of the Chinese   During the time of the Viet-Muong, there were two dialects: that of the Lowlanders and that of the Highlanders. When the Chinese came to power over the lowland Viets, Chinese characters, language, and administration were introduced. The Chinese ruled over the land for 1,000 years, and though Chinese was officially the written language, the development of the spoken language continued, with the Lowlander dialect becoming the spoken language. In the tenth century, the Highlander language was no longer a dialect, but its own language: Muong. Though the Vietnamese spoke their own language, they used Chinese characters when writing, and this was known as chữ nôm.

WORLD WAR I

The Battle of Tannenburg   The Battle of Tannenburg was fought from August 26 to August 31, 1914. It is considered Germany's greatest victory, and Russia's worst defeat. Two Russian armies, one led by General P. K. Rennenkampf, the other by A. V. Samsonov, planned on attacking East Prussia. Contact between the two armies was lost, and the Germans took advantage of Samsonov's isolated army. Within the next few days, half of his army was lost, and on August 29, Samsonov shot himself. The Germans took 92,000 Russian prisoners.

MYSTERY

The Golden Age of Detective Fiction   The period from 1920 to 1939 is referred to as the Golden Age of Detective Fiction. During this time, such prolific mystery writers as Dorothy Sayers, Agatha Christie, and Freeman Wills Crofts produced their most notable work. While Poe and Doyle brought the mystery genre to life, the writers of this time polished the genre. These books were meant to engage the reader and make the reader try to work along with the detectives. For this reason, certain rules were set in place. These rules included that the criminal should be mentioned early in the book, detectives were not allowed to be helped by intuition or accident, no supernatural solutions were allowed, and no clues could be concealed from the reader. By World War II, the genre began to decline in popularity.

LOGIC

Connectives   Connectives are used to connect sentences represented by A and B. Connectives are the "and, or, if . . . then, not, if and only if." Connectives have their own symbols. They are:

and	^
or	v
if . . . then	->
not	~
if and only if	<->

So, now the sentences about the cat look like this:

The cat is orange and the cat is a female.   (A ^ B)
The cat is orange or the cat is a female.   (A v B)
If the cat is orange, then the cat is a female.   (A -> B)
The cat is not orange.   (~A)
The cat is orange if and only if the cat is female.   (A <-> B)

✹ THE COPENHAGEN INTERPRETATION

What Is the Copenhagen Interpretation?   Niels Bohr first posed the Copenhagen interpretation in 1920. The Copenhagen interpretation states that quantum particles do not exist in one state or another, but rather all of the possible states exist at one time. Only when it is observed does a quantum particle take on a probability. Think back to Schrödinger's cat. The cat was both dead and alive. Schrödinger's cat is in fact, an example of the Copenhagen interpretation. According to the Copenhagen interpretation, the quantum suicide theory does not work because the direction of the quark can be observed, and eventually the quark will turn clockwise, killing the man.

✹ VIETNAMESE

Quốc Ngữ   Beginning in the sixteenth and seventeenth centuries, Asian languages started to become Romanized by Catholic priests in an effort to translate the Bible. French Jesuit priest Alexandre De Rhodes created quốc ngữ, the Roman-based script (using the Latin alphabet) of the Vietnamese language that is still used today. De Rhodes arrived in Vietnam in 1627, and within six months was able to preach fluently. Quốc ngữ grew increasingly popular with the people of Vietnam, and it was recognized as the official writing system of the nation following independence from the French in the beginning of the twentieth century.

WORLD WAR I

The Battle of Cambrai   The Battle of Cambrai began on November 7, 1917, and continued through December. It was the first large-scale battle in World War I where tanks were used (they were introduced in the Battle of Fiers-Courcelette of 1916). Following the failure at the Third Battle of Ypres (with conditions less than suitable), the popularity of tanks dwindled, and they were seen as prone to malfunctioning and had limited use. Though the British would lose the Battle of Cambrai, the use of tanks during this particular battle showcased the strengths of these machines.

MYSTERY

Dorothy Sayers   Dorothy Sayers published her first novel, *Whose Body*, in 1923. In *Whose Body*, Sayers introduces the detective that she would use for eleven more novels and twenty-one more stories: Lord Peter Wimsey. In the 1930s, Sayers stopped writing mystery novels, focusing on radio plays and theological dramas. In 1929, Sayers founded the Detection Club, a group of British mystery writers including members such as G. K. Chesterton and Agatha Christie.

LOGIC

Use of Parentheses   Parentheses play an important part in writing out logical arguments. If we wanted to negate a sentence, we would use the symbol $\sim$. But if we write $\sim A \wedge B$, that does not mean the entire thing is negated, but rather only A is. Parentheses help us clarify. So, we would write it out like $\sim(A \wedge B)$. Parentheses also help distinguish the sentences while working. Logic problems can be very complex, sometimes with thirty lines of derivation, so the parentheses keep it all in an orderly fashion.

THE COPENHAGEN INTERPRETATION

Wave Function   Another aspect of the Copenhagen interpretation describes wave function. According to the Copenhagen interpretation, the complete description of a wave-particle is its wave function. This means that information that cannot be derived from the wave function does not exist. For example, if a wave is spread out over a large area, the particle's location cannot be determined. Therefore, since the wave function doesn't provide a location, there is no location for the particle.

VIETNAMESE

Dialects   There are three dialects found in Vietnamese. These correspond to the three geographical regions of Vietnam. The dialects are Hanoi (Northern Vietnamese), Ho Chi Minh City (Southern Vietnamese), and Hue (Central Vietnamese). Some also believe there to be a distinction between the Northern Vietnamese dialect and the North-Central dialect. The standard language is based on the Northern Vietnamese dialect, and the dialects are, for the most part, mutually intelligible. The Geneva Accords of 1954, responsible for dividing the country into North and South Vietnam, brought on a great migration of people from the north moving to the south. When Vietnam reunified in the mid-1970s, another wave of migration occurred. As a result of these migrations, there is a significant number of southern Vietnamese speakers in the north and vice versa.

WORLD WAR I

The United States Enters the War   When the war broke out, the United States remained neutral and encouraged isolationism, even though there was pro-British propaganda spreading throughout the nation. On May 7, 1915, the *Lusitania*, a British passenger ship that brought people to and from the United States and Britain, was sunk by a German U-boat. The sinking of the ship, which had American citizens aboard, outraged the citizens of the United States. As wishes of neutrality started to wane, the British government intercepted the Zimmermann Telegram, which was from the German ambassador to Mexico, asking Mexico to attack the United States if the United States declared war on Germany. On April 6, 1917, the United States declared war on Germany.

MYSTERY

Agatha Christie   Agatha Christie lived from 1876 to 1976, and is one of the most well-known and prolific mystery writers. Her protagonist Hercule Poirot, the Belgian private detective, appeared in forty-two of her seventy-eight books, including one of her most famous novels, *The Murder of Roger Ackroyd*, which came out in 1926. Much like Sayers, Christie's novels took place in Britain's upper- and middle-class country houses, in villages, and even on trains. Agatha Christie was able to produce work that was intricately detailed, complex, slightly humorous, and carefully researched (she was even an expert on poisons).

LOGIC

The Rules of Logic   There are twelve rules of logic:

1. Assumption: You can assume anything, but you have to keep track of your assumptions
2. -> Introduction: If you presume A and then obtain B, you can write $(A \rightarrow B)$
3. ^ Elimination: If you have $(A \wedge B)$, then you can also have A and you can have B
4. Repetition: If you have A, then you are allowed to have A
5. ^ Introduction: If you have A and you have B, then you can have $(A \wedge B)$
6. -> Elimination: If you have A and you have $(A \rightarrow B)$, then you can have B
7. <-> Introduction: If you have $(A \rightarrow B)$ and $(B \rightarrow A)$, then you have $(A \leftrightarrow B)$
8. <-> Elimination: If you have $(A \leftrightarrow B)$, and you have A, then you can have B (and vice versa)
9. ~ Introduction: If you have A and find a contradiction, you can have $\sim A$
10. ~ Elimination: If you have $\sim A$ and find a contradiction, you can have A
11. v Introduction: If you have A, you can write $(A \vee B)$ no matter what
12. v Elimination: If you have $(A \vee B)$ and $(A \rightarrow C)$ and $(Y \rightarrow C)$, then you can have C

continued on next page

✵ THE COPENHAGEN INTERPRETATION

The Nature of Collapse   Another part of the Copenhagen interpretation is the collapsing of wavelengths. Since the wave function exists before any observation, the wavelength has to collapse in order for the observation to be made. If the momentum of a particle is measured, the particle's wave function changes suddenly from a wave comprised of many momenta, to the wave with only one momentum that is being measured. What you observe is the collapsing of the wavelength.

◑ VIETNAMESE

Speech Patterns   When speaking in Vietnamese, pitch, or the way words and phrases are spoken, affects the meaning. This means that Vietnamese is what is known as a tone language. There are seven types of pitch: mid-level, low, high rising, low falling, rising after a dip, low broken, and high broken. When a pitch is broken, that means it is glottalized. The language also makes use of reduplication, in which a portion of a word or the entire word itself is actually repeated. This indicates plurality, intensity, and extension, and plants, fruits, birds, and insects are often reduplicated.

WORLD WAR I

The Treaty of Versailles   The Great War ended in 1918 with the Treaty of Versailles. The treaty was made by the British prime minister, the French prime minister, and President Woodrow Wilson. As a result of the treaty, much of the land Germany had acquired over the war was given back, the German army and navy were dramatically cut down in size, Germany would not be allowed to have an air force, Germany was forced to pay £6,600 million to compensate for damages, and the country had to take complete blame for the war. The League of Nations was also created in order to prevent any further conflicts.

MYSTERY

Louise Penny   The detective novel did not die when the Golden Age of Detective Fiction ended. Today, there are still great mystery writers who uphold the traditional detective stories. Louise Penny's first book, *Still Life*, came out in 2005 to rave reviews, winning several awards, including the Dagger Award, the Arthur Ellis Award, and the Barry Award. Her work follows Chief Inspector Armand Gamache, head of Quebec's homicide department. Though set in Quebec, many elements of the English mystery novels are present. Penny currently has six books out, and she has won the Agatha Award for best mystery novel of the year four consecutive times.

LOGIC

Modus Ponens, Modus Tollens, and Hypothetical Syllogism   Modus ponens is a very straightforward law. If you have $(X \to Y)$ and you also have X, then you are allowed to have Y. This is essentially rule number six, $\to$ Elimination. Modus tollens is the reverse of modus ponens. It states if you have $(X \to Y)$ and you also have $\sim Y$, then you are allowed to have $\sim X$. Essentially, this means that if Y is false, X cannot be true. Hypothetical syllogism states if there is $(X \to Y)$ and you also have $(Y \to Z)$, then you can have $(X \to Z)$.

THE COPENHAGEN INTERPRETATION

Criticism   The most famous attempt at debunking quantum mechanics and the most well-known challenge to the Copenhagen interpretation was the Einstein-Podolsky-Rosen proposition. In 1935, Albert Einstein, Boris Podolsky, and Nathan Rosen formulated an experiment to prove that quantum mechanics was incomplete. Their proposition claimed that, assuming that nothing can move faster than the speed of light, it is impossible for something to transport from one point to another in no time. This requires communication that is faster than light, which Einstein's general theory of relativity proved did not exist.

VIETNAMESE

Useful Vietnamese Phrases   Here are some helpful phrases to use when you are traveling in Vietnam:

Hello. *Chào anh* (to a man). *Chào chị* (to a woman).
Good morning. *Chào buổi sang.*
Good afternoon. *Xin chào.*
Good evening. *Chào buổi tối.*
Good night. *Chúc ngủ ngon.*
Excuse me. *Xin lỗi.*

Thank you. *Cảm ơn ông* (to a man). *Cảm ơn bà* (to a woman).
Where's the toilet? *Cầu tiêu ở đâu?*
How much is this? *Cái này giá bao nhiêu?*
Goodbye. *Chào anh* (to a man). *Chào chị* (to a woman).

1. **What was the first significant battle fought that proved that the war would not be short and introduced trench warfare?**
   a. The Battle of Cambrai
   b. The Battle of Tannenburg
   c. The First Battle at Versailles
   d. The First Battle at the Marne

2. **Which of the following was a result of the Treaty of Versailles?**
   a. Much of the land Germany had acquired over the war was given back.
   b. Germany would not be allowed to have an air force.
   c. Germany was forced to pay £6,600 million to compensate for damages.
   d. All of the above.

3. **What mystery writer was not a part of the Detection Club?**
   a. Dorothy Sayers
   b. Louise Penny
   c. Agatha Christie
   d. G. K. Chesterton

4. **"The Murders in the Rue Morgue," published in 1841, is considered the very first mystery and was written by:**
   a. Edgar Allan Poe
   b. Dorothy Sayers
   c. C. Auguste Dupin
   d. Sir Arthur Conan Doyle

5. **Which of the following states the second rule of logic?**
   a. If you have A, then you are allowed to have A
   b. If you have A, you can write $(A \lor B)$ no matter what
   c. If you presume A and then obtain B, you can write $(A \rightarrow B)$
   d. If you have $(A \lor B)$ and $(A \rightarrow C)$ and $(Y \rightarrow C)$, then you can have C

6. **Which of the following is a negation of the term: $A \land B$.**
   a. $\sim A \lor B$
   b. $\sim (A \land B)$.
   c. $\sim (A \lor B)$
   d. $A \land \sim B$

7. **The Copenhagen interpretation contradicts:**
   a. Schrödinger's cat
   b. Collapsing of wavelengths
   c. Quantum mechanics
   d. Many-worlds theory

8. **The most well known challenge to the Copenhagen interpretation is:**
   a. The Einstein-Podolsky-Rosen proposition
   b. Quantum suicide
   c. Schrödinger's cat
   d. The many-worlds theory

9. **In Vietnamese, mid-level, low, high rising, low falling, rising after a dip, low broken, and high broken are all examples of:**
   a. Different intensities
   b. Different types of plurality
   c. Different types of pitch
   d. Different types of reduplication

10. **The Roman-based script of the Vietnamese language that is still used today is called:**
    a. Xin chào
    b. quốc ngữ
    c. Chào anh
    d. Chào chị

HISTORY: The Wright Brothers

Early Attempts at Flight Prior to the Wright Brothers, The Study of Birds, The Wright Brothers' Gliders, The *Flyer*, The First Manned Flight, The *Vin Fiz*

MATH: Probability

What Is Probability?, Probability of an Event, Complementary Events, Probability and Area, Coin Probability, Mutually Exclusive Events

LANGUAGE ARTS: Edgar Allan Poe

Poe's Early Life, The American Romantic Movement, "The Raven," His Death, Griswold's Obituary, The Poe Toaster

SCIENCE: String Theory

Theoretical Physics, Strings and Membranes, Quantum Gravity, Unification of Forces, Supersymmetry, Extra Dimensions

FOREIGN LANGUAGE: Hebrew

The Origins, Revival of the Language, Modern Israeli Hebrew, Hebrew in Judaism, Writing System, Useful Hebrew Phrases

THE WRIGHT BROTHERS

Early Attempts at Flight Prior to the Wright Brothers   Humans have always had the desire to fly. In the 1480s, Leonardo da Vinci designed a concept for a machine that had birdlike wings called the ornithopter. In 1783, Joseph Michel and Jacques Etienne Montgolfier created the first hot-air balloon, and in the 1800s, Sir George Cayley created the first gliders capable of carrying humans. In 1891, German engineer Otto Lilienthal created the first glider that could fly long distances. That same year, Samuel Langley realized that in order to fly, power was needed. He built a model plane that ran on a steam-powered engine and flew for three-fourths of a mile. However when he created a full-sized version, the aerodrome was too heavy and crashed. In 1894, Octave Chanute created the biplane. This would become the basis for the Wright brothers' design.

EDGAR ALLAN POE

Poe's Early Life   Edgar Poe was born on January 19, 1809, in Boston, Massachusetts. Poe's mother had left his father and had taken the kids with her. When Poe was only two years old, his mother died. Edgar was taken in by Frances and John Allan. Poe spent five years studying in England, and in 1826, he attended the University of Virginia. Less than a year later, Poe quit school due to drinking and being in heavy debt. The next year, he joined the army. By 1835, Poe was living in Baltimore, working as an editor of a newspaper. In 1836, Poe married his thirteen-year-old cousin and moved to New York City. In 1845, his wife would die of tuberculosis two years after "The Raven" was published.

PROBABILITY

What Is Probability?   Probability is the study of the likelihood or chance of a particular event occurring. With problems regarding probability, identifying all of the different outcomes that can actually happen is crucial to understanding how to solve the problem. When you flip a coin, you want to know what the likelihood is that you'll get heads. When you pick a card from a deck, you want to figure out the probability that the card is a seven, or that the card will be hearts. Probability is about how likely an event is to occur.

STRING THEORY

Theoretical Physics   In theoretical physics, math is used to explain aspects of nature. Often, the formulas that are designed cannot be tested with an actual model, and this is what separates theoretical physics from empirical physics. A theoretical physics theory should accurately explain and predict certain phenomena with support from known observations. String theory is one of the most well-known theories in theoretical physics, and it is often known as the "theory of everything." String theory tries to explain how gravity fits with quantum physics.

HEBREW

The Origins   Hebrew is a Semitic language, and a member of the Afro-Asiatic family. According to Judaism, Hebrew was the first language. Hebrew is a Northwest Semitic language which began around the third century B.C. The first written evidence of the language was from around the tenth century B.C., and this is what is referred to as Classic Hebrew. Around 1,700 years ago, the spoken language was displaced by Aramaic, though it remained a written language. Not until the nineteenth century was the spoken language revived.

THE WRIGHT BROTHERS

The Study of Birds   From 1897 to 1899, the Wright brothers, Orville and Wilbur, rode their bicycles to the Pinnacles, a picnic spot near Dayton, Ohio. Many birds flew around the area, and the unique geography of the Pinnacles created an updraft, perfect for large soaring birds. There they observed the birds and came to the realization that in order to fly, their model needed to be based on large birds that soar. In 1899, after observing buzzards, the Wrights came up with their wing warping theory. The Wright brothers realized that as birds soared into the wind, lift was created as a result of the air going over the surfaces that were curved. To turn, birds change the shape of their wings.

EDGAR ALLAN POE

The American Romantic Movement   Poe's writing belongs to what is known as the American Romantic movement. Literature of American Romanticism focused on nature, the power of one's imagination, and individuality. This is considered a great literary genre to come out of America. Poe's life was dark and extremely emotional, and his writings also reflected this. His work featured mystical, magical, and mysterious elements in ways that set his work apart from more realistic work. Other writers of American Romanticism include Henry David Thoreau, Walt Whitman, Emily Dickinson, Washington Irving, and Herman Melville.

PROBABILITY

Probability of an Event   In probability problems, the event is the end result. It's what we want to figure out. To figure out the probability of an event A occurring, the formula is:

$$P(A) = \frac{\text{Number of outcomes favorable to } A \text{ occurring}}{\text{Total number of equally likely outcomes}} = \frac{n(A)}{n(S)}$$

For example, every letter from the word *pizza* is written down on a piece of paper and put in a hat. What is the probability that you will pick a *z*?

$S = \{P, I, Z_1, Z_2, A\}$
$A = $ event of getting $Z = \{Z_1, Z_2\}$

$$P(A) = \frac{2}{5}$$

STRING THEORY

Strings and Membranes   When string theory was first developed in the 1970s, it was believed that strings, little filaments of energy, were one-dimensional, and came in two forms: open and closed (think of one rubber band that is broken, and another that is not). These strings, known as Type I strings, could go through five different types of interactions. Physicists believe the closed strings could describe gravity. Later it was discovered that more than just strings were required. These are known as branes, and they are sheets that the strings attach one or both ends to.

HEBREW

Revival of the Language   From the fourth century to the nineteenth century, Hebrew existed solely as a written language. In 1881, Eliezer Ben-Yehuda revived Hebrew as a spoken language based on the liturgical language.

🏛 THE WRIGHT BROTHERS

The Wright Brothers' Gliders   The Wright brothers created a series of gliders over the next three years, and even corresponded with Octave Chanute. After a successful test, they created a full-size glider, choosing Kitty Hawk, North Carolina, as the test site due to its hilly landscape, isolated location, and wind. The 50-pound, 17-foot-wingspan glider was tested at Kitty Hawk in 1900, both piloted and unmanned. A year later, the largest glider ever (weighing almost 100 pounds and with a 22-foot wingspan) was flown at Kill Devil Hills, North Carolina. Their glider faced some problems, and the Wright brothers came to the realization that their calculations were not reliable. They built a wind tunnel to test various wing shapes, and soon planned on making a new glider with a 32-foot wingspan.

✒ EDGAR ALLAN POE

"The Raven"   "The Raven," arguably Edgar Allan Poe's most famous poem, was first published on January 29, 1845, in the *New York Evening Mirror* to rave reviews. The poem tells the story of a man who desires his love who has died. He is visited by a talking bird that only says one word: "Nevermore." The man, so caught up in his imagination, believes the bird is telling him that he will never be reunited with his love. Poe has said "The Raven" discussed man's proclivity to torture himself.

➗ PROBABILITY

Complementary Events   The complimentary event is the probability that an event will not occur. This is represented as:

$$1 - P(A)$$

For example:

The probability of getting a green towel from the hamper is ¼. What is the probability of not getting a green towel?

$$P \text{ (Towel is not green)} = 1 - ¼ = ¾$$

And as you get more complex, it looks like this:

A hamper contains green and blue towels. The probability of getting a blue towel is $\frac{3}{5}$. What is the probability of getting a green towel?

A = Getting a blue towel
B = Getting a green towel
A and B are complementary events. Another way to say P(B) is to say P(A')
P(A')= P (Not getting a blue towel)

$$= 1 - P(A)$$
$$= 1 - \frac{3}{5}$$
$$= \frac{2}{5}$$

✳ STRING THEORY

Quantum Gravity   There are two basic laws in modern physics and they represent two very different areas of study: general relativity and quantum physics. General relativity studies nature on a grand scale, focusing on planets, galaxies, and the entire universe. Quantum physics, on the other hand, studies the smallest objects that can be found in nature. String theory is an attempt to unite these two very different theories, and any theory that does so is known as a theory of quantum gravity. It is believed that string theory has the most promise to unite the two.

◉ HEBREW

Modern Israeli Hebrew   In the 1880s, three types of Hebrew accents existed: Sephardi (Hispanic and Mediterranean), Ashkenazi (German), and that of Jews that were separate from both, living in Iraq, Yemen, Morocco, and Tunisia. The standard Hebrew that Eliezer Ben-Yehuda created was supposed to be based on Sephardi pronunciation and Mishnaic spelling. However, for many of the earliest speakers, Yiddish was their native tongue, and so idioms and literal translations were brought into the language from Yiddish. Instead of Sephardi phonology, the Ashkenazi style was used.

THE WRIGHT BROTHERS

The *Flyer* In 1902, the Wright brothers tested their new 32-foot-wingspan glider. Their research showed that if the glider had a moveable tail, it would actually balance the glider. The Wright brothers connected a tail to the wires responsible for warping the wings. After successful tests were performed in the wind tunnel, the brothers decided they would try to make a powered aircraft. They studied how propellers worked and created a motor and an aircraft that would be sturdy enough for the motor, as well as able to withstand the motor's vibrations. This new craft was known as the *Flyer*, and it weighed 700 pounds.

EDGAR ALLAN POE

His Death It is unknown what caused Edgar Allan Poe's death. What is known is that Poe died on October 7, 1849, in Baltimore. Days earlier, he was discovered outside of a bar, lying on a wooden plank, and brought to the hospital. Records of his hospitalization indicated that he was delirious, hallucinating, and was having tremors until he ultimately slipped into a coma. When he came out of the coma, he was at first calm, but then became increasingly delirious and combative. Four days later, he would be dead. The cause of death on his death certificate reads "congestion of the brain." Many believed this to be alcohol related; however, Poe had not had any alcohol six months prior to his death. Researchers today believe the cause of death was from rabies.

PROBABILITY

Probability and Area Problems involving probability can also have to do with finding the area of a particular geometric shape. For example:

If a dart is thrown at this circle, what is the probability it will land on the area that is shaded?

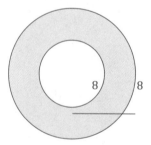

Total area: $\pi \times 16^2 = 804.25$
Area of not-shaded part: $\pi \times 8^2 = 201.06$
Area of shaded part: $804.25 - 201.06 = 603.19$, which rounded equals 603
So:

$$\frac{603}{804} = \frac{3}{4}$$

✳ STRING THEORY

Unification of Forces   There are four fundamental forces found in the universe that string theory attempts to unify: gravity, weak nuclear force, strong nuclear force, and electromagnetic force. Currently, these are four completely separate and different phenomena. String theorists believe that string theory is what unifies these forces. They believe that all four of these forces are described by strings that interacted with one another in the early stages of the universe, when energy levels were extremely high.

◑ HEBREW

Hebrew in Judaism   The Hebrew language has existed for over 2,000 years and little of the language has changed. Because of this fact, the language is deeply rooted in the Jewish religion, used for prayer and study, and the Torah, the Jewish bible, is written in Hebrew. Ashkenazi, Sephardi, and Mizrahi relate to the different pronunciations of the language, and though Modern Hebrew is established, all of these pronunciations are still used in religious ceremonies and rituals.

THE WRIGHT BROTHERS

The First Manned Flight   In order for the *Flyer* to gain enough speed to launch, the Wright brothers created a movable downhill track. On December 13, 1903, after only two tries (one of which resulted in the *Flyer* crashing), Orville Wright flew the *Flyer* for twelve seconds. This was the first piloted and powered flight in history to ever be a success. On November 9, 1904, the *Flyer II*, this time flown by Wilbur, flew for over five minutes.

EDGAR ALLAN POE

Griswold's Obituary   Rufus Wilmot Griswold was an anthologist, journalist, editor, and critic who worked with Poe and had a long-standing feud with the writer. When Poe died, Griswold wrote an obituary printed in the *New York Daily Tribune*, signed with the pseudonym Ludwig. The obituary claimed Poe was a reckless drunk, friendless, and a madman, and that he would be missed by few. In 1850, Griswold claimed to be the literary executor of a posthumous biography of Poe. The book is famous for its terribly inaccurate depiction of Poe as a drug addict and madman, and much of it was fabricated.

PROBABILITY

Coin Probability   To solve problems regarding probability with a coin, you have to use tree diagrams. These are very simple, because they are a visual way of showing all of the possible outcomes.

   If a coin is tossed 3 times, this is what it looks like:

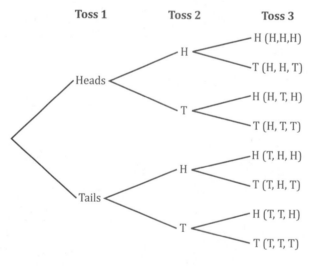

STRING THEORY

Supersymmetry   There are two types of particles in the universe: fermions and bosons. In string theory, it is hypothesized that there is a connection between these two types of particles called supersymmetry, and that for one to exist, the other has to also exist. The idea of supersymmetry was actually discovered separate from string theory, and in the mid-1970s, it was incorporated into the theory, turning it into super-string theory. Supersymmetry is still a theoretical assumption, and scientists have yet to observe the particles. Scientists believe supersymmetry to be the case because of how much energy it takes to make the particles, and that as energy spread as a result of the big bang, the particles would have collapsed into lower energies.

HEBREW

Writing System   The Hebrew alphabet, which is written from right to left, is an abjad. It consists of twenty-two letters, all consonants. The script is a "square script," and it is based on Aramaic script (or Ashurit). There is also a cursive version of the alphabet for writing. If vowels are necessary, diacritic marks are placed above or below the letters and sometimes consonants are used as vowels.

THE WRIGHT BROTHERS

The *Vin Fiz* On July 30, 1909, the United States government bought its first airplane. It was a Wright Brothers biplane, and it sold for $25,000 with an additional $5,000 because it had exceeded 40 miles per hour. In 1911, the Wright Brothers' *Vin Fiz* became the first airplane to travel coast to coast. Calbraith Perry Rogers purchased the plane from the Wright brothers and had only ninety minutes of training. The flight took a total of eighty-four days, stopped seventy times, and crash-landed so frequently that little of the original plane existed by the end of the journey.

EDGAR ALLAN POE

The Poe Toaster Beginning in 1949, 100 years after the death of Edgar Allan Poe, a mysterious man dressed in black with a white scarf started bringing three roses, a bottle of French cognac, and sometimes a note to the tombstone of Edgar Allan Poe on Poe's birthday. He did this every year until 1998, when it is believed he died and his son took over. Though there were attempts to discover the identity of the Poe Toaster, they never succeeded, and 2010 was the first year the Poe Toaster did not show up. He didn't appear the following year either, and it is believed that he too has passed away, perhaps ending a sixty-year tradition.

PROBABILITY

Mutually Exclusive Events If events cannot occur at the same time, that means they are mutually exclusive. For example, if you toss a coin and get heads, you cannot also have tails at the same time. If events are mutually exclusive, then the probability of having A or B is represented as $P(A) + P(B)$.

For example:

What is the probability of rolling a die and getting a 3 or a 4?

$$P(3) = \frac{1}{6}$$
$$P(4) = \frac{1}{6}$$
$$P(3) + P(4) = \frac{1}{6} + \frac{1}{6}$$
$$= \frac{2}{6}$$
$$= \frac{1}{3}$$

So, the probability of getting a 3 or 4 when the die is rolled is $\frac{1}{3}$.

STRING THEORY

Extra Dimensions Our universe currently has three dimensions of space, up/down, front/back, and left/right. String theory, however, can only make sense if there are more than three dimensions. And scientists have possible explanations for where these extra dimensions are. One explanation is that it is believed that there are six dimensions, and that they are curled up into sizes so small that we will never identify them. Another explanation states that the other dimensions are inaccessible because we are fixed on a three-dimensional brane, and those other dimensions extend from off of our brane.

Useful Hebrew Phrases   Here are some helpful Hebrew phrases to use when traveling to Israel (or maybe attending a service). Note that these are written phonetically.

Hello. *Shalom.*
Good morning. *Boker tov.*
Good afternoon. *Achar tzahara'im tovim.*
Good evening. *Erev tov.*
Pleased to meet you. *Na'im me'od.*
I don't understand. *Ani lo mevin* (when said by a man).
    Ani lo mevinah (when said by a woman).
How much is this? *Kama ze ole?*
Thank you. *Rav todot.*
Where's the toilet? *Eifo ha'sheirutim?*
Goodbye. *Lehitraot.*

1. **On December 13, 1903, Orville Wright flew the first piloted and powered flight for how long?**
   a. 45 seconds
   b. 12 minutes
   c. 12 seconds
   d. 45 minutes

2. **In order to successfully fly, the Wright brothers realized that they needed to base their models on:**
   a. Kites
   b. Small birds that rely on flapping their wings
   c. Large soaring birds
   d. Balloons

3. **Which of the following did literature of American Romanticism NOT focus on?**
   a. Nature
   b. Imagination
   c. Individuality
   d. Industrialism

4. **When Poe died, Rufus Wilmot Griswold wrote an obituary printed in the *New York Daily Tribune*, signed with what pseudonym?**
   a. Ludwig
   b. The Raven
   c. The Poe Toaster
   d. Baltimore

5. **Every letter from the word *cello* is written down on a piece of paper and put in a hat. What is the probability that you will pick an *l*?**
   a. $\frac{1}{5}$
   b. $\frac{2}{5}$
   c. $\frac{1}{2}$
   d. $\frac{1}{3}$

6. **A drawer contains green and red socks. The probability of getting a red sock is $\frac{3}{5}$. What is the probability of getting a green sock?**
   a. $\frac{2}{5}$
   b. $\frac{3}{5}$
   c. $\frac{4}{5}$
   d. $\frac{3}{10}$

7. **Which of the following is one of the fundamental forces found in the universe that string theory attempts to unify?**
   a. Gravity
   b. Electromagnetic force
   c. Strong and weak nuclear forces
   d. All of the above

8. **The two types of particles in the universe are:**
   a. Fermions and strings
   b. Bosons and strings
   c. Fermions and bosons
   d. Strings and branes

9. **Ashkenazi, Sephardi, and Mizrahi are examples of:**
   a. Different writing systems
   b. Different pronunciations
   c. Different dialects of Israel
   d. Different forms of Aramaic script

10. **Eliezer Ben-Yehuda is responsible for:**
    a. Making Hebrew the official language of Judaism
    b. Making Yiddish the official language of Israel
    c. Creating Sephardi
    d. Reviving the Hebrew spoken language

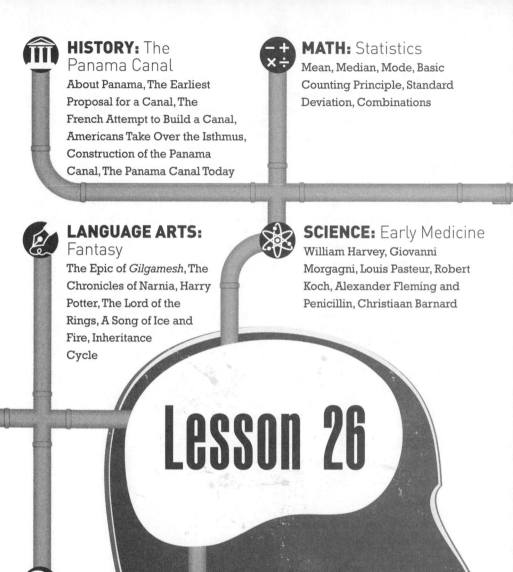

HISTORY: The Panama Canal
About Panama, The Earliest Proposal for a Canal, The French Attempt to Build a Canal, Americans Take Over the Isthmus, Construction of the Panama Canal, The Panama Canal Today

MATH: Statistics
Mean, Median, Mode, Basic Counting Principle, Standard Deviation, Combinations

LANGUAGE ARTS: Fantasy
The Epic of *Gilgamesh*, The Chronicles of Narnia, Harry Potter, The Lord of the Rings, A Song of Ice and Fire, Inheritance Cycle

SCIENCE: Early Medicine
William Harvey, Giovanni Morgagni, Louis Pasteur, Robert Koch, Alexander Fleming and Penicillin, Christiaan Barnard

Lesson 26

FOREIGN LANGUAGE: Yiddish
The Origins, The Writing System, The *Worms Mahzor*, World War II, Yiddish Today, Useful Yiddish Phrases

THE PANAMA CANAL

About Panama   Panama is the southeastern end of the isthmus that bridges North America and South America. It is also between the Pacific Ocean and the Atlantic Ocean (when standing on the highest point, the summit of Volcán Barú, you can actually see both oceans). In its entirety, it is slightly smaller than the state of South Carolina. From 1538 to 1821, Panama was part of the Spanish Empire.

FANTASY

The Epic of *Gilgamesh*   The Epic of *Gilgamesh*, which dates back to ancient Sumer, is not only the oldest fantasy story ever written, but it is the oldest story ever written. *Gilgamesh* was actually found inscribed on clay tablets. The story revolves around Gilgamesh, a king who embarks on a journey to slay a horrible beast, Humbaba, and searches for immortality. Gilgamesh was, in fact, based on a king of that time, the king of Uruk, who ruled during the twenty-sixth century B.C.

STATISTICS

Mean   In statistics, the mean is another way of saying the average. To find the average, you have to add up all of the numbers and then divide the sum by the amount of numbers that were just added together.

For example:

What is the mean of the following numbers?

$$9, 12, 14, 19, 20$$

First, you add all of the numbers together:

$$9 + 12 + 14 + 19 + 20 = 74$$

And then, since you added up 5 numbers, you will divide 74 by 5.

$$74 \div 5 = 14.8$$

EARLY MEDICINE

William Harvey   William Harvey discovered that blood flowed in one direction in the body, and that the flow of blood was continuous. He made the discovery in 1616; however, his findings were not published until 1628, in his book, *Exercitatio Anatomica de Motu Cordis et Sanguinis in Animalibus*. Not only did Harvey discover that blood flowed in one direction, but he also explained that the transformation of venous blood into arterial blood actually took place in the lungs (at the time, it was believed that this occurred in the liver).

YIDDISH

The Origins   Yiddish stems from the Ashkenazi Jewish community's borrowing of words from both German and Hebrew. Thus, it is a Germanic language, and the Sephardic Jewish community does not speak it. It is believed that Yiddish was first used around A.D. 900 to 1100, and it was the spoken language, never the written language, of the people. As centuries passed, Yiddish grew away from German, developing its own linguistic rules.

THE PANAMA CANAL

The Earliest Proposal for a Canal   The proposal to build a canal in Panama dates all the way back to 1534, when King Charles V of Spain, the Holy Roman Emperor, sought a route that would ease traveling between Spain and Peru and give the Spanish military an edge on the Portuguese. From 1788 to 1793, Spanish naval officer Alessandro Malaspina demonstrated that a canal would in fact be feasible, and he began making outlines for its construction. Other attempts to make use of the location were made in 1698 by Scotland, and in 1855 a railway was built across the isthmus. That same year, an employee of the U.S. government proposed a canal in a report.

FANTASY

The Chronicles of Narnia   The Chronicles of Narnia series is seven books written by C. S. Lewis. Included in that series are some of the best-known fantasy books of all time, such as *The Lion, the Witch and the Wardrobe*; *Prince Caspian*; and *The Magician's Nephew*. The books, written from 1949 to 1954, are set in the fictional world of Narnia, and throughout the entire series, the entire history of Narnia, from its beginnings to its end, are covered. The books often have children as the central characters, talking animals, magic, and good versus evil as a common theme.

STATISTICS

Median   The median is another way of saying the middle. Before you can do anything, the numbers have to be put in order of value.

For example: 6, 8, 10, 13, 16

Since there are five numbers, the number 10 is right in the middle, and that is our median.

However, when you have a median in between two numbers, you then take the mean of those numbers.

For example: 9, 14, 16, 17, 19, 21

The median is between 16 and 17, so you take the mean.

$$16 + 17 = 33$$
$$33 \div 2 = 16.5$$

EARLY MEDICINE

Giovanni Morgagni   Giovanni Morgagni is considered by many to be the father of pathology. His book *De Sedibus et Causis Morborum* (On the Sites and Causes of Diseases), published in 1761, is the foundation of pathological anatomy studies. Studying healthy and unhealthy bodies, Morgagni began to observe abnormalities and linked symptoms to them. The most famous discoveries to come out of this work involved myocardial degeneration, subacute bacterial endocarditis, and angina pectoris, and the impact of tuberculosis and blood clots. He also discovered that strokes came from alterations to cerebral blood vessels, and not a lesion of the brain as was believed.

YIDDISH

The Writing System   Yiddish is written with the Hebrew characters; however, the vowels are used differently. Unlike Hebrew, the Yiddish alphabet (known as *alef-beyz*) uses letters to represent vowels and pronunciation aids (if the word is originally Hebrew, however, it remains the same).

THE PANAMA CANAL

The French Attempt to Build a Canal   With the success of the Suez Canal, the French saw a canal as the best solution. They began constructing the canal on January 1, 1880, choosing Panama over Nicaragua because they believed it could best support a sea-level canal, meaning it had no locks (which raise and lower water levels in chambers in order to carry water over uneven terrain). Instead, this canal would maintain the same level all the way through and carve through the terrain. The construction was rushed and poorly planned, and the terrain proved too difficult to cut through with the machinery they had. The harsh weather and tropical fever left an estimated 22,000 people dead, and by 1888, the company funding the construction crashed, ending the building of the canal.

FANTASY

Harry Potter   One of the most successful and popular fantasy series of today is Harry Potter, written by J. K. Rowling. These seven books chronicle the story of a wizard, Harry, and his two friends as they go to Hogwarts School of Witchcraft and Wizardry, and Harry embarks on a quest to defeat the evil wizard, Lord Voldemort. One noticeable difference between the Harry Potter series and other fantasy novels, is that the world Harry lives in is actually the present day. Unlike C. S. Lewis's Narnia, Harry's world takes place in present-day London.

STATISTICS

Mode   The mode is the number that appears most frequently.
  For example: 1, 3, 5, 9, 5, 6, 5
  First, you put it in order of value: 1, 3, 5, 5, 5, 6, 9
  The mode would be 5 because it appears the most.
  You can have several modes in any problem. If there are no modes, then you put the numbers into groups.
  For example: 1, 3, 4, 11, 13, 21, 22
  There are no modes, so you group accordingly:
  0–9: 3 values; 10–20: 2 values; 20–30: 2 values

EARLY MEDICINE

Louis Pasteur   Louis Pasteur is a name that is forever associated with changing the medical world. Pasteur is responsible for discovering the existence of germs. In 1856, a man from an alcohol factory approached Pasteur, the Dean of the Faculty of Science at the University of Lille, with a question about why his vats of fermented beer kept turning sour. After analyzing samples under a microscope, Pasteur found microorganisms which he believed were responsible. Though initially scoffed at by his peers, Pasteur proved that diseases were caused by these microorganisms, and in 1881, Pasteur announced that he had discovered a way to weaken anthrax germs so that a vaccine could be created.

YIDDISH

The *Worms Mahzor*   A blessing found in a prayer book from 1272, the *Worms Mahzor*, is the oldest document of Yiddish that was embedded in a Hebrew text. This is significant for a number of reasons, one of which is that it shows that the Yiddish of this time closely resembled Middle High German and had Hebrew words infused into it. From the fourteenth and fifteenth centuries, poetry and songs written in Yiddish started appearing. The *Dukus Horant* is the oldest example of an epic poem written entirely in Yiddish.

🏛 THE PANAMA CANAL

Americans Take Over the Isthmus   In 1902, Congress gave the authority to purchase the assets of the French canal company, but it required that the United States and Colombia first form a treaty for the control and use of the canal. As negotiations with Colombia failed, the United States supported Panama's fight for independence. In the Hay-Bunau-Varilla Treaty, Panama gave the United States the rights to the area of the canal without having a Spanish translation. President Theodore Roosevelt backed a lock-based model for the canal, and in 1906, the area was cleared of yellow fever.

🍃 FANTASY

The Lord of the Rings   In 1937, Oxford professor J. R. R. Tolkien wrote a book called *The Hobbit*, which was set in a fictional Middle Earth where wizards, elves, trolls, and hobbits lived. In 1954, a trilogy, and a sequel to *The Hobbit*, was published. It was known as The Lord of the Rings. The trilogy focuses on the events following those found in *The Hobbit* and a journey to destroy a powerful ring that could destroy the world if in the wrong hands. Frodo Baggins is the main character, and he is joined by his friend and two cousins as they embark on a journey to save the world.

➕ STATISTICS

Basic Counting Principle   The basic counting principle is very simple and is used to determine the number of outcomes. In essence, the principle states that when you have A ways to do something, and B ways to do another thing, then doing both would equal A × B.

For example:

If there are 5 types of ice cream and 2 types of cones, then there are 10 (5 × 2) different combinations you can have. This problem can also be written out with a tree diagram you saw earlier in the book.

An important thing to note about this rule is that it only works if the objects or things are independent from one another.

⚛ EARLY MEDICINE

Robert Koch   Building on the work that Louis Pasteur had started, Robert Koch is most known for his involvement in anthrax and tuberculosis. While Pasteur was convinced that the microbes were the causes of disease, he was never successful in proving it. Koch however, was able to prove it. Whereas Pasteur was a research scientist, Koch was a doctor and had a great depth of knowledge relating to the human body. While studying anthrax, Koch realized that microbes from anthrax created spores that lived in the dead animal's body. These spores then turned into germs, spreading the disease. Koch would then go on to discover the germs that caused tuberculosis, proving that it was not caused by "bad air."

🗨 YIDDISH

World War II   Prior to World War II, there were 11 to 13 million Yiddish speakers. The extensive toll on the Jewish community from the Holocaust, however, led to a dramatic decline. Five million Yiddish speakers died as a result of the Holocaust (around 85 percent of all of the Jews that died). Those Yiddish speakers that did survive the Holocaust either migrated or assimilated into other countries, and with the Zionist movement believing in a monolingual approach, use of Yiddish declined.

THE PANAMA CANAL

Construction of the Panama Canal   Lieutenant Colonel George Washington Goethals was chosen to become the canal's new chief engineer, and he split the work up into thirds: the Atlantic Division, the Central Division, and the Pacific Division. The Panamanian Railroad was a great help for the Americans, as were rock drills, steam shovels, and dynamite, without which the job would have been impossible. The extreme climate and horrible accidents gave it the name "Hell's Gorge." The three-part lock division Goethals created allowed for two-way traffic; the locks are powered by electricity.

FANTASY

A Song of Ice and Fire   A Song of Ice and Fire is an ongoing series of books written by George R. R. Martin, first published in 1991. The books take place on a continent called Westeros, and a land mass east of Westeros called Essos. The main stories found in each of these books relate to a civil war in Westeros, the threat of a race of creatures known as the Others, and the quest of an exiled daughter of a murdered king to reclaim the throne. The books are told from the points of view of several characters, and all of the books are in the third person. The first book has recently been turned into a television show for HBO, *Game of Thrones*.

STATISTICS

Standard Deviation   Standard deviation, represented by σ, is the measurement of how spread out the data is. To find the standard deviation, you take the square root of the variance. The variance is the average of the squared deviations that came from the mean. To find the variance requires a few steps, but it is actually quite simple. You first must find the mean. From there, subtract the mean from each number and then square those numbers. Then, find the average of those squared numbers.

EARLY MEDICINE

Alexander Fleming and Penicillin   Alexander Fleming accidentally discovered penicillin, one of the most powerful antibiotics, on September 3, 1928. While cleaning his office, Professor Fleming found a glass plate from research he had been conducting. The plate had been coated with staphylococcus bacteria, and mold in the shape of a ring was growing on it. Around the ring, the plate was free of the staphylococcus bacteria. Fleming concluded that a substance in the mold was responsible for killing the bacteria. This mold was *Penicillium notatum*. Ten years later, the substance within the mold was found; penicillin.

YIDDISH

Yiddish Today   It is unknown how many Yiddish speakers exist today. In 2009 it was estimated that there were 1,762,320 Yiddish speakers, with one-third of that population residing in the United States; however, other reports stated the number was less than 200,000 in the United States. Some countries, including Russia, Sweden, Lithuania, and Moldova, still have Yiddish-speaking communities. In 1999, the Swedish Parliament gave Yiddish legal status as an official minority language, and government documents are published in the language.

THE PANAMA CANAL

The Panama Canal Today   In 1979, the Panama Canal Treaty went into effect, granting Panama complete control of the canal after twenty years. The Panama Canal Authority took full control of the waterway on December 31, 1999. The age of the canal and the volume of traffic are beginning to take its toll on the canal, and it has become an international traffic jam of trade. In 2006, Panamanians voted to modernize the canal, and a larger set of locks will double its capacity.

 FANTASY

Inheritance Cycle   The Inheritance Cycle is a series of ongoing books written by Christopher Paolini. The first book in the series, *Eragon*, was written by Paolini when he was just fifteen years old. After spending a year working on it, the book was self-published by his parents, and upon being discovered, was republished by a major publishing company. The books are set in Alagaësia, with the main character being Eragon, a teenage orphan, and his dragon, Saphira. The books follow Eragon as he becomes a member of the Dragon Riders and attempts to defeat the evil king who had killed past Dragon Riders fearing they would take the throne.

 STATISTICS

Combinations   For mean, median, mode, and standard deviation, you have had to put numbers in value order. But sometimes the value order is not important. When value order is not important, it is called a combination, and this is represented as $C(n,r)$. The letter n represents the number of things selected at r. This also equals $P(n,r)/r!$

For example:

If four shirts are taken from a group of eight shirts and you want to figure out how many combinations of four there could be, you would do:

$$P(8,4)/4! = (8 \times 7 \times 6 \times 5)/(4 \times 3 \times 2 \times 1) = 1680/24 = 70 \text{ combinations}$$

 EARLY MEDICINE

Christiaan Barnard   On December 3, 1967, Christiaan Barnard became the first surgeon to perform a human heart transplant. Born in South Africa, Barnard worked as a senior cardiothoracic surgeon in Cape Town. The operation lasted five hours, and even though the patient would die eighteen days later of double pneumonia, Barnard's operation was considered a success and was celebrated around the world. He introduced a new kind of surgery that has since become routine. In 1974, Barnard performed the first ever heterotopic, or "double heart" transplant, in which the patient effectively has two hearts.

 YIDDISH

Useful Yiddish Phrases   Here are some helpful Yiddish phrases to use. Note that these are spelled out phonetically:

Hello. *A gutn tog.*
Good morning. *Gutn morgn.*
Good afternoon/evening. *A gut ovnt.*
Good night. *A gute nakht.*
Pleased to meet you. *Es frayt mikh dikh tsu kenen.*
Cheers! *Zayt gesunt!*

Have a nice day. *Hot a gutn tog.*
Excuse me. *Zayt moykhl.*
Thank you. *Nishto farvos.*
How much is this? *Vi tayer iz dos?*
Where's the toilet? *Vu iz der tualett?*
I don't understand. *Ikh farshtey dos nit.*
Goodbye. *Biz shpeter.*

1. **Which of the following allowed the Americans to perform construction on the Panama Canal that the French did not have access to?**
   a. Rock drills
   b. Steam shovels
   c. Dynamite
   d. All of the above

2. **Which of the following describes Panama?**
   a. Panama is the southeastern end of the isthmus that bridges North America and South America.
   b. Panama is between the Pacific Ocean and the Atlantic Ocean.
   c. Panama is the size of Texas.
   d. A and B.

3. **Who wrote the Chronicles of Narnia?**
   a. J. R. R. Tolkien
   b. George R. R. Martin
   c. J. K. Rowling
   d. C. S. Lewis

4. **Who wrote A Song of Ice and Fire?**
   a. J. R. R. Tolkien
   b. George R. R. Martin
   c. J. K. Rowling
   d. C. S. Lewis

5. **What is the mean in the following number set: 6, 7, 9, 11**
   a. 8.25
   b. 4
   c. 7
   d. 7.5

6. **What is the median in the following number set: 9, 12, 12, 13, 14, 15, 29**
   a. 14.9
   b. 13
   c. 13.5
   d. 12.5

7. **Who discovered penicillin?**
   a. Christiaan Barnard
   b. Robert Koch
   c. Alexander Fleming
   d. Giovanni Morgagni

8. **What is Louis Pasteur responsible for?**
   a. Performing the first open heart transplant
   b. Discovering germs
   c. Discovering the cause of tuberculosis
   d. Discovering that blood flows in one direction in the body

9. **Yiddish is a combination of:**
   a. Hebrew and German
   b. German and Russian
   c. Hebrew and Russian
   d. Russian and Polish

10. **Which of the following was a prayer book that contained the oldest Yiddish writing?**
    a. Ashkenazi
    b. Sephardic
    c. *Worms Mahzor*
    d. Alef-beyz

Lesson 27

THE GREAT DEPRESSION

Economic Boom   Following World War I, America faced a time of economic expansion and the stock market had become increasingly popular. Many saw the stock market as an easy way to get rich, and as stock prices rose, people viewed stocks as a safe way to invest. Stocks were being purchased on margin, meaning people didn't have enough to actually pay for the stock, so they would pay 10 to 20 percent and the broker would pay the rest. Not only did individual people put their money in the stock market, but even companies and banks invested money in the stock market.

ALICE IN WONDERLAND

About "Lewis Carroll"   Lewis Carroll (1832–1898) was the pen name of a shy man whose real name was Charles Lutwidge Dodgson. Dodgson was a math professor at Oxford who was partially deaf and had physical deformities and a stammer. His appearance made him uncomfortable and shy around adults, but around children he was very different. Around kids, Dodgson was full of humor, highly animated, and most of all, a great storyteller. In 1856, Dodgson became close with the children of Henry George Liddell, a classics scholar who had accepted a position at one of Oxford's colleges. Liddell's daughter, Alice, would become the inspiration for Dodgson's greatest work. He would often take the children on boat rides, entertaining them with fantastical stories. Ten years later, these stories would be published.

GAME THEORY

What Is Game Theory?   Game theory is also known as the theory of social situations. Essentially, game theory involves determining the right strategies to use in situations while other competing strategies are also being used at the same time. Game theory also involves understanding how groups react. Game theory is a very useful tool, especially in economics. It can be used on a personal level, in business, and even at the national level. The assumption is that at all times, decisions made by the agents are rational. Of course, this is not always the case. Even when behavior is irrational, however, game theory can still lead to interesting findings about human nature. Though it might sound complex, game theory is actually fairly simple to understand.

ARCHIMEDES

About Archimedes   Archimedes of Syracuse was a physicist, astronomer, mathematician, inventor, and engineer, from Syracuse, Sicily, who lived from 287 to 212 B.C. He is considered to be one of the greatest mathematicians of all time, on a par with Sir Isaac Newton. Though little is known about his early life, he studied in Alexandria, attending the school Euclid had established, before returning to Syracuse. His impact on the world has been incredibly long-lasting, and his inventions and principles in math and science can still be found today. Among his most famous inventions are the catapult and the compound pulley, and he made several important contributions to the lever.

ARABIC

The Origins   Arabic is a Semitic language in the Afro-Asiatic group; however, it has preserved much of its Proto-Semitic (the predecessor to the Semitic languages) qualities. While many Semitic languages died, Arabic flourished with the rise and spread of Islam and the use of Arabic in the Qur'an. The earliest form of written Arabic appeared in the fourth century A.D., and by the seventh century, it appeared in the Qur'an.

THE GREAT DEPRESSION

Black Tuesday   On October 24, 1929, what would become known as Black Thursday, the New York Stock Exchange crashed and large amounts of people began selling their stocks. Black Thursday is considered the beginning of the Great Depression. Five days later, Tuesday the 29th, was the worst day in the history of the stock market. Panic spread and people could not sell fast enough. With everyone selling and nobody buying, stocks plummeted. That day, known as Black Tuesday, more than 16.4 million shares of stock were been sold. The next day, the stock market was closed.

ALICE IN WONDERLAND

Alice's Adventures in Wonderland   *Alice's Adventures in Wonderland* tells the story of a young girl named Alice who one day while sitting by the river sees a rabbit run past her talking about how late he is. As he goes down the rabbit hole, Alice follows him. At the bottom, Alice finds a drink labeled "drink me." As she drinks, she begins to shrink, and soon she enters a wonderland full of talking animals and interesting creatures. Each time she eats or drinks, she changes size. When the Queen of Hearts accuses the Knave of Hearts of stealing tarts, Alice tries to help out, but instead, she gets accused. The book ends with Alice back on the riverbank, awake, leaving us to wonder whether it was all just a dream or not.

GAME THEORY

Cooperative Game Theory   There are two types of game theory: cooperative and noncooperative. The main difference between the two types is found in the independence given to the players of each. In cooperative game theory, players do not know what will happen outside of what will happen with their own decisions, but they rely on the cooperation of the other players in deals or contracts. In essence, they are making decisions based entirely on what they know of their choices. An example of a cooperative game would be if there is a person willing to sell an object, and there are two different and unrelated people wanting to buy that object at their own prices. If there is bargaining between two of the three people, then there is cooperation.

ARCHIMEDES

The Archimedes Heat Ray   Archimedes invented many objects, though none have been as controversial as his supposed heat ray. In the second century A.D., it was written that Archimedes created a device that had the ability to destroy ships with fire. Anthemius of Tralles claims that he did so using glass. The Archimedes Heat Ray used mirrors that would focus the sun's light onto a ship, making the boat catch on fire. There have been many attempts at recreating the Archimedes Heat Ray. A test in 1973 resulted in an immediate explosion of the test boat; however, it is believed this was due to its tar paint. In 2005, students from MIT conducted a test that resulted in small flames, but only after an extended period of time. The Archimedes Heat Ray has been tested numerous times on the popular show *Mythbusters*, and each time it has been "busted."

ARABIC

Classical Arabic   Classical Arabic is the language that is featured in the Qur'an and classical literature, and is based on the medieval dialects of Arabic. Classical Arabic is considered a sacred language and is only used for prayer. Of the Old North Arabian languages, Classical Arabic is the only one to survive. Many symbols featured in the language are absent in the present form of Arabic.

THE GREAT DEPRESSION

Hoovervilles   Hoovervilles were the names given to the shantytowns (named after President Hoover) that formed coast to coast in the cities of the United States. The Great Depression led to widespread poverty. From 1929 to 1933, over 100,000 businesses failed and many people were left homeless with nowhere else to stay but in these shantytowns. The largest Hooverville was found in New York City's Central Park. When Hoover's term ended in 1933, unemployment was at 13 million.

ALICE IN WONDERLAND

Through the Looking Glass   *Through the Looking Glass* continues Alice's story at a later point in time. At the beginning of the story, Alice comes to the realization that she can step into the mirror, leading to an alternate world. There, she finds a book that is written backward. As she holds it up to the mirror, she reads a poem "Jabberwocky" (another one of Lewis Carroll's most famous works). As she leaves the house, she comes across several new characters, including Tweedledee and Tweedledum, the White Queen, and Humpty Dumpty (who explains "Jabberwocky" to Alice).

GAME THEORY

Noncooperative Game Theory   Noncooperative game theory involves making a decision based on the participation of the other players, but without any sort of cooperation in the form of deals or bargains. Instead, decisions are made independently. Noncooperative game theory is about working from what is known about the other players to achieve your own goals. In noncooperative game theory, all of the other players' moves and options are known by everyone else. For example, if a major retailer wanted to make a decision regarding a product, they might check with their competition to see if the decision is worth it.

ARCHIMEDES

The Golden Crown   Archimedes was approached by King Hiero II, who suspected that his goldsmith had replaced some of the gold in his new crown with silver. The king asked Archimedes to figure out if this was the case, and because it was for the gods, he was not to damage it in any way. Archimedes realized that the density of the crown could be measured by placing it in a tub of water. If the crown was made of other materials, the density would be lower than that of gold. By doing this test, it is said that Archimedes was able to conclude that the crown had been made of materials other than gold. Whether this is the method he actually used has been called into question, however, due to the fact that the differences in density are so slight (the water would have risen in centimeters).

ARABIC

Modern Arabic   Modern Arabic is the standard Arabic language of today and it is based on Classical Arabic. The Arabic language is diglossic. Essentially, what this means is that Arabic speakers speak two languages: the dialect that they speak in, and then the codified and universal form of Arabic that is used on a larger scale for things like writing, literature, television, film, and media. Modern Arabic is also used when two people of different Arabic dialects speak to one another. The spoken dialects of Arabic are rarely written.

THE GREAT DEPRESSION

The Dust Bowl   During World War I, the farms of the Southern plains in the United States were extremely profitable. The demand for wheat and corn was high, and farmers produced food for the homeland and abroad. In the 1930s, however, a combination of events would lead to the Dust Bowl. The farming practices, with much of the land deeply planted, plowed, and farmed, began to take their toll. The 1930s saw a great drought that lasted years (the worst in the history of the United States), and with the heavily plowed land, the once-prosperous agriculture was now devastated. Inches of dried soil would get swept up by the wind, darkening the skies with dust that would engulf entire towns.

ALICE IN WONDERLAND

Symbolism   Lewis Carroll's books feature quite a lot of symbolism, most significantly, the loss of childhood innocence that everyone must face. Alice's body constantly changing shape, creating a great amount of discomfort for her, is actually symbolic of puberty and the changes of the body. Throughout the books, Alice is constantly given puzzles to solve that seem completely unsolvable. This is to show that life is always full of challenges and one's expectations and the reality are not the same thing, that sometimes life is frustrating.

GAME THEORY

Decision Theory   Decision theory involves a single-person game and focuses on the forming of one's beliefs and the making of decisions that are goal oriented. Normative decision theory concentrates on how one should make a decision, and descriptive decision theory concentrates on how a decision is actually made. Decision theory is particularly useful for economists, and a popular use of decision theory states that with risky alternatives, the preferences can be seen as the maximization of the anticipated value of the money income.

ARCHIMEDES

The Archimedes Screw   Archimedes was commissioned by King Hiero II to build a huge ship, so large that it would begin taking on water, and Archimedes's solution was the creation of one of his most famous inventions: the Archimedes screw. The screw was initially used as an irrigation device and for pumping water out of ships. On the outside, the device appears as a cylinder. Inside the cylinder, a spiral blade the size of the cylinder turns. Water enters through the bottom of the cylinder, and as the spiral blade turns, the water gets raised to the top. The Archimedes screw is still being used to this day, often for pumping grains and coal.

ARABIC

Colloquial Arabic   Colloquial Arabic refers to the spoken form of the language, of which there are several different dialects. The two main divisions, however, lie between the Arabic language spoken in the Middle East and that spoken in North Africa. Dialects of Arabic are so different due in part to the various nations of the Muslim world and the influence of the languages that were spoken in these lands prior to Arabic. The five major dialects are Egyptian Arabic, Maghrebi Arabic, Mesopotamian Arabic, Levantine Arabic, and Gulf Arabic.

THE GREAT DEPRESSION

The New Deal   When Franklin Delano Roosevelt became president, he focused on reforming the nation and set forth the New Deal (a phrase he coined during his speech accepting the nomination). The New Deal was split up into two phases, one from 1933 to 1934, and the other from 1935 to 1941. The first phase concentrated on regulating agriculture and business. During the first phase, programs like the National Recovery Administration, the Agricultural Adjustment Administration, and the Federal Communications Commission were established. The second phase focused more on the working class and social legislation. It is during the second phase that Social Security was created.

ALICE IN WONDERLAND

The Significance   Lewis Carroll's work was groundbreaking for the time. Other Victorian children's books focused on giving rules for children to live by. But Lewis Carroll's stories of Alice's adventures embraced silliness and fantasy. The *Alice in Wonderland* series showed for the first time that children's books did not have to include morals or teach any sort of lessons. They showed that children books could just be fun and allow children to use their imagination and embrace nonsense and fantasy.

GAME THEORY

General Equilibrium Theory   General equilibrium theory is an economic theory first proposed in the 1870s, with its modern form created in the 1950s. In economies with multiple markets, general equilibrium theory is used to study supply and demand to show that there is equilibrium in the prices. General equilibrium theory is usually used on a macroeconomic scale for such things as analyzing stock prices, tax policy, and international trade. The private sector uses the general equilibrium theory as a model. To analyze individual markets, partial equilibrium theory is used.

ARCHIMEDES

The Claw of Archimedes   The Claw of Archimedes was a weapon created by Archimedes to protect the city wall of Syracuse. Though the actual appearance of the claw is unknown, it is believed the device was a crane that featured a grappling hook. These hooks would connect to enemy ships and either lift the boats entirely out of the water, or simply shake them enough to capsize. The claw was used during the Second Punic War, as the Romans attacked Syracuse.

ARABIC

The Writing System   Like Hebrew, the Arabic writing system is an abjad (meaning it only consists of consonants) with twenty-eight letters. While words are written from right to left, numbers are written from left to right. The system of writing is derived from Aramaic script, and, following the Latin alphabet, the Arabic alphabet is the second most widely used alphabet in the world. All of the letters have four allographs, meaning conditional forms. The forms of letters change based on where they are in the word (whether they are at the beginning, middle, or end).

THE GREAT DEPRESSION

World War II   Though Roosevelt's New Deal reform certainly helped, the Great Depression did not come to a complete end until the beginning of World War II. The amount of unemployment decreased by 7,050,000 in three years, and the amount of people serving in the military increased by 8,590,000. While the men fought overseas, women worked in the factories to produce weapons and materials for the war. Factories where vacuum cleaners had been made were now producing machine guns. By 1943, over 2 million women were employed in factories.

ALICE IN WONDERLAND

History of Publication and Beyond   When the book first came out in 1865, it received very poor reviews, with many finding it too ludicrous. Critics found the only thing praiseworthy about the book to be the illustrations. In 1866, Carroll approached his publisher about a sequel, and by the time it came out, the first book had developed a following. In the early 1860s, the Liddell family broke away from Carroll suddenly. Some say Carroll and Henry George Liddell had a dispute over work, while others believe Carroll's relationship with Alice was questionable. Though there is no hard evidence, Henry George Liddell and his wife destroyed Carroll's early letters to Alice, and the source of the split may never be known.

GAME THEORY

The Prisoner's Dilemma   One of the most famous examples of game theory is the prisoner's dilemma. In this game, two people are suspected of committing a crime and brought into separate interrogation rooms. If they both keep quiet, they can be put in jail for five years. The suspects are offered a deal: If one confesses and the other does not, the confessor will be let go and the other suspect will get twenty years. If they both confess, they will each get ten years in jail. The best strategy to take in this situation is for both to confess and get the ten year sentence, because the individual players do not know what the other person will do and have to think of their best interests. Though ten years is not the greatest outcome of the situation, strategically, it makes the most sense.

ARCHIMEDES

Work in Mathematics   Archimedes made several important discoveries in mathematics, especially in geometry. He is responsible for discovering how to find the volume of a sphere, which led him to discovering the value of pi, and how to create the formula to find the area of the space underneath a curve. Archimedes discovered the principle of buoyancy (as showcased by the golden crown study), and many believe him to be the real inventor of integral calculus (2,000 years earlier than when Isaac Newton created it).

ARABIC

Useful Arabic Phrases   Here are some helpful Standard Arabic phrases to use when traveling to an Arabic-speaking country. Note that these are spelled out phonetically:

Hello. *As-salām 'alaykum.*
Good morning. *ṣabāḥul khayr.*
Good afternoon/evening. *Masā' al-khayr.*
Good night. *Tuṣbiḥ 'alā khayr.*
I don't understand. *Lā afham.*

Excuse me. *Al-ma'dirah.*
How much is this? *Bikam hādhā?* (from a man) *Bikam hādihi?* (from a woman)
Where's the toilet? *Ayn al- ḥammām?*
Goodbye. *Ilā al-liqā'.*

1. **Which of the following contributed to the crash of the stock market?**
   a. Many saw the stock market as an easy way to get rich, and as stock prices rose, people viewed them as a safe way to invest.
   b. Stocks were being purchased on margin.
   c. Companies and banks also invested money into the stock market.
   d. All of the above.

2. **Which of the following is true?**
   a. Social Security was set up by the FCC to create jobs.
   b. The first phase of the New Deal concentrated on regulating agriculture and business.
   c. World War II made the Great Depression worse.
   d. The Dust Bowl was a series of regulations and reforms.

3. **What is one example of symbolism found in *Alice's Adventures in Wonderland*?**
   a. Alice's body changing shapes throughout the story
   b. Alice following the rabbit
   c. Humpty Dumpty explaining the poem
   d. The Queen of Hearts accusing Alice of stealing the tarts

4. **What made the *Alice in Wonderland* series so groundbreaking?**
   a. The stories embraced silliness and nonsense.
   b. They did not feature a moral or lesson at the end.
   c. They featured material that was not age-appropriate.
   d. A and B.

5. **Which of the following accurately describes general equilibrium theory?**
   a. A single-person game theory that focuses on the forming of one's beliefs
   b. A theory where a player does not know what will happen outside of their own decisions, but they rely on the cooperation of the other players with deals or contracts
   c. A theory that is used to study supply and demand in multiple markets
   d. A theory where two people are suspected of committing a crime and brought into separate interrogation rooms where they are each given options to choose from to get a lighter prison sentence

6. **In the prisoner's dilemma, what outcome makes the most sense strategically?**
   a. Confess to the crime
   b. Keep quiet
   c. Deny you did the crime
   d. Wait for your lawyer

7. **Which of the following inventions of Archimedes is still used today?**
   a. The claw of Archimedes
   b. The golden crown
   c. The Archimedes screw
   d. The Archimedes heat ray

8. **The Claw of Archimedes was used as:**
   a. An irrigation system
   b. A weapon to protect Syracuse's city walls
   c. A buoyancy test
   d. A weapon to set enemy ships on fire

9. **Which of the following is true?**
   a. Classical Arabic is spoken today; Colloquial Arabic is found in the Qur'an.
   b. Classical Arabic is spoken today, and it's the same language found in the Qur'an.
   c. Modern Arabic is found in the Qur'an and Classical Arabic is spoken today.
   d. Modern Arabic is written today and Classical Arabic is found in the Qur'an.

10. **How do you say "Hello" in Arabic?**
    a. As-salām 'alaykum.
    b. Al-ma'dirah.
    c. Lā afham.
    d. Masā' al-khayr.

ANSWER KEY: d, b, a, d, c, a, c, b, d, a

HISTORY: World War II

Invasion of Poland, Invasion of Russia, Pearl Harbor, The Holocaust, The Battle of Normandy (D-Day), End of the War

MATH: Knot Theory

What Are Mathematical Knots?, The Reidemeister Moves, Why Knot Theory Is Important, Knot Polynomials, Adding Knots, Tabulating Knots

LANGUAGE ARTS: Science Fiction

Jules Verne, H. G. Wells, Robert Heinlein, Arthur C. Clarke, Isaac Asimov, Ray Bradbury

SCIENCE: The Earth's Spheres

Lithosphere, Hydrosphere, Cryosphere, Biosphere, Atmosphere, Celestial Sphere

Lesson 28

FOREIGN LANGUAGE: Sign Language

The Origins, About Deafness, Relationship with Oral Languages, Different Types of Sign Language, Written Form, Sign Language with Primates

WORLD WAR II

Invasion of Poland On August 23, 1939, Hitler and Stalin agreed to the Nazi-Soviet Pact. The invasion of Poland was originally set for August 26, but Mussolini told Hitler that Italy was not yet ready for war, so the deadline was extended. On September 1, 1939, Adolf Hitler's Germany invaded and defeated Poland within weeks, in what was the first military engagement of World War II. Hitler believed this invasion would lead to a quick victory in this war. On September 3, Britain declared war on Germany.

SCIENCE FICTION

Jules Verne Jules Verne is one of the most well-known and celebrated science fiction authors of all time, and he is generally regarded as the "father of science fiction." His works include the classics *Twenty Thousand Leagues Under the Sea*, *A Journey to the Center of the Earth*, and *Around the World in Eighty Days*. Verne, a Frenchman, lived from 1828 to 1905, and the first English-language translations of his work appeared in the 1870s.

KNOT THEORY

What Are Mathematical Knots? In mathematics, a knot is a one-dimensional closed curve, or loop, that does not intersect, and that exists in a three-dimensional world. More than one loop is known as a link, and the separate loops are called components. The area where the loops cross over is known as the crossing. The unknot, or trivial knot, is the simplest form of a knot, and this is a loop with zero crossings. If two knots can move around without cutting and still look the same, these knots are considered the same. This process of moving a knot without cutting is known as ambient isotopy.

THE EARTH'S SPHERES

Lithosphere The lithosphere is the crust that covers the entire Earth. From the top of mountains to the ocean floor is all considered the lithosphere. The lithosphere consists of the crust, which is solid, hard, and made of minerals, and the uppermost mantle. The lithosphere has an extremely uneven surface and is around 100 kilometers thick. Tectonic plates, which cause earthquakes when they shift, are also included in the lithosphere.

SIGN LANGUAGE

The Origins The origins of sign language can be traced back to ancient Greece, where Socrates believed it only made sense for the deaf to communicate with their hands and other body parts. In 1520, Pedro Ponce de Léon created a system based on gestures to educate the deaf, mostly working with a family in Spain. From 1715 to 1780, Léon's system spread across Europe, incorporating handshakes to represent sounds. In the late eighteenth century, the National Institution for Deaf-Mutes was established in France, with the intention of instructing the deaf. In 1817, Thomas Gallaudet, an American who studied with Laurent Clerc in France, brought the sign language to America with Clerc, establishing the Connecticut Asylum for the Education and Instruction of Deaf and Dumb Persons. Clerc is responsible for much of the work that would lead to American Sign Language (ASL).

🏛 WORLD WAR II

Invasion of Russia   Hitler wished to end the war swiftly, and knew an invasion of England was not the best way to go about it. Instead, he broke his pact with Stalin and invaded the Soviet Union. The German army invaded Russia on June 22, 1941, with a devastating blitzkrieg known as Operation Barbarossa. Within one week, 150,000 Soviet soldiers had been killed or wounded. On July 3, Stalin implemented the scorched-earth policy, which required that all facilities and supplies be destroyed before retreating so the Germans could not use them. Roads, bridges, factories, and fields of crops were destroyed, slowing the German advance. The campaign lasted much longer than Hitler had anticipated, and the German armies could not withstand the Russian winter, giving the Soviets the advantage.

🌿 SCIENCE FICTION

H. G. Wells   H. G. Wells was dramatically influential in the world of science fiction literature. Among his most famous works are *The Invisible Man*, *The Island of Dr. Moreau*, *The Time Machine*, and *The War of the Worlds*. *The Time Machine*, written in 1895, is considered one of the first modern science fiction novels. Wells's *The War of the Worlds* was so influential that in 1938 Orson Welles and the Mercury Theatre on the Air adapted it into a radio program. The program, about an alien invasion, inspired panic in listeners who feared an actual alien invasion was occurring.

➗ KNOT THEORY

The Reidemeister Moves   In 1932, German mathematician Kurt Werner Friedrich Reidemeister worked with knot diagrams (that is, pictures of knots), and discovered a set of three moves that could make any knot diagram into any other type of knot diagram with the same knot. He came up with three rules: a strand could twist and untwist; one strand could be placed over the other strand (also known as the poke move); and a strand could be moved over or under a crossing (also known as a slide move).

⚛ THE EARTH'S SPHERES

Hydrosphere   The hydrosphere is 10 to 20 kilometers thick, and consists of all of the water found on Earth. This can be in solid, liquid, or gaseous form. The hydrosphere includes parts of the lithosphere and extends upward into the atmosphere for about 12 kilometers. A small amount of the hydrosphere is fresh water, meaning it is not salt water. This includes rivers, streams, and bodies of water that are precipitated into the atmosphere. The majority of fresh water, however, is frozen. Salt water makes up 97 percent of the Earth's water. As the salt water collected in the deep valleys of the surface of the Earth, oceans were created.

🖐 SIGN LANGUAGE

About Deafness   When there is a complete loss of the ability to hear out of either one or both ears, it is known as deafness. Deafness can be caused by a number of factors. It can be inherited, or caused by diseases (such as meningitis), complications at birth, the presence of ototoxic drugs, and exposure to extreme noise. Deafness can appear at birth (known as congenital deafness), or come on either gradually or suddenly. There are two main types of deafness: conductive (when transmission of sound waves is interfered with) and sensorineural (when nerve impulses cannot reach the brain). In the fourth century B.C. it was believed that deaf people were also unable to speak, and thus unteachable, and this stigma lasted with the deaf community for centuries.

WORLD WAR II

Pearl Harbor   The attack on the U.S. Naval base at Pearl Harbor is what brought America into World War II. The Imperial Japanese Navy led a surprise attack at Pearl Harbor on December 7, 1941. The Japanese launched two attacks, sinking four U.S. battleships, killing 2,400 Americans, and wounding another 1,200. The next day, on December 8, the United States declared war on Japan. President Roosevelt famously announced to the American people, "Yesterday, December 7, 1941—a date which will live in infamy—the United States was suddenly and deliberately attacked by naval and air forces of the Empire of Japan."

SCIENCE FICTION

Robert Heinlein   Robert Heinlein lived from 1907 to 1988 and is considered one of the most controversial authors of science fiction. Heinlein began his career writing for pulp magazines. He is credited for turning science fiction into a serious field within literature. His work contained political messages and dealt with the hypocrisy of religion. He wrote thirty-two novels and many short stories, with some of his best-known work being *Stranger in a Strange Land*, *Starship Troopers*, and *The Moon Is a Harsh Mistress*. His novel *Space Cadet*, from 1948, featured nuclear weapons and even cell phones.

KNOT THEORY

Why Knot Theory Is Important   Knot theory might not sound very useful at first, but it is very important in understanding some of the most complex parts of our world. Understanding knots is extremely useful in learning about enzymes that act on strands of DNA, because DNA is tangled in knots. In order for DNA to interact with enzymes, the strands must unpack. The enzymes help unpack DNA by slicing through the DNA, allowing the strands to reconnect in a less tangled manner. By thinking of DNA as a knot, one can use knot theory to understand how DNA unknots and how hard the process is, as well as understand more about enzymes.

THE EARTH'S SPHERES

Cryosphere   The cryosphere is sometimes included as part of the hydrosphere. The cryosphere refers to the parts of the planet that are so cold that water freezes into a solid form. The polar regions of the planet (North Pole, or Arctic; and South Pole, or Antarctic) are considered the main parts of the cryosphere. These areas are covered in huge ice sheets, and at the South Pole, Antarctica has an ice sheet covering the entire continent. The cryosphere is not limited to the poles. Places with extremely high elevations, like Mount Kilimanjaro in Africa, are also considered part of the cryosphere, and even seasonal areas where lakes and rivers freeze over are considered a part of it.

SIGN LANGUAGE

Relationship with Oral Languages   Sign languages do not depend on oral languages, and they have their own grammatical structures. Sign language does have something known as fingerspelling, where letters of the alphabet are represented with hand signs; however, this is only one part of sign language. In general, sign languages are completely separate from oral languages and have different paths of development. Even though British and American hearing people speak the same language and can understand each other, the American Sign Language and the British Sign Language are completely different, and deaf people speaking one cannot understand the other.

🏛 WORLD WAR II

The Holocaust   In 1933, there were over 9 million Jews living in Europe. As Adolf Hitler came to power, he promoted hatred toward the Jewish people, believing Germans were a superior race and that Jews presented a threat to the community. The Holocaust was Hitler's state-sponsored mass genocide of the Jewish people, in which approximately 6 million Jews were murdered. Jews were placed into ghettos, and then into concentration camps, and then extermination camps where they were gassed to death. Toward the end of the war, the Jewish people were placed on trains and made to go on marches, known as "death marches." As the Allied forces approached, the camps were liberated.

SCIENCE FICTION

Arthur C. Clarke   Arthur C. Clarke was born in 1917. During World War II, Clarke was involved in working with British radar. In 1945, Clarke published an article in which he proposed placing three satellites in orbit that would be able to allow global communications (this would turn out to be surprisingly successful, and Clarke is known as the inventor of the communication satellite). Clarke published many stories throughout his lifetime, and his short story, *The Sentinel*, was actually the inspiration for the Stanley Kubrick film, *2001: A Space Odyssey*.

➕ KNOT THEORY

Knot Polynomials   A knot polynomial is an example of a knot invariant—meaning a quantity that is the same value for any equivalent knots—that is a polynomial. The most well-known knot polynomial is the Alexander polynomial which was discovered in 1923. This was the only known polynomial knot until 1984, with the discovery of the Jones polynomial. The Alexander polynomial could not distinguish handedness, meaning the objects are the same unless in a mirror reflection. The Jones polynomial however, was able to distinguish handedness.

THE EARTH'S SPHERES

Biosphere   The biosphere consists of all of the living things on the planet, from the large animals to the smallest microorganisms. The biosphere includes the hydrosphere, lithosphere, atmosphere, and cryosphere. Ecological communities form within the biosphere, and these are known as biomes. The three main types of biomes are grasslands, tropical rainforests, and deserts. The majority of life found on Earth is found up to 30 meters above ground, 3 meters below the ground, and in the first 200 meters of the oceans. Though humans are part of the biosphere, scientists put human beings in a group known as the anthrosphere.

SIGN LANGUAGE

Different Types of Sign Language   There are many different forms of sign language. Although these languages emerged separately and unrelated to the spoken languages of countries and are different grammatically, they do feature manually coded languages; that is, they have incorporated the languages of their countries. Several sign languages are mutually intelligible as well. For example, Danish Sign Language, Icelandic Sign Language, and Norwegian Sign Language (which are descendants of Danish Sign Language) are, for the most part, understandable by those who speak Swedish Sign Language. An International Sign Language (IS) has been created as well, and is used at international events.

WORLD WAR II

The Battle of Normandy (D-Day)   By 1944, Germany knew the Allies would attempt to liberate Europe through an invasion of France. The Allied forces planned to land on the northwest coast of France, known as Normandy, under the codename "Operation Overlord." On June 6, 1944, the Allies landed on five beaches of the Normandy coast. The Allied forces were met with heavy resistance from the defending Germans, but eventually, they were able to make it through. The accomplishment of the Allied forces, and the failure of the Germans, put an end to Hitler's goal of a Nazi-controlled Europe.

SCIENCE FICTION

Isaac Asimov   Isaac Asimov lived from 1920 to 1992, and he is considered one of the greatest writers of science fiction. He wrote around 500 books, publishing in genres such as science, horror, comedy, and even poetry. The best-known works of Asimov are his short story *Nightfall*, the *Robot* series of novels (of which *I, Robot* is one), and the *Foundation* novels. Asimov's work even inspired the creation of the *Star Trek* character Data.

KNOT THEORY

Adding Knots   Knots become more complex through addition. The process of adding knots together is known as knot sum. Two knots can be added by cutting the knots and then joining the pairs of the ends together. The zero knot, which looks like an *O*, is a very special case. When more knots are added to it, though it is longer, its shape of the *O* remains.

THE EARTH'S SPHERES

Atmosphere   All of the air that surrounds the planet is considered the atmosphere. The majority of the atmosphere is located near the Earth's surface. The atmosphere begins at less than 1 meter below the surface of the planet and goes up to more than 10,000 kilometers. The air of the atmosphere consists of 21 percent oxygen, 79 percent nitrogen, and a small amount of carbon dioxide and a variety of other gasses. The atmosphere protects the living creatures found in the biosphere from the Sun's rays, and absorbs and emits the heat from the Sun.

SIGN LANGUAGE

Written Form   The written form of sign language also differs from the oral forms of languages. This is known as SignWriting. SignWriting was created in 1974 by Valerie Sutton, and is actually based on the graphic notation used for writing ballet steps. The system uses visual symbols to express the handshapes, facial expressions, and movements found in sign language. In other words, the alphabet shows how the hands look. SignWriting is currently the written form for twenty-seven Sign Languages.

WORLD WAR II

End of the War   Germany's control and power began to weaken. As the Soviet Union fought German forces in the Battle of Berlin, Hitler, who had been hiding in a bunker during the battle, committed suicide. On May 1, the German forces surrendered in Italy, and on the next day, the forces fighting in Berlin surrendered to the Soviets. On May 7, the war in Europe was over. On August 6 and 9, the United States dropped two atomic bombs on Japan, and on August 14, Japan surrendered.

SCIENCE FICTION

Ray Bradbury   Ray Bradbury, an American author born in 1920, has written more than 500 works. His most famous work is also perhaps one of the most controversial science fiction books ever: *Fahrenheit 451*, a novel set in a dystopian world where hedonism is celebrated and the reading of books is prohibited. Bradbury is also the author of other famous books such as *The Martian Chronicles*, *The Illustrated Man*, and *Something Wicked This Way Comes*.

KNOT THEORY

Tabulating Knots   In knots, a crossing number is a knot invariant that is the least amount of crossings in a knot diagram of a particular knot. Knots are cataloged by their crossing number. Tables include the prime knots and one submission for a knot and its mirror image. Prime knots are the knots that cannot be expressed any simpler after knot sum. Tabulation of knots can become increasingly difficult as the number of nontrivial knots of a particular crossing number increases. John Horton Conway did the first major work verifying the process of tabulating knots.

THE EARTH'S SPHERES

Celestial Sphere   The celestial sphere is actually a fictitious sphere that surrounds the Earth, with the planet being at the center. One can only see half of the sky at any time, because that is what is above the horizon. Much like the way the sun rises and sets, so too do the stars in the sky. The celestial sphere keeps record of the celestial bodies that are in our sky. Important notions of the celestial sphere include the North Celestial Pole and the South Celestial Pole (which are extensions of the North and South Poles), the Celestial Equator (which is like the equator, but it expands into the sphere), the horizon (which changes based on what position you are on), the Zenith (the point that lies directly overhead) and the Meridian (which goes from the North Pole, through the Zenith, to the South Pole).

SIGN LANGUAGE

Sign Language with Primates   Language is not only a form of communication, but a uniquely human experience. Studying whether primates have the ability to develop language could lead to some great discoveries about the earliest humans. Washoe, a chimpanzee, was the first nonhuman to ever learn sign language and communicate with humans. Since the 1960s, chimpanzees and gorillas have been learning to use sign language for communication. Koko, a gorilla, was introduced to sign language in the 1970s. In 2004, Koko was featured in news reports when she signed to her caretakers that she had a toothache and needed to go to a dentist.

1. **Which of the following was responsible for America's entry in the war?**
   a. The Battle of Normandy
   b. The Invasion of Poland
   c. The Invasion of Russia
   d. The attack on Pearl Harbor

2. **Which of the following was won by the Allied forces?**
   a. The Invasion of Poland
   b. The Invasion of Russia
   c. The Battle of Normandy
   d. The attack on Pearl Harbor

3. **Who is considered the "father of science fiction"?**
   a. H. G. Wells
   b. Ray Bradbury
   c. Isaac Asimov
   d. Jules Verne

4. **Who wrote *The Moon Is a Harsh Mistress*?**
   a. Isaac Asimov
   b. Robert Heinlein
   c. Arthur C. Clarke
   d. Ray Bradbury

5. **When more knots are added to a zero knot, the shape of the knot:**
   a. Tangles
   b. Divides into two separate knots
   c. Decreases
   d. Remains the same

6. **Which of the following is not one of the Reidemeister moves?**
   a. A strand could twist and untwist.
   b. A strand can be cut in half and then those two strands are placed on top of one another.
   c. One strand could be placed over the other strand.
   d. A strand could be moved over or under a crossing.

7. **The cryosphere is sometimes considered a part of the:**
   a. Biosphere
   b. Hydrosphere
   c. Lithosphere
   d. Atmosphere

8. **The biosphere consists of:**
   a. All of the air that surrounds the planet
   b. All of the water that is found on the planet
   c. All of the life that is found on the planet
   d. All of the crust that surrounds the planet

9. **Which of the following is true?**
   a. In general, sign languages are completely separate from oral languages and have different paths of development.
   b. In general, sign languages are based entirely on oral languages and follow the same path of development.
   c. All sign language is based on ASL.
   d. All sign language is based on IS.

10. **SignWriting is based on:**
    a. The graphic notation that was used to write ballet steps
    b. Visual symbols that express handshapes
    c. Symbols that represent letters from the Latin alphabet
    d. A and B

HISTORY: The Holocaust
Hitler's Propaganda, Concentration Camps, Ghettos, Pogroms, The "Final Solution," Liberation

MATH: Chaos Theory
What Is Chaos Theory?, The Butterfly Effect, Fractals, Strange Attractors, Misconceptions of Chaos Theory, Applications of Chaos Theory

LANGUAGE ARTS: Fairytales
Aesop's Fables, Charles Perrault, Hans Christian Andersen, The Brothers Grimm, Gabrielle-Suzanne Barbot de Villeneuve, Carlo Collodi

SCIENCE: Geologic Periods
Cambrian, Triassic, Jurassic, Cretaceous, Tertiary, Quaternary

Lesson 29

FOREIGN LANGUAGE: Hindi
The Origins, Sanskritization, Hindi Vocabulary, Dialects, Hindi Today, Useful Hindi Phrases

THE HOLOCAUST

Hitler's Propaganda   One way Adolf Hitler made the mass extermination of Jews possible was by eliciting strong feelings of ill will toward the Jewish community. He did so through propaganda by newspapers, film, art, music, books, radio, and the press. The weekly Nazi newspaper, *Der Stürmer*, meaning "The Attacker," featured caricatures of Jewish people as apelike. Films showed the Germans as superior, with an emphasis on German pride, and depicted the Jewish people as inferior, even subhuman. When Hitler came to power, he ruled with a combination of propaganda and a police state to silence any critics.

FAIRYTALES

Aesop's Fables   Even though Aesop's fables (of which there are currently over 600) are some of the most popular fairytales ever written (e.g., "The Tortoise and the Hare"), very little is known about the actual man, Aesop. It is known that Aesop was Greek and born in Thrace in the sixth century B.C. It is believed that he spent most of his life living as a slave on the island of Samos and that, though he was a slave, he was allowed many freedoms and used his fables to argue in court. It is unknown how many of the fables were actually told by Aesop and how many were just attributed to him as they were collected later on.

CHAOS THEORY

What Is Chaos Theory?   Chaos theory is the mathematical study of extremely complex systems, and more than that, it is a study of the unpredictable and uncontrollable. For example, the stock market, the weather, ocean currents, even migration patterns of birds are all extremely sensitive to any sort of change, and therefore cannot be predicted like other principles in mathematics and science (like gravity or chemical reactions). Chaos theory emerged in the early twentieth century when Henri Poincaré determined that any measurement of something, for example, an orbiting planet, could never be infinitely precise, even if it can be accurately predicted.

GEOLOGIC PERIODS

Cambrian   The Paleozoic era, the time period when life forms first began to explode in diversity, started with the Cambrian period. The Cambrian period occurred 570 to 510 million years ago. Many significant events occurred during the Cambrian period. The supercontinent Gondwana broke apart and global temperatures began rising. Oceans were considerably higher, and though life on land was sparse, it is during this time that the first invertebrates began to appear in the oceans. While Precambrian life had soft bodies, the life found in the Cambrian period featured hard shells.

HINDI

The Origins   Hindi is an Indo-Aryan language that, along with Urdu, which is the official language of Pakistan, is a descendent of a colloquial speech used in North India (the Khari Boli dialect spoken in Delhi) in the ninth and tenth centuries called Hindustani. Much of the vocabulary and grammar of Hindi and Urdu are the same, with the exception that Urdu is written in Persian script and Hindi is written in the Devanagari system. Hindi was also greatly influenced by Sanskrit, one of the oldest Indo-Aryan languages, which was also written in Devanagari.

THE HOLOCAUST

Concentration Camps   From 1933 to 1939, the Jewish people were placed in concentration camps, where they were detained under horrible conditions. The first concentration camps began appearing as early as 1933 with Hitler's appointment as chancellor. The very first concentration camp was at Dachau. Initially, these camps held political prisoners, but they would later go on to hold Jews, gays, gypsies, and those who were mentally ill, as well as anyone who opposed the regime. There were different types of concentration camps, and in 1939, forced labor camps began to appear. These required inmates to do physical labor under horrible conditions. Death was extremely common in these camps, but nothing would compare to the camps created to act out Hitler's "Final Solution."

 FAIRYTALES

Charles Perrault   Charles Perrault was born in Paris on July 12, 1628. At the age of sixty-seven, Perrault lost his job as secretary to the king's finance minister. It was then that he decided to pursue writing. He is the author of some of the most well-known fairytales that still exist today, such as "Little Red Riding Hood," "Cinderella," "Puss in Boots," and "Sleeping Beauty." These stories and four others were published in his book *Stories or Tales from Times Past; or Tales of Mother Goose*. Though these stories and plots had existed before Perrault wrote them, Perrault was the first to turn them into a work of literary art through a combination of wit and style.

 CHAOS THEORY

The Butterfly Effect   Perhaps the most well-known principle to come out of chaos theory is the butterfly effect. The butterfly effect shows how even one slight change in space/time can change giant systems. For example, there is a link between a butterfly flapping its wings in one part of the world at a precise moment in time and space, and a hurricane that happens on the other side of the world. The flapping of the butterfly's wings could alter the movement and strength of the wind, which in turn leads to something else. The butterfly effect proves that large systems are unpredictable.

 GEOLOGIC PERIODS

Triassic   The Triassic period occurred 248 to 206 million years ago, and it was the first period of the Mesozoic era, the time period when dinosaurs first started developing. There were two major extinction events in the Triassic Period, one toward the beginning (the Permian-Triassic extinction event, which is considered the most severe extinction event of life on Earth) and one toward the end (the Late-Triassic extinction event). This period is defined by the first appearance of dinosaurs (which were no more than 15 feet tall and walked on all four legs), the first mammals (which were small and lizard-like), and flying reptiles (known as pterosaurs).

 HINDI

Sanskritization   By 1950, the Constitution of India declared Hindi, more specifically the Khari Boli dialect, and the use of Devanagari as the official language and writing system (and that Hindi and English would be the two official languages used by the Central Government). The government encouraged a Sanskritization of the language (in which Sanskrit vocabulary is introduced and used). This was done in an attempt to unite the different regions and appeal to the pride Indians had in their ancient culture.

THE HOLOCAUST

Ghettos   Following the invasion of Poland in 1939, all Polish Jews were to be put in ghettos, areas of cities that were surrounded by guards, brick walls, and barbed wire. Jewish people were forced to leave their homes and belongings and were put into these ghettos. By October, Jewish people from Czechoslovakia and Austria were being deported to Poland to be put in these ghettos as well. The largest ghettos were those of Warsaw and Lodz. The conditions in Warsaw were so horrible that from 1940 to 1942, around 100,000 Jews died from disease and starvation.

FAIRYTALES

Hans Christian Andersen   Hans Christian Andersen was a Danish author who lived from 1805 to 1875 and is considered the father of modern fairytales. Andersen wrote over 150 fairytales, of which his most famous include "The Little Mermaid," "The Ugly Duckling," "The Emperor's New Clothes," and "Thumbelina." Not only did Andersen's work break through previous traditions of Danish literature by using idioms and spoken language, but only 12 of his 156 fairytales were based on folklore. The rest were completely original. His work came to influence authors such as Charles Dickens (whom he had a friendship with) and Oscar Wilde.

CHAOS THEORY

Fractals   A major part of chaos theory involves understanding fractals. Fractals are the shapes we see in everyday life, and they are complex patterns that never end and are self-similar on other scales. A fractal can be created by repeating a process in a continual loop. Fractal patterns can be seen throughout the natural world, in mountains, trees, rivers, seashells, clouds, and hurricanes. In nature, we do not see a right triangle. We see shapes the mountains and rocks create. Using chaos theory and fractals, scientists try to uncover what makes these shapes.

GEOLOGIC PERIODS

Jurassic   The Jurassic period occurred 206 to 144 million years ago, and it is considered the middle of the Mesozoic era. In the early part of the Jurassic Period, Pangaea broke up into northern and southern supercontinents. It is during this time that the most commonly known dinosaurs, such as stegosaurus, brachiosaurus, and allosaurus, lived. The dinosaurs that were herbivores were quite large in size, while the carnivores were smaller. Mammals were still relatively small (around the size of dogs), and the first bird, which resembled a dinosaur but had feathers, appeared.

HINDI

Hindi Vocabulary   The formal vocabulary in Standard Hindi comes from Sanskrit. This is the language used in radio, TV, literature, and public addresses. The language spoken by the people, however, is based on the vernacular of the various regions. This vocabulary is largely influenced by Arabic, Persian, and even English. Vocabulary can be broken down into five categories: Ardhātatsam (words that were borrowed from Sanskrit), Tatsam (words that are spelled the same way in Hindi and Sanskrit), Tadbhav (words derived from Sanskrit but spelled differently), Videshī (words that are borrowed from languages that are not Indo-Aryan), and Deshaj (words that were neither borrowed nor derived from other Indo-Aryan words).

THE HOLOCAUST

Pogroms   Pogroms, or violent attacks on Jewish populations, began in Russia in the 1800s. During the Holocaust, with the increasing resentment toward the Jewish people growing, pogroms began appearing once again. Pogroms were encouraged by the Nazi regime, leading to entire communities killing all of the Jewish people in their towns. Even when the war ended, pogroms still persisted. The most famous postwar pogrom was the Kielce Pogrom of July 4, 1946, in Poland. The surviving Jewish were met with angry mobs and forty-two Jews were killed, and fifty injured.

FAIRYTALES

The Brothers Grimm   Jakob Grimm and Wilhelm Grimm were born in 1785 and 1786, respectively. Intrigued by the Romantic movement occurring in Germany, the two brothers began collecting fairytales in the early 1800s. In 1812, the first volume, consisting of eighty-six stories, was published, and two years later, another volume of seventy stories was published. The stories were told to the brothers by peasants and villagers, and the brothers edited these stories and added footnotes to many. The work of Jakob and Wilhelm Grimm brought stories like "Cinderella," "The Frog Prince," "Hansel and Gretel," and "Rapunzel" to the masses, and their work became incredibly popular.

CHAOS THEORY

Strange Attractors   When there is a long-term pattern within a bounded chaotic system, and it is not a simple orbit or periodic oscillation, it is known as a strange attractor. With strange attractors, patterns that are not obvious will appear. The Lorenz Attractor is an example of a system that is nonlinear and dynamic, and it corresponds to the Lorenz oscillator, a three-dimensional system that evolves over a pattern that doesn't repeat.

GEOLOGIC PERIODS

Cretaceous   The Cretaceous period occurred 144 to 65 million years ago. It is the longest period found in the current eon, the Phanerozoic eon. While dinosaurs still thrived, and Pangaea continued to separate, it is during this time that flowering plants and new kinds of birds (which still could not fly) and mammals began to appear, as well as the first lizards and snakes. This period ended with the K-T extinction, one of the largest mass extinctions, in which all of the dinosaurs and large marine reptiles died off.

HINDI

Dialects   There are currently eighteen languages recognized by the Indian Constitution, and each of these languages features a wide array of dialects. There are more than ten variations of Hindi, and the dialects can be divided into two main categories: Western Hindi and Eastern Hindi. Khari Boli, which became the standard language, is a Western Hindi dialect. The dialect spoken in Mumbai (or Bombay), known as Bambaiya Hindi, is a vernacular language that is associated with the poor or young. However, due to Mumbai's role in the Indian film industry, Bambaiya Hindi appears in many of the films that come from India.

THE HOLOCAUST

The "Final Solution"   In June of 1941, Germany began to enact the "Final Solution." Mobile killing groups were created, and they gathered up all of the Jews of towns, lined them up, and shot them one by one. By 1942, six death camps, or killing centers, were established near railway lines so that the Jewish people from concentration camps could be easily transported. The Jewish people, who at this point were forced to wear yellow stars on their clothing so they could be identified as Jewish, were gathered up and taken to these death camps, where they would be gassed to death. Around 3.5 million Jewish people were killed in these camps. The largest of these camps was Auschwitz.

FAIRYTALES

Gabrielle-Suzanne Barbot de Villeneuve   Gabrielle-Suzanne Barbot de Villeneuve was a French author who lived from 1695 to 1755. She is most widely recognized as the author of "Beauty and the Beast," which was featured in a collection called *La jeune américaine, et les contes marins* (told by an old woman during a long sea voyage), published in 1740. Her story was much longer (a total of 362 pages), and the Beast was much more ferocious. A French aristocrat, Madame Jeanne-Marie Le Prince de Beaumont, took the story and rewrote it, dramatically cutting it down to size and creating the "Beauty and the Beast" that we know today.

CHAOS THEORY

Misconceptions of Chaos Theory   There are several misconceptions related to chaos theory. Chaos theory is not about proving disorder or disproving determinism. Chaos theory is not used to show ordered systems are not possible. While chaos theory shows that slight changes can have dramatic impacts, and that prediction of a state is not possible, chaos theory still states that it is plausible and possible to create a model of a system based on the behavior overall. While systems might be unpredictable, the only way to express this is with representations of a system's behaviors.

GEOLOGIC PERIODS

Tertiary   The Tertiary period occurred 65 to 1.6 million years ago. This period is divided into five epochs. During the first epoch, the Paleocene epoch, the first primates started appearing. In the Eocene epoch, aquatic mammals and modern birds started to appear. The Oligocene epoch featured toothed whales, cats, and dogs. During the Miocene epoch, primates, horses, camels, rhinos, and beaver-like animals started to appear. During the Pliocene epoch, the first ancestors of modern humans, hominids, appeared and the geography of the planet was similar to what is found today.

HINDI

Hindi Today   Hindi is one of the official languages of the Republic of India, and it is spoken as a second language in places like Fiji, Mauritius, Guyana, Trinidad, and Surinam. Around 500 to 600 million people speak Hindi, and it is believed to be the fifth most-spoken language in the world. Hindi is the native language for 40 percent of India's population, and this area is referred to as the Hindi belt.

THE HOLOCAUST

Liberation   As the Allies advanced through Germany, the concentration camps were gradually liberated. In total, an estimated 5 to 7 million Jewish people were killed as a result of the Holocaust. Around 50,000 to 100,000 remained in the Allies' zones of occupation, many refusing to ever go back to their homes, later being transported to the United States, Israel, and Palestine. The Nuremberg Trials began in October of 1945 and were presided over by American, British, French, and Russian judges. The first trial prosecuted twenty-one members of the Third Reich, including many of those responsible for the Holocaust.

FAIRYTALES

Carlo Collodi   Carlo Lorenzini, who would come to be known as Carlo Collodi, was an Italian author who lived from 1826 to 1890. Originally working as a satirical journalist, Collodi left journalism and began working as a magazine editor and theatrical censor. It is during this time that he began translating the works of Charles Perrault. Inspired by Perrault, Collodi started working on his own fairytales, and began writing "The Story of a Puppet." His story, which would later be retitled as "The Adventures of Pinocchio," was very popular. Two years after his death, the story was translated into English.

CHAOS THEORY

Applications of Chaos Theory   Chaos theory has many real-world applications, and has even been exploited by companies. In 1993, Goldstar Co. created a washing machine that used chaos theory and made clothing cleaner and less tangled. As one large pulsator rotated, another smaller pulsator would rise and fall at random times, stirring the water. Chaos theory is also applied to understanding the stock market, in predicting weather, and even understanding how the solar system works. Chaos theory has also been applied to learning more about the body, and can be used in attempting to control brain seizures and cardiac arrhythmias.

GEOLOGIC PERIODS

Quaternary   The Quaternary period, which continues to the present, started 1.8 million years ago and began with a great Ice Age. This is the age dominated by human beings and mammals. During this time, the wooly mammoth, saber-tooth tiger, and other giant mammals (known as megafauna) roamed. Today, much of the remaining megafauna are found in Africa, such as the elephant and hippopotamus. It is during the Quaternary period that the hominids evolved into modern humans (who evolved into their current form around 190,000 years ago.)

HINDI

Useful Hindi Phrases   Here are some helpful phrases to use when traveling to India. Note that these are spelled out phonetically:

Hello. *Namaste* (this can also be used for good morning, good afternoon, good evening, good night, and goodbye).
Good morning. *Suprabhāt.*
Good afternoon/evening. *Śubh dhin.*
Good night. *Śubh rātrī.*
How are you? *Āp kaise haiṅ?*

Excuse me. *Kshama kījie.*
I don't understand. *Maiṁ samajhā nahī* (said from a man); *Maiṁ samajhī nahī* (said from a woman).
How much is this? *Kitane kā hai?*
Where's the toilet? *Tāyalet kahan haiṅ?*
Thank you. *Ābhārī hōṅ.*

1. **Which of the following did Hitler use as propaganda to elicit anti-Semitism?**
   a. Newspapers
   b. Film
   c. Art
   d. All of the above

2. **The largest ghettos in Poland were:**
   a. Warsaw and Lodz
   b. Warsaw and Auschwitz
   c. Auschwitz and Lodz
   d. Auschwitz and Pogrom

3. **Which of the following is one of Aesop's Fables?**
   a. "The Adventures of Pinocchio"
   b. "Cinderella"
   c. "The Tortoise and the Hare"
   d. "Sleeping Beauty"

4. **Gabrielle-Suzanne Barbot de Villeneuve's story was altered by Madame Jeanne-Marie Le Prince de Beaumont, and the resulting story was:**
   a. "Beauty and the Beast"
   b. "The Ugly Duckling"
   c. "Hansel and Gretel"
   d. "Little Red Riding Hood"

5. **Shapes that we see in everyday life, that are complex patterns that never end, and self-similar on other scales are known as:**
   a. Butterflies
   b. Fractals
   c. Chaotics
   d. Strange attractors

6. **Which of the following can chaos theory be applied to?**
   a. Weather
   b. Stock market
   c. Migration patterns of birds
   d. All of the above

7. **The K-T extinction, in which all dinosaurs and large marine reptiles died off, occurred after the:**
   a. Cretaceous
   b. Tertiary
   c. Quaternary
   d. Jurassic

8. **In what period did the first dinosaurs appear?**
   a. Cambrian
   b. Triassic
   c. Jurassic
   d. Quaternary

9. **Much of the vocabulary and grammar of Hindi and Urdu are the same, with the exception that:**
   a. Urdu is written in Devanagari and Hindi is written in Persian.
   b. Urdu is written in Devanagari and Hindi is written in Sanskrit.
   c. Urdu is written in Persian and Hindi is written in Devanagari.
   d. Urdu is written in Persian and Hindi is written in Suprabhāt.

10. **Which of the following describes words borrowed from Sanskrit?**
    a. Ardhātatsam
    b. Tatsam
    c. Tadbhav
    d. Videshī

HISTORY: The Cold War

The Iron Curtain, The Marshall Plan, The Cuban Missile Crisis, The Space Race, The Berlin Wall, The Dissolution of the USSR

MATH: Applied Mathematics

What Is Applied Mathematics?, Computer Science, Scientific Computing, Operations Research, Actuarial Science, Statistics

LANGUAGE ARTS: Biographies

The Immortal Life of Henrietta Lacks; *Into the Wild*; *Bonhoeffer: Pastor, Martyr, Prophet, Spy*; *The Diving Bell and the Butterfly*; *A Beautiful Mind: The Life of Mathematical Genius and Nobel Laureate John Nash*; *The Autobiography of Malcolm X*

SCIENCE: Biomes

Freshwater, Marine, Desert, Forest, Grassland, Tundra

Lesson 30

FOREIGN LANGUAGE: Mayan Languages

Yucatec Maya, Huasteco, Ch'ol, Q'eqchi', Mam, Poqomchi

THE COLD WAR

The Iron Curtain   The Warsaw Pact of 1955 was a military treaty between the Soviet Union, Poland, Czechoslovakia, East Germany, Romania, Albania, Bulgaria, and Hungary in which the countries agreed that should any of them be attacked, military aid would be provided by the other countries. The Warsaw Pact was initiated by the Soviet Union as a counter to the formation of NATO. The term *Iron Curtain* was used in reference to this division within Europe, both literally and figuratively. An actual metal fence separated the West from the East in some areas, cutting off all contact.

BIOGRAPHIES

The Immortal Life of Henrietta Lacks   Henrietta Lacks, an African American woman who was a poor tobacco farmer, died in 1951 at the age of thirty-one from cervical cancer. Though Lacks has been dead for more than sixty years, her cancer cells (which were the first cells to reproduce on their own, known as "immortal" cells) are still alive today, and are considered one of the most important tools that exist in the medical world. Lacks's cells were removed from her body during a biopsy and cultured, without her permission. *The Immortal Life of Henrietta Lacks* by Rebecca Skloot tells the story of Henrietta's suffering, the celebrity of her cells, the birth of a multimillion dollar industry, and the Lacks family, who up until twenty years ago, never knew about Henrietta's cells.

APPLIED MATHEMATICS

What Is Applied Mathematics?   Mathematics can be separated into two categories: pure mathematics and applied mathematics. Pure mathematics is the study of completely abstract math. Applied mathematics, however, uses mathematical techniques in very real and specialized ways and applies math to some sciences (such as physics), engineering, industry, and business. In applied mathematics, mathematical models are used to solve and work with very real problems and applications. Applied mathematics is also used in newer fields such as computer science.

BIOMES

Freshwater   Freshwater biomes consist of ponds, lakes, streams, rivers, and wetlands. The freshwater biome has a low concentration of salt (less than 1 percent usually), and plants and animals that live in these types of locations would not be able to live in bodies of water with higher concentrations of salt. Ponds and lakes are often isolated from larger bodies of water, and have limited diversity in terms of wildlife as a result. Streams and rivers flow in one direction, ending at the ocean. Wetlands are locations with standing water such as marshes, bogs, and swamps. Wetlands support specific types of aquatic plants and have the highest amount of diversity in terms of wildlife.

MAYAN LANGUAGES

Yucatec Maya   Yucatec Maya is spoken by 800,000 people, and it is the most common form of Mayan language spoken by the indigenous people of Mexico (who are mostly found on the Yucatán Peninsula). The Yucatec Maya language is one of only three Mayan languages that features tone, with Uspantek and a dialect of Tzotzil being the other two. Though currently written with the Latin alphabet, Yucatec Maya used Mayan script (a logosyllabic system where logograms represent entire words) until the sixteenth century.

THE COLD WAR

The Marshall Plan   Following World War II, Europe was left completely devastated industrially, economically, and agriculturally, and the United States was the only major power that had not been left in ruins. In 1947, the Marshall Plan was created by the U.S. Secretary of State George Marshall to provide aid and restore political and economic stability to the Western countries. Marshall believed this plan could both rebuild the Western countries and blunt the Communist advancements. A total of sixteen nations were involved in the program, and nearly $13 billion dollars was received in financial aid.

BIOGRAPHIES

Into the Wild   Jon Krakauer's *Into the Wild* tells the story of Chris McCandless, an Honors graduate from Emory University, who traveled across the United States renouncing society and living as a vagabond. McCandless ultimately hitchhiked to Alaska to live in the wilderness. After surviving for two years on his own, McCandless starved to death. Krakauer chronicles, as best he can, McCandless's journey through interviews with people he met along his journey, his friends and family, and authorities. Though the exact details are unknown, Jon Krakauer goes to great lengths to describe the events that may have led to Chris McCandless's unfortunate death.

APPLIED MATHEMATICS

Computer Science   Computers are an integral part of society. Computer science is more than being able to build computers or write programs. At its simplest, computer science is about solving problems and understanding how information (which, in its smallest form is known as a bit) is transferred through complex algorithms and algebra, logic, and combinatorics. The field of study began in the 1940s, and since then, has become a fundamental part of everyday life. Computer science can be used to understand the big bang, earthquakes, and even genetics.

BIOMES

Marine   The marine biome includes the oceans, estuaries, and coral reefs. Oceans, which make up 70 percent of the entire planet, are the largest of the ecosystems and have a great variety of wildlife. Estuaries are the locations where the rivers and freshwater streams join the ocean. The ecosystem of estuaries is unique due to the mixtures of the different concentrations of salt. Coral reefs exist around warm and shallow water. These are found along continents and islands, and the most dominant life form is coral, which is comprised of both animal polyp tissues and algae.

MAYAN LANGUAGES

Huasteco   The Huastec (also known as Wastek) language is spoken by 120,000 indigenous people of Mexico located in northern Veracruz, Tamaulipas, and parts of San Luis Potosi. The culture of the indigenous people who spoke Huasteco was not a part of the Classic Maya civilization due to their geographic isolation; the nearest Mayan culture was around 1,000 miles from them. The Chicomuceltec language, a Mayan language that had become extinct in the 1970s and 1980s, is believed to be the closest relative to the Huastec language.

THE COLD WAR

The Cuban Missile Crisis   The Cuban Missile Crisis is considered the closest the United States ever came to a nuclear war. By the 1960s, the United States had missiles that could reach the Soviet Union, while the missiles of the Soviets could only reach as far as Europe. In 1962, the Soviets set their attention on Cuba, and began putting their intermediate-range missiles there. Photographs of the Soviet missiles in Cuba surfaced, and a naval quarantine was deployed around Cuba. Tension grew as communication between the United States and the Soviet Union continued. Finally, the Soviet Union agreed to dismantle the installations in hopes that the United States would not invade Cuba.

BIOGRAPHIES

Bonhoeffer: Pastor, Martyr, Prophet, Spy   Eric Metaxas's *Bonhoeffer: Pastor, Martyr, Prophet, Spy* tells the story of Dietrich Bonhoeffer, a Lutheran pastor who lived in Germany during the reign of Adolf Hitler. While other churches embraced Hitler's hatred toward the Jewish people, Bonhoeffer believed the role of the churches was to help the victimized Jewish people. Bonhoeffer created an illegal seminary with the purpose of training pastors, and was involved in a plot to assassinate Hitler. The assassination attempt would ultimately lead to his death only three weeks before Hitler committed suicide. Metaxas's book focuses on the personal life of Bonhoeffer and his theological ideologies and spirituality.

APPLIED MATHEMATICS

Scientific Computing   Scientific computing, also known as computational science, is different from computer science. Scientific computing involves creating mathematical models and performing quantitative analysis with computers to solve problems. Typically, scientific computing involves computational simulation. Unlike computer science, which studies the processing of information, scientific computing implements models on computers to receive and analyze information. Often, work in scientific computing is done with supercomputers, software, and programs. In scientific computing, numerical analysis is used, which uses algorithms that feature numerical approximations.

BIOMES

Desert   One-fifth of the surface of the planet is comprised of desert, and rainfall is less than 50 centimeters a year at these locations. There are four different types of desert: hot and dry, semiarid, coastal, and cold. Hot and dry deserts feature little humidity, resulting in twice the radiation from the sun. An example of a hot and dry desert would be the Mojave Desert. Cold deserts, which are found in places like Antarctica and Greenland, are on the opposite end of the spectrum, and have cold winters with a lot of snow.

MAYAN LANGUAGES

Ch'ol   There are around 130,000 indigenous people who speak Ch'ol in Chiapas, located in southeastern Mexico. The Ch'ol languages can be divided into two languages: Tila and Tumbala, and these two are mutually intelligible. It is believed that the Ch'ol languages are the closest to the language spoken during the Classic era in the Central Lowlands. Ch'olan languages are more conservative in terms of phonology and vocabulary, and it is believed they might have been treated as a prestigious language that coexisted with other dialects.

🏛 THE COLD WAR

The Space Race   With the arms race and threat of nuclear war, fear of the Soviet Union grew. On October 4, 1957, the Soviets launched the first artificial satellite into space, *Sputnik 1*. The launch was a surprise to Americans, who believed they were the leaders in technology, and many feared *Sputnik* was a weapon. The United States launched the *Explorer 1* only four months after *Sputnik*. The Soviet Union originally led in the Space Race. In April of 1961, the Soviet Union was the first to launch a man into orbit (twenty-three days later, the United States sent their first man into orbit), and in June of 1963, the Soviet Union sent the very first woman into orbit. Ultimately, the United States won the Space Race, however. In 1961, President Kennedy announced the goal of sending a man to the moon. Eight years later, that goal was achieved.

🌿 BIOGRAPHIES

The Diving Bell and the Butterfly   In 1995, Jean-Dominique Bauby, an editor, author, and journalist for the French *Elle* magazine, suffered a devastating stroke that left him in a coma for three weeks. When he awoke from his coma, he suffered from locked-in syndrome, where his mind still functioned but his body was left completely motionless. The only thing he could move was his left eyelid. In 1996, as a person said the alphabet to him, he would blink at each letter he wanted. The result was his memoir, *The Diving Bell and the Butterfly*.

➗ APPLIED MATHEMATICS

Operations Research   In operations research, also known as management science, models and concepts are used to improve problems relating to managerial issues or problems pertaining to organizations, as well as how effectively technology is used in organizations. There are many different types of techniques that can be applied to operational research, including game theory, probability theory, graph theory, statistics, and simulation. Some of the fields involved in operations research include transportation, financial engineering, marketing engineering, energy, and manufacturing. Operations research began following World War II, stemming from the work of military planners.

✳ BIOMES

Forest   There are three types of forests: tropical, temperate, and boreal. The greatest diversity in wildlife can be found in tropical forests. These forests do not experience winter, and have only two seasons, a rainy season and a dry season. Temperate forests grow in areas with well-defined seasons that have a distinct winter (such as Wisconsin or the Adirondacks). The largest of the biomes are the boreal forests. Boreal forests (also known as taiga) are found across North America and Eurasia, and seasons are defined as short and moist summers that are moderately warm and winters that are cold, dry, and long.

◐ MAYAN LANGUAGES

Q'eqchi'   In Guatemala and Belize, 500,000 people speak Q'eqchi' (or Kekchi). Q'eqchi' speakers speak Q'eqchi' as their native language and Spanish as a second language (and some do not speak Spanish at all). There are two dialects of the language: one found in Guatemala, Alta Verapaz, and Cobán, and then an "eastern" dialect that is spoken elsewhere. Two orthographies are widely used. The first was developed in the 1960s and still remains in circulation, though it is no longer the standard. In the late 1980s and early 1990s, an orthography was developed that is now the standard form used in Guatemala.

🏛 THE COLD WAR

The Berlin Wall The Berlin Wall was more than just a division between West and East Germany. It was symbolic of Democracy versus Communism. The split had also occurred in the capital, Berlin. West Berlin was actually encircled by the rest of East Germany. While West Germany experienced economic growth, East Germany, under the Soviet Union's Communist influence, had a dragging economy and individual's rights were severely restricted. By the 1950s, many residents of East Germany were fleeing to West Berlin. Once there, they were able to fly to West Germany. By 1961, 2.5 million people had left East Germany, and several attempts, with the help of the Soviet Union, were made to control West Berlin, until finally a wall was built that stretched hundreds of miles.

📖 BIOGRAPHIES

A Beautiful Mind: The Life of Mathematical Genius and Nobel Laureate John Nash John Nash is a mathematical genius. He founded game theory, worked for RAND during the Cold War, won the Nobel Prize in Economics in 1994, and even challenged Albert Einstein on a theory of quantum mechanics when he was just twenty years old. He also suffered greatly from paranoid schizophrenia. Sylvia Nasar's book, *A Beautiful Mind: The Life of Mathematical Genius and Nobel Laureate John Nash*, explores Nash's life as he suffers with his illness, becoming entangled in his own thoughts and creating amazing mathematical accomplishments.

➗ APPLIED MATHEMATICS

Actuarial Science Actuarial science involves the assessment of risk and the creation of insurance policies to mitigate the risk for finance and insurance industries. Statistics, probability, finance, and economics are all used in actuarial science. Actuarial science also allows actuaries (those who work to assess risk and create insurance policies) to be able to predict income levels that would be needed for specific retirement incomes. In order to become an actuary, you must take several exams and become certified so that you can apply and perform the science.

⚛ BIOMES

Grassland When land is dominated by grass instead of trees, it is known as a grassland. There are two types of grasslands: tropical (also known as savannah) and temperate. Savannahs have trees scattered throughout and make up about half of Africa. In order for savannahs to exist, there must be hot or warm climates and rainfall of about 20 to 50 inches a year. Unlike savannahs, temperate grasslands do not have any trees and there is more variation in temperature from winter to summer. Prairies are temperate grasslands with tall grass, and steppes are temperate grasslands with shorter grass.

🌐 MAYAN LANGUAGES

Mam In Guatemala and Mexico, half a million people speak Mam, of which, there are three types: Northern Mam (found in Huehuetenango), Southern Mam (found in Quetzaltenango), and Central Mam (found in San Marcos). Due to mountainous terrain and isolation, there are several dialects within these different types of Mam; however, even as such, the dialects are still mutually intelligible. Mam, Tektitek, and Awakatek are closely related, and together are known as the Mamean language group.

THE COLD WAR

The Dissolution of the USSR   In 1985, Mikhail Gorbachev became president of the Soviet Union, and as reform was being promoted and was desperately needed in the Soviet Union, Gorbachev introduced perestroika, a restructuring of the economy, and glasnost, which allowed for political freedom. As reforms continued throughout 1986–1990, Soviet states gained new autonomy, and Gorbachev's power and ability to hold the union together weakened. In 1991, a coup was attempted against Gorbachev. The coup failed, but Gorbachev lost support and Boris Yeltsin came to power. The USSR was dissolved and the Russian Federation was created.

BIOGRAPHIES

The Autobiography of Malcolm X   Malcolm X was one of the most important and controversial leaders during the civil rights movement. In his autobiography, he discusses his childhood growing up in Boston as the son of a Baptist minister, how his life turned to the streets and prison, and finally, his embrace of Islam. He discusses his education, which he says he got from the schools, the streets, the prisons, and his mentor. The book was written by Alex Haley transcribing interviews he did with Malcolm X, and though Malcolm read drafts, he never lived to see it in print. Haley would later go on to write *Roots*.

APPLIED MATHEMATICS

Statistics   Though statistics is the study of organization, collection, and interpretation, it often features applied mathematics (especially when dealing with statistical procedures and research, which get improved through mathematical tests). Probability, algebra, decision theory, scientific computing, and combinatorial design are all used in statistics. Statistics can also be applied to a wide range of topics, including economics, engineering, public health, marketing, biology, education, sports, and medicine.

BIOMES

Tundra   The coldest biome is known as the tundra, of which there are two types: arctic tundra and alpine tundra. Tundra include very low diversity in wildlife, very cold climates, and short growth and reproduction seasons. Arctic tundras encircle the north pole and are desert-like. Though there are several plants that thrive in arctic tundras, they are not deep root systems. Alpine tundras are found on mountains where the altitude is so high that trees cannot grow. The plants and animals are similar to those found in the arctic tundra, able to withstand the extremely cold environments.

MAYAN LANGUAGES

Poqomchi   The Poqomchi language is spoken in Guatemala by 90,000 people. There are currently two dialects of Poqomchi, a western and an eastern dialect. Poqomchi is a Poqom language, and is related to Poqomam, which is spoken by 30,000 people. Poqom languages are also related to Core Quichean languages such as K'iche' (which has the largest amount of speakers), Archi, and Tz'utujil.

1. **The Warsaw Pact was initiated by the Soviet Union as a counter to the formation of:**
   a. The USSR
   b. NATO
   c. The Berlin Wall
   d. *Sputnik*

2. **How did the Cuban Missile Crisis end?**
   a. The Soviet premier agreed to dismantle the installations of missiles in hopes that the United States would not invade Cuba.
   b. The United States invaded Cuba and took over the Soviet Union's missiles.
   c. The United States launched an attack on the Soviet Union's missiles.
   d. The United States invaded Cuba and launched a nuclear bomb at the Soviet Union.

3. **What book was written by a man who suffered from locked-in syndrome, leaving his entire body motionless except for his left eyelid?**
   a. *A Beautiful Mind: The Life of Mathematical Genius and Nobel Laureate John Nash*
   b. *Into the Wild*
   c. *The Diving Bell and the Butterfly*
   d. *The Autobiography of Malcolm X*

4. **Which of the following is true regarding Dietrich Bonhoeffer?**
   a. Bonhoeffer believed the role of the churches was to help the victimized Jewish people.
   b. Bonhoeffer created an illegal seminary for the purpose of training pastors.
   c. Bonhoeffer was involved in a plot to assassinate Hitler.
   d. All of the above.

5. **Which of the following is true?**
   a. Pure mathematics is the study of math pertaining to science and applied mathematics uses mathematical techniques in nonscientific fields.
   b. Pure mathematics is the study of completely abstract math and applied mathematics uses mathematical techniques in very real and specialized ways.
   c. Applied mathematics is the study of completely abstract math and pure mathematics uses mathematical techniques in very real and specialized ways.
   d. Applied mathematics is the study of math pertaining to science and pure mathematics uses mathematical techniques in non-scientific fields.

6. **Which of the following involves the assessment of risk and the creation of insurance policies to mitigate the risk for finance and insurance industries?**
   a. Statistics
   b. Actuarial science
   c. Operations Research
   d. Scientific computing

7. **Which of the following has the highest amount of diversity in wildlife?**
   a. Lake
   b. River
   c. Wetland
   d. Stream

8. **What are the three types of forests?**
   a. Tropical, arctic, and savanna
   b. Tropical, temperate, and boreal
   c. Boreal, savanna, and alpine
   d. Alpine, prairie, and boreal

9. **Yucatec Maya, Uspantek, and a dialect of Tzotzil are the only Mayan languages that:**
   a. Feature tone
   b. Have a writing system
   c. Have prefixes
   d. Have suffixes

10. **The closest language to that spoken during the Classic era in the Central Lowlands is:**
    a. Ch'ol
    b. Poqomchi
    c. Yucatec
    d. Poqomam

HISTORY: The Baby Boomers and the Sixties

Postwar Baby Boom, The Suburbs, The Sixties, Civil Rights Movement, Feminism, Hippies

MATH: Fermat's Last Theorem

About Pierre de Fermat, Fermat's Last Theorem, Sophie Germain, Ernst Kummer, Faltings's Theorem, Andrew Wiles

LANGUAGE ARTS: Nonfiction

A People's History of the United States, Helter Skelter: The True Story of the Manson Murders, In Cold Blood, Fast Food Nation: The Dark Side of the All-American Meal, The Education of Henry Adams, Midnight in the Garden of Good and Evil

SCIENCE: Photosynthesis

What Is Photosynthesis?, Leaf Structure, Chloroplast and Chlorophyll, Light Reactions, Dark Reaction, The Carbon Cycle

Lesson 31

FOREIGN LANGUAGE: Filipino

The Origins, Differences Between Tagalog and Filipino, The Written Language, Influence of Outsiders, Filipino Today, Useful Filipino Phrases

THE BABY BOOMERS AND THE SIXTIES

Postwar Baby Boom   The term *baby boomer* refers to a person born between 1946 and 1964. At the end of World War II in 1945, millions of men returned home. On June 22, 1944, Congress passed the GI Bill of Rights, allowing for homes and farms to be available with low interest rates and little to no down payment for GIs. As soldiers returned from war, they got married and started having families. Prior to the war, the average number of births per year was from 2.3 to 2.8 million. In 1946, however, there were 3.47 million births. In the late 1950s, there was an all-time high of 4.3 million births per year.

NONFICTION

A People's History of the United States   *A People's History of the United States* by Howard Zinn tells history unlike ever before, offering the historical context from different perspectives. For example, his first chapter deals with Columbus and the New World. He begins the chapter by telling the perspective of the Arawak Indians who met with Columbus. Zinn then provides details about the murders committed by Columbus's men, and how this is a detail that is not widely talked about in traditional history. Within every chapter of the book, Zinn goes over a major event, retells the event from new perspectives, includes events and information mainstream history has left out, and interprets how the elite attempted to maintain control.

FERMAT'S LAST THEOREM

About Pierre de Fermat   Pierre de Fermat lived from 1601 to 1665 in France. Fermat was a lawyer and government official who provided some of the most important work in number theory, analytic geometry, and calculus of probabilities. For Fermat, math was more of a hobby and he was not interested in getting his work published. In fact, the one thing he ever published was done so anonymously. Fermat created very important work relating to minima and maxima, and had a long-standing feud with René Descartes. Fermat created many theorems that he claimed to have proven, but many of the proofs have never been found. His most intriguing work was his last theorem, which remained unsolved for three centuries.

PHOTOSYNTHESIS

What Is Photosynthesis?   Photosynthesis is the process that plants and some bacteria perform to convert the energy that comes from sunlight into usable energy. The sunlight is first turned into a sugar, and then through a process called cellular respiration, the sugar is turned into adenosine triphosphate, known as ATP, a form of energy. Plants require water and carbon dioxide, and as a result of photosynthesis, oxygen is released into the atmosphere. Without photosynthesis, life would not exist. The process of photosynthesis can be summarized as:

$$6CO_2 + 6H_2O \rightarrow 6(CH_2O) + 6O_2$$

The products are $6(CH_2O)$, which is energy in the form of sugar and oxygen.

◯ FILIPINO

The Origins Filipino is a Western Austronesian language. Filipino is based on another language, Tagalog, which was spoken in Manila. It was not until 1987 that the term *Filipino* was adopted, and the language was declared the official language of the Philippines. Though little is known about the history of the language, the first written Tagalog dates to around A.D. 900. In the 1930s, the government decided that there must be an official language of the country but did not specify what the language would be. By the 1970s, more than half of the population spoke Tagalog. When Tagalog became the official language in 1987, the term *Filipino*, (originally *Pilipino*), was used to unite the people. Many feared that by using Tagalog (which was the language of the dominant group in the Philippines) there would be dominance of the Tagalog culture, and so the name of the language was changed to handle these fears and increase acceptance.

THE BABY BOOMERS AND THE SIXTIES

The Suburbs   The rise in numbers of families brought a rise in consumerism, and people began moving outside of the cities, concentrating in the suburbs. Suburbs made living in houses affordable. The first, and most famous, example of a suburban community was Levittown in Long Island, New York. Thousands of identical homes were built by Bill Levitt and his company, and suburbs like Levittown began popping up all over the nation. The rise of suburbs led to the building of new schools, strip malls, and a sense that everything was the same. Black families were originally not allowed to live in suburbs, furthering segregation.

NONFICTION

Helter Skelter: The True Story of the Manson Murders   In August of 1969, over the course of two days, a series of horrible murders occurred in Los Angeles that shook the world. The murderers were a group of young men and women who followed the leadership of Charles Manson. Written by Vincent Bugliosi, the prosecutor in Charles Manson's case, and Curt Gentry, *Helter Skelter: The True Story of the Manson Murders* tells the story of how Manson was able to coerce people into following him, details the murders and other horrible escapades of Manson's, and brings to light Manson's idea of Helter Skelter, an apocalyptic war between the blacks and the whites.

FERMAT'S LAST THEOREM

Fermat's Last Theorem   Fermat did not want his work published, and many feared it would be lost. After his death, his son began collecting his father's work. His calculations and theorems were in the form of letters and comments in books, and inside a copy of Diophantus's *Arithmetica*, was a note referring to a theorem. This would become Fermat's most famous work. Fermat's last theorem states:

If n is greater than 2 in the problem $x^n + y^n = z^n$, there are no solutions that are not non-zero integer solutions.

Fermat claimed to have discovered a "remarkable" proof of this problem that would not fit in the margins of the book. The proof was never discovered, and for three centuries mathematicians were unable to figure it out.

PHOTOSYNTHESIS

Leaf Structure   The main organs for plants to perform photosynthesis are leaves. Leaves play a critical role in allowing carbon dioxide and water in and allowing oxygen and sugar to escape. As water comes in through the roots of the plant, it is transported to the leaves via cells. A waxy layer, called the cuticle, covers the leaf. This waxy layer prevents carbon dioxide from coming in and oxygen from going out. As a result, leaves have tiny openings called stomata (*stoma* is the singular term), which allow the carbon dioxide to pass and the oxygen to enter.

FILIPINO

Differences Between Tagalog and Filipino   Though Filipino is almost identical to Tagalog, when the language was adopted as the official language, some minor changes did occur. The inclusion of new words from other languages like English and Spanish was embraced, and Western sounds and letters of the alphabet that were not previously found in Tagalog were incorporated into the Filipino alphabet. Students are taught in schools that the language is Filipino, and do not refer to it as Tagalog.

THE BABY BOOMERS AND THE SIXTIES

The Sixties By the 1960s, the baby boomers (of which there were 70 million) were now teenagers, and the innocence of the 1950s was replaced with rock and roll music, the tensions of the Cold War, the civil rights movement, the assassination of President Kennedy, experimentation with drugs, a sexual revolution, and antiwar protests. The "American Dream" that was so sought after in the 1950s started to crumble and the role of government was constantly questioned. The sixties was a period dominated by a countercultural revolution.

 # NONFICTION

In Cold Blood Truman Capote was a celebrity due to his writing and his personality. His best-known work had been romantic novels like *Breakfast at Tiffany's* (1958). After ten years abroad in Europe, Capote decided to turn to nonfiction. In 1966, *In Cold Blood* came out, and it is considered by many to be the first nonfiction novel. The subject of his book was the 1959 murders of Herbert Clutter and his wife and children in Holcomb, Kansas. Capote researched the book for five years, interviewing the two murderers and becoming very close to them. *In Cold Blood* tells the stories of both the murderers and the victims.

 # FERMAT'S LAST THEOREM

Sophie Germain Many mathematicians attempted to solve Fermat's last theorem. Though great progress was made, the theorem was far from being proved and remained famous in the math world. Sophie Germain, who lived from 1776 to 1831 in France, used the pseudonym Monsieur Le Blanc in her studies to hide the fact that she was a woman. Germain began working on the theorem, and after several years of work, believed she had made a breakthrough. Germain showed that for exponents that were prime numbers and less than 100, there were no solutions that were prime to the exponent.

 # PHOTOSYNTHESIS

Chloroplast and Chlorophyll Plant cells have specialized organelles known as chloroplasts that are not found in animal cells. The chloroplasts make sugar and starch through photosynthesis. They also contain the molecule chlorophyll, which is a pigment that absorbs the energy of light and gives plants their green color. As the sunlight hits the plant, all of the wavelengths are absorbed except for green, which gets reflected back. When the light hits the chloroplast, the chlorophyll uses the sun's energy to combine water and carbon dioxide, which leads to the creation of sugar and oxygen.

FILIPINO

The Written Language In 1593, the Spanish came to the Philippines and established colonial rule. Prior to this time, Tagalog was written in Baybayin, a form of writing known as an abugida, a system consisting of fourteen consonants and only three vowels. When the Spanish took control of the land, the Latin alphabet was introduced, and Tagalog was written using a total of thirty-two letters. When Tagalog became the national language, the alphabet changed yet again, to a system known as Abakada, which consisted of twenty letters. In 1987, the alphabet was again changed to be able to incorporate the Spanish and English influences in Filipino. This new alphabet consisted of twenty-eight letters.

🏛 THE BABY BOOMERS AND THE SIXTIES

Civil Rights Movement   One of the most significant things to come out of the 1960s was the civil rights movement, which peaked from 1955 to 1965. Though African Americans had fought for nearly a century for equal rights, and there had been some progress, it was during this time that the most substantial accomplishments were made. In 1954, *Brown v. Board of Education* made segregation in public schools unconstitutional. Among some of the most critical events that occurred during this time period was the entry of the first African American student into the University of Mississippi; the work of Martin Luther King Jr.; the protests in Birmingham, Alabama; the March on Washington; the Civil Rights Act of 1964; the assassination of Martin Luther King Jr.; and the Civil Rights Act of 1968.

🌿 NONFICTION

Fast Food Nation: The Dark Side of the All-American Meal   Fast food is part of our everyday life. If we are not eating it, then we are seeing it on television, or our children are playing with toys from fast-food restaurants. Eric Schlosser's *Fast Food Nation* examines the ever-growing industry of fast food in the United States. Schlosser goes into great detail, from the creation to the marketing of fast food, and provides plenty of interesting information on a wide variety of topics. Besides simply taking a look at what the food is made of, Schlosser looks at the industry. He discusses, for example, how fast-food companies have moved their operations to anti-union states, like Kansas, Iowa, Texas, and Nebraska, to take advantage of low wages that would not be allowed in areas like New York or Chicago.

➗ FERMAT'S LAST THEOREM

Ernst Kummer   Ernst Kummer was the next to make a major breakthrough in Fermat's last theorem. Kummer lived from 1810 to 1893 in Germany. Kummer introduced the idea of "ideal" numbers, and his work with this concept would provide great insights into the theorem. In 1843, Kummer realized that attempts made at proving Fermat's theorem didn't work because the factorization of integers could not continue on to different rings of complex numbers. Kummer claimed that ideal numbers needed to be used. This concept was critical to understanding Fermat's last theorem, ring theory, and abstract algebra.

⚛ PHOTOSYNTHESIS

Light Reactions   There are two stages to photosynthesis. They are the light-dependent process (also known as light reactions) and the light-independent process (or dark reactions). Light reactions are the processes that occur in the chloroplasts and thylakoids in which light energy is absorbed by the chlorophyll and converted into chemical energy. During this process, water is split and oxygen is released. Light reactions have two photosystems (photosystem I and photosystem II) which harvest the light. The chlorophyll in photosystem I is the stronger absorber of the light. The two products to come out of light reactions are ATP and $NADPH_2$.

Influence of Outsiders   The Spanish controlled the Philippines from 1593 until 1898. From 1898 until 1946, the Philippines was controlled by the United States. The Spanish imposed their religion, political ideologies, language, alphabet, and social and economic institutions on the people of the Philippines. As a result of the Spanish conquest, it is estimated that 40 percent of the Filipino language is comprised of either Spanish words or words derived from Spanish, and until 1987, Spanish was one of the official languages of the country. As the Americans controlled the Philippines, English was also introduced as an official language.

THE BABY BOOMERS AND THE SIXTIES

Feminism   In the 1960s, a second wave of feminism swept the nation. In 1963, Betty Friedan published a book called *The Feminine Mystique* that became wildly popular. The book criticized the constricted roles women took as mother and housekeeper. Feminists began looking at the treatment of women in relation to sex, history, and education. Feminist organizations such as the National Organization for Women (NOW) advocated for equal opportunity in the workplace and the right to an abortion (which would pave the way for *Roe v. Wade*).

NONFICTION

The Education of Henry Adams   *The Education of Henry Adams* is a very interesting book. Henry Adams, the great-grandson of John Adams and grandson of John Quincy Adams, wrote the book himself; however, it is written in the third person. The book describes Adams's early life growing up in Boston, and events in his life such as his introduction to the world of the South and the horrors of slavery. Adams goes into detail about his education at Harvard, and as he discusses his life, he discusses the realization that his formal education did not prepare him for the world at large.

FERMAT'S LAST THEOREM

Faltings's Theorem   Gerd Faltings was born in 1954, and in 1983, his work with the Mordell conjecture (created in 1922 by Louis Mordell) became very important in understanding Fermat's last theorem. The Faltings theorem actually paved the way for the solution to the problem. Faltings proved that if the value of n is greater than 2, there is a limited number of coprime integers that can be x, y, and z in Fermat's last theorem.

PHOTOSYNTHESIS

Dark Reaction   The light-independent process (or dark reaction) occurs in the stromata of chloroplasts and takes carbon dioxide from the atmosphere and turns it into glucose with the ATP and $NADPH_2$ from the light-dependent process. For this process to occur, light is not necessary and no matter how much light is available, the process can continue. A 5-carbon sugar is combined with carbon dioxide, creating a 6-carbon sugar. This sugar is then broken into fructose and glucose, which sucrose is made of.

FILIPINO

Filipino Today   The Philippines consists of 7,107 islands, with a population of around 70 million, and there are over 100 different native languages that each have their own dialects. Some of these dialects and languages are mutually intelligible, while others are not. Tagalog was chosen to be the base for the official language because it is the native language for around 25 percent of the population, the largest percentage of speakers in the Philippines. Today, Filipino and English are the languages taught in schools.

THE BABY BOOMERS AND THE SIXTIES

Hippies   The hippie movement emerged from the Beat Generation of the 1950s, which was a group of writers (such as Allen Ginsberg and Jack Kerouac) who had a bohemian lifestyle involving sexual liberation and the use of drugs. The Beat Generation was centered in New York, and several of the people associated with the movement moved to San Francisco, starting the hippie movement. Music, art, drugs, expressing love, political commentary, and protesting were critical elements to the hippie lifestyle. One of the most famous events to come out of the hippie movement was the Woodstock music festival in 1969.

NONFICTION

Midnight in the Garden of Good and Evil   John Berendt's _Midnight in the Garden of Good and Evil_ is the true story of a murder trial in Savannah, Georgia, in 1981. Similar to Capote's _In Cold Blood_, _Midnight in the Garden of Good and Evil_ is more like a novel than just an account of events. The crime, however, only sets the scene for what the book's true focus is. The book is the story of a town, Savannah, and its rich history and the quirky and colorful residents that live there.

FERMAT'S LAST THEOREM

Andrew Wiles   Fermat's last theorem was finally proved in 1994 by English mathematician Andrew Wiles, who worked at Princeton. Wiles worked in private for seven years, without ever informing any of his colleagues of the work he was doing on Fermat's last theorem. In 1993, Wiles gave three lectures at the Isaac Newton Institute in Cambridge, England. On the last day, Wiles wrote out his work on the chalkboard and ended with Fermat's last theorem. He was met with great applause. Under a peer review, some errors were found in his work, but after a year, Wiles, with the help of Richard Taylor, was able to fix the errors and prove Fermat's last theorem.

PHOTOSYNTHESIS

The Carbon Cycle   As animals produce carbon dioxide from breathing, plants take in the carbon dioxide and use it to make organic nutrients. The plants are then eaten by an animal (transferring the carbon), and then that animal is eaten by another animal (once again transferring the carbon). When plants and animals die and their bodies start to decay, carbon enters the ground. Some of that carbon will be buried and eventually turn into fossil fuel. As humans use fossil fuels, carbon is released into the atmosphere in the form of carbon dioxide gas. The carbon then travels from the atmosphere into the oceans and other bodies of water.

FILIPINO

Useful Filipino Phrases   Here are some helpful phrases to use when traveling to the Philippines:

Hello. _Mabuhay._
Good morning. _Magandang umaga._
Good afternoon. _Magandang hapon._
Good night. _Magandang gabii._
How are you? _Kumasta?_
Yes. _Oo._   No. _Hindi._
Thank you. _Salamat._
Excuse me. _Mawaláng-galang na nga hô._

I don't understand. _Naiintindihan ko hô._
Do you speak English? _Marunong ba kayong mag-Ingglés?_
How much? _Magkano?_
Where is the bathroom? _Nasaan ang banyo?_
Do you understand? _Naiintindihan ba ninyo?_
What's your name? _Anóng pangalan ninyó?_
Goodbye. _Paalam na hô._

1. **The work of the National Organization for Women paved the way for:**
   a. The Beat Generation
   b. The Jim Crow laws
   c. *Brown v. Board of Education*
   d. *Roe v. Wade*

2. **Levittown was the first example of:**
   a. A women's organization advocating equal opportunities in the workplace
   b. A suburb
   c. A civil rights protest
   d. A civil rights march

3. **Who wrote *A People's History of the United States*?**
   a. John Berendt
   b. Howard Zinn
   c. Truman Capote
   d. Henry Adams

4. ***In Cold Blood* is notable for being the first:**
   a. Book about a crime
   b. Nonfiction book
   c. Nonfiction crime novel
   d. Book that proved the innocence of the suspects

5. **Who first showed that for exponents that were prime numbers and less than 100, there were no solutions that were prime to the exponent?**
   a. Sophie Germain
   b. Andrew Wiles
   c. Louis Mordell
   d. Gerd Faltings

6. **Ernst Kummer's most significant contribution was the notion of:**
   a. Prime numbers
   b. Ideal numbers
   c. Coprime integers
   d. Exponents

7. **In the formula $6CO_2 + 6H_2O \rightarrow 6(CH_2O) + 6O_2$, what does $6(CH_2O)$ represent?**
   a. Sugar and oxygen
   b. Carbon monoxide
   c. Carbon dioxide
   d. Sucrose

8. **What are the two products that come out of light reactions?**
   a. ATP and carbon monoxide
   b. ATP and carbon dioxide
   c. Carbon dioxide and $NADPH_2$
   d. ATP and $NADPH_2$

9. **Prior to the Spanish conquest, Tagalog was written in:**
   a. Abakada
   b. Baybayin
   c. Paalam
   d. The Latin alphabet

10. **What percentage of the Filipino language is either Spanish words or words derived from Spanish?**
    a. 30 percent
    b. 40 percent
    c. 50 percent
    d. 60 percent

HISTORY: Landing on the Moon
Apollo 1, Apollo 7, Apollo 8, Apollo 9, Apollo 10, Apollo 11

MATH: Pascal's Triangle
About Blaise Pascal, Before Pascal, What Is Pascal's Triangle, Patterns and Properties, Formula for Pascal's Triangle, Fibonacci Sequence

LANGUAGE ARTS: William Shakespeare
Shakespeare's Early Life, His Work, Shakespeare's Writing Style, The Globe Theatre, Shakespeare's Sexuality, Authorship Controversy

SCIENCE: Early Humans
Lucy, *Homo Habilis, Homo Erectus, Homo Sapiens*, Neanderthals, *Homo Sapiens Sapiens*

Lesson 32

FOREIGN LANGUAGE: Swahili
The Origins, Influence of Other Languages, Spread of Swahili, The Written Language, Swahili Today, Useful Swahili Phrases

🏛 LANDING ON THE MOON

Apollo 1   The Cold War led the United States and the Soviet Union toward a new frontier: space. The *Apollo* program was created with the specific intention of having a man land on the moon. On January 27, 1967, the launch and flight crew of *Apollo 1* were conducting a simulation a month before their intended launch. The day was met with problems and delays, and at 6:30 P.M., a spark ignited inside the spacecraft, and the closed compartment was engulfed in flames. The three astronauts in the spacecraft died of asphyxiation. The cause of the spark is still unknown; however, the flammable materials within the spacecraft, combined with an oxygen-rich atmosphere and exposed wiring, were a recipe for disaster. The fire led to several changes in procedures and management for the rest of the program.

🍃 WILLIAM SHAKESPEARE

Shakespeare's Early Life   William Shakespeare lived from 1564 to 1616 in England. Very little is known of his childhood, including the date of his actual birth. Shakespeare did not attend university when he got older, which was reserved for the wealthy, and by the time he was eighteen years old in 1582, he was married. By 1589, Shakespeare, who was living in London to pursue acting and playwriting, had begun writing his first play, *Henry VI, Part I*. By 1590, Shakespeare had become a popular playwright, and in 1593, his poem *Venus and Adonis* was published and achieved great success. From 1594 until his death, Shakespeare was associated with a theater troupe called the King's Men.

➗ PASCAL'S TRIANGLE

About Blaise Pascal   Blaise Pascal was a French scientist, inventor, physicist, and mathematician who lived from 1623 to 1662. Pascal invented many things, including the wristwatch and an early form of the calculator. Pascal was a child prodigy, and at a very early age made important discoveries relating to fluids. When he was only eighteen years old, Pascal invented the Pascaline, a calculator based on a numerical wheel that featured eight dials that could be added up and used a base of ten. Though Pascal did not create Pascal's triangle, in 1653, Blaise Pascal understood the significance of the patterns of the triangle, and it is named in his honor.

⚛ EARLY HUMANS

Lucy   In 1974, a nearly complete skeleton (a total of forty-seven bones) was found in Ethiopia. This skeleton has been named Lucy, and it was an absolutely incredible discovery. Lucy, who was named after the Beatles' "Lucy in the Sky with Diamonds," lived around 3.18 million years ago, was an *Australopithecus afarensis*. She is the oldest known humanlike hominid that proved to be bipedal, meaning with the ability to stand up. Lucy stood four feet tall and weighed only 50 pounds, and it is believed that she died by falling into a river or lake and drowning.

🌐 SWAHILI

The Origins   Swahili is a Bantu language, a branch of languages in the Niger-Congo family. The language developed as a result of Arab and Persian people moving to the East African coast from A.D. 500 to 1000, and the language is a blend of Bantu, Arab, and Persian, along with other influences such as English, Portuguese, and German. While the grammar is associated with Bantu, much of the vocabulary is associated with the other languages. The word *Swahili* actually means "the coast" in Arabic. In Swahili, the word for the language is *Kiswahili*, and speakers of Kiswahili are known as Waswahilis.

LANDING ON THE MOON

Apollo 7 *Apollo* missions 4, 5, and 6 were successful unmanned flights. On October 11, 1968, *Apollo 7* tested the manned command module in orbit for the first time. While in orbit, the crew of three practiced lunar-mission maneuvers. Not only was *Apollo 7* the first manned *Apollo* flight, but it was also the first time a manned flight was broadcast on live television. The spacecraft was able to exit orbit and re-enter the atmosphere successfully, and the capsule was recovered in the Atlantic Ocean.

WILLIAM SHAKESPEARE

His Work William Shakespeare wrote some of the world's most famous comedies, tragedies, and histories, as well as sonnets and poems. The number of plays he wrote is still up for debate. The general consensus is that he wrote a total of thirty-seven plays; however, others believe that including possible lost works and collaborations, it's really more like forty. He also wrote countless poems, including 154 sonnets and two long-form narrative poems. Shakespeare wrote sonnets all of his life, and a collection of them was published in 1609 by publisher Thomas Thorpe. Since Thorpe printed the sonnets without Shakespeare's consent, it is believed that they were not intended to be published, but were actually private pieces.

PASCAL'S TRIANGLE

Before Pascal The numbers found in Pascal's triangle were well known before Blaise Pascal from the studies made by Indians in combinatorics and the study of figurative numbers by the Greeks. One of the first depictions of the numbers in the triangle is from commentary found in the tenth century of an Indian book that was written between the fifth and sixth centuries. Use of the triangle was also found in Persia at around the same time, with Persian mathematician, Al-Karaji, and later by Omar Khayyám. In fact, in Iran, it is referred to as the "Khayyam triangle."

EARLY HUMANS

Homo Habilis The first real humans lived 2.4 to 1.4 million years ago in Africa and are called *Homo habilis*. The *Homo habilis* still had apelike features; however, they were taller and had larger brains than the *Australopithecus afarensi*. The most notable thing about *Homo habilis* is that this is the first time we see tool making, and thus, *Homo habilis* marks the beginning of the Stone Age, in which tools of stone were used by early mankind (*Homo habilis* means "handy man"). *Homo habilis* did not know how to make fire yet.

SWAHILI

Influence of Other Languages The largest and most obvious influences in Swahili are Persian and Arabic. In some cases, Arabic words just completely replaced Bantu words. For example, the numbers 1, 2, 3, 4, 5, 8, and 10 are all Bantu words, but the words for 6, 7, and 9 have been replaced with Arabic words. From 1500 to 1700, the coastal towns were controlled by the Portuguese, and several Portuguese words and customs (such as Swahili bull fighting) have remained. When the British and Germans colonized the East African coast later on, Swahili began incorporating those languages as well (such as the word *baiskeli* for "bicycle").

🏛 LANDING ON THE MOON

Apollo 8   On December 21, 1968, *Apollo 8* was launched. Close to three hours after the launch, translunar injection, in which the ship is maneuvered into a trajectory that will bring it to the Moon, occurred. After sixty-nine hours and eight minutes, the spacecraft entered elliptical lunar orbit; the first manned mission to do so. At a little over eighty-nine hours, on December 25, transearth injection occurred, setting the ship into the trajectory headed toward Earth. On December 27, the capsule landed in the Atlantic Ocean and the mission was a success.

✍ WILLIAM SHAKESPEARE

Shakespeare's Writing Style   Shakespeare's plays featured blank verse, a metrical pattern that consisted of lines of iambic pentameter that did not rhyme. When passages deviated within the plays, Shakespeare would use a different poetic form or simple prose. With one exception, his sonnets were written in iambic pentameter. Shakespeare also invented words and phrases (of which there are at least 1,500 he made up). Among the many words he invented or made popular were *assassination*, *bump*, *submerge*, *frugal*, *gnarled*, *dishearten*, *obscene*, *generous*, and *monumental*.

➗ PASCAL'S TRIANGLE

What Is Pascal's Triangle?   Pascal's triangle is a number pattern in the shape of a triangle that follows a very simple concept. You begin at the top with 1 and then move down the triangle. To get the next number, you just add the two numbers above it. For example:

$$
\begin{array}{c}
1 \\
1 \; 1 \\
1 \; \mathbf{2} \; 1 \\
1 \; 3 \; 3 \; 1 \\
1 \; 4 \; \mathbf{6} \; \mathbf{4} \; 1 \\
1 \; 5 \; 10 \; 10 \; 5 \; 1
\end{array}
$$

The bold numbers show how Pascal's triangle works. When the 1 and the 2 are added up, you get 3, which gets placed below those numbers.

⚛ EARLY HUMANS

Homo Erectus   *Homo erectus* existed 1.89 million to 70,000 years ago. *Homo erectus* are the first humans to feature the body structure of modern humans, with shortened arms and elongated legs (however, their brains were ⅔ the size of ours). This indicates that humans were no longer tree climbers but adapting to life on the ground, and could walk and perhaps even run. *Homo erectus* began to travel past Africa, migrating to other continents. *Homo erectus* were also the first to make and control fire, and were the earliest hunters.

🌐 SWAHILI

Spread of Swahili   Swahili was the language of the people living on the East African coast for centuries. As interactions with countries around the Indian Ocean, such as Comoro or Madagascar, and trade and migration increased, the Swahili language spread. During the nineteenth century, the language spread to Tanzania, and it also made it to Rwanda, Uganda, Congo, Burundi, Central African Republic, Mozambique, and even as far as South Africa. Christian missionaries learned the language, and also helped spread it by translating the Gospel into Swahili.

🏛 LANDING ON THE MOON

Apollo 9   On March 3, 1969, *Apollo 9* was launched. The manned mission successfully used all of the *Apollo* lunar hardware in orbit and it was also the first use of the lunar module, a separate part with the purpose of landing, in a manned flight. The operations lasted ten days, and the crew was able to demonstrate all of the mission maneuvers. While in orbit, the crew simulated a landing using the lunar module and safety maneuvers. One of the safety maneuvers, in which the command module is inoperable and the lunar module is used as a lifeboat, was actually used during the recovery of *Apollo 13*.

📝 WILLIAM SHAKESPEARE

The Globe Theatre   Shakespeare's most well-known plays were performed at the Globe Theatre in London. The theater was built by the brother of Richard Burbage, one of the actors that worked with Shakespeare, who wrote for the troupe. From 1592 to 1593, an outbreak of the plague caused the theater to shut down, and it is during this time that William Shakespeare turned to poetry. In 1594, the Globe Theatre reopened, and Shakespeare and the troupe became extremely popular. The Globe Theatre could seat two to three thousand people, and performances were held in the afternoon using daylight. During a performance of *Henry VIII* on June 29, 1613, a cannon was fired and it set the roof on fire, burning the Globe Theatre to the ground.

➗ PASCAL'S TRIANGLE

Patterns and Properties   The first diagonal row of Pascal's triangle is made up of ones and the next diagonal row is counting numbers (1, 2, 3, 4, 5, etc). The third diagonal row is made up of triangular numbers, which follow the rule $x_n = n(n + 1)/2$. The fourth row is made up of tetrahedral numbers. If you add up the horizontal rows, you get multiples of 2:

$$
\begin{array}{ll}
1 & = 1 \\
1\ 1 & = 2 \\
1\ 2\ 1 & = 4 \\
1\ 3\ 3\ 1 & = 8 \\
1\ 4\ 6\ 4\ 1 & = 16 \\
1\ 5\ 10\ 10\ 5\ 1 & = 32 \\
\end{array}
$$

✳ EARLY HUMANS

Homo Sapiens   *Homo sapiens*, literally meaning "wise man," began to appear 250,000 years ago and came out of Africa. These humans had much larger brains, and as a result, their skulls extended forward. Homo sapiens is the genus that we are currently in, and these are considered the earliest "modern man." *Homo sapiens* were hunters and gatherers, created tools from stone, and even sewed clothing. During this time, *Homo sapiens* lived side by side with another species, *Homo neanderthalensis*, who behaved much like *Homo sapiens*.

🗣 SWAHILI

The Written Language   Swahili is an extremely easy language to learn because pronunciation is as simple as sounding out the letters. The oldest form of the written language dates back to the eighteenth century. Due to contact with Arab traders, the language was originally written in Arabic script. In the 1930s, the British attempted to standardize Swahili. The dialect found in Zanzibar, called Kiunguja, would be the standard written and spoken language, written with the Latin alphabet.

LANDING ON THE MOON

Apollo 10   *Apollo 10* was launched on May 18, 1969. The mission of the *Apollo 10* was to perform a staging of what the *Apollo 11* mission would be like, with the only exception being it would not actually land on the Moon. The *Apollo 10* mission was the first time that the complete spacecraft traveled to the Moon, making it to around 14 kilometers above the surface of the Moon, and it was the second mission that orbited the Moon. The mission lasted a total of eight days, and the crew was recovered in the Pacific Ocean.

WILLIAM SHAKESPEARE

Shakespeare's Sexuality   Though William Shakespeare married at the age of eighteen, his sexuality has constantly been an issue of controversy. It is believed that Shakespeare had several affairs with women and showed an interest in men, but the only evidence is circumstantial and is taken from analyzing his sonnets. His book of sonnets that was supposed to be private, was a collection of love poems about a young man he referred to as "Fair Lord," in which he expressed his love for him, and his book was dedicated to "Mr. W.H."

PASCAL'S TRIANGLE

Formula for Pascal's Triangle   To find a value at any spot along the triangle, the formula is expressed as:

$$\binom{n}{k} = \frac{n!}{k!(n-k)!}$$

n and k relate back to the lesson in combinations, where it looks like this: $^{n}C_{k}$
So, Pascal's triangle can also look like this:

$$\binom{0}{0}$$
$$\binom{1}{0} \binom{1}{1}$$
$$\binom{2}{0} \binom{2}{1} \binom{2}{2}$$
$$\binom{3}{0} \binom{3}{1} \binom{3}{2} \binom{3}{3}$$
$$\binom{4}{0} \binom{4}{1} \binom{4}{2} \binom{4}{3} \binom{4}{4}$$
$$\binom{5}{0} \binom{5}{1} \binom{5}{2} \binom{5}{3} \binom{5}{4} \binom{5}{5}$$

EARLY HUMANS

Neanderthals   *Homo neanderthalensis* was an entirely separate species from *Homo sapiens*. Neanderthals were much taller and stronger than the *Homo sapiens*, had larger brains than even current man, and buried their dead (implicating that perhaps this is the first sign of religion). At around 30,000 B.C., the Neanderthals died off, and no one is certain why. Some believe *Homo sapiens* killed them all, while others believe there was interbreeding between *Homo sapiens* and Neanderthals, and eventually the one species ceased to exist. In 2010, a study discovered that traces of Neanderthal DNA were found in modern human DNA.

SWAHILI

Swahili Today   Swahili is most commonly spoken in Kenya, Tanzania, Uganda, and Congo; however, it is also spoken along the eastern coast, and in parts of Somalia, Burundi, Rwanda, Mozambique, and the Comoros Islands. In Tanzania, Swahili is the official language used for government and education, and Kenya and Uganda also follow this policy (along with English). There are fifteen main dialects found in the language, with the dominant dialects being Kiunguja (found in mainland Tanzania and Zanzibar), Kimvita (found in Kenya and Mombasa), and Kiamu (found in coastal areas and the island of Lamu).

LANDING ON THE MOON

Apollo 11   *Apollo 11* was launched on July 16, 1969. On July 20, Neil Armstrong and Edwin "Buzz" Aldrin landed on the Moon and took their very first steps there. The lunar module spent twenty-one hours and thirty-six minutes on the surface of the Moon, and the crew spent two hours and thirty-one minutes outside the craft. Two days after arrival, the crew departed, taking with them 46 pounds of soil and lunar rocks. The mission lasted eight days and landed in the Pacific Ocean. *Apollo 11* was the first manned spacecraft to land on another planetary body and return home safely.

WILLIAM SHAKESPEARE

Authorship Controversy   Since the 1700s, there have been people, known as Anti-Stratfordians, questioning whether William Shakespeare actually wrote all of his plays or whether they had been written by contemporaries of his. There are three main candidates that people feel could have been the true authors of the plays Shakespeare takes credit for: Edward de Vere, Francis Bacon, and Christopher Marlowe. Edward de Vere, the seventeenth Earl of Oxford was a nobleman of Queen Elizabeth I, and many believe his life paralleled content found in Shakespeare's plays. Perhaps the strongest candidate is Francis Bacon, whose book *Promus* features 4,400 parallels in terms of thought and expression. Christopher Marlowe was a playwright who was stabbed to death in a bar fight in 1593. Some believe that he was actually a spy and that he faked his own death, and continued to write plays under the pen name, William Shakespeare.

PASCAL'S TRIANGLE

Fibonacci Sequence   If you recall from earlier, the first eight numbers in the Fibonacci sequence are: 1, 1, 2, 3, 5, 8, 13, 21. These values can be found in Pascal's triangle.

```
1 1 2 3   5   8......
         1
        1  1
       1  2  1
      1  3  3  1
     1  4  6  4  1
    1  5  10  10  5  1
```

EARLY HUMANS

Homo Sapiens Sapiens   *Homo sapiens sapiens* started to exist 90,000 years ago, and were spread across the world. In Europe, *Homo sapiens sapiens* were known as Cro-Magnons. It is with the *Homo sapiens sapiens* that we first see bows and arrows, constructed homes like huts and tents (used when following herds of animals), advanced weaponry, clothing, improved languages, and artwork. It is during this time that the famous cave paintings of Lascaux, France, were created. Anatomically speaking, the Cro-Magnons are almost identical to modern man of today.

Useful Swahili Phrases   Here are some helpful phrases to use when traveling to the eastern coast of Africa:

Hello. *Habari.*
Good morning. *Habari ya asubuhi.*
Good afternoon. *Habari ya mchana.*
Good evening. *Habari ya jioni.*
Good night. *Usiku mwema.*
How are you? *Habari yako?*
I don't understand. *Sielewi.*
Cheers! *Maisha marefu!*
Do you speak English? *Unazungumza kiingereza?*
What's your name? *Jina lako ni nani?*
Excuse me. *Samahani nipishe.*
Sorry. *Samahani.*
Please. *Tafadhali.*
How much is this? *Hii ni bei gani?*
Thank you. *Asante.*
Where's the toilet? *Choo kiko wapi?*
Goodbye. *Kwaheri.*

1. **The first successful manned *Apollo* flight was:**
   a. *Apollo 5*
   b. *Apollo 6*
   c. *Apollo 7*
   d. *Apollo 8*

2. **What was the first mission that traveled to the Moon with the complete spacecraft?**
   a. *Apollo 8*
   b. *Apollo 9*
   c. *Apollo 10*
   d. *Apollo 11*

3. **Which of the following is true?**
   a. William Shakespeare wrote tragedies, comedies, and histories.
   b. William Shakespeare wrote comedies, musicals, and horror.
   c. William Shakespeare wrote tragedies, musicals, and histories.
   d. William Shakespeare wrote musicals and horror.

4. **What is blank verse?**
   a. A metrical pattern that consists of lines of trochaic tetrameter that rhymes
   b. A metrical pattern that consists of lines of trochaic tetrameter that do not rhyme
   c. A metrical pattern that consists of lines of iambic pentameter that rhymes
   d. A metrical pattern that consists of lines of iambic pentameter that do not rhyme

5. **In Pascal's triangle, what is the third diagonal row made up of?**
   a. Multiples of 2
   b. The Fibonacci sequence
   c. Triangular numbers
   d. Tetrahedral numbers

6. **If you add up all of the horizontal rows in Pascal's triangle, the values are:**
   a. Multiples of 2
   b. The Fibonacci sequence
   c. Triangular numbers
   d. Tetrahedral numbers

7. **Lucy was an important discovery because:**
   a. She was the first *Australopithecus afarensis* ever discovered.
   b. She was proof that *Australopithecus afarensis* was bipedal.
   c. She was the first female hominid discovered.
   d. She was the tallest *Australopithecus afarensis* ever documented.

8. **One of the reasons scientists believe the Neanderthals died off is:**
   a. They assimilated with the *Homo sapiens*.
   b. They were killed off by the *Homo sapiens*.
   c. They got a severe illness that spread throughout the species.
   d. A and B.

9. **Swahili is a combination of:**
   a. Persian and Arabic
   b. Arabic, French, and Bantu
   c. Persian, Arabic, and Bantu
   d. Arabic, Italian, and Bantu

10. **How do you say "Good morning" in Swahili?**
    a. Habari ya mchana.
    b. Habari ya jioni.
    c. Habari ya asubuhi.
    d. Sielewi.

HISTORY: The Cultural Revolution in China

Mao Zedong, Great Leap Forward, Break from the Soviets, The Cultural Revolution, Tiananmen Incident, End of the Cultural Revolution

MATH: Group Theory

What Is Group Theory?, Permutation Groups, Matrix Groups, Transformation Groups, Abstract Groups, Rubik's Cube

LANGUAGE ARTS: Victorian Literature

Style of Victorian Literature, The English Novel, Children's Literature, Poetry, Scientific and Philosophical Writing, Late Victorian Period

SCIENCE: Gas Laws

Properties of Gas, Boyle's Law, Charles's Law, Gay-Lussac's Law, Avogadro's Law, Graham's Law

Lesson 33

FOREIGN LANGUAGE: Pashto

The Origins, Afghanistan, Pakistan, Dialects, Writing System, Useful Pashto Phrases

🏛 THE CULTURAL REVOLUTION IN CHINA

Mao Zedong   Mao Zedong was born in 1893. He founded the People's Republic of China, and when he was younger, he was one of the original members of the Chinese Communist Party. Mao was elected chairman of the Soviet Republic of China in 1931 and became one of the most important Communist leaders of the time. Following the Second Sino-Japanese War, the Communists and a political party called the Kuomintang fought in a civil war, and by 1949, the Communists had taken most of mainland China. The People's Republic of China was established, and Mao became chairman.

📖 VICTORIAN LITERATURE

Style of Victorian Literature   The Victorian era is the transitional period between the romantic period and the twentieth century, during the reign of Queen Victoria in Britain (1837–1901). Literature produced during this time dealt with the issues of daily life. With the rise of industrialism, reform movements involving child labor, women's rights, emancipation, and the concept of evolution heavily influenced the work, and the Victorian age is considered to be one of pessimism and doubt. Works had moral purposes, and featured ideals like love, justice, and truth.

➗ GROUP THEORY

What Is Group Theory?   As you recall from earlier, groups are an abstract term that have to satisfy four basic rules: closure, associativity, identity, and inverses. Group theory is the study of the different systems that follow these laws. For example, in the problem $a \times b = c$, group theory is not concerned with the numbers or the multiplication process, but the rule that fits that problem and understanding how those properties relate to other systems. Essentially, group theory is a study of symmetry, and has many real-world applications, especially in chemistry and physics.

⚛ GAS LAWS

Properties of Gas   Gases have three properties. Gases are easily compressed, they can easily expand, and they take up more space than any liquids or solids. Gases exert pressure, and because the molecules are spread over a wide area, gas has a low density. Many properties of gas are based on five postulates that make up the kinetic molecular theory. The kinetic theory states:

Gas is composed of molecules, and the size of these molecules is negligible compared to the distance between molecules.

Molecules move at random in straight lines, in any direction and at a wide variety of speeds.

Forces of repulsion and attraction between molecules is weak, except when colliding.

There is no kinetic energy lost when molecules collide, making the collisions elastic.

The absolute temperature of a molecule is proportional to its average kinetic energy.

☾ PASHTO

The Origins   Pashto, an Eastern Iranian language, which also goes by the name *Afghan* in the Farsi language and *Pathan* in Punjabi, is part of the Indo-Iranian language family. Pashto originated as the native language of the Pashtun people, who live between Afghanistan and Pakistan. The first written records of Pashto date back to the sixteenth century, and by the seventeenth century, the national poet of Afghanistan, Khushhal Khan Khattak, wrote in Pashto. Parts of the language borrow from Greek, dating back to the third century B.C.

THE CULTURAL REVOLUTION IN CHINA

Great Leap Forward In 1958, Mao Zedong attempted to modernize the economy of China so that it could rival America's. Mao believed industry and agriculture were to be the focus of the development project, and his plan was called the Great Leap Forward. Mao believed that in order for industry to grow, workers must be well-fed, and in order for agriculture to grow, new tools were needed. Mao believed the best way to make this happen was by making China into a series of many communes. By 1958, there were 26,578 communes and 700 million people placed into them. The Great Leap Forward was a dismal failure, and it is believed that 20 to 30 million people died from famine.

VICTORIAN LITERATURE

The English Novel During the nineteenth century, the novel became the most popular form of literature. Novels focused on portraying the difficulty of real life, where ultimately it is love, perseverance, and hard work that win out. An especially important part of the novel during this time was the depiction of the emerging and expanding middle class, a break from the aristocratic portrayals found in earlier novels. Most of the novels were published serially in journals, with the latest chapter or section appearing with each new issue and featuring intricate plots and plot twists to keep readers interested.

GROUP THEORY

Permutation Groups If you recall, permutations are rearrangements. If you have abc, a permutation of that is bca. One of the most important types of groups are permutation groups. Permutation groups are important because any group can be represented as a permutation group. If there is a group G, the elements of set M are permutations, and the group operation is the composition of the permutations in group G. Two permutations make up a group when one is the identity element, and the second one is a permutation that is the inverse of itself.

GAS LAWS

Boyle's Law Boyle's law, named after Robert Boyle, states that if temperature is constant, there is an inversely proportional relationship between volume and absolute pressure. The equation for Boyle's law is represented as:

$$pV = k$$

p is the pressure, V is the volume, and k is a constant, which is found by multiplying the pressure by the volume. Because there is an inverse relationship between volume and pressure, if the volume is doubled, the pressure would be inverted, which means that one-half of the pressure is being used.

PASHTO

Afghanistan Pashto is currently spoken in Afghanistan and Pakistan. In Afghanistan, Pashto is mostly prevalent in the south, southwest, and east, though it is also spoken in some western and northern areas. Since the eighteenth century, the kings of Afghanistan (with one exception) were ethnic Pashtuns. In 1936, Pashto was declared a national language in Afghanistan, and it is currently one of two official languages, the other being Dari (as of 1964). Pashto spread to Pakistan as a result of the Durand Line, which was established in 1893 and became a border between Afghanistan and Pakistan. One-third of the Afghan Empire was lost from the border shift, and this land became Pakistan.

🏛 THE CULTURAL REVOLUTION IN CHINA

Break from the Soviets   Following the failure of the Great Leap Forward, Mao Zedong withdrew from public life temporarily. In the 1950s, Mao's People's Republic of China and Stalin's Soviet Union were the largest communist states, and supported one another. When Stalin died, Nikita Khrushchev came to power, and began to steer away from Stalin's policies. Mao Zedong believed that Khrushchev's policies were betraying Marxism, and with the Great Leap Forward taking a horrible turn for the worse, Khrushchev stopped funding the People's Republic of China. Mao Zedong was then replaced as chairman in 1959 by his opponent; however, he retained his position with the Politburo of the Communist Party.

📖 VICTORIAN LITERATURE

Children's Literature   Children's literature changed during the Victorian era. By 1848, the work of Hans Christian Andersen was translated into English, sparking a great interest in fairytales. It is during the Victorian era, for example, that Lewis Carroll's *Alice in Wonderland* books came out and became popular. The change in children's literature is a direct result of the time period. Views on children began to shift, and child labor and required education of children came to the forefront of social issues. As more children began reading, an industry based on producing literature for them began to grow.

➗ GROUP THEORY

Matrix Groups   Matrix groups are the second most important types of group. You might recall from earlier that matrices are vector space. In a matrix group, group G is a set that consists of elements that are square matrices. A square matrix has the same vertical and horizontal dimensions. Matrix groups have invertible matrices. Matrix groups are useful for understanding objects that have symmetries. For example, matrix groups can be found in projective spaces of geometry, the study of molecules in chemistry, and the study of particle physics. Conceptually, matrix groups are very similar to permutation groups.

⚛ GAS LAWS

Charles's Law   In the 1800s, Jacques Charles and Joseph Louis-Gay Lussac studied how gas volume was affected by the gas's temperature. Charles's law, which is also called the law of volumes, shows that when heated, gas expands. Charles's law can be depicted as:

$$V \propto T$$

Other ways of showing this are: $\dfrac{V_2}{V_1} = \dfrac{T_2}{T_1}$ or $\dfrac{V_1}{T_1} = \dfrac{V_2}{T_2}$ or $V_1 T_2 = V_2 T_2$

V represents volume and T represents absolute temperature. In each formula, the volume of gas increases proportionally when the absolute temperature increases.

🗣 PASHTO

Pakistan   Pashto is not an official language in Pakistan as it is in Afghanistan, even though in the Federally Administered Tribal Areas, Khyber Pakhtunkhwa (which used to be known as North-West Frontier Province), and Balochistan Province a total of 27 million people (or 15 percent) speak the language. In Pakistan, the official languages are Urdu and English. Pashto was allowed to be used in schools as a medium of instruction for the first time in 1984. Even though Pashto has no official status, there is a long literary tradition of Pashto in Pakistan.

🏛 THE CULTURAL REVOLUTION IN CHINA

The Cultural Revolution   From 1966 to 1976, in an effort to prevent the bureaucratization and capitalization of Communism as in the Soviet Union, Mao Zedong created what would be known as the "Great Proletarian Cultural Revolution." The Cultural Revolution is now considered one of the darkest periods in China's history. All schools were closed, and the students were encouraged to join the Red Guard, which was responsible for persecuting intellectuals and teachers. The Red Guard turned increasingly more violent (over a million people died from the purges) and split into factions. Mao then enforced the People's Liberation Army to suppress the factionalism of the Red Guard. During this time period, Mao's ideology was harshly enforced. Youths were taken out of cities and forced to work in agrarian areas. Artists who made antisocialist work and ethnic minorities were highly persecuted.

🎼 VICTORIAN LITERATURE

Poetry   The most highly regarded poet during the Victorian era was Alfred, Lord Tennyson. His poetry reflected the feelings of the era, expressing melancholy and doubts about religion, yet a confidence in class. There was a movement in the middle of the nineteenth century known as the Pre-Raphaelite movement that focused on reviving the work of medieval and classical times. The greatest example of this movement can be found in Tennyson's *Idylls of the King*, which combined the story of King Arthur with ideas and issues of the modern day.

✖ GROUP THEORY

Transformation Groups   Transformation groups deal with symmetry. Both permutation and matrix groups are special types of transformation groups. These groups act on a specific space (in permutation groups, it is a set, and in matrix groups, it is a vector space), but the structure is preserved. As transformations preserve an object, there will be more symmetry. Transformation groups have two properties:

If transformations f and g belong to G, then the composition $f \circ g$, meaning $(f(g(x))$, also belongs to G.

The set G contains the inverse transformation f^{-1} with every transformation f.

⚛ GAS LAWS

Gay-Lussac's Law   Gay-Lussac's law builds upon Boyle's law and Charles's law, and actually represents two ideas. The first part is known as the law of combining volumes. This law states that gases combine in simple proportions (for example, water is simply two parts hydrogen and one part oxygen). The other part of Gay-Lussac's law is the pressure-temperature law. This law states that pressure of an amount of gas at a constant volume is proportional to the absolute temperature.

This can be expressed as: $\dfrac{P}{T} = k$ or $P \propto T$

🌙 PASHTO

Dialects   In both Pakistan and Afghanistan, there are two main dialects of Pashto. The northern dialect is known as Pakhto, and the southern dialect is simply known as Pashto. Pakhto, the northern dialect, is known for its harder sound, while Pashto sounds softer. The difference in name stems from these changes in pronunciation. In general, there are not that many morphological differences between the two dialects, and they are generally mutually intelligible. The dividing line between the two dialects passes through Paktika, where north of the line, Pakhto is spoken, and south of the line, Pashto is spoken.

THE CULTURAL REVOLUTION IN CHINA

Tiananmen Incident   Zhou Enlai, the premier who founded the People's Liberation Army, died on January 8, 1976. The Gang of Four forbade anyone to take part in any of the activities honoring his death, creating great uproar. On April 4, 1976, the eve of a festival that paid homage to the deceased, an estimated 2 million people gathered in Tiananmen Square to memorialize Zhou Enlai and express their anger over the Cultural Revolution. The next day, the people discovered that their wreaths and items for Zhou Enlai were removed, leading to outrage. A violent riot began, police cars were set ablaze, and thousands of people forced their way into government buildings.

VICTORIAN LITERATURE

Scientific and Philosophical Writing   During the Victorian era, Charles Darwin's ideas of evolution in his book *On the Origin of Species* shook the world, and writings about nature and evolution became widely popular. It is also during this time period that some great philosophers began to write. The Victorian era saw the work of John Stuart Mill, John Henry Newman, and Henry Edward Manning. Karl Marx and Friedrich Engels, the two founders of Communism, wrote their books during this time in Victorian England.

GROUP THEORY

Abstract Groups   So far, all of the types of groups have been concrete. They have used either numbers, matrices, or permutations. In the late nineteenth century, the idea of abstract groups was created. Abstract groups have abstract properties and are presented with generators and relations. An abstract group can be represented as:

$$G = < S \mid R >$$

An example of an abstract group would be the Cyclic Group, a group that is generated from one single element.

GAS LAWS

Avogadro's Law   In 1811, Italian chemist Amedeo Avogadro hypothesized that two gases with the same pressure, volume, and temperature would also contain the same number of molecules, regardless of any physical or chemical properties. Avogadro's law can be written as:

$$\frac{V}{n} = k$$

V represents the volume, n represents the number of moles (or substance) in the gas, and k is a constant.

From Avogadro's law, it was determined that the ideal gas constant (k) is the same value for any gas, which means:

$$\frac{p_1 \bullet V_1}{T_1 \bullet n_1} = \frac{p_2 \bullet V_2}{T_2 \bullet n_2} = \text{constant}$$

PASHTO

Writing System   The Pashto alphabet, which has 45 letters, is derived from the Arabic alphabet, but features letters that represent sounds not found in Arabic. All of the 28 letters from the Arabic system are used, and there are three letters in common with the Persian and Urdu alphabets. In total, there are 45 letters to the Pashto alphabet. In the late eighteenth century, the spelling system was standardized.

THE CULTURAL REVOLUTION IN CHINA

End of the Cultural Revolution   By 1968, the Chinese economy was close to collapsing and the factionalism in the Red Guard was creating havoc. In 1971, the chaos of the Cultural Revolution had died down with the People's Liberation Army. From 1972 to 1976, with both Chairman Mao and the premier in deteriorating health, there was a great struggle over whether to continue the Cultural Revolution in the succession phase. Mao's propagandists blamed the chaos of the Cultural Revolution on four people, known as the "Gang of Four" (one of whom was Mao Zedong's wife). In October of 1976, the Gang of Four were arrested, thus ending the Cultural Revolution. Mao Zedong died on September 9, 1976.

VICTORIAN LITERATURE

Late Victorian Period   The Victorian era can be divided into two parts: the early Victorian period (which ended around 1870), and the late Victorian period (which lasted from 1890 to 1918). In the late Victorian period, the principles that followed throughout the Victorian era were rejected. There was a return to fantasy, with such works as Robert Lewis Stevenson's *The Strange Case of Dr. Jekyll and Mr. Hyde*, and the emergence of the "problem novel." Problem novels focused on the institution of marriage and the role of the sexes and sexual identity.

GROUP THEORY

Rubik's Cube   Group theory sounds incredibly complicated. To understand how group theory works, think of the Rubik's Cube. The Rubik's Cube can be thought of as a mathematical group because it meets all four requirements of being a group, and permutations are each of the elements of the group. In order to solve the Rubik's Cube, you need to perform certain actions in a particular order.

GAS LAWS

Graham's Law   Graham's law deals with effusion, the process where molecules escape from a container through a hole and do not collide. Graham's law states that the rate of effusion is inversely proportional to the square root of the molecular masses. Graham's law can be written as:

$$\frac{\text{Rate}_1}{\text{Rate}_2} = \frac{\sqrt{M_2}}{\sqrt{M_1}}$$

Rate$_1$ and Rate$_2$ are the rates of effusion for the first and second gases, respectively, and M_1 and M_2 are the molar masses of the first and second gases, respectively.

PASHTO

Useful Pashto Phrases   Here are some helpful phrases to use when traveling to Afghanistan or Pakistan. Note that these are written phonetically.

Hello. *Salaam.*

Good morning. *Sahr pikheyr.*

Good afternoon. *Wradz mo pa kheyr.*

Good evening. *Maakhaam mo pa kheyr.*

Good night. *Shpa mo pa kheyr.*

Pleased to meet you. *Khwakh shum pa li do di.*

I don't understand. *Za na poheegum.*

How much is this? *Da somra di?*

Excuse me. *Bakhena ghwaarum.*

Where's the toilet? *Khakandas cheerta di?*

Thank you. *Manana.*

What's your name? *Staa num tsa dhe?*

Goodbye. *Da khoday pa amaan.*

1. **The Red Guard was responsible for:**
   a. Protecting China's borders from the Soviet Union
   b. Persecuting intellectuals and teachers
   c. Creating the Great Leap Forward
   d. Creating communes

2. **The Cultural Revolution was blamed on:**
   a. Chairman Mao
   b. Zhou Enlai
   c. The Gang of Four
   d. The Red Guard

3. **Which of the following are reasons for the wide popularity of children's literature?**
   a. Views on child labor began to change.
   b. Children were required to attend school and learn to read.
   c. The works of Hans Christian Andersen were translated into English.
   d. All of the above.

4. **What did the Pre-Raphaelites focus on?**
   a. A revival of classical and medieval work
   b. A rejection of classical and medieval work
   c. A revival of ideology from the French Revolution
   d. A rejection of ideology from the French Revolution

5. **Which of the following statements is true?**
   a. Any group can be represented as a transformation group.
   b. Any group can be represented as an abstract group.
   c. Any group can be represented as a permutation group.
   d. Any group can be represented as a matrix group.

6. **As transformations preserve an object, there will be:**
   a. More symmetry
   b. Less symmetry
   c. More abstraction
   d. Less abstraction

7. **Which law states $pV = k$?**
   a. Graham's law
   b. Charles's law
   c. Gay-Lussac's law
   d. Boyle's law

8. **Which law states $V \propto T$?**
   a. Graham's law
   b. Charles's law
   c. Gay-Lussac's law
   d. Boyle's law

9. **Why did Pashto spread to Pakistan?**
   a. The Afghanis invaded Pakistan.
   b. The Pashtun people invaded Pakistan.
   c. The Durand Line divided the area inhabited by Pakhtuns, creating Pakistan.
   d. The Durand Line forced all Pashto-speaking people to move to Pakistan.

10. **Which of the following is true?**
    a. The first written records of Pashto date back to the sixteenth century.
    b. By the seventeenth century, the national poet of Afghanistan, Khushhal Khan Khattak, was writing in Pashto.
    c. Parts of the language borrow from Greek, dating back to the third century B.C.
    d. All of the above.

ANSWER KEY: b, c, d, a, c, a, d, b, c, d

HISTORY: Vietnam War

Vietnam Following the Geneva Peace Accords, A Split in Vietnam, The Kennedy Years, The Johnson Years, Antiwar Movement, The End of the War

MATH: The Number *e*

What Is *e*?, The Natural Base, Numerical Series, Discrete Accumulation, Hyperbolic Trigonometry, Derangements

LANGUAGE ARTS: Charles Dickens

About Charles Dickens, *A Christmas Carol*, *Oliver Twist*, *David Copperfield*, *A Tale of Two Cities*, *The Mystery of Edwin Drood*

SCIENCE: Plasma

What Is Plasma?, Degree of Ionization, Temperatures, Differences Between Plasma and Gas, Magnetization, Examples of Plasma

Lesson 34

FOREIGN LANGUAGE: Afrikaans

The Origins, Phonetics and Grammar, Dialects, Afrikaans and Apartheid, Afrikaans in Post-Apartheid South Africa, Useful Afrikaans Phrases

VIETNAM WAR

Vietnam Following the Geneva Peace Accords   After 100 years of colonization by the French, the Vietnamese fought and defeated the French in the First Indochina War, forcing them to leave. The French and Vietnamese met in Geneva to sign a treaty in the summer of 1954. According to the Geneva Peace Accords, elections would be held in 1956, making the division between North and South Vietnam at the seventeenth parallel disappear. The United States, believing this would give too much power to the Communist party in Vietnam, supported the creation of the Southeast Asia Treaty Organization (SEATO) to act as a counterrevolutionary alternative. With the help of the United States and SEATO, South Vietnam established a new government as the Republic of Vietnam.

CHARLES DICKENS

About Charles Dickens   Charles Dickens is one of the Victorian era's best-known writers. Dickens's work focused on hypocrisy, injustice, and social evils, and much of his work drew upon his actual life and featured comical characters and social commentary. Dickens lived from 1812 to 1870. Like other Victorian works, his writing was often serialized, and in total, Dickens wrote fifteen novels. Some of his most famous novels include *Oliver Twist*, *Nicholas Nickleby*, *A Christmas Carol*, *A Tale of Two Cities*, *Great Expectations*, and *The Pickwick Papers*. Dickens began his career as a journalist at the age of sixteen, and he continued working in journalism for the rest of his life.

THE NUMBER e

What Is e?   The number *e*, also known as Euler's number, is one of the most famous and important irrational numbers, and it is the base of the natural logarithms. The number was first introduced in the early 1600s by John Napier, who worked with logarithms. Napier abandoned the concept of natural logarithms, instead focusing on common logarithms that had a base of ten. Leonard Euler picked up where John Napier left off, and it is Euler who is responsible for discovering the properties of *e*. The number *e* expands infinitely, with the first values of *e* being:

$e = 2.71828182845904523536\ldots$

PLASMA

What Is Plasma?   The three most well-known phases of matter are solid, liquid, and gas. There is a fourth phase, however, known as plasma, and it is the most abundant form of matter in the entire universe even though it does not have a definite form. Plasma is matter that has a very high pressure and temperature, and stars and interstellar dust feature plasma (for example, it is found on the Sun). Plasma is a combination of free electrons (which are stripped from their orbit), neutral atoms, and charged ions. Like gas and liquid, plasma is fluid; however, due to the charged particles, it both responds to electro-magnetic forces and generates electro-magnetic forces.

AFRIKAANS

The Origins   Spoken in South Africa and Namibia, Afrikaans is a West Germanic language and is a daughter language of Dutch. In the seventeenth century, the Dutch created colonies in Africa, and up until the nineteenth century, Afrikaans was considered to just be a dialect of Dutch. The language evolved, and in 1914, Afrikaans was considered a separate language and declared the official language of South Africa. Of the vocabulary in Afrikaans, it is believed that 90 to 95 percent has Dutch origins, and the rest has influences from Malay, the Bantu languages, and Portuguese.

🏛 VIETNAM WAR

A Split in Vietnam   Ngo Dinh Diem became president of the government of the Republic of Vietnam in 1956, and quickly claimed that the Communists of the North were attacking to reclaim the South. In 1957, Diem, with the aid of the U.S. military, counterattacked the North. Diem's presidency was oppressive and corrupt and was opposed by the Vietnamese people. From 1956 to 1960, the North attempted to peacefully unite the two Vietnams; however, following Diem's attacks, it was understood that a more violent overthrow was necessary. In 1960, the Communists created the National Liberation Front.

✒ CHARLES DICKENS

A Christmas Carol   Though Dickens's *A Christmas Carol* is a celebration of Christmas, at its heart the novel is a social commentary on the division of the rich and poor in Victorian England. At the time of its writing, the British government enforced what were known as the Poor Laws, which made the poor labor in horrible factories and stay in debtor's prisons. When Dickens was twelve years old, his own family was moved to a debtor's prison, and Dickens was forced to work in a shoe polish factory.

➕ THE NUMBER *e*

The Natural Base   When looking at the graphs of the exponential functions $y = f(x) = 2^x$ and $y = g(x) = 3^x$, we see a couple of things. The function that equals 2^x begins with a higher value than the function that equals 3^x, but the value of the 3^x function starts to get higher than the 2^x function when $x = 0$. As the values of the function get larger, they grow faster and the curves get steeper. When comparing the average growth rates of the functions, the average rates of f lag behind the value of the function, and the average rates for g are always slightly higher. Both curves do not coincide with the average growth rates; however, 3^x is closer. This means that the base of the exponential function lies somewhere between 2 and 3, which is e. The exponential function $y = e^x$ has an equal rate of growth to its value.

✳ PLASMA

Degree of Ionization   In order for plasma to exist, there must be ionization, where an atom is converted into an ion by removing and adding charged particles. Even a gas that has 1 percent ionized particles will exhibit properties of plasma. The degree of ionization, which is mostly controlled by temperature, is the ratio of ions to the total number of molecules. To find the degree of ionization, the formula is:

$$\alpha = n_i / (n_i + n_a)$$

n_i represents the ion density and n_a is the density of atoms that are neutral.

◐ AFRIKAANS

Phonetics and Grammar   Though Afrikaans is a daughter of the Dutch language, and as such, there are many phonetic similarities between the two, Afrikaans has grown to have several differences from Dutch. Afrikaans is a phonetic language, and one of the only Germanic languages that features nasal vowels. Afrikaans is also a simpler language than Dutch. Unlike Dutch, there aren't any long consonants or aspirations after letters *p*, *t*, and *k*, and there is no distinction of gender for nouns and no declensions. To indicate plural, an *e* or an *s* is added to words.

LESSON 34C

VIETNAM WAR

The Kennedy Years   A team sent to Vietnam by President Kennedy in 1961 to report on what was happening there stated that there was a need for military, economic, and technical aid, as well as advisors to stabilize Diem's regime and destroy the NLF. Kennedy agreed to send advisors and machines, but not troops. The plan did not work, and the NLF was becoming more successful. Another plan, called the Strategic Hamlet Program, that would place villagers into hamlets to isolate them from the NLF, also backfired. In 1963, Diem's brother raided a Buddhist pagoda, which led to massive protests in which Buddhist monks performed self-immolation. Pictures of the monks spread worldwide and created outrage, and the United States decided to support a coup. On November 1, 1963, Ngo Dinh Diem and his brother were captured and executed.

CHARLES DICKENS

Oliver Twist   *Oliver Twist* was published serially in 1837. The story was his second novel (the first being *The Pickwick Papers*, which was met with great success), but it was the first of his stories that focused on social commentary and critiquing how public institutions dealt with the poor. Dickens revisited this theme again in *Nicholas Nickleby*. One reason Dickens wrote *Oliver Twist* was because of the Poor Law Amendment Act of 1834, which stripped citizenship rights from the poor, who had to give up their political rights for financial aid and work in factories.

THE NUMBER e

Numerical Series   The numerical value of e goes on for infinity. To find the values of e, you can use several different equations:

$e = 1 + 1/1! + 1/2! + 1/3! + 1/4! + 1/5! + \ldots$
or
$1/e = 1 - 1/1! + 1/2! - 1/3! + 1/4! - \ldots$
or
$e - 1 = 1 + 1/(1 + (1/(2 + 1/(1 + 1/(1 + 1/(4 + 1/(1 + 1/(1 + 1/(1 + 1/(6 + \ldots))))))))))$
or
$(e - 1)/2 = 1/(1 + (1/(6 + 1/(10 + 1/(14 + 1/(18 + \ldots))))))$

PLASMA

Temperatures   In order to sustain ionization, extremely high temperatures are needed. (Otherwise, electrons and ions recombine, forming an atom, and the plasma turns into a gas.) Plasmas can be categorized as thermal and nonthermal. Thermal plasma has heavy particles and electrons in thermal equilibrium (meaning at the same temperature). In nonthermal plasma, electrons are much hotter, meaning they are more ionized than the ions and neutrals. The temperature of plasma is measured in kelvins, also known as electronvolts, and is the thermal kinetic energy found in each particle.

AFRIKAANS

Dialects   In the 1800s, there were three dialects of Afrikaans: Cape Afrikaans, Orange River Afrikaans, and Eastern Border Afrikaans. The Malay slaves who and spoke a form of Portuguese, influenced the Cape Afrikaans dialect. Orange River Afrikaans was influenced by the Koi languages of the Griqualand West areas and Namakwaland. The Eastern Border Afrikaans dialect evolved from those traveling out of the Cape and toward Natal. When the language was standardized, it was based on the Eastern dialect.

VIETNAM WAR

The Johnson Years When Kennedy was assassinated, Lyndon B. Johnson took over, and he was convinced that more needed to be done in Vietnam. In 1968, in the Gulf of Tonkin, two American ships were attacked by North Vietnam. The attack was used by the Johnson administration to get Congress to pass the Gulf of Tonkin Resolution, which allowed Johnson to order the bombing of North Vietnam. By 1968, North Vietnam had continued success launching attacks on southern cities, with the intention of forcing the United States to make a bargain. That year, Johnson decided not to run for re-election.

CHARLES DICKENS

David Copperfield Charles Dickens's eighth novel was *David Copperfield*, published in 1849. The book is considered the closest Charles Dickens ever got to writing an autobiography. In July of 1948, Dickens's sister, who was a model for Scrooge's sister Fan in *A Christmas Carol*, became terminally ill and died in September. Dickens intended to write an autobiography, but the process proved too painful for him, so instead, he fabricated a character and told his story through David Copperfield. In the book, many of the events that David Copperfield (whose initials are the inverse of Dickens's) goes through are dramatizations of Dickens's life.

THE NUMBER *e*

Discrete Accumulation The number *e* is also a very important part of understanding investments and loans. Using *e*, one can easily compute what the limit on the effective rate would be. For example, if you invest $100 into a bank with an annual rate of 4 percent, and your bank offers a monthly compounding, by the end of the year your investment would be worth $104.08. One can use *e* to figure out the limit on the effective rate. For example: $100 \times e^{0.04} = 104.08$.

PLASMA

Differences Between Plasma and Gas Due to the fact that it has no definite volume or form, plasma is most closely related to gas, which shares this property. It is its own form of matter, however, and plasma has several differences from gas. While gas has very low electrical conductivity, plasma has extremely high electrical conductivity that can be seen as infinite. While all gas particles behave similarly, ions, electrons, neutrons, and protons all act independently in plasma. Though for gas, two-particle collisions is the general rule, for plasma, waves that are made up of an organized movement of plasma, interact over long areas.

AFRIKAANS

Afrikaans and Apartheid The white Afrikaans community increasingly separated itself from the English-speaking community, which eventually led to the Anglo-Boer War that lasted from 1899 to 1902. Though the Afrikaners lost, they began a campaign to promote the language. In 1948, the National Party, which was Afrikaans-oriented, won the elections, and instituted apartheid and made it so that black children would only be taught the Afrikaans language. This would link the language to apartheid and the horrible political system of the National Party, and this association still remains.

VIETNAM WAR

Antiwar Movement   Johnson had wished to go to war in Vietnam and have little change in terms of everyday life back home. The Vietnam War, however, was met with a great antiwar movement. In major cities and college campuses across the United States, antiwar protests erupted. One of the most famous events occurred during the 1968 Democratic National Convention, where hundreds of thousands of people came to Chicago to protest the war, leading to a police riot.

CHARLES DICKENS

A Tale of Two Cities   Published in 1859, *A Tale of Two Cities*, Dickens's twelfth novel, was a departure in many ways for the author. The story is historical, with the backdrop being the events of the French Revolution, and is less character-driven and more focused on political events. Dickens shows both the cruelty of the French aristocracy and the suffering of the poor, justifying the need to revolt, but he also depicts the heinous deeds of those revolutionaries as they come to power.

THE NUMBER e

Hyperbolic Trigonometry   The formula for a hyperbole is $x^2 - y^2 = 1$. The x and y coordinates have hyperbolic functions known as hyperbolic cosine and hyperbolic sine, which are written as $x(v) = \cosh v$ and $x(v) = \sinh v$, where v represents the area. An example of this in the real world would be the shape of a hanging necklace, known as a catenary (which can be expressed as $y = \cosh x$). Another way of writing these equations are:

$$\sinh(v) = \frac{e^v - e^{-v}}{2}$$

$$\cosh(v) = \frac{e^v + e^{-v}}{2}$$

PLASMA

Magnetization   When a plasma is magnetized, it features a magnetic field that is so strong it can influence the movement of the charged particles. On average, a particle completes a single gyration around the magnetic field before a collision occurs, and the electrons are often magnetized, not the ions. Magnetized plasma is known as anisotropic, meaning the direction parallel to the magnetic field has properties that are different from those that are perpendicular to the magnetic field.

AFRIKAANS

Afrikaans in Post-Apartheid South Africa   Instead of being one of two official languages in South Africa, when the democratized republic was established in 1994, Afrikaans was downgraded. It is now one of eleven official languages, having lost its special and protected status. The language is still quite prevalent, however, in the media, and is beginning to see a revival in popularity. As time goes on, the language is no longer being directly associated with the oppression of apartheid and the National Party.

VIETNAM WAR

The End of the War When Richard Nixon became president, he had plans to end the war. Nixon's plan, known as Vietnamization, was to encourage the South Vietnamese to take control of the war and bring American troops back home, shifting the fighting to air attacks. During the Nixon years, the United States expanded the war into Laos and Cambodia, violating their international rights, in an attempt to crush Communist supply routes and sanctuaries. In December of 1972, the United States launched bombing raids in the largest cities of the DRV. The bombings were condemned by the international community, and Nixon had to reconsider his strategy. In 1973, the Nixon administration and the GVN signed a peace accord, and hostilities between the DRV and the United States ended. The war in Vietnam continued until April 30, 1975, when the Communists captured Saigon.

CHARLES DICKENS

The Mystery of Edwin Drood Dickens was writing a murder mystery, *The Mystery of Edwin Drood*, when he died, leaving the book unfinished and the mystery unsolved. Since his death, there have been numerous attempts to finish the book. Perhaps one of the most famous was *Drood*, a Broadway musical based on Dickens's story that makes up for the lack of an ending by asking the audience to vote on the answers to the various mysteries. The musical debuted in 1985 and won five Tony Awards, including the Best Musical category.

THE NUMBER *e*

Derangements Derangements are related to permutations. They are solutions that are "all wrong." For example, 10 guests are about to leave your home; if you wanted to figure out how many ways the coats could be randomly put on, it would be a permutation of 10. The derangements are the number of times that no person gets their own coat, or everything is wrong. There are 3,628,800 different permutations and 1,334,961 derangements. If you divide those two numbers, you get e. No matter how many people there are, the odds of getting the correct coat is $1 - 1/e$.

PLASMA

Examples of Plasma Even though plasma is found in the stars and Sun, there is evidence of plasma on the Earth's surface. Lightning, for example, is plasma, with a temperature that can reach ~28,000 Kelvin and densities of electrons that can be up to 10^{24} m^{-3}. Fluorescent lights, sparks, flames, neon signs, plasma displays, and even aurora borealis are all examples of plasma. In neon signs, for example, a glass tube is filled with gas. As the light is turned on, the gas becomes charged by the electricity, creating plasma.

AFRIKAANS

Useful Afrikaans Phrases Here are some helpful Afrikaans phrases to use when traveling to South Africa:

Hello. *Haai, Hallo.*
Good morning. *Goeiemôre.*
Good afternoon. *Goeie middag.*
Good evening. *Goeienaand.*
Good night. *Goeienag.*
How are you? *Hoe gaan dit met jou?*
Pleased to meet you. *Bly te kenne.*
Where are you from? *Waarvandaan kom jy?*

What's your name? *Wat is jou naam?*
I don't understand. *Ek verstaan nie.*
Excuse me. *Verskoon my.*
How much is this? *Hoeveel kos dit?*
Thank you. *Dankie.*
Where's the toilet? *Waar is die toilet?*
Goodbye. *Totsiens.*

1. **The United States did not send troops to Vietnam until the presidency of:**
   a. Eisenhower
   b. Kennedy
   c. Johnson
   d. Nixon

2. **Which of the following describes Nixon's plan of Vietnamization?**
   a. It was to encourage the South Vietnamese to take control of the war, bring American troops back, and have fighting done from the air.
   b. It would place Vietnamese villagers into hamlets, isolating them from the NLF.
   c. It would expand the war into Laos and Cambodia.
   d. It would support the creation of the Southeast Asia Treaty Organization (SEATO).

3. ***A Tale of Two Cities* was a departure from Charles Dickens's earlier work because:**
   a. It was the first to be published as a book and not serialized.
   b. It was a historical novel and not as character-driven.
   c. It was written in French.
   d. It steered away from political and social commentary.

4. **Which Dickens book is considered the most autobiographical?**
   a. *David Copperfield*
   b. *Oliver Twist*
   c. *The Mystery of Edwin Drood*
   d. *A Christmas Carol*

5. **Which of the following is true?**
   a. The exponential function $y = e^x$ has an equal rate of growth to its value.
   b. The exponential function $y = e^x$ has a higher rate of growth to its value.
   c. The exponential function $y = e^x$ has a lower rate of growth to its value.
   d. The exponential function $y = e^x$ is half the rate of growth to its value.

6. **Which of the following correctly finds *e*?**
   a. $e = 2 + 1! + 2! + 3! + 4! + \ldots$
   b. $e = 1 + 1! + 2! + 3! + 4! + \ldots$
   c. $e = 1 + 1/1! + 1/2! + 1/3! + 1/4! + \ldots$
   d. All of the above

7. **Which of the following is a difference between gas and plasma?**
   a. While plasma has very low electrical conductivity, gas has extremely high electrical conductivity that can be seen as infinite.
   b. While gas has very low electrical conductivity, plasma has extremely high electrical conductivity that can be seen as infinite.
   c. While gas has very high electrical conductivity, plasma has extremely low electrical conductivity that can be seen as infinite.
   d. Both gas and plasma have extremely high electrical conductivity, but only gas can be seen as infinite.

8. **At a low temperature, electrons and ions will:**
   a. Break apart from the atom
   b. Recombine and form an atom
   c. Turn into protons
   d. Turn into neutrons

9. **How much of Afrikaans stems from Dutch?**
   a. 25–30 percent
   b. 40–45 percent
   c. 90–95 percent
   d. 50–55 percent

10. **Which of the following is true?**
    a. There are no long consonants in Afrikaans.
    b. There is no distinction in gender for nouns.
    c. There are no declensions.
    d. All of the above.

ANSWER KEY: c, a, b, a, a, c, b, b, c, d

HISTORY: Korean War
Origins of the War, Surprise
Attack from North Korea, Inchon
Invasion, Dismissal of MacArthur,
End of the "Accordion War," The
End of the War

 MATH: Unsolved Math
Problems
P versus *NP* Problem, Hodge
Conjecture, Riemann Hypothesis,
Yang-Mills Existence and Mass
Gap, Navier-Stokes Equations, Birch
and Swinnerton-Dyer Conjecture

LANGUAGE ARTS:
Existentialism
What Is Existentialism?, The
Origins of Existentialism,
Existentialist Literature,
Fyodor Dostoyevsky,
Søren Kierkegaard,
Jean-Paul Sartre

SCIENCE: Anthropology
What Is Anthropology?, Physical
Anthropology, Cultural Anthropology,
Linguistic Anthropology, Archaeology,
Applied Anthropology

Lesson 35

**FOREIGN
LANGUAGE:**
Cherokee
The Origins, Sequoyah,
The Writing System,
Dialects, Creating New
Words, Useful Cherokee
Phrases

KOREAN WAR

Origins of the War   Following World War II, the Soviet Union began moving into Korea. The United States did not want Korea to become another Communist state and moved in as well. The 38th parallel was decided as the division between the part controlled by America (South Korea) and the part controlled by the Soviet Union (North Korea). During this time, the Korean people created an interim government known as the Korean People's Republic, which became increasingly more communist. The Soviet Union recognized the new government, but the United States would not, and the KPR became pro-Soviet. The United States tried to bring a free market to South Korea, but it led to elevated prices and famine. The United States handed the issue over to the UN, and elections were held including all of Korea. Following the elections, the North cut off all power to the South.

EXISTENTIALISM

What Is Existentialism?   Existentialism is the philosophical study of the meaning of existence. There are several key ideas that existentialism touches on, such as free will, the idea that human nature is made by the choices one makes in life, the idea that decisions create stress and have consequences, and that a person is at their best when struggling for life. Existentialism is very much about understanding the meaning of life on a personal level without touching on factors like wealth, social values, or other external forces.

UNSOLVED MATH PROBLEMS

P versus NP Problem   One of the most famous unsolved problems is the P versus NP problem in computer science. Posed by Stephen Cook in 1971, the problem essentially asks whether all problems that have solutions that can be efficiently checked with computers can also be efficiently solved with computers. Another way of asking the P versus NP problem is: If a problem's solutions can be verified rapidly, then can the solutions be computed rapidly? There are currently problems where there is no way to arrive at a solution quickly; however, verifying the answer can be done quickly.

ANTHROPOLOGY

What Is Anthropology?   Anthropology covers a wide area; however, it is essentially the study of humans in the past and in the present. Anthropology draws upon the social, physical, and biological sciences, as well as the humanities. Anthropology can be categorized into four different areas of study: physical (or biological) anthropology, cultural anthropology, linguistic anthropology, and archaeology. One main part of anthropology is to apply this knowledge of humans to be able to solve problems. Often, in order to address a complex matter such as the evolution of humans or spread of disease, anthropologists will have to combine these fields of study.

CHEROKEE

The Origins   The Cherokee language is one of the Iroquoian languages, and it is the only Southern Iroquoian language that is still spoken today. The language came from the Native American people living in what is now North Carolina and northern Georgia. The language is really called Tsalagi, and the word *Cherokee* was actually given by the white settlers, who had learned the word from the Creek people, for whom *Cherokee* meant "people with another language." Today, Cherokee is the healthiest of the Native American languages.

KOREAN WAR

Surprise Attack from North Korea   By 1949, most of the U.S. military had moved out of South Korea, and the United States was afraid to provide too much weaponry, with Rhee, the leader of South Korea, often talking of attacking the North. On June 25, 1950, the North Korean army crossed the 38th parallel and attacked South Korea, stunning the United States, who had no sort of plan ready. South Korea had very little weaponry (as a result of the U.S. withdrawal), while North Korea entered South Korea in Soviet tanks. The UN condemned the actions of North Korea, and in the United States, there was talk of sending General Douglas MacArthur to lead an attack.

EXISTENTIALISM

The Origins of Existentialism   Gabriel Marcel was the first to coin the term *existentialism* in the mid-1940s. However, he was certainly not the first to write on the topic. Existentialist ideas can be found in the work of Henry David Thoreau, Voltaire, and even the teachings of Buddha and in William Shakespeare's *Hamlet*. Søren Kierkegaard is considered the first existentialist, and it is a major theme found in his work related to human existence and free will, but he was not well regarded in his time. In the 1920s, Martin Heidegger, influenced by Kierkegaard's thought, worked on what he referred to as *Dasein*, or being.

UNSOLVED MATH PROBLEMS

Hodge Conjecture   In algebraic geometry, the Hodge conjecture is an unsolved problem that deals with algebraic varieties. In the twentieth century, shapes of complicated objects were becoming more understood by the idea that one could approximate the shape and then build it with simple building blocks. Manifolds are complex shapes that can be described with equations. Algebraic cycles are when more equations are added, producing smaller shapes. Then the issue arises whether one knows if a shape can be stretched into another shape or not. Hodge's conjecture attempts to show which algebraic cycles were equivalent to shapes on a manifold; however, it was never proven.

ANTHROPOLOGY

Physical Anthropology   Physical anthropology, also known as biological anthropology, studies the biological makeup of humans and early humans, as well as how humans have adapted to their environments. In order to understand our ancestors and how humans have evolved, physical anthropologists study artifacts, primates, and the fossil record, as well as the biology and genetic makeup of people who are currently living. Physical anthropology also looks at causes of death and the spread of disease, and examines the ways in which behavior, growth, and development are shaped by cultural and biological processes.

CHEROKEE

Sequoyah   If the Cherokee possessed a written language before the arrival of European settlers, it was lost in the changes wrought by Europeans from the sixteenth to the eighteenth centuries. The language itself would surely have been lost had it not been for one man, Sequoyah, who turned the language into a syllabary (and it is one of the few Native American languages with one). Having worked as a silversmith, Sequoyah learned the writing system of the white people (although he did not know the pronunciations of the letters), and the influence of the Latin alphabet can be seen in the system. Cherokee is polysynthetic, meaning that many morphemes are linked to form one word.

KOREAN WAR

Inchon Invasion   North Korea had captured most of South Korea, alarming the United States. The United Nations was persuaded by the United States to support South Korea, and 300,000 UN troops (of which, 260,000 were American) went to Korea in July of 1950, led by General MacArthur. MacArthur planned an amphibious attack at the port of Inchon. The North Koreans were driven back, and South Korea was recaptured. After reclaiming South Korea, the American troops attacked North Korea, and reached as far as the Chinese border, which worried the Chinese, and they began to attack. The Chinese used "human wave tactics," and once they were able to drive the Americans back, they recaptured North Korea and headed for South Korea. MacArthur wished to use the atomic bomb, but Truman would not have it, and instead sent more troops, which eventually drove the Chinese army back.

EXISTENTIALISM

Existentialist Literature   The ideas of existentialism were not only featured in philosophical theory, but also in literature. In fact, some of the most acclaimed existentialist work is actually found in novels and plays. Existentialist literature focused on attempting to find meaning and make sense of a world that was filled with chaos. As a result, existentialist literature often featured themes such as absurdism, alienation, and isolation.

UNSOLVED MATH PROBLEMS

Riemann Hypothesis   The Riemann hypothesis deals with the Riemann zeta function, a complex function that deals with complex numbers (i). For the Riemann zeta function, a zero of a function is not as simple as a function like $f(a + bi) = 0$. Instead, there are two types of zeros: trivial and nontrivial. Trivial zeros occur at even integers that are negative, and the nontrivial zeros appear at anything other than those, and at $\frac{1}{2} + bi$. The Riemann hypothesis suggests that all nontrivial zeros are like that, but no one has been able to prove this is the case.

ANTHROPOLOGY

Cultural Anthropology   Cultural anthropology focuses on people living today. Cultural anthropologists look at practices and patterns across cultures, especially in regard to how groups of people govern and organize themselves. An important part of cultural anthropology is that it examines the similarities and differences among societies with topics such as race, class, sexuality, and nationality. One distinction between cultural anthropology and the other types of anthropology is that researchers usually have the chance to participate and get hands-on experience, while dealing with very real topics such as ecology, health, education, the environment, development, social change, and agriculture.

CHEROKEE

The Writing System   The syllabary that Sequoyah introduced is still in use to this day. The syllabary features a total of eighty-five characters, some of which are based (in shape only) on the Latin alphabet, and is read from left to right, horizontally. Sequoyah had been introduced to English, Greek, and Hebrew letters without any knowledge of how to read them. Within a time period of just a year since the introduction of the writing system, 90 percent of the Cherokee people could read and write. Each symbol in the syllabary is representative of a syllable, not a phoneme.

KOREAN WAR

Dismissal of MacArthur Without telling anyone else, General MacArthur sent an ultimatum to China to withdraw their troops or he would attack. When Truman found out about MacArthur's actions, he was outraged and knew he had to fire MacArthur. Truman waited, however, and when Congress approved NATO, Truman needed to find another reason. News spread that MacArthur wanted to go against Truman's policies and use the Chinese Nationalist Forces to anger the People's Republic of China. When a congressman read MacArthur's plan before Congress, Truman began to discuss dismissing MacArthur. General MacArthur was fired on April 11, 1951.

 # EXISTENTIALISM

Fyodor Dostoyevsky One of the most important existentialist novelists was the Russian essayist and novelist, Fyodor Dostoyevsky, who lived from 1821 to 1881. Dostoyevsky is perhaps best known for his novels *Crime and Punishment*, *The Brothers Karamazov*, and *The Idiot*. Dostoyevsky's most important work relating to existentialism, however, was his *Notes from the Underground*. His work focused on the problem of freedom. To Dostoyevsky, man was limited by everything, including society, the economy, the church, and God. Though Dostoyevsky had extreme political and social views, he was a devout Christian.

 # UNSOLVED MATH PROBLEMS

Yang-Mills Existence and Mass Gap Physicists have been able to unify three out of the four fundamental forces (electromagnetism, the weak force, and the strong force). Chen Ning Yang and Robert Mills came up with a theory in which they suggested that strong and weak nuclear forces could be illustrated with action functionals that had more complex, non-Albelian symmetry groups. Though their theory is successful, no one is able to make any logical sense of why it works.

 # ANTHROPOLOGY

Linguistic Anthropology Linguistic anthropology is the study of languages, and more specifically, how language influences and mirrors social life and culture. Linguistic anthropology examines the role language has in establishing ideologies, belief systems, and social identities, as well as creating communication patterns and cultural representations of one's social and natural world. To study linguistic anthropology, one must take on an active role, performing interviews, and observing the use of language.

CHEROKEE

Dialects There were originally three major dialects found in the Cherokee language: the Lower dialect, the Middle dialect (known as the Kituhwa or Giduwa dialect), and the Western dialect (also known as the Overhill or Otali dialect). In 1900, the Lower dialect became extinct. The Middle dialect spoken by the Eastern band is currently the closest dialect to the original Cherokee language. The Otali dialect is the most different, containing pronunciation differences and words adopted from English.

KOREAN WAR

End of the "Accordion War" Following the dismissal of MacArthur, Matthew Ridgway controlled the U.S. effort. On April 22, 1951, the Chinese attempted to recapture Seoul, but failed. Following another failed attack, the United States believed a counterattack would be successful. By May 30, the UN/US/ROK forces were back at the 38th parallel, and both sides were at a stalemate. Truman began to push for an end to the war, and the United States contacted the Soviet Union, which was willing to negotiate. Peace talks began on July 8.

EXISTENTIALISM

Søren Kierkegaard Søren Kierkegaard was a Danish philosopher who lived from 1813 to 1855 and is one of the founders of existentialism, though much of his work was based on his faith in God. His book *Fear and Trembling* is key to the origins of existentialism. Kierkegaard attempted to understand Abraham's anxiety when God told him he had to kill Isaac, his only son, to show his faith. To understand this, Kierkegaard creates the "Knight of Faith" and the "Tragic Hero." To Kierkegaard, the Tragic Hero commits acts within social or ethical codes, which Abraham, Kierkegaard claimed, did not do. Instead, Abraham was a Knight of Faith who knew killing his son was wrong, but if he didn't do it, he would be going against God. Ethics now turns into temptation, and the Knight of Faith shows that faith is a reason to rise above ethics.

UNSOLVED MATH PROBLEMS

Navier-Stokes Equations The Navier-Stokes equations describe the motion of fluids (which are gases and liquids) in space. Though these equations are crucial in fluid mechanics, understanding of the solutions is not complete. It is believed that to explain and predict turbulence (another problem in physics that remains unsolved despite its importance and significance in engineering and science) and breeze, one can use the Navier-Stokes Equations, but relatively little is understood about the equations.

ANTHROPOLOGY

Archaeology Archaeology studies the ancestors of humans, along with their cultures and ways of life, through analyzing fossil remains and artifacts. Evidence like animal bones, pottery, and stone tools are used to learn about the culture of early humans, and their interactions with each other and their environment. In archaeology, one assumes that there are basic continuities with humans over a specific time and place; however, it is also understood that each society is living in that particular time, and is thus, a product of that time period.

CHEROKEE

Creating New Words Because the Cherokee language is polysynthetic, the ability to create new words can be easily done. For example, the word *policeman* is *didaniyisgi* (written as ᏗᏓᏂᏱᏍᎩ), which actually means "he catches them finally and conclusively." The word for *attorney* is *ditiyohihi* (written as ᏗᏘᏲᎯᎯ), literally meaning "he argues repeatedly and on purpose with a purpose." Words have also been taken from the English language and have been adopted into Cherokee (for example, *kawi* means "coffee," and the word *gasoline* is the same in Cherokee and in English).

 KOREAN WAR

The End of the War   Dwight Eisenhower became president in 1953, and no real progress had been made in the negotiations. On June 8, both sides came to an agreement with a document known as the Terms of Reference, which dealt with prisoners of war. Once the POW issue was resolved, the sides focused on a peace treaty. On July 27, 1953, China, North Korea, and the UN signed an armistice (South Korea refused). Along the 38th Parallel, a buffer zone was created between the North and South. North Korea and South Korea remained separate, and because the treaty was never signed by the South, they are technically still at war with one another.

EXISTENTIALISM

Jean-Paul Sartre   Jean-Paul Sartre was a French existentialist who lived from 1905 to 1980. Among other things, Sartre wrote novels, screenplays, and plays. One of his most famous works was his book *Being and Nothingness*, which focused on the consciousness of being. Sartre suggests that appearance is the only reality, and that there are two kinds of being: in-itself and for-itself. In-itself refers to inanimate objects that just exist without any active or passive consciousness, while for-itself refers to something that is cognizant of its awareness. When a person gazes at another person, the person goes from a being-for-itself to a being-in-itself.

UNSOLVED MATH PROBLEMS

Birch and Swinnerton-Dyer Conjecture   The Birch and Swinnerton-Dyer conjecture deals with number theory. The conjecture deals with arithmetic data, the elliptic curve, the number field, and the Hasse-Weil L-function. The Birch and Swinnerton-Dyer conjecture was deemed one of the seven most important open problems by the Clay Mathematics Institute. The Birch and Swinnerton-Dyer conjecture states that if $\zeta(1)$ is 0, then the number of rational points is infinite. If $\zeta(1)$ does not equal 0, then the number of solutions is finite.

ANTHROPOLOGY

Applied Anthropology   Applied anthropology uses the ideas and concepts of anthropology and relates them to current problems and issues of the present-day in an effort to help solve them. Applied anthropology can be used on a large scale, such as impacting the study of economic development patterns or public health methods, and it can be used on a smaller scale, for example, helping in the design of airplane seats or work stations. Essentially, what applied anthropology does is it takes anthropology, something that is mostly thought of as scholarly and academic, and applies it to the real world.

⊙ CHEROKEE

Useful Cherokee Phrases   Here are some helpful phrases to use when speaking with a Cherokee person. Note that these are written phonetically.

Hello. *O-si-yo.*
Good morning. *O-s-da sunalei.*
Good evening. *O-s-da sv-hi-ye-yi.*
Good night. *O-s-da sv-no-i.*
How are you? *(T)do-`hi-tsu?*
Thank you. *Wa-do.*
What is your name? *Ga-do-de-tsa do?*

What is this? *Do-i-s-di-hi-na?*
I don't understand. *Tla-i-go-li-ga.*
Is this where you live? *Hi `yas-di `ste nv `sv?*
What are they doing? *Ga-do-a-na-du-ne?*
Goodbye. *Do-na-da-`go-v-I* (to one person).
   Do-`da-ga-g`hv-i (to a group of people).

1. **The 38th parallel divided Korea into, North Korea and South Korea. Which of the following is true?**
   a. North Korea was controlled by the United States and South Korea was controlled by the Soviet Union.
   b. South Korea was controlled by the United States and North Korea was controlled by the Soviet Union.
   c. South Korea was controlled by China and North Korea was controlled by the Soviet Union.
   d. North Korea was controlled by China and South Korea was controlled by the Soviet Union.

2. **At the beginning of the war, South Korea had very little weaponry because:**
   a. South Korea had lost them all to China.
   b. The Soviet Union refused to provide too many weapons, fearing they would use them to attack the North.
   c. America refused to provide too many weapons, fearing they would use them to attack the North.
   d. South Korea had lost them all to Japan.

3. **Existentialism is:**
   a. The philosophical study of human reason
   b. The philosophical study of mental activity
   c. The philosophical attitude that questions whether one could obtain knowledge
   d. The philosophical study of what it means to exist

4. **Kierkegaard's Knight of Faith proves:**
   a. There is no God.
   b. Faith is a reason to rise above ethics.
   c. Acts are committed based on ethical and social codes.
   d. God did not want Abraham to really kill his son.

5. **Which of the following asks the question: "If a problem's solutions can be verified rapidly, then can the solutions be computed rapidly"?**
   a. Birch and Swinnerton-Dyer conjecture
   b. *P* versus *NP* problem
   c. Yang-Mills existence and mass gap
   d. Riemann hypothesis

6. **Which of the following suggests that all nontrivial zeros are at ½ + bi?**
   a. Birch and Swinnerton-Dyer conjecture
   b. Riemann hypothesis
   c. Yang-Mills existence and mass gap
   d. *P* versus *NP* problem

7. **Which of the following examines the similarities and differences among societies with topics such as race, class, sexuality, and nationality?**
   a. Applied anthropology
   b. Archaeology
   c. Cultural anthropology
   d. Linguistic anthropology

8. **To study the ancestors of humans, archaeology uses:**
   a. Pottery
   b. Fossil remains
   c. Stone tools
   d. All of the above

9. **Sequoyah is responsible for:**
   a. Creating a polysynthetic language
   b. Creating Kituhwa
   c. Creating Otali
   d. Creating the written Cherokee language

10. **Because the Cherokee language is polysynthetic:**
    a. It is impossible for new words to be created.
    b. The letters used from the Latin alphabet do not feature the same sounds.
    c. New words can easily be created.
    d. There are only two dialects to the language.

HISTORY: Civil Rights

Brown v. Board of Education, Rosa Parks, Project C, Desegregation of the University of Alabama, The March on Washington, Civil Rights Act of 1964

MATH: Diophantine Equations

What Are Diophantine Equations?, Examples of Diophantine Equations, Hilbert's Tenth Problem, Linear Diophantine Equations, Exponential Diophantine Equations, General Method to Use for First-Order Equations with Two Variables

LANGUAGE ARTS: Franz Kafka

About Franz Kafka, Kafka and Existentialism, "The Metamorphosis," *The Trial*, *The Castle*, *Amerika*

SCIENCE: Mitosis

Prophase, Metaphase, Anaphase, Telophase, Cytokinesis, Meiosis

Lesson 36

FOREIGN LANGUAGE: Khoisan Languages

About Khoisan Languages, Hadza, Sandawe, Khoe, Tuu, Other Click Languages

CIVIL RIGHTS

Brown v. Board of Education   On May 17, 1954, the Supreme Court announced one of the most important verdicts relating to a change in civil rights. The case revolved around Linda Brown, an African American third grader, who, in order to get to her elementary school, had to walk a mile, even though a white school was closer to her. Brown was denied access by the school principal, and the case went to the Supreme Court. The Supreme Court ruled that "separate but equal" was, in fact, not equal at all, and that segregation of public schools was unconstitutional.

FRANZ KAFKA

About Franz Kafka   Franz Kafka is considered one of the most important existentialist writer. Kafka, a Jewish man from Prague, lived from 1883 to 1924. Kafka grew up studying at German schools, which was considered the language of the elite at the time, and worked for a large insurance company. Kafka's work often explores themes of alienation and the absurdity of life. The only work published during Kafka's lifetime were his articles and short stories. His three novels, which are considered masterpieces, were unfinished when he died, and Kafka wished them to be destroyed. However, Kafka's friend Max Brod did not comply with his wishes and had them published.

DIOPHANTINE EQUATIONS

What Are Diophantine Equations?   Named after Diophantus of Alexandria of the third century, Diophantine equations are equations that feature indeterminate polynomials, where variables are only allowed to be integers. In other words, the value of variables like x and y have to be whole numbers. Diophantine equations relate to algebraic surface and algebraic curves, and involve finding the values of the integers so that the equations work out correctly. Diophantus was one of the first people that introduced symbolism into algebraic formulas. While some equations have a finite solution, others have no solution at all. You've already seen plenty of Diophantine equations throughout this book.

MITOSIS

Prophase   If you recall from earlier, mitosis is cell division. Following interphase, which prepares the cell for division, the next step in the cycle is prophase. In prophase, the chromatin will condense and become chromosomes, which have duplicated and now have sister chromatids. The chromatids are identical to each other and are connected, forming an X. The mitotic spindle, which moves the chromosomes, is formed and set up away from the nucleus. By the end of this step, the nuclear envelope is broken down into vesicles.

KHOISAN LANGUAGES

About Khoisan Languages   The Khoisan languages do not belong to any other language families, and are indigenous to eastern and southern Africa. These are the click languages found in Africa. Several of these have become extinct, most of them are endangered, and very few have a written language. These languages feature click consonants as phonemes. Though previously believed to have been related, the Khoisan languages are in fact separate from each other; however, they are grouped together because they all feature the click consonant. The name *Khoisan* is derived from the Khoi-Khoi group found in South Africa and the San group (or Bushmen) found in Namibia.

🏛 CIVIL RIGHTS

Rosa Parks On December 1, 1955, Rosa Parks boarded a bus in Montgomery, Alabama. A white passenger told her to give up her seat and move to the "colored section," which was in the back of the bus. Parks refused and, as a result, was arrested. In response to her arrest, the African American community of Montgomery, led by Reverend Martin Luther King Jr., boycotted the city's public transportation. The boycott lasted for 381 days and reduced revenue by 80 percent. On December 21, 1956, the buses were desegregated.

📖 FRANZ KAFKA

Kafka and Existentialism Kafka's work explores fully the concepts of absurdity and dread. Kafka wrote about characters in a surreal world who only wanted to be recognized and accepted by those around them. His work invokes concepts of cruelty, pity, and injustice. He placed rationality in the irrational. His work shows that there is nothing a person can do to give meaning to his or her relationship with the world.

DIOPHANTINE EQUATIONS

Examples of Diophantine Equations You have seen countless examples of Diophantine equations. The values of x, y, and z are unknown and represent real values.

The Pythagorean theorem is one example of a Diophantine equation:

$$a^2 + b^2 = c^2$$

Another example is Pell's equation, where n is a constant:

$$x2 - ny2 = \pm 1$$

The Erdős–Straus conjecture states:

$$\frac{4}{n} = \frac{1}{x} + \frac{1}{y} + \frac{1}{z}$$

This can also be stated as the polynomial equation:

$$4xyz = yzn + xzn + xyn = n(yz + xz + xy)$$

⚛ MITOSIS

Metaphase In metaphase, chromosomes are aligned along the middle of the nucleus of the cell and are held in place by microtubules of spindle fibers. This is known as the metaphase plate. Chromosomes are oriented so that kinetochores, a protein structure on the chromosomes, are facing the pole, and each tail of the chromosomes are facing each other. The organization allows for the new nuclei to receive a single copy of each chromosome when separation occurs (in the next phase).

🗣 KHOISAN LANGUAGES

Hadza Hadza is spoken by around 800 people in Tanzania, and around half of those that speak Hadza remain hunters and gatherers. The Hadza language is not related to any other Khoisan language. Even though it features clicks, the words found in the language are unique and do not originate from any other languages. It has been suggested that the Hadza people and the Jul'hoan people have the most different mitochondrial DNA found within any group of people, and that perhaps these people were the first to split from the family tree. This would suggest that their languages are the closest to the original human languages, and that the first languages featured clicks.

CIVIL RIGHTS

Project C   Martin Luther King Jr. and the Southern Christian Leadership Conference created a plan to challenge the segregation of Birmingham, Alabama, and this plan came to be known as "Project C" (for confrontation). Their strategy involved sending a message about the horrors of segregation through nonviolence, with boycotts, rallies, and peaceful demonstrations. The police reacted to these nonviolent actions with police dogs, violence, and fire hoses. On April 12, 1963, Martin Luther King was arrested. While in prison, King wrote his famous "Letter from a Birmingham Jail."

FRANZ KAFKA

"The Metamorphosis"   One of Kafka's most well-known stories is "The Metamorphosis." The story revolves around Gregor Samsa, who one day awakes to discover that he has turned into a large insect (it is never mentioned what kind). The story follows Gregor as he deals with this situation, and how his family deals with it. Ultimately, the family cannot stand to look at Gregor anymore and Gregor dies, giving the family relief that he is gone. The story deals with the absurdity of life, the disconnect between one's body and one's mind, alienation, and how much sympathy a person can have.

DIOPHANTINE EQUATIONS

Hilbert's Tenth Problem   In 1900, German mathematician David Hilbert created a list of twenty-three mathematical problems that had not been solved at the time. His tenth problem proposed a question as to whether there was an algorithm that existed that could determine if there was a solution to any random Diophantine equation. There is an algorithm that exists for first-order Diophantine equations (meaning the variables do not have any powers greater than 1). A mathematician named Matiyasevich was able to prove in Matiyasevich's theorem that it was impossible to create a general algorithm.

MITOSIS

Anaphase   The chromosomes that are paired begin to separate at the kinetochores. The kinetochores then start to move toward the poles. Once this has happened, the polar fibers will elongate, which starts to spread the poles farther apart from one another. The sister chromatids then separate, and move toward their related poles.

KHOISAN LANGUAGES

Sandawe   Around 40,000 people in Tanzania speak Sandawe. It is believed that Sandawe is related to Khoe, with its closest relatives being those languages found in Namibia and Botswana. The language features two dialects, a southeastern dialect and a northwestern dialect. The differences between the dialects include the talking speed, the dropping of some vowels, and slight grammatical differences. The language features fifteen clicks that act as consonants.

🏛 CIVIL RIGHTS

Desegregation of the University of Alabama   In 1963, George Wallace, who had run his campaign with a slogan of "segregation now, segregation tomorrow, segregation forever," became governor of Alabama. In June of that same year, the state government was barred from interfering with the admission of two African American students attending the University of Alabama. Wallace made himself the registrar of the university temporarily, and stood at the door of the building, refusing to let the students come in to register. President Kennedy called in the Alabama National Guard, and 100 members of the National Guard escorted the two students. The commander, General Henry Graham, ordered Wallace to move, telling him "step aside."

📖 FRANZ KAFKA

The Trial   The Trial tells the story of Joseph K., a young man who, on his thirtieth birthday, is visited by two warders and arrested, even though he has not done anything. K. is told to stay at home and wait for instructions. The story then follows K.'s process of dealing with the law and the untouchable court. On Joseph K.'s thirty-first birthday, he is once again visited by two warders, who bring him to a quarry and tell him to kill himself. Though K. does not fight them, he cannot do it, and they kill him.

➕ DIOPHANTINE EQUATIONS

Linear Diophantine Equations   A linear Diophantine equation is written in the form: $ax + by = c$. If the value of c is the greatest common divisor of both a and b, then there is an infinite number of solutions. A problem that meets these characteristics is known as a Bézout's identity. This is also the case when the value of c is a multiple of a and b's greatest common divisor. When the value of c is not the greatest common divisor for both a and b or a multiple of a and b's greatest common divisor, then the Diophantine equation does not have any solutions.

⚛ MITOSIS

Telophase   Once the chromatids have reached their opposite poles, new membranes begin to form around the sets of chromosomes, forming two nuclei. These two nuclei are, for the time being, in the same cell. RNA synthesis occurs and the nuclear envelop reappears, which then breaks down the chromosomes to the point that they can no longer be viewed with a light microscope.

🗣 KHOISAN LANGUAGES

Khoe   The Khoe languages, of which there are seven languages that still exist today, is the largest and most diverse of the Khoisan languages, with over a quarter-million people speaking a Khoe language. The Khoe languages were the first that European colonists were introduced to. The most well-known language is Nama, found in Namibia. Though Khoe languages make use of clicks, they are not used as much as in other Khoisan languages. There are two main branches of Khoe: Khoekhoe, found in South Africa and Namibia, and Tshu-Khwe, found in Botswana and Zimbabwe.

ⓜ CIVIL RIGHTS

The March on Washington   On August 28, 1963, a massive march was held in Washington, D.C. The march, which was intended to pressure the government to act faster, had around 300,000 demonstrators. Civil rights organizations marched for an end to segregation in public schools, the right to vote, protection from police brutality, and a law that prohibited segregation in the work place, among other things. The event featured performances from artists such as Bob Dylan and Joan Baez, readings by celebrities Paul Newman and Sidney Poitier, and most importantly, Martin Luther King delivered his "I Have a Dream" speech.

🖉 FRANZ KAFKA

The Castle   *The Castle* tells the story of K., a land surveyor, who arrives at a village to do work. The village's government office is found in a Castle above the village. The task of doing the work he was hired to do becomes increasingly more difficult for K. as he interacts in the village and bureaucracy. *The Castle* is Kafka's only book that expresses close relationships between characters. Instead of an unattainable quest, such as those found in Kafka's other works, *The Castle* is really about the lives of the villagers.

DIOPHANTINE EQUATIONS

Exponential Diophantine Equations   When there are exponents with a variable or additional variables, it is known as an exponential Diophantine equation. For example, the Ramanujan–Nagell equation states $2^n - 7 = x^2$. There is no general theory that allows one to solve these types of problems. Thus, in order to figure out the solution, one can try simple trial and error, testing out possible values and working from the solutions to see which number it should be, or methods like Størmer's theorem which is based on Pell's equation.

❋ MITOSIS

Cytokinesis   Technically, cytokinesis is not a part of mitosis; rather, it completes the cell division. After telophase, there are two nuclei in a single cell. All that is left is for the cell to divide in half. Cytokinesis actually begins during anaphase and continues simultaneously through telophase. The cell first begins to furrow, a process where it starts pinching in. The cell pinches until there are two daughter cells, each with its own nucleus. These two cells will then continue the cycle.

KHOISAN LANGUAGES

Tuu   Another language family is the Tuu languages, which consists of two clusters, and is a part of the Khoisan family (they are referred to as Southern Khoisan). The two branches of the Tuu languages are Taa and !Kwi. Once widespread, today the only !Kwi language that still exists is Nluu (which only has around a dozen elderly speakers). Taa also only has one existing language today; however, it is more robust, with around 4,200 speakers of the language. There are many similarities between the Tuu languages and the Juu languages. The Tuu languages feature what is known as bilabial clicks, which are more complex and distinct, and it is one of the only languages to do so.

CIVIL RIGHTS

Civil Rights Act of 1964   In 1963, President Kennedy proposed a new Civil Rights Act. When Kennedy was assassinated, the bill was still being worked on in Congress. On July 2, 1964, the bill was signed into law. The Civil Rights Act of 1964 made it illegal to racially discriminate in public places like restaurants, hotels, and movie theaters, and required that employers provide equal opportunities for employment. Any project that received federal funding would have it cut if it was found that there was discrimination based on race, color, or nationality. It also stated that standards must be uniform concerning the right to vote.

FRANZ KAFKA

Amerika   Kafka's *Amerika* follows the journey of Karl Rossmann, a seventeen-year-old European emigrant, who is forced to go to New York after a sex scandal with a housemaid. Unbeknownst to Karl, his uncle, Senator Jacob, is also on the boat. Senator Jacob recognizes Karl and has him stay with him, but later abandons Karl. The book then follows Karl as he interacts with people and gets various jobs, until ultimately, Karl decides to join a theater in Oklahoma. The book was never finished, but Kafka told Max Brod that it would end on that chapter, with the theme of reconciliation.

DIOPHANTINE EQUATIONS

General Method to Use for First-Order Equations with Two Variables
When given a first-order equation that has two variables, there are several steps you can take to figure it out. Instead of using x, y, and z, simplify it to x, x_2, x_3. The first step is to rewrite the equation so that it appears as $ax_2 + bx_1 = c$, so that a is larger than b. Then divide a by b, creating a quotient and a remainder (q and r). Rewrite a as: $q \cdot b + r$. Now, make the equation so that the left side looks like: $q \cdot$ term $+$ value $\cdot x_2$. Then replace term with x_3.

MITOSIS

Meiosis   Meiosis is a cell division that occurs to produce germ cells like the sperm and egg, and thus is a necessity for sexual reproduction. In meiosis, a copy of the mother's chromosomes and a copy of the father's chromosomes are taken. Four haploid cells are produced, each with one copy of a chromosome. This process is responsible for creating genetic diversity, because each cell has its own unique combination of chromosomes. A single parent cell will create four daughter cells, and each daughter cell has half the amount of chromosomes as the parent cell.

KHOISAN LANGUAGES

Other Click Languages   Not every language that features clicks is considered a Khoisan language. There are several non-Khoisan languages that feature the click consonant. The Nguni languages and Bantu languages both have the click, and even an extinct Australian language, known as Damin, featured clicks. The Bantu incorporated clicks into the languages as a result of neighboring Khoisan languages and absorption and displacement of those populations, especially through intermarriage. The Dahalo language of Kenya is believed to have gotten clicks from an earlier language, which might mean it is in the same situation as Sandawe or Hadza.

1. The idea that "separate but equal" was not actually equal first appeared in:
   a. *Brown v. Board of Education*
   b. The Boycott of Montgomery public transportation
   c. The March on Washington
   d. The Civil Rights Act of 1964

2. In response to George Wallace refusing to let African American students enter the University of Alabama, what happened?
   a. President Kennedy called in the National Guard.
   b. Riots broke out.
   c. The students were not allowed to attend the school.
   d. Martin Luther King Jr. delivered his "I Have a Dream" speech.

3. In "The Metamorphosis," what happens to the protagonist, Gregor Samsa, in the beginning of the book?
   a. He leaves for America.
   b. He travels to a village for work.
   c. He turns into a giant insect.
   d. He is arrested for a crime he did not commit.

4. Which of the following is a theme found in the work of Franz Kafka?
   a. Absurdity
   b. Alienation
   c. Injustice
   d. All of the above

5. In Diophantine equations, the value of variables x and y are:
   a. Decimals
   b. Fractions
   c. Whole numbers
   d. Imaginary numbers

6. In $ax + by = c$, if the value of c is the greatest common divisor of both a and b, then there is:
   a. Two solutions
   b. No solution
   c. An infinite number of solutions
   d. Only one solution

7. At which stage do two nuclei form?
   a. Metaphase
   b. Anaphase
   c. Telophase
   d. Cytokinesis

8. At which phase do chromosomes align along the middle of the nucleus of the cell, which are then held in place by microtubules of spindle fibers?
   a. Metaphase
   b. Anaphase
   c. Telophase
   d. Cytokinesis

9. What might the different mitochondrial DNA found in the Hadza people imply?
   a. They are the closest group of people related to Neanderthals.
   b. Original human languages featured clicks.
   c. They speak a more advanced language due to their DNA.
   d. Clicking is found in DNA.

10. The largest and most diverse Khoisan languages are:
    a. The Khoe languages
    b. The Tuu languages
    c. Sandawe
    d. Taa

ANSWER KEY: a, a, c, d, c, c, c, a, b, a

HISTORY: Gulf War

Invasion of Kuwait, Operation Desert Shield and Operation Desert Storm, Scud Missile Attacks, Battle of Khafji, End of the War, The Impact on the Soldiers

MATH: Category Theory

What Is Category Theory?, Functors, What Categories Are Made Of, Completeness and Co-Completeness, Natural Transformations, Duality

LANGUAGE ARTS: Journalism

Johann Carolus, The *Oxford Gazette*, The Civil War, Henry Stanley, William Randolph Hearst, Muckraking

SCIENCE: Types of Animals

Vertebrates, Invertebrates, and Chordates, Mammals, Reptiles, Echinoderms, Mollusks, Marsupials

Lesson 37

FOREIGN LANGUAGE: Amharic

The Origins, Grammar, Writing System, Rastafarians, Amharic Today, Useful Amharic Phrases

GULF WAR

Invasion of Kuwait From 1980 to 1988, Iraq and Iran engaged in an extremely bloody conflict that left Iraq deep in debt. On August 2, 1991, Saddam Hussein sent 100,000 troops to Kuwait. Saddam believed that Kuwait exceeded its quota in the production of oil, driving the global market prices down, and as a result Iraq was losing much-needed revenue from its oil. There were two days of intense fighting, which resulted in the Kuwaiti Armed Forces being overrun or fleeing to Bahrain and Saudi Arabia. Iraq occupied Kuwait for seven months, and during that time, Kuwait was looted and there were human rights abuses.

JOURNALISM

Johann Carolus Johann Carolus lived from 1575 to 1634, and is responsible for publishing the very first newspaper, called *Relation aller Fürnemmen und gedenckwürdigen Historien* (meaning "Collection of all distinguished and commemorable news"). The paper was published in 1605 in Strasburg when it was part of the Holy Roman Empire. Carolus made his living writing these newsletters by hand and selling them to subscribers at high prices. In 1604, Carolus bought a printing shop and began printing his newsletters. He realized that if he printed a lot and sold them cheaper, he would make more money.

CATEGORY THEORY

What Is Category Theory? Category theory is an extremely complex process that takes mathematical results that already exist and abstracts them even further. Not only does this give perspective for results, but it also unifies mathematics. This can lead to some very important outcomes. Category theory can reveal that unrelated topics in mathematics have common ideas, a proven result can create many results in other areas of math, and extremely difficult problems can be translated into problems that are easier and relate to other fields of math. Concepts are viewed as a collection of arrows and objects that satisfy specific conditions.

TYPES OF ANIMALS

Vertebrates, Invertebrates, and Chordates Vertebrates, which belong in the subphylum Vertebrata, are any animals that have an endoskeleton, or internal skeleton, with a backbone and vertebrae. Invertebrates, on the other hand, do not have an endoskeleton and do not constitute a separate subphylum, but are found in a wide variety of animal groups. Chordates are somewhere in the middle. Most chordates are vertebrates; however, not all of them are. Chordates don't have spines but have nerve chords at a stage during development. Any animal with a spine is a chordate because the nerve chord turns into the spinal cord. Humans are chordates; however, the features that make us chordates are developed in the embryo stage and no longer exist when we are grown.

AMHARIC

The Origins Spoken in Ethiopia, Amharic is a Semitic language that stems from the Ge'ez language. In the first millennium B.C., south Arabian immigrants brought the Sabean language to Ethiopia. In the next millennium, the Ethiopians had their own version of the language, with influence from the Cushitic people, known as Ge'ez. Before the tenth century, Ge'ez was no longer used as the spoken language; however, it is still used by the Ethiopian Orthodox Church. From Ge'ez came three languages: Tigrinya (which most closely resembles Ge'ez), Tigré, and Amharic.

GULF WAR

Operation Desert Shield and Operation Desert Storm   Saddam Hussein's actions created a threat to the United States, especially relating to the oil production in the Persian Gulf. With the approval of Saudi Arabia, President George H. W. Bush sent ground troops and warplanes to Saudi Arabia as Iraqi troops began approaching the borders of Saudi Arabia, indicating an interest in the oil fields. The U.S. deployment sent out to defend Saudi Arabia was known as Operation Desert Shield. It was the largest deployment since the Vietnam War. Thirty other nations joined the United States. On January 17, 1991, with the understanding that Saddam Hussein would not withdraw, Desert Shield turned into Desert Storm.

JOURNALISM

The *Oxford Gazette*   One of the most important milestones in the history of journalism was the publication of the *Oxford Gazette* in 1665. The *Oxford Gazette* was the first newspaper that was ever printed. The paper was available to every class, and most significantly, the text was separated into columns. The *Gazette* was printed twice a week under the same name, which was also a major change. Other newspapers during this time that were published twice a week would alternate titles. The *Gazette*, the official publication of King Charles II, was printed in two locations: London and Oxford. The *Oxford Gazette* later changed its name to the *London Gazette*, and it still exists to this day.

CATEGORY THEORY

Functors   Categories can be thought of as even more abstract. A category is a kind of structure, and as such, one can search for processes that preserve this type of structure. Those processes are known as functors. What functors do is associate an object of a category to another object from another category (and with every morphism in the first, a morphism in the second is associated). Functors allow one to study the relationships among a variety of classes of structures; a fundamental concept in areas such as algebraic topology.

TYPES OF ANIMALS

Mammals   There are several characteristics that differentiate mammals from other animals. Mammals have hair or fur that covers the body (even some cetaceans, i.e., whales and dolphins, have a thin covering of hair); they are warm-blooded, meaning they are capable of regulating the temperature of their bodies; and they give birth to babies that are fully formed. Cetaceans are considered mammals because they breathe air with lungs, give birth to live offspring, have some hair, and are warm-blooded, just like humans, cats, dogs, elephants, and primates.

AMHARIC

Grammar   Amharic is considered to be a pro-drop language. This means that pronouns can be dropped when speaking and are in some way inferable. Sentences without any elements emphasized will not feature independent pronouns. In Amharic, the verbs agree with the person, gender, and number of the subject. Gender is expressed in several different ways, and nouns are either masculine or feminine. The feminine gender not only indicates sex, but it is also used when indicating something little or when expressing sympathy or tenderness.

GULF WAR

Scud Missile Attacks   Iraq had Scud missiles, tactical ballistic missiles developed by the Soviet Union that were designed to carry chemical and nuclear warheads. Casualties from Scuds ranged from extensive to very little. On January 17, Iraq fired a total of seven Scud missiles at Israel, which the Israelis were prepared for. The United States pleaded with Israel to not counterattack, which Israel agreed to, due to the fact that the United States promised to target and destroy all Scud missile sites in Iraq.

JOURNALISM

The Civil War   By the American Revolution, newspapers were fairly common. By 1800, there were more than 200 newspapers in the United States. These newspapers, however, were not independent and objective pieces, but usually ways for political parties to get their messages across. The Civil War, however, changed the way newspapers wrote. Reporters were hired to act as war correspondents and report on what was happening. With the rail system and the telegraph, information could travel faster. Due to how much it cost to send telegraph messages, the writing had to be concise. This molded the way stories are written to this day.

CATEGORY THEORY

What Categories Are Made Of   A category, known as C, is made up of three entities. Class ob(C) features elements that are referred to as objects. Class hom(C) features elements that are morphisms (which are really arrows). The morphism (known as f) features a source object that is unique (known as a) and an object it targets (known as b), so it would be expressed as: $f: a \rightarrow b$ (which can be stated as f is a morphism from a to b). The last mathematical entity that a category is made up of is a binary operation (shown as $\circ$). This is known as the composition of morphisms, and can be broken down as this:

$$\text{hom}(a, b) \times \text{hom}(b, c) \rightarrow \text{hom}(a, c)$$
$$f: a \rightarrow b \quad \text{and} \quad g: b \rightarrow c \quad \text{is written as } g \circ f$$

TYPES OF ANIMALS

Reptiles   Reptiles have several distinct characteristics. Though they breathe air through their lungs like mammals, they are cold-blooded, meaning they do not have the ability to regulate the temperature of their bodies. In other words, the temperature of their bodies is dependent on the temperature of their environment. Reptiles live on land and in water, their bodies are covered in scales, and most lay eggs (vipers and boas are two examples of reptiles that give birth to live young, but this is uncommon for reptiles). The largest group of reptiles is snakes and lizards.

AMHARIC

Writing System   The writing system of Amharic is based on the writing system of Ge'ez and it is known as Fidel. The writing system is an abugida (based on consonants), and the characters represent a combination of consonants and vowels. There are thirty-three characters in Fidel that each have seven forms. Like other Semitic languages, the symbols are very similar to one another, and the roots of words are consonants with vowels that are merely supplemental. Amharic is one of the few African languages that has its own writing system.

🏛 GULF WAR

Battle of Khafji   On January 29, the Battle of Khafji was fought, lasting for a total of three days. Four days prior to the battle, the U.S. forces noticed the Iraq forces building up behind the border of Kuwait, reinforcing artillery and bunkers. On the night of January 29, the U.S. marines were in position, ready for an attack, and Soviet-built tanks approached. A convoy of Iraqi tanks followed, signaling the international sign of surrender—their cannons faced the opposite direction. The cannons suddenly swung around and began firing, and the Iraqis gained control of Khafi for the time being. The Allies attacked with air support and a barrage of fire, and it proved to be too powerful for Saddam's forces. By January 31, Iraq's offensive was finished.

📝 JOURNALISM

Henry Stanley   The daily newspapers produced in New York continued to redefine journalism. Henry Stanley became a special correspondent for the *New York Herald* in 1867. In 1866, the famous Scottish missionary and explorer of Africa, David Livingstone, went to Africa once again to study the Nile River. Dr. Livingstone vanished and was not heard from for a long time. *The New York Herald* sent Henry Stanley to Africa in search of Dr. Livingstone in 1871. In November of 1871, Stanley found Dr. Livingstone, and said the famous line, "Dr. Livingstone, I presume?" This was the beginning of investigative reporting.

➗ CATEGORY THEORY

Completeness and Co-Completeness   Initial objects occur if there is exactly one morphism for every other object $f: S \to X$, while terminal objects occur if there is exactly one morphism for every other object $f: X \to T$. Objects can also go through pushout and pullback. If, in a category, all pullbacks exist and there is a terminal object, it is finitely complete. If there is a category where all pushbacks exist and it has an initial object, then it is finitely co-complete.

⚛ TYPES OF ANIMALS

Echinoderms   Echinoderms live in the ocean and do not have a brain, eyes, or heart. These animals do have (for the most part) mouths on the bottom of their bodies, an anus at the top, and many arms that radiate symmetrically from the center of the animal. The most common echinoderms are starfish and sea urchins. These creatures also have tube feet, which are tentacle-like and have suction pads that enable the creatures to move. Some, such as the starfish, are carnivorous; others feed on plankton, while still others eat detritus.

☪ AMHARIC

Rastafarians   The word *Rastafarian* is from the Amharic language. The Emperor of Ethiopia from 1930 to 1974, Haile Selassie I, was known as Ras Tafari, a combination of the Amharic word *Ras* which meant "head" (with the same meaning that the word *Duke* would have), and Haile Selassie I's given name, Tafari. Rastafarians consider Haile Selassie I to be the returned Messiah and reincarnation of Jesus, though he himself, an Orthodox Ethiopian Christian, did not associate with the religion or believe that he was the reincarnation of God.

GULF WAR

End of the War   The war ended by a series of ground attacks that lasted three days, and constant bombing from above. On February 24, Allied troops entered Iraq, targeting Kuwait City, west of the Iraqi flank, and then past the Iraqi lines. The next day, marines got to Kuwait City and the retreat route of the western flank was cut off. The third day was one of the largest tank battles ever, and the Americans were able to destroy the Iraqi tanks without losing a single one. On February 26, as Iraqi troops retreated, they set fire to around 700 oil wells. A large convoy of Iraqi troops formed along a major highway, which was bombed from above. On February 27, 1991, President Bush declared that Kuwait was liberated and that the war was over.

JOURNALISM

William Randolph Hearst   William Randolph Hearst lived from 1863 to 1951. The son of a self-made millionaire, Hearst studied journalism at Harvard. While he was still at Harvard, Hearst told his father he wanted to run the *San Francisco Examiner*, and on March 7, 1887, William Randolph Hearst became the owner of *The Examiner*. In 1895, Hearst bought *The New York Morning Journal*, where he competed against his fellow Harvard classmate and mentor, Joseph Pulitzer (and if you recall from the lesson on World War I, these two men are responsible for yellow journalism).

CATEGORY THEORY

Natural Transformations   A relation between two functors is known as a natural transformation. Natural transformations allow for the transforming of one functor into another functor while also respecting the arrangement of morphisms of the categories. Besides the concepts of categories and functors, natural transformations is one of the most basic concepts in category theory.

TYPES OF ANIMALS

Mollusks   Mollusks were one of the first creatures that inhabited the planet, with fossils of mollusks dating back to over 500 million years ago. On the outside, mollusks feature a hard shell that covers a soft organ. Mollusks can be found on both land and water. For example, oysters, clams, octopus, squid, slugs, and snails are all examples of mollusks. While some mollusks move by ejecting water from their bodies like the squid and scallop, others move with a "foot" (like slugs and snails), and still others, like clams and oysters, do not move, but rather stay stationary in one spot.

AMHARIC

Amharic Today   In the thirteenth century, Amharic was the official language of the court in Highland Ethiopia, as well as the dominant language spoken. Today, Amharic is the national language of Ethiopia and spoken in all of the provinces. The language currently has 25 million speakers. Outside of Ethiopia, there are 2.7 million people who speak Amharic. Amharic literature first appeared in the nineteenth century.

🏛 GULF WAR

The Impact on the Soldiers   When U.S. soldiers returned home, many began experiencing symptoms such as nausea, rashes, cramps, short-term memory, difficulty breathing, headaches, and even birth defects. This came to be known as Gulf War Syndrome. In 1994, a panel created by the National Institutes of Health ruled out biological and chemical warfare as the cause. As recently as 2008, it was declared that the evidence suggested that nerve gas, an anti-nerve-gas agent, and pesticides that were used for sand flies might be what caused the syndrome.

JOURNALISM

Muckraking   After World War I, investigative journalists began exposing abuses and corruption from businesses and the government. Theodore Roosevelt praised the ideas behind this activity, but believed the journalists' methods were irresponsible. One of the most famous muckrakers was Upton Sinclair, who wrote *The Jungle* in 1906. The book looked at the food and drug industry. After President Roosevelt read his book, he ordered that the meat-packing industry be investigated. Due to Sinclair's work, the Meat Inspection Act was passed that same year.

CATEGORY THEORY

Duality   In category theory, every theorem or definition features a dual. The dual can be found by reversing the direction of the arrows. If something is true in category C, then this means that the dual will also be true in C^{op}, or the opposite category. Similarly, if something is not true in C, then its dual is not true in C^{op}. Oftentimes, C^{op} is abstract and does not have to be a category that comes from a mathematical performance. When this is the case, the category D is said to be in duality with C when D and C^{op} are what is known as "equivalent as categories."

✷ TYPES OF ANIMALS

Marsupials   Marsupials are a special type of mammal. The most common marsupials are found in Australia (the kangaroo, koala, and wallaby); however, there are marsupials in South America and Central America. North America has only one type of marsupial, the Virginia opossum. Marsupials feature an abdominal pouch that they use to carry their young. The mothers give birth early and the baby is not yet fully developed. The baby then climbs to the mother's pouch from the birth canal, where it continues to mature for weeks (and sometimes months).

AMHARIC

Useful Amharic Phrases   Here are some helpful Amharic phrases to use when traveling to Ethiopia. Note that these are written phonetically.

Hello. *Sälam.*

Welcome. *In kwahn deh-na meh tash* (to a man). *In kwahn deh-na meh tah* (to a woman).

Good morning. *əndämn adäru* (the ə is a schwa).

Good afternoon. *əndämn walu.*

Good evening. *əndämn amäshu.*

Pleased to meet you. *Siletewaweqin dess bilognal.*

I don't understand. *Algebagnim.*

Excuse me. *Yiqirta.*

Thank you. *Ameseginalehugn.*

Where are you from? *Irswo keyet not?*

What's your name? *Simi man new?* (to a man) *Simish man new?* (to a woman)

Thank you. *Ameseginalehugn.*

Goodbye. *Chow.*

1. **On January 17, Iraq fired a total of seven Scud missiles at Israel. The United States pleaded with Israel not to counterattack, which Israel agreed to do because:**
   a. The United States promised to give Iraq's artillery to Israel.
   b. The United States promised Israel the oil in the region when the war was over.
   c. The United States promised Israel could own the land when the war was over.
   d. The United States promised to target and destroy all Scud missile sites in Iraq.

2. **The Battle of Khafji lasted a total of:**
   a. Three days
   b. Three weeks
   c. Three months
   d. Three years

3. **Henry Stanley was the first:**
   a. Newspaper publisher
   b. Investigative reporter
   c. Muckraker
   d. War correspondent

4. **Which of the following is a result of the Civil War?**
   a. Reporters were hired to act as war correspondents.
   b. Due to how much it cost to send telegraph messages, the writing had to be concise.
   c. Newspapers reported on current events instead of the message political parties wanted to get out.
   d. All of the above

5. **The processes that preserve the structure of categories are known as:**
   a. Fractals
   b. Functors
   c. Functions
   d. Functels

6. **If, in a category, all pullbacks exist and there is a terminal object, it is:**
   a. Finitely complete
   b. Finitely incomplete
   c. Finitely co-complete
   d. Infinitely complete

7. **Humans are:**
   a. Vertebrates
   b. Invertebrates
   c. Chordates
   d. A and C

8. **A starfish is an example of:**
   a. A mollusk
   b. A marsupial
   c. A reptile
   d. An echinoderm

9. **Amharic is a:**
   a. Romance language
   b. Germanic language
   c. Semitic language
   d. Khosian language

10. **The writing system of Amharic is:**
    a. An abugida
    b. A Ge'ez
    c. A Rasta
    d. A selassie

HISTORY: Y2K

What Was Y2K?, Response by the U.S. Government, International Response, Panic, Solutions, Errors from Y2K

MATH: Prime Numbers

What Are Prime Numbers?, The Fundamental Theorem of Arithmetic, Euclid's Theorem, The Largest Known Prime, Trial Division, Prime Gaps

LANGUAGE ARTS: Joseph Pulitzer

Early Life, His Early Career in Publishing, *The New York World*, Yellow Kid, Journalism Schools, Pulitzer Prize

SCIENCE: Stem Cells

What Are Stem Cells?, Unique Properties of Stem Cells, Embryonic Stem Cells, Adult Stem Cells, Induced Pluripotent Stem Cells, Use of Stem Cells

Lesson 38

FOREIGN LANGUAGE: Spiritualism, Mediums, and Talking to the Dead

Spiritualist Beliefs, Mediums, Communication with the Dead in Other Religions, Emanuel Swedenborg, Houdini's Quest, How to Conduct a Séance

Y2K

What Was Y2K? In an effort to save memory on computers, it was common that for all computer software from the 1960s to the 1980s two digits were used to represent a year instead of four digits. By the 1990s, people began to realize that this meant the numbers would become 00 in the year 2000, and that computers would interpret this to mean 1900. This would throw computers off completely. This bug, which existed not only in software but in firmware as well, would be a major threat to the financial, banking, utility, telecom, manufacturing, and airline industries.

JOSEPH PULITZER

Early Life Joseph Pulitzer was born in Budapest in 1847. In 1864, when Pulitzer was just eighteen years old, he came to America and enlisted in the army and fought for the Union in the Civil War. Following the war, Pulitzer moved to St. Louis, Missouri, and worked driving a taxi, waiting tables, and caring for mules. Pulitzer soon became a reporter on a local German newspaper, joined the Republican Party, and was nominated for state legislature. Even though his district was Democratic, Pulitzer won the election.

PRIME NUMBERS

What Are Prime Numbers? A prime number is a whole number greater than 1 that can only be divided by 1 and itself. Examples of prime numbers are:

2, 3, 5, 7, 11, 13, 17, 19, 23 . . .

There is an infinitude, or infinite set, of prime numbers and this concept was first demonstrated by Euclid in 300 B.C. A whole number that can be divided by numbers other than itself and 1 is known as a composite number. Furthermore, any whole number that has a value greater than 1 is either composite or prime.

STEM CELLS

What Are Stem Cells? Stem cells are a very special type of cell because during their early life and growth stages, they can actually develop into many different types of cells. Another very important feature of stem cells is that in a living body, they can be used as a repair system and divide infinitely, replenishing the other cells. During division of stem cells, the new cells can either turn into different types of cells that have a specific function or they can remain as stem cells. Under certain conditions, stem cells can actually turn into tissue or become organ-specific cells that carry out particular functions.

SPIRITUALISM, MEDIUMS, AND TALKING TO THE DEAD

Spiritualist Beliefs Spiritualism is a monotheistic religious movement that appeared in the nineteenth century. By the year 1897, there were more than 8 million followers in Europe and the United States. As accusations of fraud grew, Spiritualist churches began to appear, where spiritualism is still practiced to this day. Spiritualists believe in communicating with spirits of those who have passed on. They believe that after the death of the physical body, the soul lives on and that the soul can still improve and learn. In spiritualism, communicating with the dead is done by people who are gifted with the ability to do so. These people are known as mediums.

🏛 Y2K

Response by the U.S. Government   The United States Government passed the Year 2000 Information and Readiness Disclosure Act on October 19, 1998. The Act was intended to promote the sharing of information related to the Y2K problem from the private sector, and for their help, the companies were provided with a limited amount of protection and exemption from antitrust policies. The White House worked with FEMA, which was independent at the time and created websites as a form of outreach. Federal agencies had their own task forces associated with Y2K and worked with the private sector. The United States spent $300 billion dollars in preparation for Y2K.

JOSEPH PULITZER

His Early Career in Publishing   In 1872, Joseph Pulitzer purchased the *St. Louis Post* for $3,000, as well as a German newspaper. The profits from the *Post* were able to pay for his law school education. In 1878, Pulitzer, who had started a law firm, closed it and purchased the *St. Louis Dispatch*, which had been in trouble. He combined the *Post* and *Dispatch* into one paper, and focused on writing about corruption, gambling, tax fraud, and lotteries. He made it his goal to clean up and repair St. Louis.

➗ PRIME NUMBERS

The Fundamental Theorem of Arithmetic   The fundamental theorem of arithmetic states that all integers that are positive and larger than 1 can be written as the product of one or many primes so that it is unique except, perhaps, for the order of prime factors. What this theory says is that primes are the building blocks of numbers that are natural or composite. Prime factorization is the process of finding out what prime numbers make up a natural number. For example, if you wanted to find the prime factors of 18, you would do:

$$18 \div 2 = 9$$
$$9 \div 3 = 3$$
$$18 = 3^2 \times 2$$

⚛ STEM CELLS

Unique Properties of Stem Cells   Stem cells are not like any other cells found in the body, and they have three properties, no matter the source. Stem cells have the capability to divide and renew themselves over long periods of time, a characteristic that blood cells, muscle cells, and nerve cells do not have. Stem cells are not specialized, meaning they do not have functions like carrying oxygen or pumping blood. Instead, they create specialized types of cells. The process of creating a specialized cell from an unspecialized cell is known as differentiation.

☾ SPIRITUALISM, MEDIUMS, AND TALKING TO THE DEAD

Mediums   Mediums communicate with the dead to provide messages to the living. There are two types of mediums: physical mediums and mental mediums. Physical mediums usually only work with séances. This is because anyone sitting next to the medium will see and hear what is going on around them. With mental mediums, the process is in the mind of the medium. There are three forms that mediums identify: clairvoyance (seeing the spirit), clairaudience (hearing the spirit), and clairsentience (sensing the thoughts and presence of the spirit).

Y2K

International Response   Funded by the World Bank, the International Y2K Co-operation Center was established and met on December 11, 1998. Among the things discussed at the meeting were planning for crises, testing computers, and communication among countries. The IY2KCC intended to promote worldwide programs, promote coordination with geographic areas, and promote communication and support from the private sectors.

JOSEPH PULITZER

The New York World   In 1883, at the age of thirty-six, Pulitzer bought the *New York World* for a total of $346,000 from its owner, who was reportedly losing $40,000 a year on the paper. Pulitzer made the paper focus on scandals, sensationalized stories, and human-interest pieces, and used the paper to expose fraud and abuses. In 1909, Pulitzer was indicted when the *New York World* reported that the U.S. government fraudulently paid $40 million dollars to the French Panama Canal Company. Pulitzer was indicted for libeling Roosevelt. The case was dismissed, however, and it was a very important moment concerning freedom of the press.

PRIME NUMBERS

Euclid's Theorem   As previously stated, prime numbers are infinite. This is actually a theorem, known as Euclid's theorem. There are many proofs that show Euclid's theorem to be true. Euclid showed this with his own proof. His proof stated that if you have a list of prime numbers, there will always be another one after the last number you've written. If P is the product of the prime numbers and $q = P + 1$, the answers produced will be either prime or not prime. Though this doesn't only give prime answers, it proves the number of primes goes on infinitely.

STEM CELLS

Embryonic Stem Cells   The stem cells taken from embryos are known as embryonic stem cells. These cells are mostly derived from the embryos of eggs fertilized in vitro, which are then donated for further research. These cells are then grown in the laboratory. If grown under proper conditions, embryonic stem cells can remain undifferentiated. If they begin clumping together, they will differentiate spontaneously and begin to form various types of cells. When scientists attempt to generate a specific type of cell, they control the differentiation. Today, scientists have "recipes" that tell them how to make particular cells.

SPIRITUALISM, MEDIUMS, AND TALKING TO THE DEAD

Communication with the Dead in Other Religions   Though Spiritualism derived from Christianity, many other religions have a similar concept of being able to talk to the dead. In indigenous religions and animism, shamans contact the dead and the spiritual world. Animists believe that shamans can talk not only to the dead, but also with the spirit of nature. Sufism, which is considered a mystical branch of Islam, believes that communication with the dead is possible as well. There are also some Wiccan religions that believe the dead can talk to humans.

Y2K

Panic   Y2K created a mass panic, and people began preparing for a disaster. Insurance companies began selling policies that covered the Y2K crisis, stores began stocking up on food and even began selling freeze-dried foods. People feared the stock market would crash and that planes would stop working and fall from the sky. A survey of 14,000 people found that more than half of the people were going to take cash out of their bank accounts that would last them two to six weeks.

JOSEPH PULITZER

Yellow Kid   During World War I, Pulitzer and Hearst were competing with one another in the newspaper industry using yellow journalism. In 1886, the *New York World* incorporated a color section, and was one of the first papers to do so. Pulitzer hired cartoonist Richard F. Outcault, and he created *Hogan's Alley*, featuring his character, the Yellow Kid, one of the world's first newspaper comics, which became immensely popular. William Randolph Hearst was extremely impressed with the work of Pulitzer, and bought Outcault from the *New York World to* join his paper. Pulitzer then hired George Luks to create the Yellow Kid series.

PRIME NUMBERS

The Largest Known Prime   Since Euclid has proven that prime numbers go on infinitely, mathematicians have been trying to discover larger prime numbers that exist. The Electronic Frontier Foundation even awards prizes for those who find the next largest prime numbers. Many of the largest prime numbers are called Mersenne numbers, named after the seventeenth-century monk who created the formula $M^p = 2^p - 1$. Of the ten highest prime numbers found, the top nine are Mersenne primes, and the tenth is the highest non-Mersenne prime. Currently, the largest prime is $2^{43,112,609} - 1$.

STEM CELLS

Adult Stem Cells   Adult stem cells are undifferentiated cells that exist around differentiated cells in a tissue or organ and have the ability to renew and differentiate to create some or all of the specific types of cells in the tissue or organ. In living organisms, stem cells repair and maintain the tissue they exist in. Whereas the embryonic stem cell is derived from the embryo, scientists still do not know where the adult stem cells are derived from, and they have been identified in the brain, heart, teeth, skin, skeletal muscle, testes, ovarian epithelium, liver, blood vessels, peripheral blood, and gut.

SPIRITUALISM, MEDIUMS, AND TALKING TO THE DEAD

Emanuel Swedenborg   Emanuel Swedenborg lived from 1688 to 1772. At the age of fifty-six, Swedenborg, who was a Swedish scientist, inventor, and philosopher, claimed to have had a spiritual awakening. Swedenborg began having dreams and visions, and he believed he was chosen by God to reform Christianity with a new doctrine. Following his supposed awakening, Swedenborg published eighteen books, with his most well-known book being *Heaven and Hell*. In his *Life on Other Planets*, Swedenborg claimed he had communicated with spirits from the Moon, Mars, Mercury, Saturn, Venus, and Jupiter. The fact that he had not communicated with spirits from Neptune or Uranus, which had not been discovered yet, has raised concern over his credibility.

Y2K

Solutions   The Y2K problem was solved in several different ways. Dates were expanded, meaning the two-digit years in programs, databases, and files were changed to four-digit years. For databases whose size was too large to change, codes that were six-digit year/month/day were changed into three-digit days and three-digit years (this was known as date repartitioning). In the process of windowing, the two-digit years were kept, and the programs had to determine the century only when it was needed for a specific function. This process required installations of code and was much simpler than expanding the dates.

JOSEPH PULITZER

Journalism Schools   In 1892, Joseph Pulitzer approached the president of Columbia University about creating the first ever journalism school, and offered to pay for it. Pulitzer was turned down; however, in 1902, the new president of Columbia University took him up on his offer. The journalism school, however, was not created until after Pulitzer's death. In his will, Pulitzer left Columbia University $2 million dollars, and the Columbia University Graduate School of Journalism was created in 1934. By the time Columbia University created the school, the University of Missouri, from the sway of Pulitzer, had created the Missouri School of Journalism.

PRIME NUMBERS

Trial Division   Trial division is an extremely complex process with a very simple idea. The basic concept of trial division is to see if a number that is going to be factored (n) can be divided by a number greater than 1 but less than that number (n). This means that one has to test whether n is divisible by a number that is not itself. You begin by two and work your way up. If a number is not divisible by two, it will not be divisible by four (because four is divisible by two). This rule applies for any multiples. So from that, we can determine that the only numbers worth testing are prime numbers.

STEM CELLS

Induced Pluripotent Stem Cells   An induced pluripotent stem cell (iPSC) is an adult cell that is reprogrammed into an embryonic cell-like state with the use of viruses. This is done by forcing the cell to express factors and genes that are important for keeping the important properties of embryonic stem cells. Scientists do not know if embryonic stem cells and iPSCs differ in any important ways. Use of iPSCs has been very important in developing drugs and modeling diseases. Scientists hope to use iPSCs with transplantations. Using the viruses to change the adult cells needs further studying, however. Scientists have noticed that introduction of the viruses can cause cancers.

Houdini's Quest   Famous magician and escape artist Harry Houdini made it a lifetime goal of his to debunk mediums and show the world that they were fraudulent. He would attend several séances dressed in disguise and expose their tricks to reporters and policemen. He even hired researchers to learn about the psychics in the audience of his performances, so that when it was show time, he would invite them to the stage and outsmart them. Houdini began to include in his own performances the how-to process of creating a séance. Before Houdini died, he told his wife that if it was possible to communicate to the dead, he would pass a code on to her. On the tenth anniversary of his death, Houdini's wife held a séance on the radio. After none of the mediums could break the code (though they claimed to), Harry's wife said that Houdini did not come through and that it was finished.

Y2K

Errors from Y2K   Though the crisis was averted, there were some errors that occurred on January 1, 2000. A webpage on the national weather forecasting system of France showed a map with the date 01/01/19100. On the website of the U.S. Naval Observatory (where the official time of the country is kept), the date was reported as Jan. 1, 19100. In Japan, equipment that monitored radiation stopped working at midnight and an alarm went off at a nuclear power plant. In two states of Australia, machines used for validating bus tickets stopped working.

JOSEPH PULITZER

Pulitzer Prize   Joseph Pulitzer died at the age of sixty-four in 1911. In Pulitzer's will, he made very specific provisions for the creation of a prize; however, he allowed for changes to occur. The prizes would be four awards in journalism, four awards in letters and drama, four scholarships, and one award in education. The first Pulitzer Prizes were awarded in 1917. The Board of the Pulitzer Prize has since made additional awards, including categories like music, online journalism, and multimedia. The Pulitzer Prize has even been given to cartoonists.

PRIME NUMBERS

Prime Gaps   When there is a sequence of numbers and there are no prime numbers that show up, it is called a prime gap. Another way to think of prime gaps is it is the difference between two successive numbers that are prime. For example:

Primes: 2 3 5 7 11 13 17...

Gaps: 1 2 2 4   2   4....

Mathematically, this is written as: $g_n = P_{n+1} - P_n$

In this formula, g_n is the nth prime gap and P_n represents the nth prime number.

STEM CELLS

Uses of Stem Cells   Stem cells can be used for a wide variety of things. Human stem cells can be used when testing drugs. For example, stem cells are currently used for screening anti-tumor drugs. Perhaps the most impressive way stem cells can be used, however, is for cell-based therapies. Stem cells offer the possibility of renewing and replacing cells and even generating tissues. This would allow treatment of ailments and diseases such as Alzheimer's, stroke, heart disease, burns, diabetes, rheumatoid arthritis, and osteoarthritis by healing destroyed tissue.

How to Conduct a Séance

Step 1. Gather your participants (there should be at least three people) around a round table. The table makes a symbolic circle that is needed.

Step 2. Choose your medium. It can be a person among your group or someone who has had experience talking with the dead.

Step 3. Place a simple, natural food that is aromatic at the center of the table and light candles (at least three—the more the better) and dim the lights.

Step 4. Sit around the table and join hands.

Step 5. To summon the spirit, the medium must say: "Our beloved [name of the spirit], we bring you gifts from life into death. Commune with us, [name of the spirit], and move among us." Wait for something to happen. If nothing happens, repeat Step 5.

Step 6. When there is communication, have your medium ask simple questions with yes or no answers (one noise for yes, two noises for no).

Step 7. If the situation gets out of control and you need to end the séance, break the circle, put out the candles, and turn on the lights. If not out of control and you have finished your questions, thank the spirit, tell them to go in peace, break the circle, put out the candles, and turn on the lights.

1. **Y2K was a problem because computers would interpret the year 2000 as:**
   a. The Year 0
   b. The Year 1000
   c. The Year 1900
   d. The Year 100

2. **What was the purpose of the Year 2000 Information and Readiness Disclosure Act?**
   a. To establish a system that monitored Internet activity
   b. To promote the sharing of information related to the Y2K problem from the private sector
   c. To assemble the other countries of the world and discuss Y2K
   d. To put an end to the private sector

3. **Pulitzer made the *New York World* focus on scandals, sensationalized stories, and:**
   a. Economics
   b. Poverty
   c. Sports
   d. Human-interest pieces

4. **Yellow Kid was the first:**
   a. Investigative journalist
   b. Comic strip character published in newspapers
   c. Newspaper Joseph Pulitzer purchased
   d. Book awarded the Pulitzer Prize

5. **What is important about Euclid's theorem?**
   a. It provided a formula that would only find prime numbers.
   b. It found the largest known prime.
   c. It created trial division.
   d. It proved that there is an infinite amount of prime numbers.

6. **To use trial division, you have to:**
   a. Divide by all of the prime numbers
   b. Multiply by all of the prime numbers
   c. Divide by all of the numbers that are not prime
   d. Multiply by all of the numbers that are not prime

7. **Which of the following is a property of a stem cell?**
   a. The ability to divide and renew itself over a long period of time
   b. Not having a specialization
   c. The ability to create a specialized cell
   d. All of the above

8. **What is differentiation?**
   a. The process of creating a specialized cell from an unspecialized cell
   b. The process of creating an unspecialized cell from a specialized cell
   c. The process of turning an adult cell into an embryonic cell
   d. The process of turning an embryonic cell into an adult cell

9. **What is clairsentience?**
   a. Seeing the spirit
   b. Hearing the spirit
   c. Sensing the thoughts and presence of the spirit
   d. Having your body overcome by the spirit

10. **What is clairvoyance?**
    a. Seeing the spirit
    b. Hearing the spirit
    c. Sensing the thoughts and presence of the spirit
    d. Having your body overcome by the spirit

ANSWER KEY: c, b, d, b, d, a, d, a, c, a

HISTORY: War on Terror

9/11, The War on Terror, War in Afghanistan, War in Iraq, Fighting in Pakistan, Death of Osama bin Laden

MATH: Infinity

The Symbol, Aristotle, Galileo's Paradox, Cantor's Set Theory, Finitism, Real Analysis

LANGUAGE ARTS: Propaganda Techniques

Bandwagon, Glittering Generalities, Plain Folks, Transfer, Assertion, Card Stacking

SCIENCE: DNA

What Is DNA?, Structure, Protein Synthesis, Replication, Discovery of DNA, Uses of DNA

Lesson 39

FOREIGN LANGUAGE: Extinct Languages

Dalmatian, Ubykh, Tsetsaut, Eyak, Polabian, Apalachee

WAR ON TERROR

9/11 On September 11, 2001, a series of attacks would change the course of United States history. Four commercial passenger jet airliners were hijacked by nineteen al-Qaeda terrorists. Two of the planes crashed into the twin towers of the World Trade Center in New York City. Within two hours, both of the towers collapsed (killing 2,752 people, including 343 firefighters and 60 police officers). The third plane crashed into the Pentagon (killing 184 people). After hearing about the other two attacks, passengers and crew aboard the fourth flight attempted to retake the plane, and the plane crashed near Shanksville, Pennsylvania (killing all forty-four people on board). In 2004, Osama bin Laden took responsibility for the attacks.

PROPAGANDA TECHNIQUES

Bandwagon One of the most common forms of propaganda that appears during both times of war and peace is known as bandwagon. Bandwagon plays a very important role in modern-day advertising. Bandwagon is the idea that a person should do something or join in because everyone else is also doing it. Essentially, what bandwagon does is create a winning side and a losing side, and you know when something is winning because there are more people on that side. In modern advertising, a new form of bandwagon has appeared. This new bandwagon says something along the lines of everyone else is doing something, and if you don't, you will miss out.

INFINITY

The Symbol The symbol for infinity, ∞, is known as a lemniscate. This comes from the Latin word *lemniscus*, which means "ribbon." In John Wallis's *De Sectionibus Conicis* of 1655, the symbol is used for the very first time. It is unknown why Wallis chose the symbol. Some believe that it was derived from the Roman numeral for the number 1,000. This number was actually derived from the Etruscan numeral and appeared as CIↃ (this was also used at the time to mean "many"). Others believe that the symbol came from the last letter of the Greek alphabet, omega (ω).

DNA

What Is DNA? Deoxyribonucleic acid, or DNA, is the genetic makeup of each cell in our body, and every characteristic of any living organism and most viruses. Almost every single cell in the body has the same DNA. The DNA is located inside of the nucleus of the cell (called nuclear DNA), though some DNA can also be found in the mitochondria (which is known as mDNA or mitochondrial DNA). Information is stored in the DNA as a code of four chemical bases. The bases are guanine (G), adenine (A), thymine (T), and cytosine (C). There are around 3 billion bases in human DNA. Of those bases, 99 percent are the same in every human.

EXTINCT LANGUAGES

Dalmatian The Dalmatian language was a Romance language spoken in Croatia. The words stemmed from Latin, and the Latin alphabet was used, although it also featured diacritical marks. The Dalmatian language had two dialects. The dialect of the north was known as Vegliotian, and the dialect found in the south was known as Ragusan. As the Slavic people came to the land, the language started to fade away. In 1898, the last speaker of Dalmatian died. There still exist some Dalmatian words in modern-day Croatian, such as the words for *onion* and *rainwater reservoir*.

WAR ON TERROR

The War on Terror   Following the attacks of September 11, the Bush administration declared a war on terrorism. The objectives of the war were to defeat terrorists and their organizations (including Osama bin Laden and Abu Musab al-Zarqawi), strengthen the international efforts in combating terrorism, deny any forms of support or sanctuary to terrorist organizations, reduce conditions that terrorists can exploit, and defend U.S. interests at home and abroad. In October of 2001, Operation Active Endeavor was launched by NATO with the purpose of preventing any movements of weapons of mass destruction or terrorists.

PROPAGANDA TECHNIQUES

Glittering Generalities   Glittering generalities are common in the political world and in advertising. Glittering generalities are words that are associated with extremely valued concepts, but with individual subjects, these words have a different meaning. This type of propaganda throws in important concepts, and by doing so, demands approval. For example, often food will feature on their label extremely general and vague terms such as "new" or "homemade." Often politicians will express their policies as being "in defense of democracy," a very broad phrase that is more about conveying an idea or belief.

INFINITY

Aristotle   Aristotle distinguished between two different types of infinity. There was potential infinity and actual infinity. Aristotle believed that natural numbers were potentially infinite due to the fact that they did not have a greatest number. Aristotle did not believe, however, that numbers were actually infinite, but rather that it was impossible to think of all of the natural numbers as complete. He believed the idea of actual infinity did not make sense, and so only potential infinity was allowable. Aristotle believed actual infinity to be a paradox because it is something that is complete yet consists of an infinite amount of something.

✸ DNA

Structure   DNA is a double-helix molecule that consists of two chains. A single chain is a strand that is made up of a large amount of nucleotides, or chemical compounds, that are linked together. The nucleotides are made up of three things: deoxyribose (a sugar molecule in the center of the nucleotide), a phosphate group (which links to the deoxyribose of the other chain), and one of the bases (A, G, T, or C). When the two chains come together, they form the double-helix shape. Bases are always paired accordingly: A with T and C with G.

◖ EXTINCT LANGUAGES

Ubykh   Ubykh was a northwest Caucasian language that was once spoken in Turkey and the eastern coast of the Black Sea, Sochi. When the Russians came in 1864, the Ubykhs left Sochi and founded a series of villages in Turkey (Hacı Osman, Masukiye, Hacı Yakup, and Kırkpınar). The language had a total of eighty-four consonants and only two vowels. Over time, Turkish and Circassian were adopted, and on October 7, 1992, the last speaker of Ubykh passed away. Before his death, linguists collected a great number of audio recordings and took notes on the language. There has been an interest in reviving the language.

🏛 WAR ON TERROR

War in Afghanistan   On October 7, 2001, the War in Afghanistan began with the launch of Operation Enduring Freedom. The goal of Operation Enduring Freedom was to dismantle the al-Qaeda organization, end its use of Afghanistan as its base, remove the Taliban, and find Osama bin Laden. The first phase of Operation Enduring Freedom saw the Taliban get thrown out of power in Kabul. In 2002, Operation Anaconda was launched to destroy any al-Qaeda and Taliban that remained. The Taliban came together in Pakistan and unleashed offensives on the coalition forces. Fighting between the Taliban and coalition forces is still ongoing, though peace talks are underway.

📋 PROPAGANDA TECHNIQUES

Plain Folks   The plain folks method of propaganda is about convincing others that your views reflect the views of the common, everyday folk, and that you have the interests of the common person in mind. Often local accents, idioms, or jokes are used to create the sense of familiarity. Other methods include limiting one's vocabulary, including stutters, and not pronouncing words perfectly. These errors can come across as sincere to the viewer. Often, glittering generalities are used with the plain folks strategies, making the broad ideas seem more valid.

➗ INFINITY

Galileo's Paradox   Galileo came up with a surprising paradox relating to infinity. Galileo noticed that if you remove half of the set of equal numbers, there are as many numbers remaining in the set as before. For example, if you remove all of the odd numbers from a set, you will only have the even numbers remaining. If you then pair the natural numbers (n) with $2n$ which is even, the set that has the even numbers is equinumerous (meaning they have the same cardinality) to the set that had all natural numbers. In other words, if you had infinity, you still have infinity.

⚛ DNA

Protein Synthesis   Inside the DNA are instructions for how to produce protein. Proteins are made up of amino acids, which also determine the function and structure of the protein. The sequence of nucleotide bases in the DNA determine the sequence of amino acids. A triplet (three nucleotide bases) specifies an amino acid. GAC, for example, is the codon (genetic code) for leucine. When the DNA molecule separates into two strands, protein synthesis occurs. Transcription begins, where a part of the strand turns into a template for a new strand, known as messenger RNA. This RNA then attaches to ribosomes, and through translation, amino acids are linked and a protein is formed.

◉ EXTINCT LANGUAGES

Tsetsaut   Tsetsaut was an Athabaskan language spoken by a North American indigenous people in northwestern British Columbia. Just about all of the information we have about Tsetsaut is from 1894, when it was recorded by anthropologist Frank Boas. Boas recorded the language from two slaves of Nisga'a, one of Canada's Native American communities. The work Boas did with these two slaves was enough proof that the language they spoke was a separate branch of Athabaskan. The Tsetsaut people called themselves Wetaɬ. The word *Tsetsaut* comes from an Anglicization that was given by the Nisga'a and Gitksan people.

WAR ON TERROR

War in Iraq   In March 2003, the War in Iraq began. First, Iraq was attacked from the air, and then ground forces went in. Though the reasons for the war have been questioned, the Bush administration claimed that it was part of the war against terrorism and that Iraq housed terrorists and weapons of mass destruction. In April 2003, Baghdad fell and the government of Saddam Hussein dissolved soon after. President Bush announced the war was over; however, an insurgency occurred that actually led to more casualties than the initial invasion. No weapons of mass destruction were found. In December 2003, Saddam Hussein was captured, and in 2006, he was hanged. U.S. combat ended on September 1, 2010, with Operation New Dawn.

PROPAGANDA TECHNIQUES

Transfer   Often used in the political world and during times of war, transfer is an attempt to link two separate things so that the audience thinks of them both in the same way. Transfer usually deals with negative things. By linking blame of one politician to blame of their entire political party, transfer is occurring. Transfer can also be positive, however. If a highly respected organization approves or backs another organization or event, then prestige is being transferred. Common examples of transfer are also found in symbols. The flag, for example, has come to represent the entire nation.

INFINITY

Cantor's Set Theory   Georg Cantor came to the realization that one cannot count to infinity, but one can compare sets to see if they are the same size by finding a one-to-one matching of the elements within the sets. The size of any set is known as cardinality. Sets are known as infinite if elements can be removed without reducing the cardinality. When there is the same cardinality as there are natural numbers, the set is called countable. Cantor's theorem states if there is a set X, there is at least one set that is raised to the power of X, and that is cardinally bigger than X.

DNA

Replication   Before a cell divides, the DNA is replicated. This occurs in the nucleus, and involves the polynucleotides separating. These then act as a model for a new complementary chain to be made. When chains separate, nucleotides attract complementary nucleotides, which are joined by hydrogen bonds. This forms the rungs of the new DNA. The phosphate group of a nucleotide is linked to the deoxyribose of the adjacent nucleotide by an enzyme known as DNA polymerase. The process continues, resulting in a new molecule that has a double helix.

EXTINCT LANGUAGES

Eyak   Eyak was a Na-Dené language, which were related to Athabaskan languages. Eyak was spoken in Alaska, and the last speaker of Eyak, Marie Smith Jones, died on January 21, 2008, in Cordova, Alaska. Though she had nine children, none of them learned the language. Several factors led to the extinction of the Eyak language. Though the introduction of the English language and the suppression of aboriginal languages took part in the extinction, it was also brought on by the migration of the Tlingit people, which led to a merging of Tlingit and Eyak.

WAR ON TERROR

Fighting in Pakistan   After the attacks of September 11, Pakistan sided with the United States following an ultimatum given by President Bush. The president of Pakistan, Pervez Musharraf, said he was against Islamic extremism and pledged that Pakistan was committed to fighting terrorism. In 2002, Pakistan made some very important arrests within jihadi organizations, including al-Qaeda officials of high rank. In 2004, the Pakistan Army launched 80,000 troops to remove al-Qaeda and the Taliban. When the Taliban in Afghanistan fell, many fled to Pakistan, where they were subsequently killed and captured. Currently, there is still a Taliban Pakistani resistance fighting in Pakistan.

PROPAGANDA TECHNIQUES

Assertion   A common form of propaganda used in advertising and politics is known as assertion. Assertion is an enthusiastic or energetic statement presented as a fact even though it is not actually the case. Assertions imply that the idea is just accepted, that there is no explanation needed. When a product is advertised as "the best," unless they have evidence to prove their claim, this is an assertion. The advertisers want the public to just agree without seeking out any other information. Assertions can be extremely dangerous, and can lead to lies.

INFINITY

Finitism   There is also a field of math that rejects the notion of infinity. This is known as finitism. Finitism states that objects cannot exist unless they are constructed in a finite amount of steps from natural numbers. One of the leading researchers was David Hilbert. A concept even stronger than finitism is known as ultrafinitism. Ultrafinitists deny the existence of infinite sets of natural numbers because they can never actually be completed. Both finitism and ultrafinitism are forms of constructivism, which holds that in order to prove the existence of a mathematical object it must be constructed.

DNA

Discovery of DNA   In 1868, Swiss physician Friedrich Miescher discovered what he referred to as "nuclein." In reality, these were the nucleic acids. In 1951, the complete DNA molecule was discovered by three scientists, Francis Crick, James Watson, and Maurice Wilkins. By the 1940s, scientists understood that DNA was composed of amino acids and was the basic genetic makeup of life. They did not know, however, what the molecule looked like. Using x-ray diffraction, the scientists were able to conclude that DNA was a double helix. In 1962, the three scientists received the Nobel Prize for their contributions to science.

EXTINCT LANGUAGES

Polabian   Polabian was a West Slavic language. The Polabian language was spoken by the Polabian Slavs around the Elbe River in what is present-day northeastern Germany, and use of the language dates back to the first millennium A.D. The language became extinct during the eighteenth century and was replaced with German when the German Empire conquered the Polabian lands. Today, although Polabian does not exist, there are two Sorbian languages spoken that are related to Polabian. The Polabian language has similarities to older phases of Sorbian and Polish languages.

 WAR ON TERROR

Death of Osama bin Laden   On May 2, 2011, ten years after the attacks of September 11, Osama bin Laden was killed. The operation was called Operation Neptune Spear, and was ordered by President Obama. A team of United States Navy SEALs from the United States Naval Special Warfare Development Group (or SEAL Team Six) raided the compound in Pakistan where bin Laden had been living. Following the raid, bin Laden's body was taken to Afghanistan to be identified and then was buried at sea following Muslim practices. On May 6, his death was confirmed by al-Qaeda.

 PROPAGANDA TECHNIQUES

Card Stacking   Card stacking is about not telling your audience the full truth. Someone performing card stacking omits or holds back contrary information and only puts out the information that best benefits his or her perspective or goal. Card stacking is very effective because it gives someone the ability to present the truth, but still manage to manipulate what is being put out in the world.

INFINITY

Real Analysis   There are some basic formulas regarding infinity, indicating its limitlessness. For example, $x \to \infty$ and $x \to -\infty$ show that x can grow and decrease without bound. If every t is $f(t) \geq 0$, then:

$\int_{-\infty}^{\infty} f(t)\, dt = \infty$ shows the area under $f(t)$ is infinite

$\int_{-\infty}^{\infty} f(t)\, dt = n$ shows that the area under $f(t)$ equals n, and thus, is finite.

$\int_{a}^{b} f(t)\, dt = \infty$ shows $f(t)$ doesn't bound an area that is finite from a to b

DNA

Uses of DNA   DNA is astounding for a number of reasons. Medically speaking, DNA gives insights into the evolutionary past of mankind; it helps people understand diseases, drugs, and birth defects; and DNA can help people understand how to cure genetic mutations and illnesses. DNA is also used to identify people involved in crimes and paternity tests. DNA testing even helped solve the mystery of the missing Romanov children. The last Russian czar (Nicholas II) and his family were executed in 1918. Later, it was found that two children were missing from the mass grave. In 1991, two bodies were found 70 meters away from the grave of Nicholas II, and with DNA, it was proven that these were his two daughters.

EXTINCT LANGUAGES

Apalachee   The Apalachee people lived in the Florida Panhandle (the northwestern part of the state), but they currently reside in Louisiana. The Apalachee language is a Muskogean language. Of the Muskogean languages that existed, Chickasaw, Alabama, Creek-Seminole, Choctaw, Koasati, and Mikasuki are still spoken today. Apalachee and Hitchiti are the only two that are extinct. The language became extinct due to tribal enemies and disease brought on from the Europeans. Due to the Europeans' actions in the eighteenth century, the Apalachee people migrated to Louisiana.

1. **What happened during the first phase of Operation Enduring Freedom?**
   a. Saddam Hussein was executed.
   b. The Taliban were thrown out of power in Kabul.
   c. Osama bin Laden was executed.
   d. Baghdad fell.

2. **What operation marked the end of combat in Iraq?**
   a. Operation New Dawn
   b. Operation Iraqi Freedom
   c. Operation Neptune Spear
   d. Operation Enduring Freedom

3. **Which of the following propaganda techniques uses local accents, idioms, or jokes to create the sense of familiarity?**
   a. Bandwagon
   b. Plain folks
   c. Transfer
   d. Card stacking

4. **Which of the following propaganda techniques states a person should do something because everyone else is also doing it?**
   a. Bandwagon
   b. Plain folks
   c. Transfer
   d. Card stacking

5. **Which of the following did Aristotle think could only make sense?**
   a. Finitism
   b. Ultrafinitism
   c. Actual infinity
   d. Potential infinity

6. **What states if there is a set X, there is at least one set that is raised to the power of X, and that is cardinally bigger than X?**
   a. Aristotle's Theorem
   b. Hilbert's Theory
   c. Galileo's Paradox
   d. Cantor's Theorem

7. **Which of the following is NOT a base found in DNA?**
   a. Guarana
   b. Guanine
   c. Adenine
   d. Cytosine

8. **What is deoxyribose?**
   a. An amino acid
   b. A sugar molecule
   c. A messenger RNA
   d. A phosphate

9. **Dalmatian was spoken in:**
   a. Croatia
   b. The Florida Panhandle
   c. Turkey
   d. British Columbia

10. **Anthropologist Frank Boas worked closely with this language, producing the most well known work about it:**
    a. Apalachee
    b. Polabian
    c. Tsetsaut
    d. Eyak

ANSWER KEY: b, a, b, a, d, d, a, b, a, c

HISTORY: Israeli-Palestinian Conflict

History of the Land, Palestinian State, Terror from Palestine, Repression from Israel, Hamas, Recognizing Israel

MATH: Logarithms

What Are Logarithms?, Basic Rules of Logarithms, Expanding Logarithms, Simplifying Logarithmic Expressions, Change-of-Base Formula, Applications of Logarithms

LANGUAGE ARTS: Editing Strategies

Editing and Proofreading, Your Target Audience, Start with the Sentences, Move On to the Words, Grammar, Spelling, and Punctuation, Proofreading

SCIENCE: RNA

Messenger RNA, Ribosomal RNA, Transfer RNA, Small Interfering RNA, Precursor Messenger RNA, RNA Therapeutics

Lesson 40

FOREIGN LANGUAGE: Endangered Languages

Karaim, Votic, Dyirbal, Chong, Sarikoli, Chuvash

ISRAELI-PALESTINIAN CONFLICT

History of the Land   The history of Israel and Palestine is a very complex one. In ancient times, the land was known as Judea and it was the land of the Jewish people. When the Romans conquered the land, it was renamed Palestine. This land was then conquered and inhabited by Arabs for more than 1,000 years. With the Zionist movement, the Jewish people wished to return to Israel. The Balfour Declaration of 1917 stated that Britain wished to turn Palestine into a national home for the Jewish people, upsetting the Arabs that lived there. Riots broke out and the British stopped immigration of the Jewish people to Palestine. After the Holocaust, the British once again began allowing Jewish people to move to Palestine. In 1947, the land was divided into a Jewish and Arab state.

EDITING STRATEGIES

Editing and Proofreading   Editing and proofreading are not interchangeable. They are two very important processes to use during the finishing process of writing. Editing is about making sure terminology is used correctly. It's ensuring that every term that is used is the right term. Often, research is an important part of the editing process. Proofreading, however, is about scanning your writing to make sure that everything is grammatically sound, and that there are no syntax or spelling errors. The meaning of the words does not matter. This is about whether or not the structure is correct.

LOGARITHMS

What Are Logarithms?   Maybe the most useful concept in arithmetic that can be used in all sciences, logarithms are ways to express a power that a fixed base, or number, is raised to so that a given answer is produced. Common logarithms have a base of ten, while natural logarithms have a base e. Here are some basic logs:

$\log(10) = 1$
This is because $10^1 = 10$
$\log(100) = 2$
This is because $10^2 = 100$
$\log(2) \approx 0.3$
This is because $10^{0.3} = 2$
The opposite of a log, which is known as an antilog, looks like this:
$\text{antilog}(2) = 100$
With antilogs, you are just raising the base (10) to the power of x (in this case 2).

RNA

Messenger RNA   Messenger RNA, also known as mRNA, is the single-stranded molecule that is responsible for encoding a chemical blueprint for the process of protein synthesis. Messenger RNA has a copy of the genetic information found on a strand of DNA. Whereas DNA has the genetic information in the nucleus, messenger RNA transports that information out of the nucleus to the cytoplasm. It is in the cytoplasm that the proteins are put together. As mentioned earlier, messenger RNA goes through transcription and then translation.

ENDANGERED LANGUAGES

Karaim   Karaim is a Turkic language that has influences from Hebrew similar to the way the Ladino or Yiddish languages do. The language is spoken by the Crimean Karaites, who are followers of Karaite Judaism. The language is spoken in Crimea, Poland, western Ukraine, and Lithuania. Currently, there are only six speakers alive.

ISRAELI-PALESTINIAN CONFLICT

Palestinian State   The Arab people did not accept the division of the land, and war between Palestine and Israel broke out. The Jewish people expanded their territory after a victory, leaving hundreds of thousands of Palestinians refugees. The two-state solution was finally agreed upon in 1988. Violence and land settlement continued, however, and in September of 2000, there was open conflict. The Road Map Peace Plan is a plan that was issued by the Bush administration to create a Palestinian state in peace.

EDITING STRATEGIES

Your Target Audience   Once your writing is finished, it is of absolute necessity that you go back and edit. Your first draft should never be your final draft. Think about your audience. Who are you writing this for? Is it a technical audience? Do you need to explain any technical terms you have included or will they know what you're talking about? How old is your audience? If you are writing for children, they have a shorter attention span than adults. Think about the length of your sentences. Make sure what you have written is appropriate for the people who are going to be listening to or reading it.

LOGARITHMS

Basic Rules of Logarithms   Just like you can add exponents when there is the same base, logarithms follow a similar rule. Here are the three main rules for logarithms. Note, these only work when the bases are identical:

$$\log_b(m) + \log_b(n) = \log_b(mn)$$

This means that when adding logs with the same base, you multiply the numbers inside of the log.

$$\log_b(m) - \log_b(n) = \log_b(m/n)$$

When subtracting logs with the same base, divide the numbers inside the logs

$$n \bullet \log_b(m) = \log_b(m^n)$$

When there is a multiplier, it turns into an exponent on everything that is in the log, and vice versa.

RNA

Ribosomal RNA   Ribosomes create proteins. A part of the ribosome is known as ribosomal RNA, or rRNA. This type of RNA creates polypeptides (which are groups of amino acids that proteins are made of). A ribosome is an extremely small structure found in the cytoplasm. The ribosome has two subunits, and both of the units contain ribosomal RNA and protein. However, from these units, a startling discovery has been made, leading scientists to believe that the origin of life lies in RNA. This is because the larger of the two units of the ribosome features a chemical reaction. This chemical reaction turns genetic information into the beginning of the proteins, and only rRNA is located there.

ENDANGERED LANGUAGES

Votic   Votic is spoken by the Votes people of Ingria (which is part of Russia). It is related to Estonian and is part of the Finnic subgroup within the Uralic language family. It is only spoken in two villages, Krakolye and Luzhitsy, and by 2005, only twenty speakers remained.

ISRAELI-PALESTINIAN CONFLICT

Terror from Palestine   Many Palestinian parties and underground groups were created with the sole intention of destroying Israel through violence. The Palestine Liberation Organization is the only group that has renounced this and honors the right of Israel to exist. As a result, Israel allowed the Palestine Liberation Organization to enter the Gaza Strip and West Bank. From this action, most of the area is independently controlled by Palestinians. Palestinian terrorism has continued, however, by those objecting to the agreements made by the PLO. The violence and resistance of the Palestinians against the Israelis became known as "Intifada."

EDITING STRATEGIES

Start with the Sentences   Look at your sentences carefully. This does not mean simply looking over sentences to see if there are any typos (which you'll get to later on). Pay attention to the punctuation you have included in your writing. Errors can be distracting for readers. Do any sentences seem clichéd or hackneyed? Make every sentence count. If you are finding sentences that don't seem to have any meaning, get rid of them or rewrite them so that they have a purpose. Eliminate any wordiness or repetition that does not help your writing. If every sentence begins with the same word, change it up a bit to keep it more exciting.

LOGARITHMS

Expanding Logarithms   When logs have a lot of information in them, they should be taken apart by using the rules until each log only has one thing inside of it.

For example, if you want to expand $\log_3(4x)$, you break it down as this:

$$\log_3(4) + \log_3(x) = \log_3(4x)$$

Your answer is $\log_3(4) + \log_3(x)$. You should not try to then find the value of $\log_3(4)$ in your calculator, but rather, leave it as is. Here is another example:

$$\log_5(25/x) = \log_5(25) - \log_5(x)$$
$$\log_5(25/x) = 2 - \log_5(x)$$

RNA

Transfer RNA   Transfer RNA, also known as tRNA, is responsible for reading the code and carrying amino acids that will go into the developing protein. Every amino acid has transfer RNA, and there are around twenty different tRNAs. The transfer RNA has an anticodon that reads the codon of the messenger RNA. The reading process occurs by matching base pairs with hydrogen bonds. All transfer RNAs have anywhere from seventy-five to ninety-five nucleotides. Transfer RNAs have also been known to be used in processes other than ribosome-dependent translation.

ENDANGERED LANGUAGES

Dyirbal   Dyirbal is an Aboriginal language of Australia and a member of the Pama–Nyungan language family. Dyirbal is spoken in northeast Queensland by a total of five people. The language is well known to linguists due to its features. There are only four places of articulation in Dyirbal, compared to other Aboriginal languages, which feature six. However, what really makes this language famous is its noun class system, which features four different types: man and animate objects, women, violence and fire, fruit and vegetables, and anything else that is considered miscellaneous.

ISRAELI-PALESTINIAN CONFLICT

Repression from Israel   In response to Palestinian violence, Israel limited the amount of Palestinians that could enter Israel and created very strict border checks. The checkpoints became sources of violence on both sides, with attacks by Palestinians and accidental killings of Palestinians by the border control. In 2002, Israel launched an operation known as Defensive Wall, which reoccupied land in the West Bank that had been relinquished to Palestinians. Israel Defense Forces created more checkpoints, destroyed homes, and killed thousands of Palestinians in an effort to discourage suicide bombings.

EDITING STRATEGIES

Move On to the Words   The words you choose are, obviously, very important. Look through your writing thinking about the words you have used. Think of active versus passive voice, point of view (first, second, third person), and concepts like emotionalism and neutrality. Your words should be chosen in relation to the message you want to give, how you want the audience to interpret them, and who your audience is.

LOGARITHMS

Simplifying Logarithmic Expressions   Simplifying logarithmic expressions is essentially doing the reverse of expanding logarithmic expressions. Instead of breaking it down into many parts from one large part, you are given many parts and are asked to create one large logarithm.

For example, if you were asked to simplify $\log_4(x) + \log_4(y)$, you would do:

$$\log_4(x) + \log_4(y) = \log_4(xy)$$

To simplify $3\log_3(x)$, remember to make the multiplier the exponent inside of the log. It would look like this:

$$\log_3(x^3)$$

No matter how complicated the problem might look, the processes are very simple.

RNA

Small Interfering RNA   Small interfering RNA, also known as siRNA, play an important role during the translation process. The small interfering RNA take part in what is known as RNA interference, or RNAi. The small interfering RNA strand (which is double-stranded) has a phosphate group and, at the end, a hydroxyl group. During translation, this hydroxyl group interferes by binding and creating the degradation of the messenger RNA at certain sequences. This prevents the creation of certain proteins based on the sequence of nucleotides and interferes with gene expression, a process that can help in defending against viruses.

ENDANGERED LANGUAGES

Chong   The Chong language, a Western Pearic language and part of the Eastern Mon-Khmer language family, is spoken in parts of Thailand and Cambodia. There are a total of 5,500 speakers of Chong (500 in Thailand and 5,000 in Cambodia). The language didn't have a writing system until 2000, when a version of the Thai writing system was simplified and introduced. Following the introduction of the writing system, teaching materials for the language appeared for the first time. In Thailand, there are ongoing efforts to revitalize the language.

ISRAELI-PALESTINIAN CONFLICT

Hamas   Hamas (short for Harakat Al-Muqawama Al-Islamia) is a group of radical Islamic fundamentalists who mostly operate in the Gaza Strip. Hamas wishes to create an Islamic Palestinian state and destroy Israel, and uses politics and terrorism in pursuit of their goal. In the 2006 election, a majority of the seats in the legislature of Palestine were won by Hamas. Many large-scale suicide bombings and attacks on military targets have been conducted by Hamas. Hamas has not turned any of its violence toward the United States. Attacks are only aimed at Israel and its territories.

EDITING STRATEGIES

Grammar, Spelling, and Punctuation   Think back to the lessons on grammar and punctuation. Have you used your commas, semicolons, apostrophes, and colons correctly? Are you able to explain the reason you used the specific marks that you chose? Check for words that are commonly confused. These can be tricky sometimes and can go right past you without even noticing (for example, there is a big difference between the words *affect* and *effect*, and *then* and *than*). All of these might seem like very small, minute details, but they can create big distractions for the reader.

LOGARITHMS

Change-of-Base Formula   If you wish to calculate a log that doesn't have a base of 10, you have to use what is known as the change-of-base formula. This formula states:

$$\log_b(x) = \frac{\log_d(x)}{\log_d(b)}$$

For example, if you wanted to convert $\log_4(9)$ to base 5, you would do:

$$\log_4(9) = \frac{\log_5(9)}{\log_5(4)}$$

Using the change-of-base formula is useful for locating plot-points of a graph that is a nonstandard log (that is, a log that does not have a base of 10).

RNA

Precursor Messenger RNA   A single strand of messenger RNA, which is considered immature, is known as the precursor messenger RNA (pre-mRNA). Precursor Messenger RNA is created by the process of transcription within the nucleus of a cell by a DNA template. Upon being processed, the precursor messenger RNA turns into the mature messenger RNA, or simply, the messenger RNA. After being processed, the new strand of mRNA is exported from the nucleus and translated into the protein, thus starting the cycle.

ENDANGERED LANGUAGES

Sarikoli   The Sarikoli language is a southeastern Iranian language and a member of the Pamir language group. The language is spoken in China by the Tajik people. In China, it is known as the "Tajik language" even though it is not the language spoken in Tajikistan. There are currently around 20,000 speakers of Sarikoli, with most living in Taxkorgan Tajik Autonomous County of southern Xinjiang Province, and others living close to the Pakistan-Chinese border in the Pakistani-controlled part of Kashmir. Even though Sarikoli is related to the Wakhi language, the two are not mutually intelligible.

ISRAELI-PALESTINIAN CONFLICT

Recognizing Israel   Many Palestinians want Hamas to recognize Israel so that peace can be negotiated. Though Hamas recognizes that Israel exists, they refuse to recognize the land as a Jewish state and do not plan on making peace. Leaders from the United States and Europe have refused to work with Hamas or provide any aid to Palestine until Hamas has recognized Israel and disarms. Even though a large majority of Palestinians want peace, Hamas has refused to listen to them, and will not recognize Israel and will not give up on an Islamic Palestinian state.

EDITING STRATEGIES

Proofreading   Once you have made any changes that needed to be done, your last step is to proofread. There are several steps one can take during the proofreading process. First, be aware of your strengths and weaknesses. If punctuation is not your strong suit, make sure to check every sentence for punctuation errors. One very effective way to proofread is to read what you've written from bottom to top and from right to left. By doing this, mistakes will stick out like a sore thumb. You should also scan your paper all the way through for any typos. Reading your writing out loud will also give new insights into your writing and help you spot any errors.

LOGARITHMS

Applications of Logarithms   Logarithms have very real applications in both math and non-math subjects alike. The nautilus, for example, is a cephalopod that has a large shell. The chambers of the shell are approximate copies of the last chamber that are scaled by a constant number. This same idea can be found in mathematics, and it is known as the logarithmic spiral. Logarithms are used to measure the strengths of earthquakes (which is known as the Richter Scale) and how bright stars are. They are even used in psychology (where Hick's law uses a logarithm to explain the time it takes a person to choose an alternative and the amount of choices they are faced with).

RNA

RNA Therapeutics   Scientists have realized the significance of RNA in many ways. Not only can the molecule be tested with new drugs, but it can provide insight into the formation of diseases. New therapies and treatments are being created based on RNA. RNA acts as a messenger and informs cells (cancer or normal) what proteins to make. Scientists are attempting to have RNA disrupt the message of cancer before it is made. Others are attempting to create an mRNA sequence that will bind to oligo-nucleotides that will target a therapeutic protein.

ENDANGERED LANGUAGES

Chuvash   The only surviving language of the Oghur branch, Chuvash is a Turkic language that is spoken in the Chuvashia region of Russia (where it is an official language). The writing system of Chuvash is based on Cyrillic. Chuvash is spoken by 1,640,000 people. Even though Chuvash is a Turkic language, it is not mutually intelligible with other Turkic languages. Other languages of the Oghur branch include Turkic Avar, Khazar, Bulgar, and maybe Hunnic.

1. **What was operation Defensive Wall?**
   a. A series of terrorist attacks launched by Hamas on Israel
   b. Israel's reoccupation of land in the West Bank that had been relinquished to Palestinians
   c. Israel's allowing the Palestine Liberation Organization to enter the Gaza Strip and West Bank
   d. An operation where the British stopped immigration of the Jewish people to Palestine

2. **What did the Balfour Declaration of 1917 state?**
   a. Britain wished to turn Palestine into a national home for the Jewish people.
   b. Britain wished to turn Israel into a national home for the Arab people.
   c. The United States wished to turn Palestine into a national home for the Jewish people.
   d. The United States wished to turn Israel into a national home for the Arab people.

3. **Which of the following is an example of editing?**
   a. Changing 's to s'
   b. Changing a semicolon to a colon
   c. Changing a sentence that reads as clichéd or hackneyed
   d. Correcting a misspelled word

4. **Which of the following is an example of proofreading?**
   a. Replacing a comma with a semicolon
   b. Changing a sentence that had no meaning into one that has meaning
   c. Replacing words with words that incite emotion
   d. Using words that relate to the audience

5. **What does $\log_b(m) + \log_b(n)$ equal?**
   a. $\log_b(m\text{-}n)$
   b. $\log_b(m/n)$
   c. $\log_b(m+n)$
   d. $\log_b(mn)$

6. **What does $n \cdot \log_b(m)$ equal?**
   a. $\log_b(mn)$
   b. $\log_b(m^n)$
   c. $\log_b{}^n(m^n)$
   d. $\log_b{}^n(m)$

7. **What does ribosomal RNA do?**
   a. It targets cancer cells.
   b. It creates polypeptides.
   c. It turns immature mRNA into mature mRNA.
   d. It carries amino acids into the developing protein.

8. **What process does the small interfering RNA take part in?**
   a. Translation
   b. RNA interference
   c. Transcription
   d. RNA therapy

9. **Which of the following is an Aboriginal language of Australia with a total of five speakers remaining?**
   a. Chuvash
   b. Sarikoli
   c. Dyirbal
   d. Votic

10. **Which of the following is a Turkic language that had influences from the Hebrew language?**
    a. Votic
    b. Karaim
    c. Chuvash
    d. Sarikoli

Index

Note: Page numbers in **bold** indicate category topic lists. Page numbers in *italics* indicate quizzes.

History

American Revolution, **107**, 108, 109, 110, 111, 112, 113, *114*

ancient Egypt, **17**, 18, 19, 20, 21, 22, 23, *24*

baby boomers and the sixties, **251**, 252, 254, 255, 256, 258, 259, *260*

civil rights, **295**, 296, 297, 298, 299, 300, 301, *302*

Civil War, **139**, 140, 141, 142, 143, 144, 145, *146*

Cold War, **243**, 244, 245, 246, 247, 248, 249, *250*

Columbus and New World, **99**, 100, 101, 102, 103, 104, 105, *106*

Constitution, **115**, 116, 117, 118, 119, 120, 121, *122*

Crusades, **75**, 76, 77, 78, 79, 80, 81, *82*

Cultural Revolution (China), **271**, 272, 273, 274, 275, 276, 277, *278*

French Revolution, **131**, 132, 133, 134, 135, 136, 137, *138*

Gandhi, **171**, 172, 173, 174, 175, 176, 177, *178*

Great Depression, **219**, 220, 221, 222, 223, 224, 225, *226*

Gulf War, **303**, 304, 305, 306, 307, 308, 309, *310*

Holocaust, **235**, 236, 237, 238, 239, 240, 241, *242*

Huns, **25**, 26, 27, 28, 29, 30, 31, *32*

Industrial Revolution, **123**, 124, 125, 126, 127, 128, 129, *130*

Israeli-Palestinian conflict, **329**, 330, 331, 332, 333, 334, 335, *336*

Korean War, **287**, 288, 289, 290, 291, 292, 293, *294*

Magna Carta, **41**, 42, 43, 44, 45, 46, 47, *48*

Mesopotamia and first civilizations, **1**, 2, 3, 4, 5, 6, *7*

Middle Ages, **67**, 68, 69, 70, 71, 72, 73, *74*

Ming Dynasty, **91**, 92, 93, 94, 95, 96, 97, *98*

moon landing, **261**, 262, 263, 264, 266, 268, *270*

Ottoman Empire, **33**, 34, 35, 36, 37, 38, 39, *40*

Panama Canal, **211**, 212, 213, 214, 215, 216, 217, *218*

Reformation, **49**, 50, 51, 52, 53, 54, 55, *56*

Renaissance, **83**, 84, 85, 86, 87, 88, 89, *90*

Rome, **57**, 58, 59, 60, 62, 64, 65, *66*

Russian Revolution, **179**, 180, 181, 183, 184, 185, 187, *188*

Salem witch trials, **163**, 164, 165, 166, 167, 168, 169, *170*

Spanish-American War, **147**, 148, 149, 150, 151, 152, 153, *154*

Vietnam War, **279**, 280, 281, 282, 283, 284, 285, *286*

War of 1812, **155**, 156, 157, 158, 159, 160, 161, *162*

War on Terror, **321**, 322, 323, 324, 325, 326, 327, *328*

World War I, **189**, 190, 191, 192, 194, 195, 197, *198*

World War II, **227**, 228, 229, 230, 231, 232, 233, *234*

Wright brothers, **199**, 200, 201, 202, 204, 206, 208, *210*

Xia Dynasty, **9**, 10, 11, 12, 13, 14, 15, *16*

Y2K, **311**, 312, 313, 314, 315, 316, 318, *320*

Holocaust, **235**, 236, 237, 238, 239, 240, 241, *242*

Horror fiction, **171**, 172, 173, 174, 175, 176, 177, *178*

Humor, **179**, 180, 181, 183, 184, 185, 187, *188*

Hungarian, **147**, 148, 149, 150, 151, 152, 153, *154*

Huns, **25**, 26, 27, 28, 29, 30, 31, *32*

Icelandic, **115**, 116, 117, 118, 119, 120, 121, *122*

Inca mathematics, **17**, 18, 19, 20, 21, 22, 23, *24*

Industrial Revolution, **123**, 124, 125, 126, 127, 128, 129, *130*

Infinity, **321**, 322, 323, 324, 325, 326, 327, *328*

Israeli-Palestinian conflict, **329**, 330, 331, 332, 333, 334, 335, *336*

Italian, **25**, 26, 27, 28, 29, 30, 31, *32*

Japanese, **163**, 164, 165, 166, 167, 168, 169, *170*

Journalism, **303**, 304, 305, 306, 307, 308, 309, *310*

Kafka, Franz, **295**, 296, 297, 298, 299, 300, 301, *302*

Khosian languages, **295**, 296, 297, 298, 299, 300, 301, *302*

Knot theory, **227**, 228, 229, 230, 231, 232, 233, *234*

Korean language, **155**, 156, 157, 158, 159, 160, 161, *162*

Korean War, **287**, 288, 289, 290, 291, 292, 293, *294*

Language arts

Alice in Wonderland, **219**, 220, 221, 222, 223, 224, 225, *226*

alphabet, **25**, 26, 27, 28, 29, 30, 31, *32*

biographies, **243**, 244, 245, 246, 247, 248, 249, *250*

Braille, **91**, 92, 93, 94, 95, 96, 97, *98*

Charles Dickens, **279**, 280, 281, 282, 283, 284, 285, *286*

composition, **17**, 18, 19, 20, 21, 22, 23, *24*

debating, **155**, 156, 157, 158, 159, 160, 161, *162*

dialects, **99**, 100, 101, 102, 103, 104, 105, *106*

Edgar Allan Poe, **199**, 200, 201, 202, 204, 206, 208, *210*